Corporate Environmental Strategy
and Competitive Advantage

DEDICATIONS

Sanjay Sharma
To my parents, Madan Mohan and Sushma Sharma, my life partner, Pramodita, and my daughter, Smita, for their constant love and support

J. Alberto Aragón-Correa
To Maria, my wife, the source of much joy, encouragement, and love

Corporate Environmental Strategy and Competitive Advantage

Edited by

Sanjay Sharma

Wilfred Laurier University, Canada

J. Alberto Aragón-Correa

University of Grenada, Spain

NEW PERSPECTIVES IN RESEARCH ON CORPORATE
SUSTAINABILITY

Edward Elgar

Cheltenham, UK • Northampton, MA, USA

Published by
Edward Elgar Publishing Limited
Glensanda House
Montpellier Parade
Cheltenham
Glos GL50 1UA
UK

Edward Elgar Publishing, Inc.
136 West Street
Suite 202
Northampton
Massachusetts 01060
USA

A catalogue record for this book
is available from the British Library

ISBN 1 84542 005 5

Printed and bound in Great Britain by MPG Books Ltd, Bodmin, Cornwall

Contents

Figures

Tables

Contributors

J. Alberto Aragón-Correa obtained his PhD degree from University of Seville and he is the head of the Department of Management and an assistant professor at the School of Economics and Business, University of Granada, Spain, and visiting professor at the Rotterdam School of Management, Erasmus University, The Netherlands. He teaches strategic management and environmental management. His research interests include strategic behaviour of firms, organizations and natural environment, and small firms. His research has been published in the most prestigious Spanish journals and English language journals such as the *Academy of Management Journal*, the *Academy of Management Review*, *Sustainable Development* and the *Journal of Business Research*.

Frank Boons is an associate professor at the Erasmus Centre for Sustainability and Environmental Management, Rotterdam University, The Netherlands, As an organizational and economic sociologist, his interest is in the dynamics of inter-organizational processes that relate to sustainable development. Currently, his work focuses on the ways in which individuals that represent firms, governmental agencies, and NGO's, enact the concept of sustainability. He has published in journals such as *Business Strategy and the Environment*, *Journal of Industrial Ecology and Environmental Politics*, a special issue on organizations and the environment of the *International Journal of Management and Organization*. He has co-authored a book *The Changing Nature of Business* (2000).

Per Christensen is a professor in environmental planning at the Department of Development and Planning at Aalborg University, Denmark. He has for many years studied the implementation of environmental regulations in a broader context, encompassing among others the inspiration from institutional theories. This has mainly concerned the implementation of new forms of regulation related to the topic of cleaner production, as well as experiences on implementing environmental management systems in industries. Lately these interests are moving more in the direction of how to develop EMS into LCM or life cycle management.

Enrique Claver-Cortés is a professor in business management at the University of Alicante, Spain. He earned his PhD degree from the

University of Valencia, Spain. His current research includes strategic management, human resource management, quality management and environmental management.

Rafel Crespí-Cladera is a professor of business economics at the Universitat de les Illes Balears (UIB), Spain and Family Business Banca March Chair. He obtained his PhD from the Universitat Autonoma of Barcelona (UAB). His research is mainly on empirical corporate governance, focused on Spanish and European Corporations. He has been visiting researcher at Tilburg University, The Netherlands and Oxford University. Currently he is the coordinator of a doctorate in economics management and organization jointly offered by the UAB, UIB and the Universidad Publica de Navarra.

Jesús Ángel del Brío is doctor cum laude of business administration at Universidad de Oviedo. He has taught firm organization at Universidad de Oviedo since 1995 and he has been the assistant master in human resource management in the Universidad Carlos III. His research work has been directed toward the study of environmental management from several points of view. In these topics, he has published in books and journals including *Ecological Economics, Eco-Management and Auditing, Environmental Practice, Environmental Quality Management, International Journal of Production Research, International Journal of Quality and Reliability Management, Resources, Conservation and Recycling, Technovation* and *Total Quality Management*. He has published a book entitled *Medio ambiente y empresa: de la confrontación a la oportunidad* with Beatriz Junquera.

Esteban Fernández has successively been appointed bachelor and doctor of business administration at Universidad de Oviedo, Spain. He is professor of firm organization at Universidad de Valladolid and at Universidad de Oviedo. His research work has been directed towards the study of technology, production management, strategy and environmental management. His studies on environmental management have been published in several national and international journals, such as *Ecological Economics, International Journal of Human Resource Management, International Journal of Quality and Reliability Management* and *Total Quality Management.*

Beatriz Junquera is doctor cum laude of business administration at the Universidad de Oviedo, Spain. She has taught firm organization at the Universidad de Oviedo since 1991. She has studied strategic technology management, innovation management, environmental management, environmental strategy's effects on firm's performance, and female entrepreneurs. She has published in books and journals including *Ecological Economics, Eco-Management and Auditing, Environmental Practice, Environmental Quality Management, International Journal of Human Resource Management, International Journal of Production Research, International Journal of Quality and Reliability Management, International Journal of Technology Management, Resources, Conservation and Recycling, Technovation* and *Total Quality Management*. She has published a book entitled *Medio ambiente y empresa: de la confrontación a la oportunidad* with Jesús del Brío.

George I. Kassinis is an assistant professor of management in the Department of Public and Business Administration of the University of Cyprus. He received his PhD in public policy from Princeton University. His research interests include strategy, environmental management and stakeholder management. His work has been published in *Strategic Management Journal, Production and Operations Management, Journal of Environmental Planning* and *Management, and Environmental Impact Assessment Review*. He is a member of the editorial review board of *Progress in Industrial Ecology* and a member of the Academy of Management, the Strategic Management Society and the International Association for Business and Society.

Manfred Kirchgeorg is a professor at HHL-Leipzig Graduate School of Management, Germany, where he holds the chair for marketing management. His research revolves around environmental management, sustainability marketing, stakeholder marketing and corporate brand management. Manfred is involved in a number of scholarly organizations, including the Federation of University Professors in Business Administration. He was chairman of the Environmental Management Commission of the Federation in 2003 and 2004. He has been a visiting professor at various universities in the United States, Canada, Brazil, Switzerland and Singapore. He is involved in national and international consulting and research projects, and has published several books and a large number of articles in learned journals and collaborative volumes.

Jesper Møller Larsen is employed in the technical department of Aabybro Kommune, a middle-sized municipality in Northern Jutland. He graduated in 2002 with an MSc in environmental management), writing a thesis concerning green networking and self-regulation among municipalities and companies in Denmark. At present he is, amongst others, responsible for physical planning, waste management, Agenda 21, and corporate affairs (pollution prevention) in the municipality.

Martin Lehmann is a PhD student in environmental management at the Department of Business Studies at Aalborg University, Denmark. His research interests include environmental management and institutional and organizational change, especially as it relates to ecological modernization and networks. His dissertation investigates how networks and public–private partnerships contribute to the dissemination of knowledge, capacity development and conceptual developments of environmental management practices and sustainability. He is focusing his research on both developing and developed countries; especially Thailand, where he has first-hand working experience, and Denmark.

María D. López-Gamero is an assistant lecturer in business management at the University of Alicante, Spain. She is a PhD candidate at the University of Alicante. Her current research focuses on environmental management.

Henning Madsen is an associate professor at Department of Information Science, the Aarhus School of Business. He has an MSc in mathematical economics from the University of Aarhus and a PhD in business economics from the Aarhus School of Business. His research results have been published in international journals and presented at international conferences and research meetings. He is currently involved in research projects focusing on environmental management, social networks and entrepreneurship, and trends in managerial and organizational development. He has received the ANBAR Citation of Excellence Reward.

Alfred A. Marcus is professor of strategic management and organization at the Carlson School of Management. He has taught at Carlson School since 1984. He is the author of articles in journals such as the *Academy of Management Journal* and *Academy of Management Review*, and many books including a strategy textbook, *Management Strategy: Achieving Sustained Corporate Advantage* (New York: McGraw Hill, 2005). His PhD is from Harvard and his bachelor's and master's degrees are from the University of Chicago. Resources for the Future published his most recent book on environmental issues in 2002 under the title of *Reinventing Environmental Regulation*. This book was written with Don Geffen and Ken Sexton. Other books on environmental issues that Professor Marcus has either authored, co-authored or edited are: *Better Environmental Decisions*, Island Press (1999) (with K. Sexton, K. Easter and T. Burkhardt); *Business and Society: Strategy, Ethics, and the Global Economy*, Richard D. Irwin (1996); *Controversial Issues in Energy Policy*, Sage, 1992; and *Managing Environmental Issues*, Prentice-Hall (1992) (with J. Post and R. Buchholz).

Fernando Matías-Reche is an assistant professor at the School of Economics and Business, University of Granada, Spain. He teaches human resource management and organizational behaviour. His research interests include outsourcing, organizations and natural environment, and small firms. His research has been published in some of the most prestigious Spanish journals and English language journals such as the *Journal of Business Research*.

José F. Molina-Azorín is a senior lecturer in business management at the University of Alicante, Spain. He earned his PhD degree from the University of Alicante. His research focuses on relationships between strategy, quality management and environmental management.

Francina Orfila-Sintes is a professor of business economics at the Universitat de les Illes Balears (UIB), Spain. She has a PhD from the UIB. Her research is mainly on innovation, services and environmental management. She has been visiting researcher at Roskilde University, Denmark.

Catherine A. Ramus is an assistant professor at the Donald Bren School of Environmental Science and Management, University of California, Santa Barbara. She teaches organizational behaviour and team dynamics, negotiation and environmental management. Her research interests in the field of corporate environmental management include how organizations can support employee-led environmental problem-solving and value creation, and how organizations can attract and retain employees through commitment to socially and environmentally sustainable practices. Her research has been published in journals such as the *Academy of Management Journal*, *California Management Review*, the *Journal of Management Education*, and the *Journal of World Business*. She has held positions at the United States Environmental Protection Agency and IMD International, where she conducted research with companies that were interested in improving their environmental management practices. She has a doctorate from HEC at the University of Lausanne, a master's degree from Harvard's Kennedy School of Government in Public Administration, and an undergraduate degree in economics and political science from the University of California at Berkeley.

Nigel Roome is chair of Sustainable Enterprise and Transformation at Erasmus University Rotterdam. He publishes on topics that relate to business and technology to environmental management, sustainable development, corporate social responsibility and global change, including books such as *Sustainability Strategies for Industry*, Island Press (1998) and *The Ecology of Information and Communications Technologies*, Greenleaf

Publishing (2002). In 2003 the World Resources Institute acknowledged his pioneering contribution to the curriculum for sustainable enterprise and corporate responsibility. He has worked with companies, trade associations, professional institutes and the voluntary sector in Europe and North America and advised with the World Bank, European Community and governments in Canada, USA, UK and Mexico. In particular, he chaired a European Commission expert group on sustainable and competitive product systems and authored its report, found at: europa.eu.int/comm/research/growth/pdf/etan-report.pdf.

Sanjay Sharma is a professor of strategic management and sustainability at Wilfrid Laurier University. His doctoral dissertation from the University of Calgary won the Best Dissertation Award from the Social Issues in Management Division of the Academy of Management in 1996. He has received several research awards including the Jossey Bass/New Lexington Press Award for the Best Academy of Management Paper on Organizations and the Natural Environment (1997), Best Strategy Paper at the Administrative Sciences Association of Canada (2003) and the ANBAR Citation of Excellence (1999). He was awarded a Fulbright Fellowship in 2001–2002 and has received several research grants from the Social Sciences and Humanities Research Council of Canada (SSHRC). He has served on the Council's Research Funding Adjudication Committee and his biography has been listed in *Who's Who in Canadian Business* for the last few years. His research has been published in the *Academy of Management Review*, *Academy of Management Journal*, *Academy of Management Executive*, *Strategic Management Journal*, *Journal of Applied Behavioral Science*, *Business Strategy and the Environment*, *Journal of Asian Business*, *Journal of Strategic Marketing* and *Revue Francaise de Gestion*, among others. His books include *Research on Corporate Sustainability: The Evolving Theory and Practice of Organizations in the Natural Environment* and *New Perspectives in Research on Corporate Sustainability: Stakeholders, the Environment, and Society* (both co-edited with Mark Starik) published in 2003 by Edward Elgar. Before pursuing an academic career, he worked for 16 years as a senior manager with multinational corporations. Sanjay is the past chair of the ONE Interest Group at the Academy of Management.

Andreas C. Soteriou is an associate professor of operations management in the Department of Public and Business Administration of the University of Cyprus. He holds a PhD degree in business administration from the University of Southern California. His primary research interests focus in the areas of operations management, quality and productivity improvement in the service sector. His work has been published in journals such as

Management Science, Decision Sciences, Manufacturing and Service Operations Management, the *Journal of Operations Management, Production and Operations Management*, the *European Journal of Operational Research*, and *Interfaces*. He is an associate editor of the *Journal of Applied Mathematics and Decision Sciences* and a member of the editorial review board of the *Journal of Operations Management*.

Juan J. Tarí-Guilló is a senior lecturer in business management at the University of Alicante, Spain. He earned his PhD degree from the University of Alicante. His current field of research is total quality management.

John P. Ulhøi is professor of organization and management theory and director of an inter-institutional doctoral school in Org and Mngt in Denmark. His most recent publications appear in journals such as *Journal of Business Venturing, Journal of Organizational Behavior* and *Management Decision*. He has served as an editorial board member for a variety of journals. He has served as a board member of several internal organizations, including the TIM division of the Academy of Management. Professor Ulhøi has acted as international research evaluator for the EU Commission, the Office for Scientific Affairs in Belgium, the Norwegian Research Council, the Danish Social Science Research Council and the European Foundation for Management Development in Brussels among others.

Monika I. Winn is an associate professor of strategy, corporate environmental management and sustainability at the University of Victoria's Faculty of Business in British Columbia, Canada. Her research revolves around corporate sustainability management, organizational and institutional change, and sustainable entrepreneurship, and often has international scope. She has published research articles both on strategic and on institutional change, corporate greening, organizational learning, corporate environmental leadership, and stakeholder research methodology. She is actively involved in a number of scholarly organizations, and is a founding member and past chair of the Academy of Management's ONE Group (Organizations and the Natural Environment). She is engaged in consulting and executive education on sustainability leadership.

1. Corporate environmental strategy and competitive advantage: a review from the past to the future

Sanjay Sharma and J. Alberto Aragón-Correa

During the 1960s, books such as Rachel Carson's *Silent Spring* raised awareness about the negative health and environmental impacts of emissions from smoke stacks, effluents flowing into water bodies, and toxic chemicals improperly disposed of by businesses. As a consequence, the general level of public awareness about environmental issues during this period was based on a negative view of business as a polluter (for example Jorgensen, 1991; Morrison and Dunlap, 1986). At the same time, in the US, the 1960s were marked by increasing societal awareness of the issues of human rights and quality of life, putting increased pressure on corporations to respond to the concerns of radical environmental groups such as Greenpeace about damage to the natural environment cased by their operations (Buccholz, 1993). Therefore early models discussing the integration of the natural environment into organizational decision-making and strategy were primarily derived from the deep ecology literature. Rather than addressing the issue of competitive advantage of firms, they presented a conflict between the economy and ecology and thus between corporate financial performance and environmental performance.

These models were prescriptive world-views and the lenses through which organizations were supposed to interpret their relationship with the natural environment, usually dichotomously as either 'against' or 'for' the environment. Some models even saw a conflict between technology and ecology (Orr, 1992). These paradigms were supposed to guide and influence the organization and its leadership via the individual consciousness of its actors or managers (Harman, 1987, 1992a, 1992b, 1992c), similar to the role of individual managers and leaders as moral actors in organizational decision-making for ethical and socially responsible practices and decisions (Ackerman, 1975; Wood, 1991).

A dominant perspective on the firm's economic and environmental performance conflict was the dichotomy between the dominant social paradigm (DSP) and the new ecological paradigm (NEP) (Buttel and Flinn, 1976; Catton and Dunlap, 1978, 1980; Dunlap and Van Liere, 1978, 1983, 1984). The DSP was frequently cited in early ecological literature as an 'old paradigm' (Capra, 1992) that was predominantly the Western, and primarily Eurocentric, world-view. Some dimensions discussed in the DSP–NEP dichotomy included beliefs and values of organizations that support economic growth, faith in material abundance, support for individual rights, support for property rights, laissez-faire government, and faith in science and technology (Dunlap and Van Liere, 1984). Robertson (1985) contrasted the DSP and NEP paradigms as the hyper-expansionist (HE), and the sane, humane, ecological (SHE) paradigms. The former is urban, anthropocentric and characterized by rational intellectual detachment, while the latter is countrywide, ecological and experientially intuitive and emphatic.

As more pragmatic continuums of ecological paradigms emerged, they provided space for organizations to begin to think about potential ways to reconcile their economic and ecological performance. At one extreme of his continuum, Colby (1990) labelled the neo-classical economic belief system as the frontier economic paradigm (FEP). At the other extreme he redefined the new ecological paradigm (NEP) and labelled it deep ecology. Between these two polar opposites, Colby described three other pragmatic paradigms for classifying organizational environmental strategy or behaviour as: environmental protection, resource management and eco-development. These represented a progression away from neo-classical economics paradigms of exploitation of nature to progressive viewpoints that allowed firms to pursue their core objectives of profits and competitive advantage while preserving and conserving nature. At that time a few international organizations also began to examine the effects of business on the natural environment via publications of handbooks and guidelines for an appropriate business management–natural environment interface. Examples include publications sponsored by the International Labor Organization (Evan, 1986; North, 1992), the Commission of the European Communities handbook on environmental information, opinion and education (Winter, 1988) and the World Bank's reports, including those on global environmental diagnosis (World Bank, 1992).

These more pragmatic discussions provided the background for business and management theorists to develop models urging the inclusion of ecological considerations into management decisions that also accommodated the achievement of corporate economic goals. Models included the 'sustaincentric' paradigm that urged the integration of elements such as waste assimilation, conservation, dematerialization, and inclusiveness into corporate operations (Gladwin et al., 1995) and 'eco-centric' approaches to organizational theory (Shrivastava, 1995). This embedding of ecology into organizational functioning encouraged more practical approaches toward corporate sustainability. For example Starik and Rands (1995) adopted an open systems view to examine how the organization was situated in, and interacting with, a multilevel web of stakeholders within a larger ecosystem.

Moreover the theoretical discussions presented in the *Academy of Management Review* Special Forum on Ecologically Sustainable Organizations (1995) presented arguments to contradict early discussions which proposed that strategies for reducing corporate impacts on the natural environment were similar to social issues such as employment equity and strategic issues such as changing technological environments. It became clearer that the natural environment has a systemic impact on business firms, ranging from the inputs they consume, to their processes and operations, to the products and services they produce, extending to the waste generated by consumption of their products or services (Shrivastava, 1992). On the other hand, organizational responses to a social issue such as employment equity may require a firm only to alter its human resources practices. Similarly responses to strategic issues such as technological change may require increased resource commitments to research and development and innovation efforts. However response on the organization–natural environment interface requires a consideration of the systemic consequences of each action through the entire value chains of a firm and its suppliers and customers. Therefore it was important for researchers to examine the impact on financial performance and competitive advantage of such fundamental changes in corporate operations.

Hart's (1995) natural resource-based view of the firm was one of the early systematic approaches to this challenge. He argued that organizations could develop capabilities that would help them not only develop environmental strategies of pollution prevention, clean technologies, product stewardship and sustainable development, but also achieve competitive advantage. It is not surprising that such approaches resonated better with businesses and their managers seeking to understand how to incorporate the demands of multiple stakeholders for making their operations more sustainable, while delivering shareholder value, meeting the needs of consumers and incorporating the objectives of other stakeholders such as employees and local communities.

Indeed subsequent research studies have shown that compared to regulatory compliance and pollution control via end-of-pipe clean-up of wastes that have already been generated, proactive environmental strategies that focus on preventing pollution at source are more likely to contribute to improved economic performance and competitive advantage (for example Aragón-Correa, 1998; Hart and Ahuja, 1996; Klassen and McLaughlin,

1996; Russo and Fouts, 1997; Sharma and Vredenburg, 1998). Proactive pollution prevention environmental strategies include the redesign of processes and products to reduce material and energy use, adoption of cleaner technologies with lower or zero wastes and lower material and energy inputs, product stewardship for take-back, dismantling, recycling and reuse of products, and ultimately the redefinition of the business model, for example to lease services generated by a product rather than sell higher volumes of the product (such as Interface's switch to leasing 'floor comfort' instead of selling carpet).

The link between proactive environmental strategy and competitive advantage has been a strong motivator and driver for businesses in incorporating environmental considerations into their strategy and undertaking more fundamental strategic change toward sustainability. Accordingly the chapters in this volume examine the complex relationship between corporate environmental strategy and firm performance and competitive advantage.

THE EARLY YEARS OF BUSINESS STRATEGY RESEARCH

The concept of sustainable development developed in 1987 by the report of the United Nations World Commission for the Environment and Development (UNWCED, also known as the Brundtland Commission Report) was influential in the emergence of a focus on the relationship between environmental strategy and competitive advantage in the organization and natural environment literature. This report focused on simultaneous economic development, ecological preservation and social equity by defining sustainable development as a form of development or progress which meets our present requirements without jeopardizing the ability of future generations to meet theirs (UNWCED, 1987). The UNWCED definition offered the potential for reconciling economic development and social equity with environmental preservation.

Adopting the UNWCED theme, Stephen Schmidheiny, a businessman and the commerce and industry adviser at the 1992 United Nations World Conference on the Environment and Development in Rio, gathered a group of 48 business leaders from all over the world to create the Business Council for Sustainable Development (BCSD) (Schmidheiny, 1992). The BCSD recognized the importance and urgency of corporate attention to sustainability issues, and especially highlighted the potential of win–win situations where proactive environmental strategies could lead to improved firm performance and competitive advantage. This sparked increasing business practitioner and academic interest in corporate sustainability and environmental management.

Based on this definition proposed by UNWCED (1987), a number of early business and management books discussed the broad issues at the interface of firm performance and the natural environment. These ranged from reflections on environmental aspects of economic development including issues of growth and sustainable development, the costs of pollution, energy efficiency, the green consumer and the advantages of environmental management (Cairncross, 1991); the relationship between quality and the natural environment, and methods for the assessment of environmental impacts (Welford and Gouldson, 1993); linkages between the natural environment and various functional departments of an organization (Elkington et al., 1991); and technical diagnostic tools for environmental management (Hansen and Jorgensen, 1991; Kolluru, 1994). Kolluru's (1994) handbook of environmental management contained a few chapters with a stronger connection between business strategy and the natural environment including for instance Bringer and Benforado's (1994) ideas on total quality environmental management (TQEM).

Early research analysing the relationship between environmental management and strategic management discussed some of the implications of the environmental issues for competitive advantage (for example Buzzelli, 1991; Bhat, 1992; Roome, 1992; Taylor, 1992) and the market advantages of understanding environmental behaviour and meeting the needs of environmentally conscious consumers (for example Balderjahn, 1988; Gill et al., 1986). However most of the early literature was exploratory and lacked rigour. Describing this early literature on organizations and natural environment during the 1980s, Roberts (1992: 41) suggested that 'some of this literature is trivial and amounts to little more than the provision of green window dressing to disguise the activities of companies where the environmental impact day to day of operation remains unchanged'. Similarly Purser et al. (1995: 1055) criticized such literature as based on 'simple moralistic exhortation or guilt inducing rhetoric'.

Perhaps the most influential early work is Porter's (1991) one-page article in *Scientific American* known as the 'Porter's hypothesis', which argued that stringent environmental regulations would drive firms toward improved efficiency and international competitiveness. Similarly Porter and van der Linde (1995) suggested that lower cost and differentiation benefits could be achieved by firms adopting proactive environmental strategies. While these articles were anecdotal and conceptual and did not integrate ecological aspects of business management paradigms (Gladwin et al.,

1995; Shrivastava, 1994; Shrivastava, 1995c; Purser et al., 1995), they were an excellent source of ideas for the systematic development of later empirical research on the subject.

One of the main problems facing researchers studying the business–natural environment interface was that management and organization theories had ignored the natural environment and its interaction with business operations (Gladwin et al., 1995; Shrivastava, 1994; Shrivastava, 1995c). There were no theoretical guidelines to help integrate research on the natural environment with the extant management and organizational theories. Therefore at this stage the field lacked rigorous empirical research that could be published by top-tier journals. In order to generate a more rigorous empirical and theoretical focus, some management journals began to publish special issues with focus on organizations and the natural environment to help spark future research and thinking in the area.

The *Columbia Journal of World Business* published a special issue in 1992 with 30 contributions divided into five categories: toward sustainable development, markets, agreement processes, regional politics, energy and technology, and corporate environmentalism. The editorial stated that one of the purposes of the issue was to 'elevate the debate surrounding the issues of corporate environmentalism and sustainable development to new more productive levels' (Erdman, 1992: 6). A special issue of *Business Horizons* in 1991 centred on the ethical and social responsibility implications of corporate environmental management.

The special issue of the *Academy of Management Review* on 'Ecologically sustainable organizations' (1995, **20** (4)) was a key reference point in consolidating research on the subject. Two articles in the special issue were focused on the relationship between corporate environmental strategy and competitive advantage. Hart developed the 'natural resource-based view of the firm' and introduced propositions stating three environmental strategies capable of generating capabilities to develop the organization's competitiveness: pollution prevention, product stewardship and sustainable development. He also developed arguments to show how competitive environmental practices could be based on total quality management, cross-functional capability and a shared vision of sustainability. He highlighted the positive consequences of these practices on competitiveness of the firms, such as the reduction of emissions and costs, and the development of new clean technologies. Continuing and building on his earlier arguments during that time (Shrivastava, 1994, 1995a, 1995b), Shrivastava (1995c) suggested four ways in which organizations could be competitive and simultaneously contribute to ecological sustainability: total quality environmental sustainability, ecologically sustainable competitive strategy, swap technology and reduction of the effect of towns on ecosystems. This special issue laid the foundations for increased rigour in the examination of the relationship between corporate environmental strategy and firm economic or financial performance.

THE ENVIRONMENTAL STRATEGY–FINANCIAL PERFORMANCE RELATIONSHIP

As compared to the early years described above, the progress of research on organizations and the natural environment during the second half of the 1990s and during the early 2000s has been impressive. While the publications may not have necessarily increased in number, their impact is significantly higher because they are being published in top-tier management research journals. Moreover this research has successfully integrated theoretical perspectives on ecologically sustainable organizations into extant management and organizational theories. In this proliferating literature on organizations and the natural environment, we focus on the stream of research that explores the relationship between environmental strategy and competitive advantage from three perspectives: consequences of strategies in response to environmental regulations, the relationship between generic business strategies and environmental strategy, and the link between environmental strategy and firm performance.

Entry Barriers of Regulatory Response

Several empirical and theoretical studies examining corporate responses to environmental legislation indirectly supported the competitive value of proactive environmental approaches. For example Dean and Brown (1995) studied the obstacles and advantages to new firm entry in sectors with advanced environmental legislation. Although they found mixed results, their study showed that environmental legislation is an overall obstacle to the entry of new firms, with favorable consequences for the incumbents. Rugman and Verbeke (1998) studied how environmental legislation may allow space for the development of strategies that positively affect multinational firms' financial and environmental performance. Nehrt (1998) showed that organizations which outstrip their competitors in advanced environmental practices and investments in technologies may obtain benefits if environmental legislation affecting the firm and the competitive scenario met certain conditions.

Generic Business Strategies and Environmental Strategy

Some arguments for the relationship between proactive environmental approaches and competitive advantage were based on the central role environmental strategy could play in developing a firm's generic business strategies (Shrivastava, 1995b). The rationale for the relationship was based on lower costs, improved efficiency or differentiation obtained through environmental practices (Porter, 1980). Judge and Douglas (1998) verified the competitive benefits of incorporating environmental criteria into the organization's strategic planning. Aragón-Correa (1998) empirically showed that firms with a prospector strategy (Miles and Snow, 1978), that continually developed entrepreneurial, engineering and administrative processes to search for new technologies, were more likely to be proactive in their environmental practices. The traditional perspectives about the negative economic risks and consequences of advanced environmental approaches were gradually replaced by ideas that financial and environmental benefits could be obtained simultaneously in a win–win effect (Elkington, 1994).

Environmental Strategy and Financial Performance

Empirical research has helped address the mainly anecdotal debate about the relationship of an organization's environmental strategy and its financial performance. The early perspectives ranged between those which argued that responding to environmental legislation leads to increased costs and loss of competitiveness (for example Walley and Whitehead, 1994) to others which argued that stringent environmental regulations would drive firms toward improved efficiency and international competitiveness (for example Porter, 1991).

In examining major positive and negative environmental events such as environmental awards and/or crises and accidents, Klassen and McLaughlin (1996) found a positive relationship between financial performance (as measured by stock market performance) and positive environmental events. Nehrt (1996) found a positive relationship between rapid environmental investment and profit growth in chemical bleached paper pulp manufacturers. Russo and Fouts (1997) found a positive relationship across a multi-sector sample, showing that the relationship was stronger in high-growth industries.

However the studies examining the direct connection between environmental strategies and financial performance had two important limitations that muddied their conclusions. First, the method of assessment could conceal the latent relationships and parameters which could be the real explanations of the improved performance. For example improved productivity associated with environmental strategies could be a factor in improved profitability rather than the environmental practices themselves. Indeed Klassen and Whybark (1999) showed that moderate environmental practices may generate important competitive and environmental improvements if associated with other management changes, and not otherwise. Second it was not possible to analyse whether the relationship (positive or negative) was sustainable over time. Most studies were cross-sectional and a longitudinal perspective needed to be adopted to examine this relationship.

Research adopting the resource-based view partially avoided these limitations by examining the association of proactive environmental approaches with capabilities that can lead to more sustainable competitive advantages, instead of analysing the direct relationship between environmental strategy and financial performance. The stream of research from the resource-based view of the firm has become the dominant research perspective examining the relationship between business strategy and the natural environment.

THE NATURAL RESOURCE-BASED VIEW OF THE FIRM

The natural resource-based view draws from the resource-based view (RBV) of the firm which argues that a firm's competitive advantage depends upon its ability to accumulate, generate and deploy unique and valuable resources and capabilities (Amit and Schoemaker, 1993; Barney, 1991; Peteraf, 1993; Rumelt, 1984; Wernerfelt, 1984). Resources are the factors which are owned and controlled by the business, while capabilities are the skills that the firm has to use in a coordinated way to achieve goals (Amit and Schoemaker, 1993: 35). The resources can be tangible (buildings, computers, money) and intangible (information, patents, reputation) (Hall, 1993), while capabilities are intangible and can be related to several skills such as an organization's ability to innovate, learn and/or absorb knowledge.

As discussed above, Hart (1995) was the first to expressly integrate the RBV into a discussion of environmental strategy and competitive advantage. He developed propositions based on three interconnected strategies: pollution prevention, product stewardship and sustainable development. He argued that the basic capabilities required for proactive environmental approaches included the tacit capability of continuous improvement as a basis for pollution prevention, the complex capability of cross-functional management to support a product stewardship strategy, and the rare ability to establish a shared vision for a sustainable development strategy.

This research stream can be classified into two broad categories: the competitive outcomes of capabilities that help generate proactive environmental strategies, and the antecedents for the generation and deployment of these capabilities.

The Outcomes of Environmental Capability Generation

Sharma and Vredenburg (1998) and Marcus and Geffen (1998) empirically showed that the incorporation of proactive environmental approaches in organizations had a positive effect on their financial performance via the development of different organizational capabilities. Sharma and Vredenburg's (1998) pioneering study identified three organizational capabilities – stakeholder integration, continuous higher-order learning and continuous innovation – in their analysis of firms with proactive environmental strategies in the Canadian oil industry. In addition to finding similarities with the capabilities proposed by Hart (1995), they identified an underlying dynamic process in which the opening up of an organization to new knowledge from external constituents sparked organizational learning and innovation that, in turn, enabled response to stakeholder concerns.

Russo and Fouts (1997) explained the link between environmental strategy and firm performance as being a result of environmental innovation complemented by the capabilities of organizational commitment and learning, cross-functional integration, and increased employee skills and participation in firms that engaged in pollution prevention rather than pollution control. Christmann (2000) stressed that organizational capabilities associated with pollution prevention technologies would lead to cost advantage only if a firm also possessed the complementary capabilities of process innovation and implementation. Similarly Klassen and Whybark (1999) found that a capability of developing and deploying manufacturing initiatives collectively into an environmental technology portfolio would help firms improve their manufacturing and environmental performance simultaneously. Such deployment involves continuous improvement, innovation and the integration of total quality management into operations.

Marcus and Geffen (1998) found that firms with the capabilities of searching for outside talent, technology and ideas, and of organizational learning, were likely to acquire external capabilities that enabled improved environmental performance. They showed how proactive electric utilities acquired capabilities from their major suppliers and deployed them to improve their own environmental practices. Drawing on Miles and Snow's

(1978) typology, Aragón-Correa (1998) argued that certain strategic postures represented organizational competences and found that firms maintaining a 'prospector' posture in their entrepreneurial, engineering and administrative functions exhibited proactive environmental approaches.

Thus the stream of research from this perspective has unpacked and examined the importance of capabilities such as stakeholder engagement (Marcus and Geffen, 1998; Sharma and Vredenburg, 1998), innovation (Christmann, 2000; Klassen and Whybark, 1999; Russo and Fouts, 1997), higher-order learning (Sharma and Vredenburg, 1998), strategic proactivity (Aragón-Correa, 1998), and cross-functional coordination (Russo and Fouts, 1997). Research has also examined the internal and external antecedents that facilitate the generation and deployment of these valuable capabilities, which in turn enable a firm to adopt proactive environmental strategies.

The Antecedents of Environmental Capability Generation

The two areas in the environmental strategy and competitive advantage research that hold the greatest promise relate to process issues of how capabilities are generated and acquired by firms, and under what conditions they are deployed effectively in generating competitive advantage. This is an emerging focus of research and the antecedents of environmental capability generation can be categorized into internal organizational variables, managerial roles, attitudes and interpretations, and exogenous and contingent factors.

Shrivastava (1995b, c) argued that generation of capabilities for proactive environmental approaches would require, in addition to technological resources, managerial skills based on total quality management (TQM). A stream of research has examined the importance of employee roles, interpretations and attitudes in the generation of a proactive environmental strategy. These include the importance of managerial interpretation of environmental issues as opportunities rather than threats (Sharma, 2000), employee attitudes that favour environmental protection (Cordano and Frieze, 2000), the positive effect of goal clarity and shared employee responsibility on organizational learning and employee creativity in developing proactive environmental strategies (Ramus and Steger, 2000), the championing of environmental issues (Andersson and Bateman, 2000), and the influence of the functional background of managers on environmental commitment of the firm (Aragón-Correa et al., 2004).

A few studies have examined the influence of exogenous factors on the development and acquisition of competitively valuable internal environmental capabilities. For example Marcus and Geffen (1998) longitudinally examined how electric generation firms acquired pollution prevention competencies as a result of interactions between conflicting institutional (government and market) forces and individual firm capabilities of organizational learning and search for talent and technology. Majumdar and Marcus (2001) found that strategic choice of environmental strategies by electric utilities in the United States was contingent upon whether or not environmental regulations allowed them discretion in their technology investments. Moreover those authors argued that flexible regulations were more likely to result in competitive advantage because they allowed firms to adopt efficient and productive technologies. Russo and Fouts (1997) found that industry growth moderated the relationship between environmental strategy and organizational performance because it required riskier investments, entailed organic management structures and promoted greater interest in intangible assets such as reputation, all of which contributed to improved organizational economic performance.

Recently Hart and Sharma (2004) examined the processes via which engaging distant stakeholders from the fringe of a company's network helps stimulate capability generation for radical innovation to create competitive imagination for the future. Finally, Aragón-Correa and Sharma's (2003) contingent resource-based framework offered a systematic view of how variables in a firm's general business environment such as uncertainty, complexity and hostility moderate the deployment of organizational capabilities for developing a proactive environmental strategy and the generation of competitive advantage from proactive environmental approaches.

The chapters in this volume were selected for their contribution to knowledge in these two main areas: the antecedents and the outcomes of environmental capability generation.

THE CHAPTERS IN THIS VOLUME

The chapters in this volume have been selected from the proceedings of the first Gronen Workshop on Research on Advanced Environmental Management: Opportunities and Capabilities held in Granada, Spain in April 2004. The papers at the Gronen conference were first reviewed by the conference scientific committee and then subsequently went through a minimum of two editorial reviews and revisions for this volume. The papers were selected based on their novelty and innovativeness, and the rigour of conceptual and empirical research in the area of environmental strategy, organizational capabilities and competitive advantage.

Gronen is an acronym for the Group of Research on Organizations and Natural Environment. The inspiration for its creation arose at the Academy of Management meetings in Seattle in 2003 where a group of North American and European scholars agreed to promote activities via an open network of scholars focused on rigorous research in organizations and natural environment. Gronen was set up with five main objectives: (1) to foster and facilitate rigorous research; (2) to encourage creative ideas about innovative ways of protecting the planet and its ecosystems; (3) to promote personal interactions and collaborations between scholars analysing the relationships between natural environment and organizations; (4) to foster geographical, methodological and paradigmatic heterogeneity in organizations and the natural environment research; and (5) to be flexible in developing initiatives such as workshops, conferences, symposia and web-based interactive forums to promote a scholarly community in order to achieve the first four objectives.

The next three chapters focus on conceptual discussions of the external and internal antecedents of environmental capability building including public policy, stakeholder engagement, managerial and organizational values, and human resource practices, and the outcomes of such capabilities in terms of environmental innovation. The following six chapters embed these discussions in the context of specific sectors such as small and medium-sized enterprises, the services industry, the hotel industry, the manufacturing sector and Danish industry. These six chapters include four empirical studies that support several theoretical bases for the environmental capability and competitive advantage linkages. The last three chapters adopt a more macro approach, urging 'outside-in' rather than 'inside-out' oriented capabilities to detect and prepare for extreme environmental events, and the development of sustainable clusters of innovation and green networks to tackle sustainability problems that transcend organizational boundaries.

Chapter 2 by Marcus examines the antecedents of competitive capabilities that can lead to proactive environmental approaches in such areas as pollution prevention and new product development. He proposes that the main drivers for the acquisition of these capabilities are public policies, the values and beliefs of managers, and the negotiation processes via which resource allocations are made. Since institutional forces such as public policies and regulations are filtered through unique psychological (managerial) and organizational processes, the same set of pressures will lead firms to develop unique and different capabilities for generating their environmental strategies. Thus he argues that institutional forces will not lead to isomorphic responses but rather strategic choice based on the unique capabilities that are developed by each firm. His arguments highlight the importance of managerial interpretations of environmental issues as opportunities or threats (Sharma, 2000) and existing managerial attitudes toward environmental protection (Cordano and Frieze, 2000).

Marcus makes a useful distinction between competences and capabilities. He argues that capabilities are the building blocks of competencies, and complementary and co-specialized capabilities can be integrated to generate a competence of strategic environmental management. An interesting research area of investigation arising from his discussion relates to managerial decision-making processes: the complex negotiations and the interplay between managerial morality and ethics about 'doing the right thing' and the dictates of environmental legislation and public policy and a firm's obligations to maximizing shareholder wealth. Analysing these processes will help us understand how firms invest in technologies, skills and resources to generate capabilities for building a proactive environmental management competence.

In Chapter 3, Sharma accords similar importance to managerial interpretations in the generation of capabilities required for innovations that enable firms to develop proactive environmental approaches. Balancing the often conflicting objectives of social equity, ecological integrity and economic growth creates complexity in strategic decision-making because of the number and diversity of stakeholders impacted upon by the firm's operations. As such, sustainability solutions transcend organizational boundaries and an effective understanding requires an integration of perspectives from a wide range of external and internal stakeholders. An organizational capability of engaging and integrating perspectives of diverse stakeholders can influence organizational innovation at two levels: by altering organizational knowledge structure and by transforming managerial interpretations of sustainability issues from threats to be averted into opportunities to be sought. A capability of integrating and absorbing stakeholder knowledge helps a firm to analyse the ecological impact of product life cycles and also to design products for the environment, since radical innovation requires the insights of multiple thought worlds or interpretive schemas of communities who think differently. Social intercourse helps managers evaluate complex and conflicting external information, and the potential for learning is higher when the firm faces an ambiguous environment.

This chapter concludes with a research agenda that emphasizes a longitudinal mapping of processes via which firms dynamically develop the capabilities to engage stakeholders, absorb and integrate knowledge, and develop the capability for innovating products, processes and business models for a proactive sustainability strategy. Similar to Marcus's chapter, this chapter emphasizes strategic choice and argues that self-motivated business innovation has greater potential for generating sustainable business models compared to prescriptive regulations that specify technologies and processes which may conflict with an organization's economic objectives.

In Chapter 4, Ramus adopts a more micro perspective on strategies for creating an alignment between individual and organizational values for environmental preservation to enable the generation and deployment of capabilities for proactive environmental approaches. She argues that people, and not organizations, make the decisions to adopt technologies, to implement environmental policies and to manage environmental impacts in a more sustainable manner, and therefore the organizational context and managerial values matter. Emphasizing the importance of achieving fit between organizational and individual values on environmental preservation, Ramus develops a conceptual model of how individual and organizational value systems determine individual motivations to perform environmental tasks within the organizational context. She integrates individual motivation variables including personal disposition, self-efficacy and expectancy surrounding both the task and the desired outcome, personal perceptions of organizational norms, and situational strength that includes well-recognized rules of conduct, availability of rewards and a strong rewards–performance relationship. She recommends issue-selling strategies when individual values for environmental preservation are stronger than the organization's, and organization design and motivational strategies when individuals do not share the organization's strong values for environmental protection. The chapter presents a useful research agenda.

Chapter 5 by Aragón-Correa and Matías-Reche focuses on an often under-represented and under-researched context: small and medium-sized enterprises (SMEs). They make the case that theories and research developed in the large firm context may not be completely applicable for SMEs. Focusing on the antecedents of environmental capabilities, they argue that their flexibility, entrepreneurial orientation and unified organizational cultures may place SMEs in an advantageous position to generate competitive capabilities such as shared vision for sustainability, stakeholder engagement, and 'prospector'-oriented search for innovative solutions for proactive environmental approaches. Their arguments hold promise for making the SME sector, which constitutes a significant proportion of the global economy, environmentally proactive. They caution however that SMEs must develop systematic and holistic approaches toward environmental problems rather than isolated capabilities in order to achieve competitive benefits.

In contrast to the previous conceptual chapters, Chapter 6 by Kassinis and Soteriou is an empirical study that focuses on the outcomes rather than the antecedents of environmental capability generation in another less-researched area, the services industry (the European hospitality industry). They make the case for research on environmental strategies of service companies because of certain distinctive characteristics such as the limited choices of technologies for pollution prevention, simultaneous production and consumption of services, and the involvement of the consumer as a co-producer. Thus organizational boundaries are more diffuse and interactions are more instantaneous during the service creation and consumption process, as the values, beliefs and reactions of customers interact with those of the employees of the firm. Their study examined the nature of the relationship between environmental management practices and performance in the context of services. Specifically they investigated whether the use of such practices by a service firm is positively related to performance through the mediating effect of enhanced customer satisfaction and loyalty, by looking at the impact of environmental practices on the external portion of the service profit chain. They found that the relationship between environmental practices and market performance is not direct but rather indirect when they detected a positive relationship between environmental practices and customer satisfaction, between customer satisfaction and loyalty, and finally between loyalty and market performance of the firm.

The Kassinis and Soteriou study further highlights the importance of the capabilities (customer satisfaction) that mediate the link between proactive environmental practices and performance of the firm. Generating customer satisfaction and loyalty is not dependent on environmental practices alone but is a complex capability that is organization specific and socially complex, which requires anticipating and responding to the environmental values and beliefs of customers appropriately.

In a similar research context, the Balearic Islands hotel industry, in Chapter 7 Crespi-Cladera and Orfila-Sintes examine the organizational antecedents that drive the generation of environmental innovation. Adding to the characteristics of services discussed in the previous chapter, they argue that competitiveness in tourism is intrinsically linked to the conservation of the environment since this is what attracts the tourists to the destination. However the tourism activity contributes to the deterioration of the very resource on which it depends, and may in turn result in significant losses in competitiveness to the point of the definitive decline of the destination. Moreover any environmental improvements undertaken by an individual hotel in making the destination attractive also benefits the local industry as a whole. Their study found that hotels which belonged to a chain or a business group, were owner managed, were larger in size, had a greater intensity of utilization and offered a wider range of services were more likely to develop capabilities for undertaking environmental innovations. They found that pressure from tour operators did not influence this capability. Their findings point to the importance of reputation management and resource availability (belonging to chains and larger size), longer-term commitment to a community (owner management) and size of ecological footprint (intensity of use and range of services offered) as driving factors. It is possible that tour operators generally do not focus on environmental attributes of a destination unless they specialize in eco-tourism.

In contrast to the emphasis on services in the previous two chapters, the next two chapters focus on the manufacturing sector. In Chapter 8 Claver-Cortés, Molina-Azorín, Tarí-Guilló and López-Gamero conduct a useful review of extant empirical research studies to find parallels and relationships between quality management, environmental management and firm competitiveness via cost and differentiation advantages. Drawing on the RBV, they develop a model which proposes that the resources and capabilities that need to be generated and deployed for undertaking both total quality management (TQM) and proactive environmental strategy are similar, and can lead to lower costs and differentiation advantages. They argue for a dynamic process in which both TQM and environmental strategy help develop the firm's resources and capabilities and these resources and capabilities in turn improve both the TQM and environmental practices, and enhance competitiveness.

Chapter 9 by del Brío, Fernández and Junquera is an empirical study in manufacturing firms that confirms the arguments presented by Claver-Cortés et al. in the previous chapter. Their study found that an integrated eco-manufacturing strategy is likely to have positive competitive outcomes for a firm. Their results revealed improvements in corporate and product image, relationships with external and internal stakeholders, and product quality as a consequence of the implementation of environmental practices in factories with advanced environmental objectives, leadership in environmental efficiency and manufacturing capabilities for quality. Innovation and international growth improved as a consequence of the implementation of environmental practices in factories with advanced environmental objectives, with strategically integrated environmental issues, with leadership in environmental efficiency, with just-in-time production systems, and with manufacturing capabilities for product customization. On the other hand, innovation and international growth worsened in factories that focused only on legislation compliance. Finally, efficiency improved in factories with manufacturing capabilities for manufacturing flexibility. Their study confirms the important mediating role played by environmental capabilities in generating competitive advantage for a firm undertaking proactive environmental approaches.

In contrast to the previous nine chapters, in Chapter 10 Ulhøi and Madsen strike a cautionary note on the importance of market and competitive drivers for generating proactive environmental approaches. They present data from a longitudinal study initiated in 1995 and repeated every fourth year. They report that regulations are still the most important driver in influencing corporate environmental practices, even though public policy that provided incentives for proactive environmental practices would be useful. They also argue that the short-term result orientation of business prevents managers from undertaking long-term changes and building capabilities for proactive approaches to environmental issues. They conclude that it is not so much that self-regulation and the EMS approach are wrong per se, but that relying solely on such approaches is inadequate. What is really required is a paradigm shift that would involve industry accepting its ethical and social responsibilities. However they expect that this is unlikely to happen without significant pressure from stakeholders, which they find weakening over time. Readers should view these results in the Danish context of the study. Certainly studies in the North American context indicate evidence for increasing pressure of multiple stakeholders on corporations for undertaking proactive environmental practices (for example Henriques and Sadorsky, 1999; Sharma and Henriques, 2005) and the increasing development of capabilities by firms for undertaking proactive approaches.

In Chapter 11 Winn and Kirchgeorg contend that the growing number of increasingly extreme natural disasters puts us on the verge of a radical paradigm shift regarding the relationship between ecological, societal and economic systems – one in which the environment should be assigned a significantly higher status. As multinational corporations face increasingly massive ecological discontinuities, new perspectives, firm capabilities and long-term strategies for survival will be required for a new era of management characterized by extreme upheaval, destruction and chaotic change. These capabilities, rather than focus on balance, stability and integration, will be designed to enhance the resilience of organizations and their adaptability. Thus organizational capability generation processes will shift from an 'inside-out' orientation to an 'outside-in' orientation similar to the perspectives presented by Hart and Sharma (2004).

The last two chapters agree with the Winn and Kirchgeorg perspective and contend that ecological sustainability is an urgent problem that cannot be tackled by individual organizations. In Chapter 12 Boons and Roome argue that sustainable development cannot be achieved by one organization alone and that we need to examine sustainable enterprise in clusters of innovation. Such clusters can take the form of supply chains, localized forms of industrial ecology, knowledge networks, technology development, or local or regional partnerships for sustainable development. Firms need a different set of capabilities to manage their interactions in such clusters. These capabilities utilize the tacit knowledge developed in clusters to deal with the complexity in systems change, processes of multi-actor interaction and intervention in systems. Similar to Starik and Rands (1995), this chapter adopts an open system perspective to propose that the critical capabilities for managing clusters of innovation include those for: (1) the technical management of ecological impacts; (2) the integration of economic, social and ecological values; (3) the identification and management of the appropriate system levels and boundaries; (4) the engagement and integration of other actors; (5) the development of trust between the cluster actors; (6) the coordination between different levels of governmental agencies (local, regional, national, international); (7) unlearning to break existing routines, assumptions, frames of reference and routines; and (8) the balancing of tension between experimentation in the clusters and the need for organizational stability.

Finally, Lehmann, Christensen and Larsen present an empirical study of one type of cluster discussed by Boons and Roome. They examined the Green Network in Denmark that has been in existence for around ten years since 1994 and includes 200 companies and ten public bodies that range from county authorities and municipalities to the Danish Working Environment Authority. They found that the network developed three unique capabilities effectively: (1) for keeping abreast of all the important developments; (2) for absorbing what they found important and putting aside (decoupling) influences that did not fit into their visions and programmes; and (3) for translating new influences from the institutional field quickly. The network developed two capabilities to a limited degree: (4) for getting rid of old institutions; and (5) for reactivating old ideas. The Green Network was successful in developing a capacity of detachment so that project groups could be easily shut down if a project was no longer necessary, viable or of interest to the members. The network also succeeded in making member companies take an overview of their environmental impacts so that they could address problems in a systematic and preventative way. They found significant continuity in the people, companies and administrative bodies making up the network. They conclude that the network has become a learning organization with the capacity to absorb new ideas from its environment and translate them to its own needs.

FUTURE RESEARCH DIRECTIONS

Each chapter in this volume offers several suggestions for future research directions and also for measuring the constructs and relationships developed. Some of the major research issues and intriguing ideas that arise at the intersection of these chapters are discussed in this section.

One theme that emerges clearly is that in examining capabilities, we need to emphasize investigation methods that enable a longitudinal examination of dynamic processes. This is stressed, among other chapters, in the chapters by Marcus, Sharma, and Boons and Roome. The Lehmann et al. study is the only empirical examination in this volume that adopts a longitudinal analysis of capability generation in networks. This remains a major gap not only in organizations and the natural environment research but also in the RBV research. While some argue that by their very nature, capabilities are difficult to identify and measure, we suggest that ethnographic or grounded research (Glaser and Strauss, 1967) designs that enable the mapping of evolution and changes in organizational processes and routines can effectively measure these dynamic processes. The natural resource-based view offers the greatest potential for motivating organizations to undertake proactive environmental approaches and therefore scholars need to continue to refine their research methodologies and capability measurement processes.

Second, managerial cognitions are critical filters through which external influences are interpreted and integrated into internal decision-making processes and capability generation and deployment. Marcus and Sharma emphasize the critical role of managers as mediators between external influences and the internal organizational context, while Ramus emphasizes the criticality of aligning the organizational context and values in shaping pro-environment employee behaviour. It may be argued that individual psychology is as difficult to measure as the organizational routines and processes that constitute organizational capabilities. However in the measurement of managerial cognitions, attitudes, interpretations, values and beliefs, the organizational behaviour literature has drawn on a rich source of rigorously developed measures and scales in the psychology literature. This gives us hope that developing reliable measures for evolving and dynamic organizational capabilities is a challenge that can be met.

Third, researching capability generation requires holistic research perspectives at multiple levels of analysis. The Marcus and Sharma chapters elaborate on the connections between public policy, institutional, inter-organizational, stakeholder, intra-organizational and managerial variables in the generation and deployment of competitive capabilities to develop proactive environmental strategies accompanied by competitive advantage. Carefully constructed research designs at multiple levels of analysis can reveal at what stage societal, institutional and stakeholder forces become less important influences on the development of proactive environmental strategies, and internal variables such as managerial interpretations and values, and organizational capabilities, become more important. What is the dynamic process via which internal managerial interpretations and competitive capabilities are influenced by, and shape, the external forces?

Fourth, Marcus argues that capabilities are the building blocks of a competence and that proactive environmental strategy can be considered a competence. In a recent article, Aragón-Correa and Sharma (2003) similarly argue that a proactive environmental strategy is a dynamic mega-capability that helps a firm align its strategy with the changing general business environment. We need research that identifies different configurations of co-specialized and complementary capabilities that generate proactive environmental approaches and competitive advantage in different contexts and contingent situations.

Fifth, even though Aragón-Correa and Matías-Reche propose that SMEs may develop unique capabilities for proactive environmental strategy or develop similar capabilities faster than larger organizations, this contradicts the extant research that finds a positive relationship between organization size and environmental proactiveness (Russo and Fouts, 1997; Sharma, 2000). In fact the Crespí-Cladera and Orfila-Sintes chapter in this volume also finds a positive effect of size on environmental innovation. Therefore we need comparative research studies that map the distinct capabilities of smaller and larger organizations and examine how these contribute differently to competitive advantage for firms. We also need to understand in which situations, and under which contingencies, size is important.

Sixth, Kassinis and Soteriou, and Crespí-Cladera and Orfila-Sintes, make a case for why services are different from manufactured goods. However their studies do not reveal specifically how the characteristics of services such as simultaneous production and consumption, the involvement of the consumer as a co-producer, and the conflict between a destination's environmental attractiveness and the negative effects of tourism affect the generation and deployment of capabilities for proactive approaches. Once again comparative studies of service and manufacturing firms (for example del Brío, Fernández, and Junquera's study) could examine the distinctive capabilities within each type of industry and how the greater involvement of the consumer in the production process of service firms and the close association of the consumption experience (destination) with environmental attractiveness enables the generation of such capabilities.

Seventh, does the national context matter and in which ways does it matter? Ulhøi and Madsen present a pessimistic future for environmental strategy and competitive advantage research. Is this because Danish firms have already achieved a certain level of environmental proactiveness that firms in other countries are still striving for, and further progress needs fresh public policy initiatives? Is this because the institutional environment and societal and stakeholder expectations and priorities have changed?

Comparative cross-cultural studies are important to understand the influence of national context.

Finally, the role of clusters or networks and other forms of inter-organizational collaboration is critical for finding the urgent solutions to the global sustainability problems that our planet faces. The last three chapters discuss some of the capabilities firms need to undertake and manage successful multi-stakeholder partnerships for sustainable innovation. With limited success of global initiatives on issues such as climate change, there is great urgency for researchers to focus on studies that examine the antecedents and outcomes of capability generation for achieving sustainable outcomes at a regional, national and global level, while enhancing the achievement of core competitive objectives of network members.

REFERENCES

Ackerman, R.W. (1975), *The Social Challenge to Business*, Cambridge, MA: Harvard Business Publishing.
Amit, R. and P.J.H. Schoemaker (1993), 'Strategic assets and organisational rent', *Strategic Management Journal*, **14**, 33–46.
Andersson, L.M. and T.S. Bateman (2000), 'Individual environmental initiative: Championing natural environmental issues in US business organizations', *Academy of Management Journal*, **43**, 548–70.
Aragón-Correa, J.A. (1998), 'Strategic proactivity and firm approach to the natural environment', *Academy of Management Journal*, **41**, 556–67.
Aragón-Correa, J.A., F. Matías-Reche and M.E. Senise-Barrio (2004), 'Managerial discretion and corporate commitment to the natural environment', *Journal of Business Research*, **57**, 964–75.
Aragón-Correa, J.A. and S. Sharma (2003), 'A contingent resource-based view of proactive corporate environmental strategy', *Academy of Management Review*, **28**(1), 71–88.
Balderjahn, I. (1988), 'Personality variables and environmental attitudes as predictors of ecologically responsible consumption patterns', *Journal of Business Research*, **17**, 51–6.
Barney, J.B. (1991), 'Firm resources and sustained competitive advantage', *Journal of Management*, **17**(1), 99–120.
Bhat, V.N. (1992), 'Strategic planning for pollution reduction', *Long Range Planning*, **25**, 54–61.
Bringer, R.P. and D.M. Benforado (1994), 'Pollution prevention and total quality environmental management', in R.V. Kolluru (ed.), *Environmental Strategies Handbook*, New York: McGraw Hill, 165–88.
Buccholz, R.A. (1993), *Principles of Environmental Management: The Greening of Business*, Englewood Cliffs, NJ: Prentice Hall.
Buttel, F.H. and W.L. Flinn (1976), 'Economic growth versus the environment: survey evidence', *Social Science Quarterly*, **57** (September), 410–20.
Buzzelli, D. (1991), 'Time to structure and environmental policy strategy', *Journal of Business Strategy*, March–April, 17–20.

Cairncross, F. (1991), *Costing the Earth*. Boston, MA: Harvard Business School Press.

Capra, F. (1992), 'Five criteria of systems thinking', *The Elmwood Quarterly*, **8**(4), 9–10.

Catton, W.R. and R.E. Dunlap (1978), 'Environmental sociology: a new paradigm', *American Sociologist*, **13**, 41–9.

Catton, W.R. and R.E. Dunlap (1980), 'A new ecological paradigm for post-exuberant sociology', *American Behavioural Scientist*, **24**, 15–47.

Christmann, P. (2000), 'Effects of "best practices" of environmental management on cost advantage: the role of complementary assets', *Academy of Management Journal*, **43**, 663–80.

Colby, M.E. (1990), 'Environmental management in development: the evolution of paradigms', World Bank Discussion Paper no. 80, Washington, DC: World Bank.

Cordano, M. and I.H. Frieze (2000), 'Pollution reduction preferences of US environmental managers: applying Ajzen's theory of planned behavior', *Academy of Management Journal*, **43**, 627–41.

Dean, T.J. and R.L. Brown (1995), 'Pollution regulation as a barrier to new firm entry: Initial evidence and implications for future research', *Academy of Management Journal*, **38**, 288–303.

Dunlap, R.E. and K.D. Van Liere (1978), 'The new environmental paradigm: a proposed measuring instrument and preliminary results', *Journal of Environmental Education*, **9** (Summer), 10–19.

Dunlap, R.E. and K.D. Van Liere (1983), 'Cognitive integration of social and environmental beliefs', *Sociological Inquiry*, **53** (2/3), 333–41.

Dunlap, R.E. and K.D. Van Liere (1984), 'Commitment to the dominant social paradigm and environmental concern: an empirical examination', *Social Science Quarterly*, **65**(4), 1013–28.

Elkington, J. (1994), 'Towards the sustainable corporation: win–win–win business strategies for sustainable development', *California Management Review*, winter, 90–100.

Elkington, J., P. Knight and J. Hailes (1991), *The Green Business Guide*. London: Gollancz.

Erdmann, P.B. (1992), 'Editor's note', *Columbia Journal of World Business*, **27**(3–4) (Focus issue: Corporate Environmentalism), 6–7.

Evan, H.Z. (1986), *Employers and the Environmental Challenge*, Geneva: International Labour Office.

Gill, J.D., L.A. Crosby and J.R. Taylor (1986), 'Ecological concern, attitudes, and social norms in voting behavior', *Public Opinion Quarterly*, **50**, 537–54.

Gladwin, T.N., J.J. Kennelly and T. Krause (1995), 'Shifting paradigms for sustainable development: implications for management theory and research', *Academy of Management Review*, **20**, 874–907.

Glaser, B.G. and A.L. Strauss (1967), *The Discovery of Grounded Theory: Strategies for Qualitative Research*, Chicago, IL: Aldine.

Hall, R. (1993), 'A framework linking intangible resources and capabilities to sustainable competitive advantage', *Strategic Management Journal*, **14**, 607–18.

Hansen, P.E. and S.E. Jorgensen (eds) (1991), *Introduction to Environmental Management*, Amsterdam: Elsevier.

Harman, W. (1987), 'From organizations to organism', in W. Harman (ed.), *A New View of Business and Management: Participative Wholes and Autonomous*

Parts – the Organ Metaphor in Science and Societal Change, Sausalito, CA: Findhorn Foundation.

Harman, W. (1992a), 'The role of business in a transforming world', *Business Ethics*, **6**(2), 28–30.

Harman, W. (1992b), 'Managerial effectiveness and value systems: Indian insights', in W. Harman (ed.), *The Shifting Meaning of Managerial Effectiveness*, Calcutta: Institute of Noetic Sciences.

Harman, W. (1992c), 'Toward a conscious metaphor in science', *Noetic Sciences Review*, **24**, 35–7.

Hart, S.L. (1995), 'A natural-resource-based view of the firm', *Academy of Management Review*, **20**, 874–907.

Hart, S.L. and G. Ahuja (1996), 'Does it pay to be green? An empirical examination of the relationship between emission reduction and firm performance', *Business Strategy and the Environment*, **5**, 30–7.

Hart, S.L. and S. Sharma (2004), 'Engaging fringe stakeholders for competitive imagination', *Academy of Management Executive*, **18**(1), 7–18.

Henriques, I. and P. Sadorsky (1999), 'The relationship between environmental commitment and managerial perceptions of stakeholder importance', *Academy of Management Journal*, **42**, 87–99.

Jorgensen, S.E. (1991), 'Introduction', in P.E. Hansen and S.E. Jorgensen (eds), *Introduction to Environmental Management*, Amsterdam: Elsevier, 1–12.

Judge, W.Q. and T.J. Douglas (1998), 'Performance implications of incorporating natural environmental issues into the strategic planning process: an empirical assessment', *Journal of Management Studies*, **35**, 241–62.

Klassen, R.D. and C.P. McLaughlin (1996), 'The impact of environmental management on firm performance', *Management Science*, **42**, 1199–1214.

Klassen, R.D. and D.C. Whybark (1999), 'The impact of environmental technologies on manufacturing performance', *Academy of Management Journal*, **42**, 599–615.

Kolluru, R.V. (ed.) (1994), *Environmental Strategies Handbook*, New York: McGraw Hill.

Majumdar, S.K. and A.A. Marcus (2001), 'Rules versus discretion: the productivity consequences of flexible regulation', *Academy of Management Journal*, **44**, 170–79.

Marcus, A.A. and D. Geffen (1998), 'The dialectics of competency acquisition: pollution prevention in electric generation', *Strategic Management Journal*, **19**, 1145–68.

Miles, R. and C. Snow (1978), *Organizational Strategy, Structure and Process*, New York: McGraw Hill.

Morrison, D.E. and R.E. Dunlap (1986), 'Environmentalism and elitism: a conceptual and empirical analysis', *Environmental Management*, **10**, 581–9.

Nehrt, C. (1996), 'Timing and intensity effects of environmental investments', *Strategic Management Journal*, **17**, 535–47.

Nehrt, C. (1998), 'Maintainability of first mover advantages when environmental regulations differ between countries', *Academy of Management Review*, **23**, 77–97.

North, K. (1992), *Environmental Business Management: An Introduction*, Geneva: International Labour Organization.

Orr, D. (1992), *Ecological Literacy: Education and the Transition to the Postmodern World*. Albany, NY: State University of New York Press.

Peteraf, M. (1993), 'The cornerstones of competitive advantage: a resource based view', *Strategic Management Journal*, **14**, 179–91.

Porter, M.E. (1980), *Competitive Strategy: Techniques for Analysing Industries and Competition*, New York: Free Press.

Porter, M.E. (1991), 'America's green strategy', *Scientific American*, April, 168.

Porter, M.E. and C. van der Linde (1995), 'Green and Competitive', *Harvard Business Review*, September–October, 120–34, 196.

Purser, R.E., C. Park and A. Montuori (1995), 'Limits to anthropocentrims: toward an ecocentric organization paradigms', *Academy of Management Review*, **20**, 1053–89.

Ramus, C.A. and U. Steger (2000), 'The roles of supervisory support behaviors and environmental policy in employee "ecoinitiatives" at leading-edge European companies', *Academy of Management Journal*, **43**, 605–26.

Roberts, P. (1992), 'Business and the environment: an initial review of the recent literature', *Business Strategy and the Environment*, **1**(2), 41–50.

Roome, N. (1992), 'Developing environmental management strategies', *Business Strategy and the Environment*, **1**(1), 11–24.

Rugman, A.M., and A. Verbeke (1998), 'Corporate strategies and environmental regulations: an organizing framework', *Strategic Management Journal*, **19**, special issue, 363–75.

Rumelt, R.P. (1984), 'Toward a strategic theory of the firm', in R. Lamb (ed.), *Competitive Strategic Management*, Englewood Cliffs, NJ: Prentice-Hall, 556–70.

Russo, M.V. and P.A. Fouts (1997), 'A resource-based perspective on corporate environmental performance and profitability', *Academy of Management Journal*, **40**, 534–59.

Schmidheiny, S. (1992), *Changing Course: A Global Business Perspective on Development and the Environment*, Cambridge, MA: MIT Press.

Sharma, S. (2000), 'Managerial interpretations and organizational context as predictors of corporate choice of environmental strategy', *Academy of Management Journal*, **43**, 681–97.

Sharma, S. and I. Henriques (2005), 'Stakeholder influences on sustainability practices in the Canadian forest products industry', in press, *Strategic Management Journal*, **26**(2), 159–80.

Sharma, S. and H. Vredenburg (1998), 'Proactive corporate environmental strategy and the development of competitively valuable organizational capabilities', *Strategic Management Journal*, **19**, 729–53.

Shrivastava, P. (1992), 'Corporate self-greenewal: strategic responses to environmentalism', *Business Strategy and the Environment*, **1**(3), 9–21.

Shrivastava, P. (1994), 'CASTRATED environment: GREENING organizational studies', *Organization Studies*, **15**, 705–26.

Shrivastava, P. (1995a), 'Ecocentric management for a risk society', *Academy of Management Review*, **20**, 118–37.

Shrivastava, P. (1995b), 'Environmental technologies and competitive advantage', *Strategic Management Journal*, **16**, 183–200.

Shrivastava, P. (1995c), 'The role of corporations in achieving ecological sustainability', *Academy of Management Review*, **20**, 936–60.

Starik, M. and G.P. Rands (1995), 'Weaving an integrated web: multilevel and multisystem perspectives of ecologically sustainable organizations', *Academy of Management Review*, **20**(4), 908–35.

Taylor, S.R. (1992), 'Green management: the next competitive weapon', *Futures*, **24**, 669–80.

The Academy of Management Review (1995), 'Special topic forum on ecologically sustainable organizations', **20**(4), 873–1115.

UNWCED – United Nations World Commission on Environment and Development (1987), *Our Common Future*, New York: Oxford University Press.

Walley, N. and B. Whitehead (1994), 'It's not easy being green', *Harvard Business Review*, **72**(3) 46–52.

Welford, R. and A. Gouldson (1993), *Environmental Management and Business Strategy*, London: Pitman Publishing.

Wernerfelt, B. (1984), 'A resource-based view of the firm', *Strategic Management Journal*, **5**, 171–80.

Winter, G. (1988), *Business and the Environment: A Handbook of Industrial Ecology with 22 Checklists for Practical Use and a Concrete Example of the Integrated System of Environmentalism Business Management*, Hamburg: McGraw Hill.

Wood, D.J. (1991), 'Corporate social performance revisited', *Academy of Management Review*, **16**(4), 691–718.

World Bank (1992), *Development and the Environment*, New York: Oxford University Press.

2. Research in strategic environmental management[1]

Alfred A. Marcus

The Brundtland Commission defined sustainable development as meeting 'the needs of the present without compromising the ability of future generations to meet their own needs' (World Commission on Environment and Development, 1987). To achieve sustainable development, it is necessary to recognize the interdependence of the economy, the environment and the community and to take better account of the long-term view in decision-making processes. Since the Brundtland Commission report was first issued there has been ample discussion of what sustainable development is, with little real resolution. Business sustainability is nearly as hard to define. An example may be the efforts some firms made to introduce elements of strategic environmental management (SEM). SEM rests on the assumption that businesses can maximize returns to investors at the same time as they minimize environmental harm. SEM research is about aspects of environmental management that build competitive advantage at the same time as improving the environment. Examples would be pollution prevention that lowers a firm's costs, and the introduction of environmentally friendly products and services that enable a firm to obtain premium prices. Pollution prevention shows companies how to save money, because pollution is a form of inefficiency – it indicates that scrap, harmful substances and energy are not being used completely or effectively. Introducing new products shows companies how to enhance their earnings. Companies can make big jumps in product development. Innovations are open in such areas as miniaturization, weight reduction, design for reuse and repairability.

How do firms acquire capabilities in pollution prevention and new product development that improve environmental protection? There is relatively little systematic research that explains the acquisition of such capabilities. Some of the existing research on the acquisition of competitive capabilities focuses on sources internal to the firm. For instance Penrose's early writings suggest that capabilities emerge as the unintended consequences of growth and expansion as managers find new uses for surplus resources (Penrose, 1957). Chandler argues that the knowledge and skills

27

underlying capabilities are developed from trial and error learning, feedback and evaluation in solving problems (Chandler, 1992). Taken together, this body of work portrays firms as generating capabilities through an incremental and path dependent process of learning from their own experiences (Nelson and Winter, 1982). More recently strategy researchers have started to examine how firms derive capabilities externally by learning from their inter-organizational ties. By participating in ongoing networks of alliances and exchange, they gain access to network resources that assist them in the discovery of new opportunities (Gulati et al., 2000). Network resources are a form of social capital found in the relations between firms (Coleman, 1988). Through such networks, firms learn about capabilities and by means of internal absorptive capacities they use this information to their advantage, to create competitive abilities in such areas as pollution prevention and new product development (Cohen and Levinthal, 1990).

In this chapter, I argue that there is yet another way to explain the origins of competitive capabilities in such areas as pollution prevention and new product development. There are more distant forces unrelated to what happens inside the firm and the proximate ties firms have with other companies. System-wide properties, such as long-standing and elementary logics that are embedded in public policies and the values and beliefs of managers, exert pressures on firms and contribute in significant ways to the acquisition of capabilities for environmental protection like those in pollution prevention and new product development (Marcus and Geffen, 1998). In the model I propose, the drivers for the acquisition of these capabilities are public policies and the values and beliefs of managers. These are filtered through psychological and organizational processes, which lead different firms to respond to the same set of pressures differently. The overall model is one of pressures and response, and the important question is how managers perceive, understand and negotiate their solutions in response to these pressures (Hoffman, 2000).

In this chapter, I raise a number of research questions related to this model. The first section discusses more completely the resource-based view of competitive environmental management and offers a novel explanation of some of its key concepts. The second section examines the role that public policies play in the acquisition of competitive capabilities for environmental protection. The next two sections focus on two of these capabilities: pollution prevention and new product development. The fifth section considers the impact of values and beliefs on the acquisition of these capabilities, and the sixth section raises questions about environmental negotiations. How do managers negotiate their solutions to these pressures? The final section sums up this discussion.

THE RESOURCE-BASED VIEW OF COMPETITIVE ENVIRONMENTAL MANAGEMENT

Among many economists, the idea that expenditures on the environment positively affect firms remains controversial (Majumdar and Marcus, 2001). Standard economic assumptions are that spending on environmental protection imposes significant costs and slows productivity improvements, but Porter argued that environmental challenges, by inducing firms to economize, can improve their productivity (Porter, 1991). Based on the evidence from several case studies, Porter and van der Linde concluded that environmental spending can in fact enhance a firm's competitiveness (Porter and van der Linde 1995a, b). A considerable body of work now supports the idea that sometimes it 'pays to be green' (Gladwin, 1993; Hart, 1995; Shrivastava, 1995; Russo and Fouts, 1997). In the years since Porter and van der Linde (1995a, b), a number of management scholars have explored these claims and offered their own frameworks for addressing the relationship between environmental protection and competitive advantage (Klassen and Whybark, 1999). Much of the work has relied on the resource-based view of the firm (RBV), and thus it is worth considering in greater detail what the RBV is. It is a view rather than a theory, an evocative description instead of a series of logically deduced and tightly related falsifiable propositions (Miller and Shamsie, 1997). Often it has been criticized for being tautological in nature, with the distinctions between its concepts being at best subtle (Priem and Butler, 2001). A better understanding of the RBV therefore may be necessary if we are to have a full blown understanding of competitive environmental advantage based on it.

Often there is confusion about the fundamental concepts in the RBV. There are important differences among resources, capabilities and competencies that are worth noting. The concept of a resource comes from economic theory. In economics, resources are mainly financial capital, labour and physical property. Tangible and protected by legal rights, they have prices and can be possessed and owned, transferred and traded, and bought and sold in the market (Hall, 1992, 1993). Capabilities and competencies are less measurable, analysable, understandable and tradable than resources; they cannot be as easily owned, transferred, bought or sold. According to some researchers, they are the cumulative outcomes of historical processes (Levinthal and Myatt, 1994). As a result, they resist social engineering (Barney, 1991). They cannot be easily acquired, and have more value in deterring competition. They may be compared to recipes, software, and artistic sense and technique, while financial capital, labour and physical property may be compared to ingredients, hardware, brushes, canvasses and paint (Winter, 1987; Itami and Roehl, 1987).

In the RBV, the terms 'capabilities' and 'competencies' often used are interchangeably as synonyms that connote capacities, endowments, skills and aptitudes (Bogner et al., 1999). Though frequently substituted for each other, the literature also suggests that there are significant differences between them (Prahalad and Hamel, 1990). Capabilities are 'building blocks' which 'aggregate' into competencies (Prahalad and Hamel, 1990: 84). Capabilities suggest potential, while competencies connote achieved proficiencies. Capabilities represent a system's separate components, while competencies represent its realized wholes. According to Prahalad and Hamel, companies may have many capabilities – 30 or more – but few competencies – less than five or six (Prahalad and Hamel, 1990: 84). Competencies allow the organization to tie together its complementary and co-specialized capabilities. They provide for synergy among closely connected and supportive elements, make significant contributions to perceived customer benefit and provide 'potential access to a wide variety of markets' (Prahalad and Hamel, 1990: 84). Since they involve a complex harmonization of parts, they are hard to imitate. Indeed the more complex the integration of separate elements, the more difficult it is to comprehend and copy a competency and the easier it is for a firm to establish and sustain a competitive position based on a competency it acquires.

A competence in environmental management establishes a valuable competitive position that is hard to imitate, reproduce and duplicate. It rests on many constituent capabilities such as pollution prevention and toxic reduction, full cost analysis, auditing, design for the environment, product stewardship, industrial ecology, total quality environmental management, collaboration with environmental and other non-governmental organizations, ties to trade associations, relationships with firms in the same and different industries, policy formalization manifested in environmental policy statements and reports, CEO and board involvement, and so on. How these different elements relate and cohere, how they are built up over time and come together to form an overall competence in environmental management, is an important question that deserves further research. Very little research has been done on this important question. In the retail food industry for instance, the creation of such a competence might begin with practices like newspaper, plastic and paper recycling, but to these practices others could be added (Marcus et al., 2001). A grocer could engage in advanced recycling (recycling of wooden pallets, cooking oil, meat, fat and bones, or plastic bags). It could become involved in consumer education and offer environmental products and services. It might have to provide training for its managers and employees to develop these capabilities. Its employees might be asked to use such techniques as systematically collecting and reporting information on the grocer's wastes and energy usage.

Competence in environmental management is composed of many constituent elements built up over time. The elements have complex relationships among them. To form a coherent whole, the firm's environmental capabilities have to be brought together and related in complex ways. The more complex the relations among the separate elements, the harder it is to copy or duplicate the competence the firm has acquired, and the more valuable it may be in providing competitive advantage.

A large literature deals with business competencies and a similar one has started to emerge with respect to a competency in environmental management. Hart, Shrivastava, Sharma and Vredenburg, and Christmann were among the first to consider environmental management as a competency that can provide the firm with business as well as environmental advantages. Hart, taking a 'natural-resource-based view of the firm', argued firms that developed capabilities in pollution prevention, product stewardship and sustainable development could achieve competitive as well as environmental advantage (Hart, 1995). Shrivastava argued that techniques and methods that minimized environmental impacts, reduced costs and/or enhanced sales could become a tool for competitive advantage (Shrivastava, 1995). In a study of companies in the Canadian oil and gas industry, Sharma and Vredenburg found that firms which took a proactive approach to environmental issues had unique organizational capabilities, such as stakeholder integration and continuous higher order learning and innovation (Sharma and Vredenburg, 1998). Christmann demonstrated a link between environmental best practices and competitive advantage in the chemical industry based on the existence of complementary capabilities in process innovation and implementation (Christmann, 2000). Firms with higher levels of matching assets gained larger cost advantages than firms with lower levels.

Though an impressive amount of work has been done, additional research is needed in understanding what an environmental competence really is, how it is created, what the capabilities upon which it is based are, how they are related, how the connections among these capabilities build up over time, why they might lead to competitive advantage, and how and why some firms rather than others acquire them. The process through which capabilities emerge can be vague and difficult to reconstruct because it is often based on idiosyncratic, trial-and-error efforts. Firms sometimes develop capabilities by accident rather than by planning, with learning occurring from failure as much as from success (Collins and Porras, 1994; McGrath et al., 1995; Sitkin, 1996). Even if the practices and techniques underlying a capability are explicitly defined, effective implementation may depend on associated know-how and skill in the firm (that is complementary assets) that are not articulated.

PUBLIC POLICIES

I have established that capabilities and competencies are important, but what drives their acquisition? Where do they come from? Capabilities and competencies cannot be taken as given (Ghemawat, 2001). Managers must develop them. They have to search for new ideas and methods, compare practices to the best in their industry, evaluate practices in other industries, and experiment. Inasmuch as these activities make the acquisition of additional capabilities and competencies possible, they have been referred to as a dynamic capability (Eisenhardt and Martin, 2000). A dynamic capability is 'the capacity of a firm to renew, augment, and adapt its core competencies over time' (Teece et al., 1997). The proactive environmental strategy to which Aragón-Correa and Sharma and Aragón-Correa refer is a dynamic capability (Aragón-Correa and Sharma, 2003; Aragón-Correa, 1998). An important question that researchers should ask is: to what extent does a dynamic capability give rise to both business and environmental competencies? Do they have common antecedents in the same underlying dynamic capability?

Because a business competency primarily yield private benefits that firms can fully appropriate, a dynamic capability is likely to be the main factor that brings it into existence. However with regard to a competence in environmental management, there are likely to be other causes that bring it into existence; this is because the acquisition of this competence does not produce benefits solely for the firm. When a given level of environmental protection is achieved, those who pay for it cannot exclude others from enjoying it (Marcus, 1996). The resulting gain is available to society at large, not just those directly tied to the firm. Because environmental protection is a type of public good, whose full value a firm cannot entirely appropriate, factors other than a dynamic capability may be needed to motivate its acquisition. Government's role obviously is quite important.

Government's role however means more than just regulation. To capture the richness and complexity of the firm–government interface, the focus should be on a broad array of public policies. Not enough research has been carried out on this broad array of policies. Another issue that should be researched is that firms do not merely respond to these policies. They exert considerable influence on the policy process and help create policies to which they must then respond. This too deserves additional scrutiny.

Whereas environmental regulation generally refers to legally binding mandates imposed by the government on firms and other polluters, environmental policy refers to a much broader range of policies and programmes that includes not only regulations but voluntary government–industry agreements, joint research and development efforts, government information dissemination programmes, grants, subsidies, transfers, taxes and other initiatives. In studying the relationship between competitive advantage and considerations of the natural environment, a much richer conception is possible if the focus is on broadly conceived environmental policies rather than just regulation. This is because the firm's capabilities and competencies are affected not only by environmental regulations, but also by the full range of policies and programmes.

The RBV suggests that firms will respond by trying to align their capabilities and competencies with the full spectrum of their policies. Their aim will be to enhance their capabilities and competencies so they can obtain sustained competitive advantage from these policies. While considerations of bounded rationality may restrict them to some degree, the managers of firms, if they are able to see clearly the linkages between different environmental policy types and their company's competitive advantage, will try actively to manage the public policy interface to their benefit. Not only will they participate in rule-making procedures with the goal of bringing about regulations that protect and exploit their capabilities and competencies, and blocking regulations that threaten their capabilities and competencies, but for the same reasons they will also try to exert influence on voluntary government–industry agreements, joint research and development efforts, government information dissemination programmes, grants, subsidies, transfers, taxes and other initiatives.

With regard to regulation, the argument that the win–win solutions are achievable usually rests on the assumption that a shift in regulations is needed to make them more effective and efficient. There is already a rich literature on how to improve regulations. Davis, Jaffe and Palmer, and Porter and van der Linde agree that spending on less flexible regulation is likely to retard productivity, while spending on more flexible regulation is likely to enhance it (Davis, 1977; Jaffe and Palmer, 1997; Porter and van der Linde, 1995a). A large body of organizational and public policy research supports this view (Marcus, 1988a, b). The first researcher to make this claim may have been Follet, in a classic essay 'the giving of orders', where she argues that when given orders people should have the opportunity to think independently and show initiative (Follett, 1995). Indeed several authors have found that flexible rules have a positive effect on performance because they stimulate entrepreneurship, creativity and risk-taking, while an excessively procedures and rule-centred culture stifles innovation (Burgelman, 1984; Kanter, 1986; Lawrence and Dyer, 1983; Strebel, 1987; Katz and Kahn, 1978; Eisenhardt, 1989). Flexible rules allow implementers to move beyond formal compliance to identification and internalization (Kelman, 1961). Linder and Peters for instance see value in implementers having the flexibility to adapt and redefine policies as they proceed. They maintain that when those that implement a policy play an active role in their design, the results are likely to be better (Linder and Peters, 1987). Scholars such as Lipsky, Rein and Rabinowitz, Elmore, Thomas, Berman, and Palumbo, Maynard-Moody and Wright have found that when implementers are given greater flexibility, they have greater knowledge of contradictory demands and conflicting imperatives at the point of delivery, and their performance therefore is better (Lipsky, 1978; Rein and Rabinovitz, 1978; Elmore, 1979; Berman, 1980; Thomas, 1979; Palumbo et al., 1983).

Criticisms of the current system of regulation have common elements, which point to the inflexibility of current regulations as being a barrier to the acquisition of environmental competencies by firms (Marcus et al., 2002). While the environmental regulatory system since the passage of major environmental legislation starting with the Clean Air Act in 1970 has achieved considerable improvements, even those with strong environmental values often view it as being costly and prescriptive, slow in issuing permits, focused on separate media rather than larger problems, and in need of updating to meet newly emerging problems. Most US environmental protection laws and regulations, especially those pertaining to emissions to air and discharges to waterways, set end-of-pipe technology-based standards based on the level of efficiency of pollution control devices available for a particular production process. Although alternative solutions can be employed, the regulatory outcome is far more certain if a plant manager installs the best available control devices. Thus innovations in pollution prevention, which reduce the use of toxic materials or internally recycle such materials, are not properly recognized or encouraged within the current system. Other critiques of the system are insufficient local inputs and a paperwork burden that stifles innovation.

Economists for a long period of time have been critics of the current US approach and have sketched elements of an alternative that might be more supportive of companies acquiring competencies in environmental management.[2] They base their thinking on the idea that the full harm caused by pollution and other assaults on natural systems are not adequately incorporated into the price system. As a free good with no price, nature tends to be overused. To correct this defect in markets, economists have made many proposals that move away from rigid command-and-control regulation and toward flexible approaches where creativity and innovation can flourish. The model that economists propose maximizes reliance on market mechanisms when allocation of resources is at stake; imposes pollution taxes (or trading in pollution rights) in proportion to the harms caused by pollution; establishes, to the extent possible, standards based on environmental outcomes and not on current technical solutions; introduces rigorous harm-based standards responsive to the latest advances in

scientific thinking; provides the public with clear, understandable information about the state of the environment; allows stakeholders a greater
role as watchdogs and guardians of the public interest; breaks down the
media by media (air, water and land) focus of regulatory laws, rules and
enforcement so that environmental impact, production and use can be
understood holistically; and encourages life cycle analysis, design for the
environment, total product responsibility and other system-wide approaches that would enable companies to acquire competence in environmental management. Environmental protection would be a more
integrated part of the management process. Companies would start with a
product's earliest design phase so that the environmental impact and
natural resource demands of production distribution and consumption
would be considered at an early stage along with market potential, costs of
production and distribution, and servicing problems. More research is
needed on this alternative – what it would take to get it implemented, and
what effects it would have on the acquisition of competencies in environmental management.

POLLUTION PREVENTION CAPABILITIES

For now, the question I would like to raise is the extent to which a regulatory system of this nature would encourage the further acquisition of innovative environmental management capabilities in pollution prevention
(P2). In theory the concept of P2, or reducing potential pollution at input
stages rather than at the output stage, makes good economic sense. The
goal is waste reduction. By increasing throughput, lowering rework rates
and scrap, and using less material and energy per unit of production, a
company can save money, enhance efficiency and become more competitive. The US government however long remained tied to end-of-pipe regulation (Freeman et al., 1992). Right-to-know provisions and the Toxics
Release Inventory (TRI) reporting programme in the 1987 Superfund
Amendments provided an initial impetus to P2. The 1990 Clean Air Act
barely mentioned P2. Congress passed the Pollution Prevention Act in
1990, which was designed to measure, coordinate and assist in implementing P2, but all this Act did was set up an information clearinghouse office
that gave awards to small businesses, used enforcement agreements to
commit violators to P2, and conducted research. The agency tried a voluntary reduction programme to get businesses to voluntarily reduce 17 chemicals including cadmium, chromium, nickel and toluene 33 per cent by 1992
and 50 per cent by 1995. The purpose of the Green Lights programme was
to get businesses to install energy-efficient lighting.

Chemical manufacturers were encouraged by their manufacturing association to start P2 programmes. Many companies did set up these programmes. They inventoried wastes and releases, evaluated impacts, established and implemented reduction plans, and practiced outreach. Successful P2 demanded attention to product and process design, plant configuration, information and control systems, human resources, R&D, the suppliers role, and organization. A team had to be assembled, a method for measuring P2 determined, process flow diagrams and material balance diagrams prepared, and a tracking system for materials set up. Operational and material changes then had to be considered, including process and production changes and material substitutions. A frequent target of P2 programmes was reduction of industrial solvents. For such programmes to succeed, employee involvement and recognition were important. Companies with notable programmes included 3M, Chevron, Dow, General Dynamics, IBM and Monsanto.

Despite the impressive efforts some firms made, this capability in environmental management was not fully adopted. Why was a capability in pollution prevention less than completely acquired by firms? There are a number of reasons including the following: (1) despite the financial benefits, managers viewed P2 as an extension of existing regulatory programmes that they regarded as costly and burdensome; (2) many managers believed their environmental accounting systems were not adequate to measure the true costs and savings; (3) many managers considered the risks of changing production processes to be too high; (4) many believed that investments in P2 would yield less return than other investments that they believed to be of greater strategic importance. More research is needed on why P2 and other cost-saving environmental management capabilities such as design for the environment, life-cycle analysis, environmentally conscious manufacturing, green marketing and industrial ecology have not been more frequently and fully acquired by firms.

NEW PRODUCT DEVELOPMENT CAPABILITIES

There is another environmental capability that needs further investigation as to its origins. Why have firms not used it to a greater extent? We need to know what stalls the new product development process in many firms, where environmentally sound technologies have barely got off the ground. There are many examples. A prominent one is in the area of energy. Electric utilities produce vast environmental impacts. The Environmental Protection Agency estimated that the industry generated 70 per cent of all US sulphur dioxide emissions and 30 per cent of all US nitrogen oxides

(US Environmental Protection Agency, Office of Air Quality Planning and Standards 1993). It was a major contributor to greenhouse gases, releasing more than 500 million tonnes of carbon per year (US Environmental Protection Agency, Office of Air Quality Planning and Standards 1993). Automobiles are another example where vast amounts of pollution are generated because of energy consumption. Energy efficiency and renewable energy (EERE) businesses have developed products and services that would help consumers save or replace traditional forms of energy such as oil, coal, natural gas and nuclear power. This sector includes manufacturers whose products or services save energy in residential or commercial buildings (for example energy-efficient windows, lighting components, insulation materials, appliances); save energy in industrial processes or settings (for example process controls, thermostats, heat recovery systems, ventilators); reduce energy use in commercial buildings or industrial settings (for example demand side management programmes, energy audits, training and software for energy systems); and/or produce renewable energy or alternate fuel products (for example photovoltaic products, wind power systems, whole tree biomass systems). While many EERE businesses are new firms, others are new businesses within larger, more established firms, but even the new businesses within larger firms represent ventures that are entrepreneurial in nature and are subject to the same forces that affect start-up firms.

A critical question that needs further investigation is why EERE businesses, as a whole, remain in a state of 'prolonged gestation' (Marcus and Anderson, 2001). Unlike other promising sectors of the 1970s (for example personal computers), they have not fully taken off. Some of the factors that kept this sector in a prolonged state of gestation were relatively low energy prices for conventional fuels starting in the 1980s, a pullback in government subsidies that occurred around the same time, and partially, as a consequence, a relatively low level of consumer demand. Other factors were performance uncertainties, high costs and insufficient development of infrastructure and supporting industries in the value chain. These supporting industries might have supplied valuable inputs and assisted in manufacturing, distribution, marketing, sales and/or service.

We would hope that such businesses could evolve and move through the stages of introduction, growth and business maturity as they are propelled forward by increases in sales. Not all businesses however pass smoothly through these stages. The duration varies across businesses, with some showing promise but failing to take off, and some sitting still for long periods of time neither gathering momentum nor dying. To move from initiation to take-off, critical mass and momentum are needed. This process can unfold over a very long period of time (Van de Ven and Garud, 1989). Indeed some businesses moved from origin to take-off in just two years while others take more than 50 years (Aldrich and Fiol, 1994).[3] The range of take-off time is great, and founders and entrepreneurs need considerable commitment if they are to succeed.

Commitment is especially needed between start-up and take-off, since it is in this period that many founders just give up – their interest wanes, they lose patience and they do not have the determination or the resolution to deal with setbacks that occur. Many are forced to abandon the venture because of circumstances they cannot effectively control, such as few customers, technological glitches, waning financial support and negative cash flow. Others quit before they even confront these negative conditions, simply because they grow tired or lose interest. In comparison to the number of businesses founded, relatively few survive, and even fewer take off (Hannan and Freeman, 1989). To increase the chances of success, a great deal of commitment is needed. Between start-up and take-off, the obstacles that must be overcome are formidable and those in charge of running a business must maintain their commitment.

A capability for new product development rests on ongoing commitment. Though EERE businesses floundered, many founders did not give up. A question that deserves research is why did they not give up. Why did they remain committed to this industry? A theory of commitment to businesses with an unknown future is needed. While there are many studies of who entrepreneurs are and why they start new ventures, little attention has been paid to the factors that affect commitment, yet it appears to be an important factor in explaining why some green products and services will take off and others fail (Shane and Venkataraman, 2000). Abandoning a business in the interim between initiation and take-off dooms it to failure even when there may still be promise.

We need additional research to understand better what constitutes a capability in new product development. An important aspect of this research would be to investigate why businesses that can meet environmental needs fail to take off, and what can be done about it.

VALUES AND BELIEFS

Values and beliefs may play an important role in both the acquisition of P2 and new product development capabilities. Ethical obligations are reflected in how managers define their firms' missions (Sethi and Falbe, 1987). Some firms' missions are narrow and focused with the main concern being profitability. However other firms have broad missions that are inclusive of different stakeholders and their needs. Community relations, customer welfare and employee morale may be among these firms' top priorities. If a firm's mission is narrow, it may not even engage in basic environmental practices, but if it is broad it may go much further in the area of acquiring environmental capabilities. The relationship between a firm's mission and its acquisition of environmental management capabilities needs to be further explored.

Another question is the origin of values and beliefs. Where do managers get them from? Specifically, how do managers acquire a long-term commitment to an industry with an uncertain future like EERE? One possibility is that actions to educate key business stakeholders may lead proponents of new green products and services to believe that the businesses in which they are participating are attractive, that their products and services are superior, and that disruptive exogenous change will take place that will be positive to the endeavours they have undertaken. The more that they act to educate key business stakeholders, the more their beliefs are likely to grow. By engaging in actions to convince key business stakeholders, they firm up their convictions and build confidence in the rightness of their values and beliefs. Their actions reinforce the values and beliefs, and the values and beliefs in turn reinforce the actions in a recursive cycle (Salancik, 1977).[4]

In trying to educate key business stakeholders, proponents of green products and services may come to believe in the conditions that justify their continued commitment to green entrepreneurship.[5] The proponents of green products and services endeavour to frame the unknown in a way in which it will become believable. Competing for the right to be taken for granted, they rely on rhetoric – consistent stories, encompassing symbolic language and behaviours to gain legitimacy for their activities (Aldrich and Fiol, 1994). They use their powers of persuasion to overcome resistance and scepticism (Dees and Starr, 1992).

We need to know more about this act of creating values, norms, rules, beliefs and assumptions. We need to understand the role of persuasion in commercializing green products and services. We also need to know what sustains the optimism of the proponents of green products and services (Camerer and Lovallo, 1999). Is it a belief that basic conditions that block full commercialization will change? That is do these people to a greater extent than others believe that dynamic, disruptive, exogenous factors will alter the existing landscape (Brouwer, 1991)? Do they believe that shocks and upheavals from a variety of sources will fundamentally alter the way the system works, what products and services are valued and where economic opportunities lie? We need more research on their beliefs because the capability for new product development rests on these beliefs.

NEGOTIATIONS

Managers have an array of environmental capabilities that they may acquire, which they can consolidate and build into a competence in environmental management. So far I have argued that there are likely to be two main forces – public policies and values and beliefs – that stimulate the acquisition of capabilities and competencies in environmental protection. Managers confront public policy pressures and must consider their values and beliefs. Long-standing and elementary logics embedded in public policies and in their values and beliefs exert pressures on them. In light of these pressures, how do they negotiate solutions? We need a theory of negotiations that will inform practice as well as advance research. As there is not room enough here for a full theory, I simply sketch some of the elements that might go into it (Ramus and Marcus, forthcoming). I rely heavily on Raiffa for this analysis, but understand that a fuller theory would have to draw on other theorists of negotiations (for example see Wade-Benzoni et al., 2002) (Raiffa, 1982; Wade-Benzoni et al., 2002).

Raiffa makes much of the fact that environmental negotiations typically are multi-party in nature. He maintains that there is a vast difference in the difficulty in coming to an agreement in a negotiation with three parties as compared to two. With each additional party that joins the negotiation, the complexity of reaching agreement increases as groups and sub-groups form around particular issues and additional bargaining takes place, making it more difficult to reach agreement. Raiffa also notes that not all negotiating parties are internally monolithic. It is commonly the case in environmental negotiations that each party might comprise people who are from the same organization, but whose interests differ. By design, members of the negotiating team typically represent different organizational interests. There might be a single person at the head of the team who tries to aggregate these interests but in a complex organization that person will have problems melding together competing factions. Another factor that adds to the difficulty of reaching agreement is the number of issues on the table. On the face of it, it would seem that the more issues, the more complex the negotiations and the harder it would be to reach agreement. If the issues were highly technical, as is often the case in environmental negotiations, it would only add to the difficulty. Different parties with different beliefs regarding the 'facts' – the scientific and technical realities being debated – would have a hard time agreeing. The added complexity can prevent the parties from arriving at a solution, but the upside of ambiguity and of having more than one issue on the table is the potential it provides to satisfy all the parties. It gives them more to work with in their effort to find joint gains. Joint benefits arise because the different parties attach different values to the different issues. In this way, the benefits available to the parties grow and it may be possible to come to terms when otherwise an agreement was out of reach.

Outside mediators or arbitrators are customarily referred to as 'third parties', even when there are more than two disputants. If a third party can be brought in – a trained, outside facilitator – then one would think that the prospects for a settlement would improve. Raiffa holds that third party intervention can improve the chances for a settlement. However empirical studies show that third parties do not always have this beneficial effect. In a fascinating analysis in which Leach and Sabatier examined 50 randomly selected watershed partnerships in California and Washington between 1999 and 2001, they found that there was a statistically significant negative relationship between the involvement of a trained outside facilitator and agreement (Leach and Sabatier, 2003). Leach and Sabatier comment that 'despite their best intentions' the paid facilitators evoked 'feelings of resentment' (Leach and Sabatier, 2003: 167). Their 'professional training in the arts of consensus building' in fact was 'a detriment' (Leach and Sabatier, 2003: 167). It lead the facilitators 'to devote excessive amounts of time to "getting the process right"', thereby delaying the important substantive negotiations that had to take place (Leach and Sabatier, 2003: 167).

In most environmental negotiations the parties have a long-standing relationship and a history of negotiating around similar issues. The parties observe each other's behaviour to determine whether they can trust each other and work together. Through trial and error they may discover if mutual rewards are possible. Repeated interactions therefore may be a necessary element in forging cooperative solutions. The nature of repeated negotiations amongst the same parties is that each disputant is concerned about its reputation. According to Raiffa, this concern with reputation can lead to cooperative behaviour and honesty, but it also can lead to friction that builds up over time and spoils the atmosphere for negotiations (Raiffa, 1982). With repetition, each party may want to build a reputation for toughness to obtain long-term rather than short-term rewards. When parties interact repeatedly, they can develop into long-standing adversaries. The history and content of their prior opposition plays a disproportionate role. The parties seek not just an advance over the status quo, but one based on the weight and legitimacy of claims they have historically made. These claims are no longer tied to specific issues but are related to an underlying sense of fairness about their cause (Marcus et al., 2002). If the parties think they are dealing with 'strident antagonists' and malevolent, untrustworthy characters whose promises are suspect, then it is unlikely that an agreement can be reached (Raiffa, 1982).

More research is needed on resistance to resolution and the intractability of many environmental disputes. These disputes demotivate the parties from moving forward and establishing constructive win–win outcomes. Without such outcomes, the barriers to strategic environmental management increase.

CONCLUSION

Establishing a distinctive competence for managing the physical environment is important, as it can mean less waste, fewer emissions, less accidents, lower costs and better integrated systems. To the extent that this competence is tacit, casually ambiguous, rare, firm specific and adds value to customers through product differentiation or lower costs, it provides competitive advantage. Indeed many companies have made substantial advances in reconciling their business and environmental goals. They have created 'win–win' solutions where being 'green', rather than being a cost of doing business, has become an impetus for the development of new market opportunities and innovation. However these instances of win–win outcomes are not easy to realize. System-wide properties, such as long-standing and elementary logics that are embedded in public policies and in values and beliefs, exert pressures on firms and stand in the way of the acquisition of these competencies. Managers have to negotiate the approaches they take. How they negotiate their responses is vitally important.

The progress of sustainable business and in turn the solution to some of the world's most pressing environmental problems is likely to hinge on answers to questions such as these: What is a 'green' business practice? Which of these practices are indeed profitable? And what do we mean by 'profitable'? Are we talking about the short run or the long run? Are we concerned with return to investors or productivity? How are these different elements linked in understanding the effects of business investments? Which are the 'right' things to do, regardless of whether they are profitable, however profitability is defined? What are the obstacles – internal to the firm and external to it (for instance the firm's relations to companies in its supply chain, to financial markets, to government bodies and advocacy groups) – that prevent the firm from adopting these practices? What can be done to overcome these barriers? To what extent are actions called for by the public sector? What kind of public sector actions are needed and under what conditions? Which public sector actions work best in getting the firm to become more sustainable? When can voluntary private sector actions (information disclosure and/or self-regulation for instance) replace or supplement private sector actions? When can so-called 'market' mechanisms like pollution charges or taxes best be used? Questions such as these have been discussed in this chapter.

Some business leaders no longer view environmental protection as just a constraint. They see it as an opportunity to lower costs through such means as pollution prevention, and to meet new customer demands by offering products that fulfil human needs with less environmental impact. These business leaders have gone further than others in integrating their economic goals with the goals of environmental protection. They have shifted from litigious, anti-regulatory attitudes and behaviours to new cooperative attitudes. This shift is redefining their relationships with suppliers, distributors, customers and financial markets as well as with government bodies of all types, environmental advocacy groups and international institutions.

A key proposition of SEM is that investments in environmental protection can have a positive impact on the corporate bottom line. This proposition however may not always hold. It needs to be tested: under what circumstances do investments in SEM actually lead to a positive return to businesses? Answering this question is important, for if it can be demonstrated that there are positive returns, and that these returns are likely to be higher than alternative investments, then the burden on managers is to show why they are not moving in this direction. From a strictly agency perspective (the primary obligation of managers is to maximize returns to shareholders), why are corporate leaders not making the pollution control and prevention investments that have proven to be profitable? The reason may be various institutional and organizational barriers both internal to the firm and external to it. The study of these barriers and how to overcome them is a very important area of SEM research. It is where traditional management research with its attempts to develop an empirically based, behaviorally driven theory and to understand idiosyncrasies in firm decision-making through the lens of organizational theories can play a powerful role and make an important contribution alongside economic theory.

There may be other motives for managers to make sustainable investments as well as profits, and these motives are also worthy of investigation. Thus it is important to sort through which investments would be made, even if they were not profitable. These investments might be made for a number of reasons. On the one hand, the public policy process gives firms little choice. Regulation compels firms to make these investments. Laws coerce them. They have to comply with legal dictates. But an interesting question is that given the fact that firms have to comply, what explains the ways firms exercise discretion in how they comply? With the exact same legal requirement in place, a similar facility facing nearly identical challenges to another facility may take a different approach. How do we best understand this exercise of autonomy?

Beyond the public policy process, there is another factor that may motivate firms to invest in sustainable projects. Another possibility is that these investments are made because a sufficient number of influential managers with power in the firm believe that it is the 'moral' or 'ethical' thing to do. They believe that making these investments is the 'right' thing. But what is ethical in this context? How is it to be determined and how can it be translated into effective managerial decision-making, when there are so many pressures on managers just to do what is profitable, and not do what is right?

NOTES

1. This chapter relies heavily on the many outstanding research collaborators and co-authors I have had over the years. I have blatantly borrowed some of their best ideas. I am heavily indebted to (in alphabetical order): Marc Anderson, Magali Delmas, Don Geffen, Tim Hardin, William McEvily, Sumit Mujumdar, Catherine Ramus and Ken Sexton.
2. For instance see Dorfman and Dorfman (eds) (1972). There are countless other works that have made this type of argument.
3. The average time to move from initiation to take-off was 29 years and the standard deviation was 15 years (Aldrich and Fiol, 1994).
4. As Salancik (1977: 62) writes, commitment is 'a state . . . in which an individual becomes bound by his (or her) actions'.
5. This reasoning is supported both by the literature on institutionalization and structuration, as Barley and Tolbert (1997: 93) argue, the 'web of values, norms, rules, beliefs, and taken-for-granted assumptions' in which people 'are suspended' are of people's 'own making'.

REFERENCES

Aldrich, H. and C. Fiol (1994), 'Fools rush in: the institutional context of industry creation', *Academy of Management Review*, **19**, 645–70.
Aragón-Correa, J. Alberto (1998) 'Strategic proactivity and firm approach to the natural environment', *Academy of Management Journal*, **41**(5), 556–67.
Aragón-Correa, J. Alberto and Sanjay Sharma (2003), 'A contingent resource-based view of proactive corporate environmental strategy', *Academy of Management Review*, **28**(1), 71–88.
Barley, S. and P. Tolbert (1997), 'Institutionalization and structuration: studying the links between action and institution', *Organization Studies*, **18**, 93–117.
Barney, Jay (1991), 'Firm resources and sustained competitive advantage', *Journal of Management*, **17**(1), 99–120.
Berman, P. (1980), 'Thinking about programmed and adaptive implementation: matching strategies to situations', in H. Ingram and D. Mann (eds), *Why Policies Succeed or Fail*, Beverly Hills, CA: Sage Publications, 205–31.
Bogner, W.C., H. Thomas and J. McGee (1999), 'Competence and competitive advantage: towards a dynamic model', *British Journal of Management*, **10**(4), 275–90.

Brouwer, M. (1991), *Schumpeterian Puzzles*, Ann Arbor, MI: University of Michigan Press.

Burgelman, R.A. (1984), 'Managing the internal corporate venturing process', *Sloan Management Review*, **25**(2), 33–48.

Camerer, C. and D. Lovallo (1999), 'Overconfidence and excess entry', *American Economic Review*, **89**, 306–17.

Chandler, A. (1992), 'Organizational capabilities and the economic history of the industrial enterprise', *Journal of Economic Perspectives*, **6**(3), 79–100.

Christmann, Petra (2000), 'Effects of "Best Practices" on environmental management', *Academy of Management Journal*, **43**(4), 663–80.

Cohen, W.M. and D.A. Levinthal (1990), 'Absorptive capacity: a new perspective on learning and innovation', *Administrative Science Quarterly*, **35**, 128–52.

Coleman, J.S. (1988), 'Social capital in the creation of human capital', *American Journal of Sociology*, **94**, S95–S120.

Collins, J.C. and J.L. Porras (1994), *Built to Last: Successful Habits of Visionary Companies*, New York: Harper-Business.

Davis, K.C. (ed.) (1977), *Discretionary Justice: A Preliminary Inquiry*, Urbana, IL: University of Illinois Press.

Dees, J.G. and J.A. Starr (1992), 'Entrepreneurship through an ethical lens: dilemmas and issues for research and practice', in D.L. Sexton and J.D. Kasarda (eds), *The State of the Art of Entrepreneurship*, Boston, MA: PWS-Kent, 89–116.

Dorfman, R. and N. Dorfman (eds) (1972), *Economics of the Environment*, New York: Norton.

Eisenhardt, K.M. (1989), 'Agency theory: an assessment and review', *Academy of Management Review*, **14**(1), 57–74.

Eisenhardt, K.M. and J.A. Martin (2000), 'Dynamic capabilities: what are they?', *Strategic Management Journal*, **21**, 1105–21.

Elmore, R.F. (1979), 'Mapping backward: using implementation analysis to structure policy decisions', chapter presented at the annual meeting of the American Political Science Association, Washington, DC.

Follett, M.P. (ed.) (1995), *Prophet of Management*, Boston, MA: Harvard Business School Press.

Freeman, H., T. Harten, J. Springer, P. Randall, M.A. Curran and K. Stone (1992), 'Industrial pollution prevention: a critical review', *Journal of the Air and Waste Management Association*, May, 618–56.

Ghemawat, P. (2001), *Strategy and the Business Landscape*, Upper Saddle, NJ: Prentice Hall.

Gladwin, T. (1993), 'The meaning of green', in J. Schot and K. Fischer (eds) *Environmental Strategies for Industry*, Washington, DC: Island Press, pp. 37–63.

Gulati, R., N. Nohria and A. Zaheer (2000), 'Strategic networks', *Strategic Management Journal*, **21** (Special Issue), 203–16.

Hall, R. (1992), 'The strategic analysis of intangible resources', *Strategic Management Journal*, **13**, 135–44.

Hall, R. (1993), 'A framework linking intangible resources and capabilities to sustainable competitive advantage', *Strategic Management Journal*, **14**, 607–18.

Hannan, M.T. and J.H. Freeman (1989), *Organizational Ecology*, Cambridge, MA: Harvard University Press.

Hart, S. (1995), 'A natural resource based view of the firm', *Academy of Management Review*, **20**(4), 986–1014.

Hoffman, Andrew J. (2000), *Competitive Environmental Strategy: A Guide to the Changing Business Landscape*, Washington, DC: Island Press.

Itami, H. and T. Roehl (1987), *Mobilizing Invisible Assets*, Cambridge, MA: Harvard University Press.

Jaffe, A. and K. Palmer (1997), 'Environmental regulation and innovation: a panel data study', *Review of Economics and Statistics*, **79**(4), 610–19.

Kanter, R.M. (1986), 'When a thousand flowers bloom: structural, collective, and social conditions for innovation in organizations', working chapter, Harvard School of Business, Boston, MA.

Kelman, H.C. (1961), 'Processes of opinion change', *Public Opinion Quarterly*, **25**, 608–15.

Katz, D. and R. Kahn (1978), *The Sound Psychology of Organizations*, New York: Wiley.

Klassen, R.D. and D.C. Whybark (1999), 'The impact of environmental technologies on manufacturing performance', *Academy of Management Journal*, **42**, 599–615.

Lawrence, P.R. and D. Dyer (1983), *Renewing American Industry*, New York: Free Press.

Leach, L. and P. Sabatier (2003), 'Facilitators, coordinators, and outcomes', in R. O'Leary and L.B. Bingham (eds), *The Promise and Performance of Environmental Conflict Resolution*, Washington, DC: Resources for the Future Press, 148–75.

Levinthal, D. and J. Myatt (1994), 'Co-evolution of capabilities and industry', *Strategic Management Journal*, **15**, 45–62.

Linder, S.H. and B.G. Peters (1987), 'A design perspective on policy implementation: the fallacies of misplaced prescription', *Policy Studies Review*, **6**(3), 459–75.

Lipsky, M. (1978), 'Standing the study of public policy implementation on its head', in W.D. Burnham and M.W. Weinberg (eds), *American Politics and Public Policy*, Cambridge, MA: MIT Press, 391–402.

McGrath, R., I. MacMillan and S. Venkatraman (1995), 'Defining and developing capability', *Strategic Management Journal*, **16**, 251–75.

Majumdar, S. and A. Marcus (2001), 'Rules versus discretion: the productivity consequences of flexible regulation', *Academy of Management Journal*, **44**(1), 170–80.

Marcus, A. (1988a), 'Implementing externally induced innovations: a comparison of rule-bound and autonomous approaches', *Academy of Management Journal*, **31**(2), 235–56.

Marcus, A. (1988b), 'Responses to externally induced innovation: their effects on organizational performance', *Strategic Management Journal*, **9**, 387–402.

Marcus, A. (1996), *Business and Society: Strategy, Ethics, and the Global Economy*, Chicago, IL: Irwin Press.

Marcus, A. and M. Anderson (2001), 'Why "fools" stay in: persistence in the pursuit of an opportunity business excellence and competence acquisition', Strategic Management Research Center Working Paper Series, University of Minnesota Carlson School of Management.

Marcus, A., M. Anderson and B. Spielmann (2001), 'Business excellence and competence acquisition', working paper, Strategic Management Research Center, University of Minnesota.

Marcus, A. and D. Geffen (1998), 'The dialectics of competency acquisition', *Strategic Management Journal*, **19**(12), 1145–68.

Marcus, A.A., D.A. Geffen and K. Sexton (2002), *Reinventing Environmental Regulation: Lessons from Project XL*, Washington, DC: Resources for the Future.

Miller, D. and J. Shamsie (1997), 'The resource-based view of the firm in two environments', *Academy of Management Journal*, **39**(3), 519–43.

Nelson R. and S. Winter (1982), *An Evolutionary Theory of Economic Change*, Cambridge, MA: Harvard University Press..

Palumbo, D.J., S. Maynard-Moody and P. Wright (1983), 'Measuring degrees of successful implementation: achieving policy versus statutory goals', chapter prepared for presentation at the Western Political Science Association meetings, Seattle.

Penrose, E. (1957), *The Theory of the Growth of the Firm*, Oxford: Basil Blackwell.

Porter, M.E. (1991), 'America's greening strategy', *Scientific American*, **264**, 168.

Porter, M. and C. van der Linde (1995a), 'Green and competitive', *Harvard Business Review*, **73**(5), 120–33.

Porter, M. and C. van der Linde (1995b), 'Toward a new conception of the environment–competitiveness relationship', *Journal of Economic Perspectives*, **9**(4), 97–118.

Prahalad, C.K. and G. Hamel (1990), 'The core competence of the corporation', *Harvard Business Review*, May–June, 79–91.

Priem, R. and J. Butler (2001), 'Is the resource based view a useful perspective for strategic management research?', *Academy of Management Review*, **26**(1), 22–40.

Raiffa, H. (1982), *The Art and Science of Negotiation*, Cambridge, MA: Harvard University Press.

Ramus, Catherine A. and Alfred A. Marcus (forthcoming), 'Examining barriers to negotiated environmental agreements', *International Journal of Organizational Theory and Behavior*.

Rein, M. and F.F. Rabinovitz (1978), 'Implementation: a theoretical perspective', in W.D. Burnham and M.W. Weinberg (eds), *American Politics and Public Policy*, Cambridge, MA: MIT Press, 307–35.

Russo, M. and P. Fouts (1997), 'A resource-based perspective on corporate environmental performance and profitability', *Academy of Management Journal*, **40**(3), 534–60.

Salancik, G.R. (1977), 'Commitment and the control of organizational behavior and belief', in B.M. Staw and G.R. Salancik (eds), *New Directions in Organizational Behavior*, Malabar, FL: Robert E. Krieger, 1–54.

Sethi, P. and C. Falbe (eds) (1987), *Business and Society: Dimensions of Conflict and Cooperation*, Lexington, MA: Lexington Books.

Shane, S. and S. Venkataraman (2000), 'The promise of entrepreneurship as a field of research', *Academy of Management Review*, **25**, 217–36.

Sharma, S. and H. Vredenburg (1998), 'Proactive corporate environmental strategy and the development of competitively valuable competencies', *Strategic Management Journal*, **19**, 729–54.

Shrivastava, P. (1995), 'The role of corporations in achieving ecological sustainability', *Academy of Management Review*, **20**(4), 936–60.

Sitkin, S. (1996), 'Learning through failures: the strategy of small losses', in M.D. Cohen and L.S. Sproul (eds), *Organizational Learning*, Thousand Oaks, CA: Sage Publications.

Strebel, P. (1987), 'Organizing for innovation over an industry cycle', *Strategic Management Journal*, **8**, 117–24.

Teece, David J., Gary Pisano and Amy Shuen (1997), 'Dynamic capabilities and strategic management', *Strategic Management Journal*, **18**(7), 509–33.

Thomas, R.D. (1979), 'Implementing federal programs at the local level', *Political Science Quarterly*, **94**, 419–35.

US Environmental Protection Agency, Office of Air Quality Planning and Standards (1993), *The Plain English Guide to the Clean Air Act, EPA-400-K-1993–01*, Washington, DC: Environmental Protection Agency.

Van de Ven, A. and R. Garud (1989), 'A framework for understanding the emergence of new industries', *Research on Technological Innovation, Management and Policy*, **4**, 192–225.

Wade-Benzoni, K.A., A.J. Hoffman, L.L. Thompson, D.A. Moore, J.J. Gillespie and M.H. Bazerman (2002), 'Barriers to resolution in ideologically based negotiations: the role of values and institutions', *Academy of Management Review*, **27**(1), 41–57.

Winter, S. (1987) 'Knowledge and competence as strategic assets', in D. Teece (ed.), *The Competitive Challenge*, Cambridge, MA: Ballinger.

World Commission on Environment and Development (1987), *Our Common Future*, Oxford, UK and New York, US: Oxford University Press.

3. Through the lens of managerial interpretations: stakeholder engagement, organizational knowledge and innovation

Sanjay Sharma

Scholars generally agree that the path to corporate sustainability requires the balancing of improved economic performance with smaller ecological footprints and the promotion of social equity by organizations (Gladwin et al., 1995; Starik and Rands, 1995). Businesses have developed a great deal of understanding about ways in which they can innovate to improve economic performance. However innovations that integrate the social and ecological dimensions with economic criteria are new for them. Moreover the social and environmental impacts of business cannot be assessed and understood based on internal information and knowledge alone. Such impacts are felt and perceived by a variety of external stakeholders. The understanding of stakeholders about the impact of corporate activities on their quality of life, health, air and water quality, recreational activities, habitats, species, global climate and a variety of other social and environmental parameters is evolving.

Interactions with stakeholders can help construct a firm's understanding of sustainability via its interactions with, and influences on, business operations (Hoffman, 1997; Jennings and Zandbergen, 1995; Sharma and Henriques, 2005). A firm's social embeddedness affects its strategy and practices (Baum and Dutton, 1996; Granovetter, 1973). Businesses focus primarily on economic performance and enhancing shareholder wealth. External stakeholders such as local communities, environmental NGOs, international regimes, and regulators, better understand the social and ecological impacts of business. Hence sustainability solutions transcend organizational boundaries (Westley and Vredenburg, 1991) and an effective understanding requires an integration of perspectives from a wide range of external and internal stakeholders.

Firms need an ongoing dynamic process for integrating these evolving perspectives from a wide range of external and internal stakeholders if they are to enhance their understanding of their social and environmental impacts and potential innovative solutions to strengthen their performance on social, environmental and economic criteria. However balancing the three seemingly conflicting objectives of economic, social and environmental performance creates ambiguity, complexity and uncertainty in strategic decision-making. This is because of the larger number and diversity of stakeholder issues and concerns affected by, or affecting, the firm's operations. Stakeholders such as aboriginal groups and environmental NGOs become increasingly important in the business environment while the range of concerns of conventional stakeholders such as consumers become diverse and include the environmental and social attributes of a product or service. Some stakeholders such as suppliers and customers may be collaborative and willing to work with the firm to improve its social and environmental impacts, while others may be adversarial and threaten or disrupt corporate operations.

Integrating the perspectives of diverse stakeholder groups, some of whom may be adversarial to the organization, has the potential to influence organizational knowledge and innovation in two ways. First, by transforming how managers interpret or make sense of sustainability, that is the interaction between economic, social and environmental criteria (Sharma, 2000; Sharma et al., 1999). These interpretations in turn influence organizational strategy and actions (Dutton and Jackson, 1987; Jackson and Dutton, 1988; Sharma, 2000). Second, by altering the organizational knowledge structure based on interactions with stakeholders within the domain of sustainability leading to innovations of sustainable products, processes and business models.

Therefore firms that engage their stakeholders within the domain of sustainability can potentially affect managerial understanding, interpretations and knowledge. Altered individual managerial knowledge interacts with the firm's internal knowledge base or its absorptive capacity potentially to result in organizational innovation in products, services, processes and business models that are sustainable. This chapter draws on the strategic issues diagnosis, and knowledge-based and resource-based views of the firm, to present a broad research framework to examine the organizational capabilities that channel the external knowledge flows created by stakeholder engagement into higher-order learning and sustainable organizational innovation.

CAPABILITY OF STAKEHOLDER ENGAGEMENT

Knowledge about sustainability embedded in a firm's stakeholder network is much greater than that residing in the firm or any individual stakeholder.

A firm's 'communities of interaction' (Nonaka, 1994: 15) are effective at generating, amplifying, transferring and recombining knowledge (Dyer and Nobeoka, 2000; Kogut, 2000; Nonaka, 1994). Through stakeholder exchanges, a firm begins to appreciate and understand the possibilities for action (Nahapiet and Ghoshal, 1998) to balance conflicting stakeholder influences within the sustainability domain. This requires a focus on both the exploration for information and the exploitation of existing knowledge (Levinthal and March, 1993; Van den Bosch et al., 1999). Exploration involves exchanging and combining information and experiences of individual stakeholders in interactions from the formal-hierarchical to the informal-social (Moran and Ghoshal, 1996; Nahapiet and Ghoshal, 1998; Nonaka, 1994).

External stakeholders want to influence a firm's sustainability practices because it possesses resources that will help them achieve their ecological and social objectives such as preserving natural habitats or human rights. The stakeholder influence can be direct or indirect via other stakeholders, and by withholding resources (finances, approvals) or by dictating changes in a firm's policies and operations (usage strategies) (Frooman, 1999), and collaborative or adversarial (Sharma and Vredenburg, 1998).

A stakeholder's intensity of commitment to a sustainability issue and its focus on the short-term versus long-term impacts of corporate operations influence its knowledge of sustainability and views of a firm's actions. Stakeholders may focus on social and ecological impacts such as the preservation of a habitat, species, community or the heritage of future generations. The intensity of their stake may vary from a short-term focus on individual events such as an oil spill or protecting a stand of temperate rain forest (for example Clayquot Sound on Vancouver Island in British Columbia) to a long-term focus on the sustainability impacts of a firm's processes (for example chlorine bleaching), inputs (for example forestry practices), technologies (for example nuclear power) and business models (for example selling versus leasing).

Stakeholders may be local and interact directly with the firm, or global and concerned about an overall technology or business process related to the industry in which the firm operates. Local stakeholders include investors, local communities, domestic customers, employees, state or provincial regulators, local NGOs, local and national media, and domestic suppliers. Global stakeholders include regulators in overseas markets, NGOs such as Greenpeace, international regimes such as the UNCED and WTO, overseas customers and suppliers, and communities affected by the operations of the firm's contractors or the use and disposal of the firm's products, or deforestation and soil depletion caused by the firm's suppliers to provide it with inputs. Global stakeholders such as Greenpeace, that adopt highly visible sustainability policies such as the elimination of the fossil fuel industry, influence the firm only indirectly via local stakeholders. Also an international NGO may ally with a labour union in a developing economy to improve working conditions and human rights by pressuring firms in that country to adopt minimum standards. Prominent activists or public figures such as musicians and actors sometimes take up the causes of indigenous people indirectly affected by the firm's value chain.

Local stakeholders have a greater impact on information and knowledge flow into an organization due to direct and frequent interactions with a firm. Local customers and suppliers may collaborate with a firm to find sustainable solutions, as compared to overseas customers and suppliers who could locate alternative businesses globally. Similarly state or national environmental regulations will have a greater impact on corporate operations because firms can circumvent regulations in foreign markets by selling in alternative markets. For example facing stringent regulations and consumer boycotts in European markets over their sustainability practices, several Canadian pulp and paper firms shifted their sales to Asian markets rather than invest in fundamental changes in their operations (Sharma, 1999).

Moreover stakeholders with economic stakes are likely to protect their own economic interests by collaborating with the focal firm to help develop knowledge about more sustainable usage of resources provided by them. For example banks and insurance companies may demand environmental certification, audits or reporting. The recent signing of the Equator Principles for sustainable project financing by the world's 20 largest banks implies that such pressures will increase. Customers and suppliers may request changes in products, packaging or distribution. Stakeholders with non-economic interests may not only withhold resources such as approvals and licenses, or contest new projects during environmental assessment processes, but also withhold legitimacy. For example local media may support environmental groups by not giving the firm an equal opportunity to present its perspective. Non-economic stakeholders may also exercise influence via economic stakeholders. The pathways for information flow and knowledge development may depend on how the firm engages such stakeholders.

In these various forms of direct and indirect interactions with stakeholders, a firm may choose either to avoid and disengage or actively engage with such stakeholders. The former strategy is unlikely to add to the firm's knowledge base and innovation capability. However engaging with a diversity of stakeholders in a dynamic and ongoing process that reaches out to fringe stakeholders that are weak, non-legitimate and silent has the potential of generating more diverse and disconfirming ideas and information that challenges a firm's current conventional wisdom (Hart and Sharma, 2004). Firms with proactive sustainability initiatives have been found to have a capability of engaging stakeholders and generating external information that helps them foster sustainable innovations (Sharma and Vredenburg, 1998). The depth of such a capability varies from integration of supplier and customer knowledge for product stewardship (Hart, 1995) or technological development (Marcus and Geffen, 1998), to integration of information from collaborative and adversarial economic and non-economic stakeholders for continuous learning (Sharma and Vredenburg, 1998), and ultimately to radical transactiveness designed to generate competitive imagination for the future (Hart and Sharma, 2004).

To transform a variety of stakeholder influences – adversarial and collaborative – into knowledge about sustainable practices, a firm must allow information to flow freely within the network and into the organization. An effective stakeholder engagement capability includes gatekeepers, trust building, and managing the interface for engaging stakeholders.

Gatekeeping

As the meaning and understanding of sustainability evolves within stakeholder networks, the firm needs gatekeepers to monitor the objectives and influences of stakeholders and translate this information for the internal constituents of the firm. A centralized environmental scanning department will not be effective in high knowledge exploration environments where the required dimensions of knowledge absorption are flexibility and scope, not centralized efficiency, which is important under conditions of information exploitation (Cohen and Levinthal, 1990):

> For technical information that is difficult for internal staff to assimilate, the gatekeeper both monitors the environment and translates the technical information into a form understandable to the research group. In contrast, if external information is closely related to ongoing activity, then external information is readily assimilated and gatekeepers or boundary-spanners are not so necessary for translating information. (Cohen and Levinthal, 1990: 132)

Gatekeepers may be environmental managers (Aragón-Correa et al., 2004), marketing managers, corporate community relations managers and others who interact with external publics. They must empathize with differences in perspectives (Clarke and Roome, 1999; Heugens et al., 2000), and understand the relevance of different perspectives to their firm's operations, and the impact of the firm's operations on external stakeholders' objectives. They must also be able to engage adversarial stakeholders and thus not only understand sustainability issues but also be trained in its language as spoken by various stakeholders (Clark and Roome, 1999; Hart and Sharma, 2004). To illustrate, after the Brent Spar debacle, in 1997 Shell

Expro (UK) sent its employees to workshops with facilitators from Natural Step and the Environment Council to train them to help catalyse the firm's Sustainable Development Business Plan in ongoing consultation with stakeholders (May et al., 1999). Similarly, before entering into a Sustainable Development Agreement with its community and NGO stakeholders in 1997, Formosa Plastics (Texas) compiled academic, scientific, social, religious, environmentalist, government and industrial literature related to sustainability. A conceptual model was completed, identifying how sustainability concepts applied to its facilities at all levels, and distributed to employees and key employees were trained in the sustainability concepts used by stakeholders (Blackburn et al., 1999).

Gatekeepers codify sustainability information from stakeholders to facilitate learning and decision-making by the organization. For example Royal Dutch/Shell guaranteed success of lessons learnt from stakeholder integration in its Camisea project in Peru by documenting and disseminating these lessons. At the same time, maintaining the continuity of gatekeepers is important to protect this learning (May et al., 1999). The gatekeepers also need to balance contradictory stakeholder demands through joint conflict management with input for all stakeholder concerns (Bazerman and Neal, 1984) as well as through monitoring and honest and open lines of communication to anticipate and avoid future conflicts (Kale et al., 2000). Conflict management engenders feelings of procedural justice and generates trust and commitment (Kim and Mauborgne, 1998) between the firm and its stakeholders.

Trust Building

Trust between a firm and its stakeholder groups is an agglomeration of trust between individuals in these organizations (Kale et al., 2000; Palay, 1985; Ring and Van de Ven, 1994) based on close personal ties (Macaulay, 1963). Mutual trust, respect and friendship between individual members of organizations generate relational capital (Kale et al., 2000). Diversity in stakeholder networks provides rich access to information but it is the quality of relationships (that is trust) that enables the full realization of the knowledge creation potential (Kale et al., 2000). Trust facilitates the intense and complex communication processes needed to transfer tacit knowledge across organizational boundaries (Hagg and Johanson, 1983; Tsai, 2000) and reduce the risk of opportunism. Trust facilitates knowledge creation in contexts of high ambiguity (Boisot, 1995) and is an 'indispensable base for facilitating . . . constructive "collaboration" for sharing experiences and knowledge creation' (Nonaka, 1994: 24). Trust allows organizational decision-makers to adopt a long-term perspective critical for building sustainable communities by diffusing norms of mutual gain, forbearance and reciprocity across the network (Powell, 1990; Rowley, 1997; Rowley et al., 2000).

Transparency and free exchange of information (Doz and Hamel, 1998; Hamel, 1991) lead to future knowledge flows due to the confidence that one partner will not exploit the vulnerabilities of the other (Barney and Hansen, 1994; Bradach and Eccles, 1989). This is knowledge-based trust (Gulati, 1995) that emerges as partners interact and learn about each other, rather than deterrence based on utilitarian considerations (Gulati, 1995). Trust is achieved via both gatekeepers and transparent corporate reporting systems. For example in 2000, Bill Ford Jr, chairman of Ford Motor Company, astounded the automobile industry by admitting that its popular sport utility vehicles (SUVs) contributed to global warming and were a safety concern for smaller cars. He was also open about Ford's plans for continuing to manufacture gas-guzzling SUVs to generate profits to develop environmentally friendly technologies. Ford's stakeholders including environmental groups responded favourably to this announcement (Welch, 2000; *The Economist*, 2000).

Free exchange requires the provision of information about the firm's sustainability impacts to stakeholders. This information is generated through audits and reporting via special environmental or sustainability reports. The firm should correct any incorrect or incomplete information stakeholders have, while providing all relevant information that will lead them to collaborative solutions. To illustrate, Alcoa's employees worldwide have access to benchmark technologies, information and resources via the Alcoa intranet library, learning centre, performance data and links to important EHS documentation (Schmandt and Tankha, 1999).

Stakeholder Interface Management

An effective stakeholder engagement capability requires managing an interface structure that facilitates trust-building and open information flows between the focal firm and the stakeholders. Tacit knowledge transfer requires intense interaction and cannot be transferred in large group meetings or during formal negotiations (Dyer and Nobeoka, 2000; Marsden, 1990; von Hippel, 1988). 'Much richer patterns of relationship and interaction are important where the meaning of information is uncertain and ambiguous or where parties to an exchange differ in their prior knowledge' (Nahapiet and Ghoshal, 1998: 253). Therefore effective knowledge management within a social network requires appropriate coordinating principles (Kogut, 2000), governance mechanisms (Dyer and Singh, 1998) in the form of committees and meetings, and an interaction infrastructure

(Dyer and Nobeoka, 2000; Nonaka, 1994; Van den Bosch et al., 1999) as well as inter-organizational knowledge-sharing routines (Dyer and Singh, 1998) to foster an ongoing multilateral dialogue rather than interactions only during crises. The interface structure should also include a memory bank or databases that detail the history of each relationship including stakeholder objectives as well as points of agreement and disagreement.

Such structures for economic stakeholders may include annual general meetings, financial reports, customer and supplier conventions, regular meetings with and surveys of customers and suppliers, and regular reports. Non-economic stakeholders such as regulators conduct inspections and require regular reports on emissions, effluents, air quality, employee welfare and working conditions. Firms interface with local communities and NGOs through open houses, community surveys, focus groups, partnering with local educational institutions, community awareness and education, and joint action committees. Fringe and distant stakeholders can be engaged by networking from the core to the periphery and by 'putting the last first' to hear the voices of the weak, powerless and non-legitimate (Hart and Sharma, 2004).

Interface coordination should be supplemented by internal coordination mechanisms to balance the information generated by gatekeepers, as each may be subject to different stakeholder influences and information. Firms need to ensure that the stakeholder voices emerging from operations and facilities considered less central or critical to the firm's operations are not drowned out by those emerging at high-visibility facilities or the head office. Conflicting stakeholder claims need to be understood and integrated so that their objectives are met in the best possible way. This may require coordination meetings of gatekeepers and operations managers of different units, and rotating operations managers among units.

For example after its reputation suffered during the Brent Spar and Nigerian incidents, Royal Dutch/Shell initiated a review of societal relations and an understanding of society's expectations. Round tables in 14 countries, interviews with Shell executives and external parties, focus groups with stakeholders, and surveys on reputation management uncovered weaknesses in achieving ecological and social objectives. Following this, Shell undertook formal partnerships with NGOs to facilitate learning on sustainability. These included the Natural Step and the Environment Council that helped develop Shell Expro's (UK) first Business Plan for Sustainable Development (1998), Pro-Natura that helped develop the Camisea Project's sustainable plan, and SustainAbility that helped implement Shell's triple bottom line strategy (May et al., 1999).

An effective stakeholder engagement capability requires the institutionalization of organizational routines to monitor and input stakeholder information via gatekeepers, and build trust via open and transparent information flows, and the effective management of the stakeholder interface to coordinate firm–stakeholder linkages. Firms can get better at generating knowledge from stakeholder interactions as they gain more experience (Amburgey et al., 1996; Anand and Khanna, 2000; Dyer and Singh, 1998; Lyles, 1988), making them attractive partners for other stakeholders. Increased experience reduces internal barriers to integrating external knowledge by providing information on the likely behaviour of other stakeholders, alleviating risk and enhancing willingness to form further linkages (Ahuja, 2000). The capability of stakeholder engagement is organizationally specific because it is socially complex or 'collective' (Spender, 1996) and depends on links outside and inside the organization (Cohen and Levinthal, 1990).

Stakeholder engagement only provides the conduit through which external perspectives can begin to flow into the organization. The challenge is to ensure that these perspectives are not ignored or misinterpreted, but rather become sources of organizational knowledge development and innovation. Managerial interpretations play a pivotal role in filtering external information into the organization.

THROUGH THE LENS OF MANAGERIAL INTERPRETATIONS

Uncertainty, complexity and ambiguity that characterize the domain of sustainability for organizations are an appropriate context for managerial sensemaking and interpretation of strategic issues (Weick, 1995). Managerial ignorance can be addressed via increased amounts of information. However uncertainty, complexity or ambiguity is often characterized by too much information rather than too little, whose resolution requires discussion, dialogue and sensemaking (Weick, 1995). The diversity of social, economic and environmental stakeholders that characterize the sustainability domain represent a complexity of often conflicting information, resulting in uncertainty and ambiguity about organizational actions and strategy.

One way to resolve such uncertainty or ambiguity is for managers to interpret the complex information emerging via stakeholder engagement into broad categories that facilitate decisions and actions. In their study of North American oil and gas firms Sharma (2000) and Sharma et al. (1999) found that reactive and proactive strategies of environmental responsiveness were a reflection of managerial interpretations of escalating environmental regulations and NGO and local community pressures for social and environmental responsibility, as either threats or opportunities.

As proposed by Dutton and Jackson (1987), they found managers that interpreted environmental issues as threats tended to see these issues as negative for their organization, over which they had little or no control, and with a potential to adversely affect their jobs and organizational performance (that is constrain outputs and profits). On the other hand, managers in firms with proactive environmental strategies viewed environmental issues as opportunities. They saw these as positive for their organization, over which they had control, and with a potential for generating gains for them personally or for organizational competitiveness.

Sharma (2000) and Sharma et al. (1999) found that the saliency of a threat or opportunity categorization for managerial cognitions and actions relevant to environmental issues could be shaped by the organizational context, which created an opportunity frame for managerial decision-making via providing managers with resources, information, discretion and commensurate reward and performance evaluation systems, while labelling and legitimizing these issues as positive and central to the organization's core mission and strategy. While the influence of the internal organizational context is undeniable in altering managerial perceptions, a manager's social community of interaction also influences his or her interpretation of strategic issues. In situations of ambiguity where the meaning of sustainability and expected responses are being socially constructed, managers can be expected to take cues from the stakeholders that they interact with in their work and personal lives for guidance concerning correct behaviour. Such psychologically weak or equivocal situations 'stimulate groups to engage in collective sense making and construct their own version of reality' (House et al., 1995: 94; Volkema et al., 1996).

Positive external influences from a manager's community of interaction about sustainability issues may override any negative signals within the organization. As a result of these external influences, managers may begin to transform other's negative interpretations within the organization, by initiating the process of issue legitimization of the saliency and importance of sustainability within the corporate identity. Similarly a manager's communities of interaction may help him or her overcome ambiguity by providing greater information about the meaning of sustainability, the environmental and social impacts of organizational operations, and potential solutions. This helps overcome managerial perceptions of lack of control over decision-making related to sustainability practices.

Finally, stakeholders may help provide managers with arguments to make a business case for more proactive sustainability performance to their peers and executive leadership. Making a business case for proactive sustainability practices helps managers overcome the perceptions of loss related to sustainability issues. Managers may already have developed potential solutions for overcoming the negative environmental and/or social impacts of organizational operations, but their actions may be constrained by an internal organizational context that creates perceptions of sustainability issues as threats. These managers may use a crisis (such as the need for transformation of the organizational process due to the ratification of the Kyoto Protocol) to push through their innovations. Burgelman and Sayles (1986), in their study on internal corporate venturing, showed how a research scientist who had been working on new types of insulation for years and was having trouble getting his work supported, was able to make a case for funding innovations in insulation products during the oil embargoes in the 1970s and the dramatic increase in the price of energy.

Therefore managerial interpretations of sustainability issues as opportunities rather than as threats will create positive organizational frames for innovation and are a lens through which external knowledge that flows in via stakeholder engagement is filtered into the organization. Managers may choose to label the external information negatively as a threat to the organization that requires strategies of avoidance and political lobbying, or positively as an opportunity that poses challenges for generating competitive imagination for future products, processes and business models (Hart and Sharma, 2004) via innovative solutions.

Fostering Sustainability Commitment

To create an opportunity frame for employees, firms need to foster managerial commitment to sustainability. Sustainability is a new paradigm for business (Shrivastava, 1995) and a foundation for future competitiveness (Hart, 1997; Hart and Milstein, 1999). To develop sustainability knowledge, firms need to create the conditions for sustaining a focus on sustainability. Rands and Marcus (1991) argued that only environmentally driven managers would fundamentally change corporate environmental strategies, and Cordano and Frieze (2000) emphasized the need to change managerial attitudes for improved pollution prevention performance. Sharma (2000) and Sharma et al. (1999) found that the legitimization of environmental leadership in the corporate identity contributed to the framing of environmental issues as opportunities and contributing positively to future competitive positions.

An organizational commitment to sustainability requires a strategic vision articulated publicly in corporate mission or vision statements. By devoting personal time and attention to sustainability issues and by emphasizing why sustainability is crucial to the growth and survival of the firm, the top management signals the strategic importance of sustainability to corporate strategy and corporate identity (Dutton and Dukerich, 1991; Sharma, 2000; Sharma et al., 1999). This issue labelling (Sharma, 2000) sends consistent signals to employees and builds and sustains commitment. Robert Browne of BP and Bill Ford, Jr of Ford Motor Company are examples of CEOs who have broken ranks with industry to publicly proclaim sustainable corporate visions.

As ambiguity prevents stakeholders from verifying that the firm actually behaves as it says it will (McEvily et al., 2000) transparency or a sharing of information with stakeholders is critical to maintaining sustainability commitment. Sustainability reports, audits, strategic plans, future product and service streams, and visible commitments of resources (Dixit and Nalebuff, 1991; McEvily et al., 2000) are signals to stakeholders about the incorporation of their concerns, objectives and inputs (Noda and Bower, 1996).

For example, Royal Dutch/Shell developed such a commitment by disseminating consistent sustainability information to its hundreds of divisions scattered worldwide and monitoring the progress of sustainability thinking across its complex decentralized structure (May et al., 1999). Shell's UK unit achieved commitment through employee training and also seeking every employee's input. Any employee was allowed to take time off to pursue sustainable activities. Shell also provided regular updates and feedback on progress through email and newsletters to show employees how their suggestions were being implemented (May et al., 1999). At its Camisea project, Shell set creative and modest targets to sustain commitment, rather than grand costly goals that seemed impractical (May et al., 1999).

To channel external knowledge constructively and productively through the lens of managerial interpretations to generate organizational innovation by integrating it with internal knowledge about operations and competitiveness requires that the organization possesses or generates a capability of disruptive or higher-order learning.

CAPABILITY FOR HIGHER ORDER LEARNING

The knowledge-based view of the firm (Conner and Prahalad, 1996; Kogut and Zander, 1992; Grant, 1996; Nonaka, 1994) emphasizes that in an uncertain environment, 'any organization that dynamically deals with a changing environment ought not only to process information efficiently but also create information and knowledge' (Nonaka, 1994: 14). Integrating sustainability knowledge into corporate strategy involves balancing seemingly conflicting social, ecological and economic objectives requiring higher-order learning (Argyris and Schön, 1978), a reinterpretation of existing information, and developing new understandings of surrounding events and influences (Fiol, 1994). 'When the organization faces non-recursiveness that cannot be dealt with by existing knowledge, it might try to create a new order of knowledge by making use of the fluctuation itself' (Nonaka, 1994: 28).

A capability of higher-order learning helps a firm combine external information with existing internal knowledge to generate knowledge that helps resolve conflicts between its social and ecological impacts, and economic performance (Sharma and Vredenburg, 1998). This capability is developed by building and improving organizational routines[1] for sharing explicit and tacit knowledge within the organization (Cohen and Levinthal, 1990; Levitt and March, 1988; Nelson and Winter, 1982; Nonanka, 1994), combining new information with organizational memory (Nahapiet and Ghoshal, 1998), enhancing absorptive capacity (Cohen and Levinthal, 1990) and changing the cognitive mindsets of decision-makers (Boeker, 1997; Sharma, 2000).

Following Van den Bosch et al. (1999), the organizational processes required for this capability may be categorized into combinative capabilities that enable the integration of external knowledge to generate higher-order learning. First, systems capabilities include top management direction on sustainability objectives, the labelling of sustainability issues as important for the firm (Sharma, 2000), and policies, procedures and manuals to integrate explicit knowledge. Second, coordination capabilities consist of sustainability training, job rotation, information-sharing committees, benchmarking of sustainability performance against jointly developed indicators, incentive and reward systems, and liaison between gatekeepers and managers responsible for strategic and operational decisions that enables internal transfer of tacit knowledge, and participative decision-making to help absorb that knowledge. Third, socialization capabilities foster a collective identity (of a sustainable organization) and managerial interpretations of sustainability issues as opportunities (Sharma, 2000). To illustrate, Royal Dutch/Shell facilitates coordination on sustainability information and widespread employee involvement by inviting them to forums and seminars, appointing team leaders to allocate responsibility for sustainability learning, and providing regular updates and feedback on sustainability practices, information from outside parties and alternative viewpoints (May et al., 1999).

Integrating varied and multiple stakeholder voices into strategic decision-making potentially alters organizational knowledge structures (Brown and Duguid, 1991; Nonaka, 1994) and thus affects organizational innovation.

ALTERED ORGANIZATIONAL KNOWLEDGE AND INNOVATION

Hart (1995) argued that integrating external stakeholder knowledge would help a firm analyse product life cycles in terms of their ecological impact, and design better products for the environment. Sharma and Vredenburg (1998) found that openness to external stakeholder influences, or a capability of stakeholder integration, would lead to continuous learning and innovation within organizations. Similarly in describing innovation within an organizational context, Dougherty (1992) argued that innovation requires the insights of multiple 'thought worlds' or interpretive schemas of different communities who think differently from each other.

Uncertainty that characterizes organizational decisions and practices related to sustainability often triggers breakdowns of human perception (Winograd and Flores, 1986) which may force managers to reconsider their fundamental world-views (Nonaka, 1994). Social intercourse helps managers evaluate complex and conflicting external information (Powell and Brantley, 1992). Therefore the potential for learning is higher when the firm faces an ambiguous environment (Anand and Khanna, 2000) that encourages social interaction.

A firm's 'communities of interaction' (Nonaka, 1994: 15) are effective at generating, amplifying, transferring and recombining knowledge (Dyer and Nobeoka, 2000; Kogut, 2000; Nonaka, 1994). Organizational knowledge is not simply the sum of individual knowledge (Nelson and Winter, 1982) but is 'inextricably located in complex, collaborative social practices' (Nahapiet and Ghoshal, 1998: 246) within and outside organizational boundaries (Brown and Duguid, 1991; Nonaka, 1994: 24). 'The diversity of knowledge that resides within a network is much greater than that which resides in a single firm. Consequently, if a network's members can "cooperate in a social community", superior learning opportunities will be generated' (Dyer & Nobeoka, 2000: 352).

Managers in firms that create forums or mechanisms for intense stakeholder exchanges (Hart and Sharma, 2004) can begin to appreciate and understand the possibilities for action (Nahapiet and Ghoshal, 1998) to balance conflicting stakeholder influences within the sustainability domain. This is because during times of crisis or extreme ambiguity, the negotiated order of information flows may change (Dutton and Jackson, 1987; Peterson, 1998; Tyre and Orlikowski, 1994), so that input from external stakeholders may become more important than the conventional information channels within the organization. This allows for the transfer of disconfirming information that managers would normally disregard or discount. A collective understanding of the social and ecological impacts of a firm's operations may lead to a reorientation of norms, world-views and frames of reference (Shrivastava and Mitroff, 1982).

This requires a focus on both the exploration for information and the exploitation of existing knowledge (Levinthal and March, 1993; Van den Bosch et al., 1999). Exploration involves exchanging and combining information and experiences of individual stakeholders in interactions from the formal-hierarchical to informal-social (Moran and Ghoshal, 1996; Nahapiet and Ghoshal, 1998; Nonaka, 1994). Influences from economic stakeholders such as suppliers and customers will generate exploitative knowledge that may help the firm improve operating efficiencies and economic performance. On the other hand, stakeholders with social and ecological concerns without an economic stake in the focal firm and with an adversarial stance may have radical ideas about business models with implications for future competitive advantage (Hart and Sharma, 2004). Sustainable solutions require that the firm both exploit and explore for information by harnessing and managing knowledge flows in a network of both economic and non-economic as well as collaborative and adversarial stakeholders. This will allow the firm to develop new perspectives and challenge conventional wisdom to increase its understanding of the complexities of sustainability practices (Heugens et al., 2000).

THE WAY FORWARD: A RESEARCH AGENDA

Stakeholder pressures for organizational sustainability increase the complexity of the business environment, requiring the balancing of the seemingly conflicting objectives of a firm's social and environmental stakeholders with those of its economic stakeholders (Gladwin et al., 1995; Starik and Rands, 1995). This challenges managerial frames of reference and business world-views and catalyses organizational learning and the reorienting of organizational processes. Firms with stakeholder engagement and higher-order learning capabilities can harness sustainability knowledge in stakeholder networks of not only collaborative economic stakeholders but also adversarial stakeholders with social and ecological concerns (Heugens et al., 2000). These are dynamic capabilities that consist of competitively valuable organizational sub-capabilities of gatekeeping, trust building, stakeholder interface management, maintaining sustainability commitment, systems capability, coordination capability and socialization capability.

Capabilities of stakeholder engagement and higher-order learning are competitively valuable because they are dynamic and path dependent on, and embedded within, a unique configuration of evolving stakeholder linkages and relationships. They may also lead to the development of organizational social capital which helps the firm extend its stakeholder network for further sustainability knowledge creation. These capabilities lead to short-term competitive benefits of organizational innovation in the form of waste reduction, better products and lower energy and material use (Hart, 1995), and long-term benefits including more customer-focused business models and products, operational legitimacy, reputation and competitive imagination (Hart and Sharma, 2004).

Research Implications

The theoretical framework in this chapter is developed within the context of organizational change toward sustainability. It is also a general model of managing complex change in business environments characterized by multi-stakeholder influences. However most other complex changes in the current business environment, such as the adoption of internet technologies, require input primarily from economic stakeholders and secondarily from social stakeholders. Few other contexts are more suitable than sustainability for examining how multi-stakeholder influences can drive systemic change in business (Jennings and Zandbergen, 1995; Gladwin et al., 1995; Shrivastava, 1995; Starik and Rands, 1995).

Testing the validity of this process requires longitudinal mapping of knowledge flows from stakeholder networks and their integration with internal knowledge to generate sustainable innovations. This requires multiple case studies of those firms in different industries and contexts that are embedded in complex stakeholder environments with multiple influences driving change toward sustainability. Industries such as forestry, energy, mining and chemicals face competitive global environments with pressures from both economic stakeholders to focus on short-term financial performance and shareholder value, and social and ecological stakeholders to improve their sustainability performance.

Research requires longitudinal mapping of interactions and processes at the stakeholder network level (external influences and embedded knowledge), the firm–stakeholder interface (socialization and communication between gatekeepers and stakeholders), and the organizational level (capability generation, mobilization and utilization, and sustainability knowledge creation). Potential stakeholder knowledge influences can be examined via the extent to which a focal firm is individually (rather than as a member of the industry or of the business community) subject to scrutiny by stakeholders, the focus of stakeholders on short-term impacts versus fundamental business processes, the local versus global locus of stakeholder focus, the objectives and concerns of stakeholders (social, ecological or economic), the pattern of communications between the stakeholders, and the strength of ties between the firm and its various stakeholders. These ties can be assessed based on economic measures of resource dependence as well as on the extent to which stakeholders influence organizational reputation, legitimacy and project approvals.

Examining the stakeholder engagement capability requires research at the firm–stakeholder interface to map the evolution of communication patterns and exchanges between the gatekeepers and stakeholder representatives. The changes in the respective attitudes of gatekeepers and stakeholders toward each other (collaborative versus adversarial), and the commonality of sustainability perspectives, goals and objectives, need to be explored. Examining this capability also requires studying the characteristics and sustainability training of gatekeepers, the pattern of conflict resolution, the formal and informal firm–stakeholder coordination and exchange mechanisms, and their respective attitude changes toward each other indicative of trust building. Learning and knowledge creation can be assessed by mapping the changes in internal managerial and organizational processes and routines, internal information flows and coordination structures, and increases in managerial understanding and knowledge of sustainability. Examining sustainability commitment involves studying top management commitment to sustainability via corporate mission statements and sustainability policies, and managerial interpretations of sustainability issues as opportunities versus threats (Sharma et al., 1999; Sharma, 2000).

Innovation outcomes can be examined via process changes involving waste, energy and material reductions that reduce negative environmental and social impacts, improved or new products that are also designed for lower environmental and social impact, and changes in business models that have positive sustainability impacts (such as Interface's switch to leasing floor comfort instead of selling new carpets). Assessing overall sustainability performance will require examining improvements to ecosystem health and social equity all along the firm's value chain via the operations of its suppliers, contractors and dealers, and product or service usage by consumers.

Mapping and describing the processes by which firms with a proactive sustainability strategy integrate knowledge from external and internal stakeholders to generate and deploy capabilities, and thereby innovate to enhance their competitiveness, promises to help organizations balance their economic objectives with their social and environmental impacts. Self-motivated business innovation has greater potential for generating sustainable business models compared to prescriptive regulations which specify technologies and processes that may conflict with an organization's economic objectives. This research will require comparisons between leaders and laggards in sustainability practices in several industry sectors to understand knowledge generation, capability development and innovation.

NOTE

1. Routines in this context are 'regular pattern of interactions among individuals that permits the transfer, recombination, or creation of specialized knowledge' (Dyer and Nobeoka, 2000: 347).

REFERENCES

Ahuja, G. (2000), 'The duality of collaboration: inducements and opportunities in the formation of interfirm linkages', *Strategic Management Journal*, Special Issue, **21**, 317–43.

Amburgey, T.L., T. Dacin and J.V. Singh (1996), 'Learning races, patent races, and capital races: strategic interaction and embeddedness within organizational fields', in J.A.C. Baum and J. Dutton (eds), *The Embeddedness of Strategy*, chapter 13, Greenwich, CT: JAI Press, pp. 303–22.

Anand, B. and T. Khanna (2000), 'Do firms learn to create value? The case of alliance', *Strategic Management Journal*, Special Issue, **21**, 295–315.

Aragón-Correa, J.A., F. Matias-Reche and M.E. Senise-Barrio (2004), 'Managerial discretion and corporate commitment to the natural environment', *Journal of Business Research*, **57**, 964–75.

Argyris, C. and D.A. Schön (1978), *Organizational Learning*. Reading, MA: Addison-Wesley.

Barney, J.B. and M.H. Hansen (1994), 'Trustworthiness as a form of competitive advantage', *Strategic Management Journal*, Winter Special Issue, **15**, 175–90.

Baum, J.A.C. and J.E. Dutton (1996), 'The embeddedness of strategy', in P. Shrivastava, A.S. Huff and J.E. Dutton (eds), *Advances in Strategic Management*, chapter 13, Greenwich, CT: JAI Press, 3–40.

Bazerman, M. and M. Neal (1984). *Negotiating Rationally*, New York: Free Press.

Blackburn, J., D. Bailey and L. Peyton (1999), 'Formosa Plastics Corporation (Texas)', in M. Hastings (ed.), *Corporate Incentives and Environmental Decision Making*, Texas: HARC, 53–78.

Boeker, W. (1997), 'Strategic change: the influence of managerial characteristics and organizational growth', *Academy of Management Journal*, **40**(1), 152–70.

Boisot, M. (1995), *Information Space: A Framework for Learning in Organizations, Institutions and Cultures*, London: Routledge.

Bradach, J.L. and R.G. Eccles (1989), 'Markets versus hierarchies: from ideal types to plural forms', *Annual Review of Sociology*, **15**, 97–118.

Brown, J.S. and P. Duguid (1991), 'Organizational learning and communities-of-practice: toward a unified view of working, learning and innovation', *Organization Science*, **2**, 40–57.

Burgelman, R.A. and L.R. Sayles (1986), *Inside Corporate Innovation: Strategy, Structure and Managerial Skills*, New York: Free Press.

Clark, S. and N. Roome (1999), 'Sustainable business: learning-action networks as organizational assets', *Business Strategy and the Environment*, **8**, 296–310.

Cohen, W.M. and D.A. Levinthal (1990), 'Absorptive capacity: a new perspective on learning and innovation', *Administrative Science Quarterly*, **35**, 128–52.

Conner, K. and C.K. Prahalad (1996), 'A resource-based theory of the firm: knowledge versus opportunism', *Organization Science*, **7**(5), 477–501.

Cordano, M. and I.H. Frieze (2000), 'Pollution reduction preferences of US environmental managers: applying Ajzen's theory of planned behavior', *Academy of Management Journal*, **43**(4), 627–41.

Dixit, A.K. and B.J. Nalebuff (1991), *Thinking Strategically*, New York: Norton.

Dougherty, D. (1992), 'Interpretive barriers to successful product innovation in large firms,' *Organization Science*, **3**, 179–203.

Doz, Y. and G. Hamel (1998), *Alliance Advantage: The Art of Creating Value through Partnering*, Boston, MA: Harvard Business School Press.

Dutton, J.E. and J.M. Dukerich (1991), 'Keeping an eye on the mirror: image and identity in organizational adaptation', *Academy of Management Review*, **34**, 517–54.

Dutton, J.E. and S.E. Jackson (1987), 'Categorizing strategic issues: links to organizational action', *Academy of Management Review*, **12**, 76–90.

Dyer, J.H. and K. Nobeoka (2000), 'Creating and managing a high-performance knowledge-sharing network: the Toyota case', *Strategic Management Journal*, **21**, Special Issue, 345–67.

Dyer, J. and H. Singh (1998), 'The relational view: cooperative strategies and sources of interorganizational competitive advantage', *Academy of Management Journal*, **23**(4), 660–79.

The Economist (2000), 'Guzzler puzzler', 20 May, 74.

Fiol, C.M. (1994), 'Consensus, diversity, and learning in organizations', *Organization Science*, **5**(3), 403–20.

Frooman, J. (1999), 'Stakeholder influence strategies', *Academy of Management Review*, **24**(2), 191–205.

Gladwin, T.N., J.J. Kennelly and T.S. Krause (1995), 'Shifting paradigms for sustainable development: implications for management theory and research', *Academy of Management Review*, **20**(4), 874–907.

Granovetter, M.S. (1973), 'The strength of weak ties', *American Journal of Sociology*, **78**, 1360–80.

Gulati, R. (1995), 'Does familiarity breed trust? The implications of repeated ties for contractual choices', *Academy of Management Journal*, **35**, 85–112.

Grant, R. (1996), 'Prospering in dynamically-competitive environments: organizational capability as knowledge integration', *Organization Science*, **7**(4), 375–87.

Hagg, I. and J. Johanson (1983), *Firms in Networks: A New View of Competitive Power*, Stockholm: Business and Social Research Institute.

Hamel, G. (1991), 'Competition for competence and inter-partner learning within international strategic alliances', *Strategic Management Journal*, **12**, 83–103.

Hart, S.L. (1995), 'A natural-resource based view of the firm', *Academy of Management Review*, **20**(4), 986–1014.

Hart, S. (1997), 'Beyond greening: strategies for a sustainable world', *Harvard Business Review*, **75** (1), 66–76.

Hart, S.L. and M.B. Milstein (1999), 'Global sustainability and the creative destruction of industries', *Sloan Management Review*, **41**(1), 23–33.

Hart, S.L. and S. Sharma (2004), 'Engaging fringe stakeholders for competitive imagination', *Academy of Management Executive*, **18**(1), 7–18.

Heugens, P.M.A.R., F.A.J. van den Bosch and C.B.M. van Riel (2000), 'Capability building through non-cooperative stakeholder relationships: a case study', proceedings of the International Association of Business & Society Annual Meetings, Burlington, VT, March.

Hoffman, A.J. (1997), *From Heresy to Dogma: An Institutional History of Corporate Environmentalism*, San Francisco, CA: New Lexington Press.

House, R., D.M. Rousseau and M. Thomas-Hunt (1995), 'The meso paradigm: a framework for the integration of micro and macro organizational behavior', in B.M. Staw and L.L. Cummings (eds), *Research in Organizational Behavior*, Greenwich, CT: JAI Press, vol. 17, 71–114.

Jackson, S.E. and J.E. Dutton (1988), 'Discerning threats and opportunities', *Administrative Science Quarterly*, **33**, 370–87.

Jennings, P.D. and P.A. Zandbergen (1995), 'Ecologically sustainable organizations: an institutional approach', *Academy of Management Review*, **20**, 1015–52.

Kale, P., H. Singh and H. Perlmutter (2000), 'Learning and protection of proprietary assets in strategic alliances: building relational capital', *Strategic Management Journal*, Special Issue, **21**, 217–37.

Kim, W.C. and R. Mauborgne (1998), 'Procedural justice, strategic decision making and the knowledge economy', *Strategic Management Journal*, **19**(4), 323–38.

Kogut, B. (2000), 'The network as knowledge: generative rules and the emergence of structure', *Strategic Management Journal*, Special Issue, **21**, 217–317.

Kogut B. and U. Zander (1992), 'Knowledge of the firm, combinative capabilities and the replication of technology', *Organization Science*, **3**, 383–97.

Levinthal, D. and J. March, (1993), 'The myopia of learning', *Strategic Management Journal*, Special Issue, **14**, 95–112.

Levitt, B. and J.G. March (1988), 'Organizational learning', *Annual Review of Sociology*, **14**, 319–40.

Lyles, M.A. (1988), 'Learning among joint venture-sophisticated firms', in F.K. Contractor and P. Lorange (eds), *Cooperative Strategies in International Business*, Lexington, MA: Lexington Books, 301–16.

Macaulay, S. (1963), 'Non-contractual relations in business: a preliminary study', *American Sociological Review*, **28**, 55–67.

Marcus, A.A. and D. Geffen (1998), 'The dialectics of competency acquisition: pollution prevention in electric generation', *Strategic Management Journal*, **19**, 1145–68.

Marsden, P.V. (1990), 'Network data and measurement', *Annual Review of Sociology*, **16**, 435–63.

May, P.H., V. da Vinha and N. Zaidenweber (1999), 'Royal Dutch/Shell', in M. Hastings (ed.), *Corporate Incentives and Environmental Decision Making*, Texas: HARC, 79–117.

McEvily, S., S. Das and K. McCabe (2000), 'Avoiding competence substitution through knowledge sharing', *Academy of Management Review*, **25**(2), 294–311.

Moran, P. and S. Ghoshal (1996), 'Value creation by firms', in J.B. Keys and L.N. Dosier (eds), *Academy of Management Best Paper Proceedings*, 41–5.

Nahapiet, J. and S. Ghoshal (1998), 'Social capital, intellectual capital, and the organizational advantage', *Academy of Management Review*, **23**, 242–66.

Nelson, R. and S. Winter, (1982), *An Evolutionary Theory of Economic Exchange*, Cambridge, MA: Belknap Press.

Noda, T. and J.L. Bower (1996), 'Strategy making as iterated process of resource allocation, *Strategic Management Journal*, **17** (Summer), 159–92.

Nonaka, I. (1994), 'A dynamic theory of organizational knowledge', *Organization Science*, **5**, 14–37.

Palay, T. (1985), 'Avoiding regulatory constraints: contractual safeguards and the role of informal agreements', *Journal of Law, Economics and Organizations*, **1**, 155–75.

Peterson, M.F. (1998), 'Embedded organizational event: the units of process in organizational science', *Organization Science*, **9**, 16–33.

Powell, W.W. (1990), 'Neither market nor hierarchy: network forms of organization', *Research in Organizational Behavior*, **12**, 295–336.

Powell, W.W. and P. Brantley (1992), 'Competitive cooperation in biotechnology: learning through networks?', in N. Nohria and R.C. Eccles (eds), *Networks and Organizations: Structure, Form and Action*, Boston, MA: Harvard Business School Press, 366–94.

Rands, G. and A. Marcus (1991), 'Toward theory "E": the environmentally sensitive manager', Paper presented at the Strategic Management Society Annual Research Conference, Toronto, October.

Ring, P.S. and A.H. Van de Ven (1994), 'Developmental processes of cooperative interorganizational relationships', *Academy of Management Review*, **19**, 90–118.

Rowley, T. (1997), 'Moving beyond dyadic ties: a network theory of stakeholder influences', *Academy of Management Review*, **22**, 887–910.

Rowley, T., D. Behrens and D. Krackhardt (2000), 'Redundant governance structures: an analysis of structural and relational embeddedness in the steel and semiconductor industry', *Strategic Management Journal*, **21**, Special Issue, 369–86.

Schmandt, J. and S. Tankha (1999), 'Alcoa', in M. Hastings (ed.), *Corporate Incentives and Environmental Decision Making*, Texas: HARC, 11–22.

Sharma, S. (1999), 'Sustainability thinking and practice in the Canadian forest products industry', best paper proceedings of the Eighth International Greening of Industry Conference, November, Chapel Hill, NC.

Sharma, S. (2000), 'Managerial interpretations and organizational context as predictors of corporate choice of environmental strategy', *Academy of Management Journal*, **43**(4), 681–97.

Sharma, S. and I. Henriques (2005), 'Stakeholder influences on sustainability practices in the Canadian forest products industry', *Strategic Management Journal*, **26**(2), 159–80.

Sharma, S., A. Pablo and H. Vredenburg (1999), 'Corporate environmental responsiveness strategies: the importance of issue interpretation and organizational context', *Journal of Applied Behavioral Science*, **35**(1), 87–108.

Sharma, S. and H. Vredenburg (1998), 'Proactive corporate environmental strategy and the development of competitively valuable organizational capabilities', *Strategic Management Journal*, **19**(8), 729–53.

Shrivastava, P. (1995), 'The role of corporations in achieving ecological sustainability', *Academy of Management Review*, **20**(4), 936–60.

Shrivastava, P. and I.I. Mitroff (1982), 'Frames of reference managers use: a study in applied sociology of knowledge', in R. Lamb (ed.), *Advances in Strategic Management*, Greenwich, CT: JAI Press, 161–82.

Spender, J.C. (1996), 'Making knowledge the basis of a dynamic theory of the firm', *Strategic Management Journal*, Winter Special Issue, **17**, 45–62.

Starik, M. and G.P. Rands (1995), 'Weaving and integrated web: multilevel and multisystem perspective of ecologically sustainable organizations', *Academy of Management Review*, **20**(4), 908–35.

Tsai, W. (2000), 'Social capital, strategic relatedness and the formation of interorganizational linkages', *Strategic Management Journal,* **21**, 925–39.

Tyre, M.J. and W. J. Orlikowski (1994), 'Windows of opportunity: temporal patterns of technological adaptation in organizations', *Organization Science*, **5**, 98–118.

Van den Bosch, F.A.J., H.W. Volberda and M. de Boer (1999), 'Coevolution of firm absorptive capacity and knowledge environment: organizational forms and combinative capabilities', *Organization Science*, **10**(5), 551–68.

Volkema, R.J., K. Farquhar and T.J. Bergmann (1996), 'Thirdparty sensemaking in interpersonal conflicts at work: a theoretical framework', *Human Relations*, **49**, 1437–54.

Von Hippel, E. (1988), *The Sources of Innovation*, New York, NY: Oxford University Press.

Weick, K.E. (1995), *Sensemaking in Organizations,* Foundations for Organizational Science series, Thousand Oaks, CA: Sage.

Welch, D. (2000), 'It isn't easy going green alone', *Business Week*, 29 May, 54.

Westley, F. and H. Vredenburg (1991), 'Strategic bridging: the collaboration between environmentalists and business in the marketing of green products', *Journal of Applied Behavioral Science*, 27, 65–91.

Winograd, T. and F. Flores (1996), *Understanding Computer and Cognition*, Reading, MA: Addison-Wesley.

4. Context and values: defining a research agenda for studying employee environmental motivation in business organizations[1]

Catherine A. Ramus

People, not organizations, decide on the actions that affect organizational performance (Milgrom and Roberts, 1992). People have the power to propel organizations in the direction of more environmentally sustainable ways of doing business.[2] Some people have more influence than others over decisions made in organizations, as a result of their hierarchical positions (for example CEOs, line managers), functional backgrounds (for example product designers, environmental managers), personal qualifications (for example skilled as issues sellers or champions in an organizational setting) or the like (Aragón-Correa et al., 2003; Crane, 2000); however all employees have the potential to influence an organization's environmental actions through their individual initiatives (Ramus and Steger, 2000). My underlying assumption in writing this chapter is that people matter, and researchers of corporate environmental management should be concerned with studying what motivates them to take environmental actions.

Today technology, management systems and policies and procedures exist to facilitate environmental protection in business organizations. For example Dormann and Holliday (2002) of the World Business Council for Sustainable Development showed that environmental technologies exist which can fuel sustainable development using fewer resources and less energy. Other researchers have shown that larger firms have adopted a set of beyond-compliance environmental policies (Graham and Havlick, 1999; Ramus, 2002; Ramus and Montiel, 2004) and systems that facilitate environmental management in business organizations (Delmas, 2002; Steger, 2000). The capacity and knowledge to transform businesses into more environmentally sustainable organizations are being developed, but whether organizations act to protect the natural environment is highly dependent on individuals' choices. People – not organizations – make the decisions to adopt technologies, to implement environmental policies and to manage environmental impacts in a more environmentally sustainable manner.

Hoffman (2003) argued that managers (and employees) are increasingly reconciling professional and personal value systems by promoting social change and, in so doing, are finding greater satisfaction within organizations (Chatman, 1991). Nearly three-quarters of Americans consider themselves to be environmentalists (Roper Starch Worldwide, 1995). But organizational barriers (for example organizational structures, practices and cultures) often prevent individuals from exercising their environmental values in the workplace (Fineman, 1996, 1998; Post and Altman, 1994; Ramus and Steger, 2000). Moreover environmental values, as compared to other social values, can be particularly salient to individuals when they see that pollution from their workplace can cause environmental harm to valued objects (nature, animals, the Earth) and people (offspring, family members, friends, community members) (Stern and Dietz, 1994).

In keeping with Chatman (1991), Hoffman (1993, 2003), and Howard-Grenville and Hoffman (2003), the premise of this chapter is that there is a potential advantage to business organizations in supporting individuals who act on their environmental values. This is because in acting on their environmental values people become more satisfied and productive at work (Chatman, 1991; Schneider, 1987), and because firms can harness environmental ideas to gain competitive advantage (Ramus, 2001; Ramus and Steger, 2000). Therefore as Hoffman (2003: 205) stated, 'organizations must develop new proficiencies to understand the basic motivations behind an employee's decision to act as an organizational entrepreneur'.

The first step toward this understanding is the development of a research agenda aimed at answering the following question: Why might an individual in an organizational setting be motivated to implement an environmental initiative or action aimed at improving the organization's environmental performance? This research agenda is not new; rather, it is in keeping with the organizational 'greening' literature that has recognized the importance of human resource management (environmental training; environmental objectives in performance appraisal; rewards for environmental actions, including environmental considerations in job design, candidate recruitment and selection; and so on) for achieving strategic organizational greening objectives (Callenbach et al., 1993; Dechant and Altman, 1994; Egri and Hornal, 2002; Milliman and Clair, 1996; Ramus and Steger, 2000; Russo and Fouts, 1997; Starik and Rands, 1995; Wehrmeyer, 1996). This research agenda has been contributed to, in part, by the literature on championing environmental issues in organizations, including works by Andersson and Bateman (2000) and Bansal (2003) among others, as well as the work on values and leadership by Egri and Herman (2000).

What has not been achieved in previous research is a uniting of organizational behaviour and psychology literatures and thinking with corporate environmental management research. These literatures can help us to understand how individual values and behaviours are influenced by an individual's perceptions of the organizational context, and how individual cognitions of the degree of support received from the work environment affect individual motivation to perform environmental actions. These literatures can also clarify our understanding of the relationship between values, behaviours and context. The unique contribution of this chapter is not only its bringing together the psychology, organizational behaviour and corporate environmental management research. Just as important, I use some of the learning from this synthesis to develop a conceptual model of how individual and organizational value systems determine individual motivations to perform environmental tasks within the organizational context. This conceptual model emphasizes the complexity that exists when considering individual–organization fit related to environmental issues.

The blueprint for this chapter is as follows. I draw from previous research to provide insights into both the organizational factors related to the context, and individual dispositional factors that might affect individual motivation to behave in such a way as to improve the environmental performance of the business organization. To this end, I describe the variables that can influence an individual's environmental behaviours within an organization and the factors that can influence those variables. Next, I use the values literature to define individual and organizational environmental values. From these values constructs I develop a model that shows how individual values and organizational values might affect individual motivations related to environmental protection and sustainability. I conclude with a discussion of some of the research questions that come out of this way of looking at individual environmental motivation in organizations.

FACTORS INFLUENCING INDIVIDUAL MOTIVATION

The psychology literature provides some understanding of the role of values in motivating individual environmental behaviours (McKenzie-Mohr et al., 1995; Stern and Dietz, 1994).[3] This literature suggests that individual values alone will not determine environmental actions (used here as synonymous with environmental behaviours). But the psychology research has not focused on individual environmental behaviours in organizations. The organizational behaviour literature emphasizes the importance of organizational context, and from this literature we learn that context must be considered when undertaking to understand what motivates individual environmental behaviour in an organizational setting. According to Rousseau and Fried (2001: 1) organizational context includes variables such as organizational characteristics (for example culture and norms, type of environmental strategy), demographic factors (industry, region of operations, gender and age of workforce and so on.), level of analysis including hierarchical level and work function, and pressures from the external environment (including institutional factors and stakeholder pressures). Although organizational context is broadly defined in the organizational behaviour literature, for our purposes here we need to focus on controlling for those factors that affect individual motivations to perform environmental actions. From the corporate environmental management literature we know that factors which affect individual environmental motivation include perceived incentives and disincentives to act, such as social norms in the organization (implicit rules regarding how people should behave that are often embedded in organizational policies, leader behaviours and so on) and self-efficacy beliefs, related to the environmental task and desired outcome, that are often influenced by supervisor and team mate behaviour, training and skill development and other elements of the organizational context such as the strength of the situation (Killmer and Ramus, forthcoming; Mischel, 1968, 1973; Ramus and Steger, 2000; Shamir, 1991). I discuss these factors in greater detail below.

INDIVIDUAL BEHAVIOURAL INTENT TO ACT IN AN ENVIRONMENTALLY RESPONSIBLE MANNER

To reiterate, the dependent variable I am interested in is individual motivation (behavioural intent) to perform an environmental task that will positively influence the organization's environmental performance and sustainability. Organizational behaviourists have long tried to understand individual task motivation within organizations. From research in organizational behaviour, we learn that an individual's intent to act (which is an accurate predictor of actual behaviour) can be measured using behavioural intent motivation models, which are based upon Vroom's (1964) expectancy research (Ajzen and Fishbein, 1973; Fishbein, 1963; Fishbein and Ajzen, 1975; Walker and Thomas, 1982). Killmer and Ramus (forthcoming) created a behavioural intent model for environmental behaviours in organizations. This model indicated that people make decisions based upon their personal predispositions, expectancy beliefs related to the task and the outcome, and organizational norms. Note that in addition to the three sets of variables in the Killmer and Ramus research I also include in this chapter a discussion of situational strength as an important contextual variable within organizational norms. Killmer and Ramus's variables are in keeping with Bansal's (2003) results highlighting the importance of individual-level concerns and organizational-level values. Killmer and Ramus's work differs from Bansal's however in that it proposes the inclusion of expectancy variables that allow researchers to measure the role of self-efficacy beliefs related to the task and desired outcome in individual decision-making concerning environmental actions. Inclusion of expectancy variables is supported by the behavioural intent literature (Ajzen and Fishbein, 1973; Fishbein, 1963; Fishbein and Ajzen, 1975; Walker and Thomas, 1982). Each of the three sets of variables (personal predisposition, expectancy beliefs related to the task and the outcome, and organizational norms) in turn can be influenced by a number of factors. Below, I present these variables and discuss factors that may influence the variables. See Table 4.1 for the list of variables and factors. Those readers interested in a more complete discussion of the factors affecting environmental motivation and their derivation should refer to Killmer and Ramus (forthcoming) for more information.

Personal Predisposition

Individuals enter organizations with a set of values, attitudes, beliefs and skills that will have important effects on their decisions about performing environmentally responsible tasks. These pre-existing values, attitudes and beliefs are referred to here as a 'personal predisposition' toward the behaviour (Hines et al., 1987; Killmer and Ramus, forthcoming; Sivek and Hungerford, 1990). The psychology literature shows us that there is an important link between values, attitudes and beliefs about the behaviour (all of which make up personal predisposition). Environmental attitudes are influenced by personal values (Stern and Dietz, 1994), which in turn affect individual environmental behaviours within business organizations (Egri and Herman, 2000). Environmental beliefs (about the objective of the behaviour) are influenced by the individual's underlying value system (Stern and Dietz, 1994).

Personal predisposition is defined as the employee's values, attitudes and beliefs that influence the decision to perform the environmental task. It should be noted that a person's predisposition toward creative activities in general, not just the person's environmental values, attitudes and beliefs, will also influence the decision to perform environmental tasks. The socialization process involving opinions of family members, friends, other community members and the public at large will influence behavioural intent through this variable. As the psychology literature notes, knowledge and

Table 4.1   Variables affecting an individual's environmentally related behaviour in an organization, and factors affecting these variables

Variables	Description of variables	Factors affecting variables
Personal predisposition	Includes individual values, attitudes and beliefs (see Stern and Dietz, 1994)	**Values, attitudes and beliefs are influenced by** • Opinions of others external to the organization including family, friends and community members (i.e., the socialization process influences values, attitudes and beliefs) • Knowledge and experience related to the natural environment
Expectancy and self-efficacy beliefs (related to task and desired outcome)	Two parts to efficacy beliefs: • Does the individual believe she or he will successfully accomplish the environmental task? • Does the individual believe that accomplishing the environmental task will lead to the desired outcome? (see Hostager et al., 1998)	**Task belief is influenced by** • Prior experience in accomplishing the same or similar task • Training/skills/knowledge that leads individuals to believe they can successfully accomplish the task • Supervisory behavioural support, or lack thereof, for the task (see Ramus and Steger, 2000 for list of supervisory behaviours) • Group/team/colleague behaviours that support or fail to support the task
	Desired outcome may be different for different tasks and different individuals	**Desired outcome belief is influenced by** • Different factors that depend on desired outcome

76

Organizational environmental norms (motivational force related to the perceived social beliefs within the organization about the environmental behaviour)	Individual behaviour affected by perceptions of organizational norms. Organizational norms affected by internal and external stakeholders, which in turn influence the organization's motivation for protecting the natural environment (e.g. compliance, profit, stakeholder relations)	Manifestations of commitment and norms are • policy implementation • CEO/top management (or lowercase in the item below) behaviours (which are influenced by the same set of variables that influence individual behaviours) • Organizational response to individual concerns
Situational strength	Existence of individual environmental goals, rewards and organizational norms and management systems that indicate their (not sure what 'their' refers to) relative importance to the business	Moderated by supervisor behaviour, top management behaviour, and behaviour of others in the organization

experience related to the natural environment will also have an important influence on personal predisposition toward the environmental task (McKenzie et al., 1995; Stern and Dietz, 1994). With respect to corporate greening, Cordano and Frieze (2000), Egri and Herman (2000) and Rands (1990) demonstrated that pre-existing values are a determining factor in employee motivation to protect the natural environment in business settings.

Expectancy and Self-Efficacy Beliefs

Expectancy related to the environmental task and to the desired outcome need to be measured separately, as the literature shows them to be separate constructs (Behling and Starke, 1973). Expectancy related to an environmental task is the belief that the individual has concerning whether he or she will successfully accomplish the task. It is related to self-efficacy. Bandura (1977: 193) pointed out that 'the strength of people's conviction in their own effectiveness is likely to affect whether they would even try to cope with a given situation'. One's belief in one's own ability to complete a desired task or reach a desired outcome has a direct influence on one's behaviour (Bandura, 1986; Bandura and Wood, 1989; Thomas and Velthouse, 1990). Factors influencing one's self-efficacy related to an environmental task include the person's prior experience in accomplishing (or failing to accomplish) the same or a similar task; training, skills and knowledge that leads the individual to believe in (or fail to believe in) his or her own ability related to accomplishing the task; supervisor behaviours that either support or fail to support the individual in performing the task; and group, team and other colleagues' behaviours that either support or fail to support the individual in performing the task.

The second expectancy variable is related to one's desired outcome. Different individuals may have different desired outcomes. Hostager et al. (1998) delineated 12 potential desired outcomes for environmental actions in business settings. These included societal- and organizational-level motivators such as a cleaner environment, decreased waste, sustainability, profits, market share and growth, along with individual-level motivators such as salary or wages, promotions, status, pride, accomplishment and challenge related to the accomplishment of the task. Different parties influence different desired outcomes. For instance if someone performs an environmental task in order to improve his or her chance of promotion, then having support from one's supervisor signalling that the task will be advantageous to one's career might be highly important. Alternatively, if one performs an environmental task because of an intrinsic motivation to solve an environmental problem, then the attitude of one's supervisor toward the task may be less instrumental in achieving the desired outcome of pride or accomplishment.

Organizational Environmental Norms

Individual motivation will be affected by the person's perception of organizational environmental norms, defined here to include the signals of top management and other organizational levels regarding commitment related to protecting the natural environment. (I suggest including individual perceptions of supervisor and team or colleagues' behaviours in the expectancy variables, not in the organizational environmental norms variable. This simplifies the development of the measures and is supported by the literature which shows that individuals perceive supervisor support separately from organizational support; see Ramus and Steger, 2000.) Organizational environmental norms are not directly measurable, but a person's perceptions of the social beliefs of the organization are measurable. Quite a number of influences on organizational environmental norms have been identified, including the values of the individuals in the organization, and pressures from the external environment that influence the organization's motivation to protect the natural environment. Manifestations of organizational environmental norms include environmental policy commitment and implementation, CEO and/or top management behaviours (which can be influenced by the same variables that influence individual behaviours) and organizational responses to the environmental concerns of individuals within the organization.

Situational Strength

I include situational strength under the heading of organizational environmental norms, but I describe it separately because it is a concept that is not generally understood or measured explicitly in corporate environmental management studies of individual motivation.

Situational strength is an important element of organizational context that should be controlled for (Mischel, 1968, 1973; Shamir, 1991). Mischel's work showed that situational strength is more important than personality in determining behaviour, adding evidence that organizational context is a highly important variable to include in studies. Strong situations are characterized by clear goals, well-recognized rules of conduct, availability of rewards and a strong rewards–performance relationship. They tend to produce uniformity in behaviour. In the case of environmental management within an organizational setting, a strong situation exists when there are clear environmental goals for both the organization and the individual, when there are clear environmental norms that reinforce environmental behaviour (for example environmental considerations are part of decision-making and are regularly discussed) and when rewards exist that reinforce the desirability of environmental tasks. 'Weak' situations, in contrast, feature unclear goals, ambiguous rules of conduct, uncertain availability of rewards (desirable outcomes) and an imprecise link between performance and desired outcomes. 'Weak' situations produce more variance in behaviour. Most individuals in organizations face relatively weak situations related to protecting the natural environment, resulting in large variances in behaviour related to environmentally oriented tasks.

INDIVIDUAL AND ORGANIZATIONAL ENVIRONMENTAL VALUES

From a conceptual perspective, it is interesting to explore how these variables interact with one another. To do this, I eliminate some of the complexity involved in considering all these variables simultaneously. Individual and organizational values are clearly important to individual environmental motivation (Bansal, 2003; Killmer and Ramus, forthcoming). Therefore I offer a conceptual framework that looks at these two sets of values at the same time. In this way, we can start to see how individual motivation to perform an environmental task can be understood through considering the relationship between individual environmental value orientations (personal predispositions) and the organization's environmental values (and related organizational norms).

Hines et al. (1987) and Stern and Dietz (1994) showed that individual values and perceptions of moral responsibility are associated with environmental behaviours. The psychology literature makes it clear however that values are not completely determinant of environmental behaviour.[4] A value, according to Rokeach (1973: 5), is an 'enduring belief that a specific mode of conduct or end-state of existence is personally or socially preferable to an opposite or converse mode of conduct or end-state of existence'. Individuals tend to possess a core set of values that does not change much over time (Rokeach, 1973; Schwartz, 1992). Stern and Dietz (1994) explain the relationship between values, beliefs, attitudes and behaviours. Value orientations (individuals can hold several value orientations at one time) take shape during the socialization process. These values, according to Rokeach (1968: 160), are criteria 'for guiding [and] for developing and maintaining attitudes toward relevant objects and situations'. These value orientations may affect beliefs about the consequences of actions on an environmental object that one values. According to Stern and Dietz (1994), four value orientations affect environmental behaviour: egocentric (focused on self), altruistic (moral obligation to prevent or ameliorate harm), biospheric (moral norms regarding the treatment of non-human objects) and traditional (focused on valuing family security, elders, honesty and loyalty). The results of their empirical work showed that all environmentally relevant beliefs may be influenced by values. Beliefs about consequences to the natural environmental (that occur as a result of behaviours) largely determine the behaviour of the actor. Thus understanding a person's underlying values and beliefs can be one means by which to understand that person's motivation (or behavioural intent) toward an environmental initiative. I will discuss this further below, when I set up a conceptual model that can explain individual environmental actions in a business setting.

Organizational values are a different construct from individual values. Organizational values, according to Rokeach (1979: 50), are 'socially shared cognitive representations of institutional goals and demands'. Organizational values are related to organizational culture in that they provide the decision rules for interpreting signals within the organizational environment (Rokeach, 1973). According to Schein (1985: 15), 'all cultural learning ultimately reflects someone's original values, their sense of what "ought" to be, as distinct from what is'. Thus we see that individual values ultimately influence both the culture of the organization and its values. This is important for our purposes here because below I set up a framework whereby in the first instance individual and organizational environmental values are separate, but one can expect that over time the values of one might influence the values of the other, and vice versa. This is in part the basis for the environmental championing literature (Andersson and Bateman, 2000; Bansal, 2003; Stern, 1992), which acknowledges the important role of individuals in facilitating organizational responses that protect the natural environment. It is also important to note that both individual and organizational values are relatively stable over time.

VALUES-BASED CONCEPTUAL MODEL

I will now present the dynamics of a simple two-by-two model that includes individual and organizational environmental values. Imagine a situation in which a new employee has decided to join a firm.[5] Just as individuals hold a variety of different environmental values, so too there is evidence of a spectrum of environmental value systems in organizations. (For example see the research in Sharma et al., 1999.) In this framework, both the set of potential individual environmental values (personal predisposition) coming with the new employee and the set of potential organizational environmental values existing in the organization (signalled through organizational norms) fall somewhere on a continuum from 'extremely concerned' to 'extremely unconcerned' about environmental protection and/or sustainable development. As explained above, the values orientation of an individual and an organization are expressed in different terms, but these values are discernible. An individual joining an organization will be able to discover information about the organization's environmental values through signals such as whether the environment is mentioned in the company core values, the content and availability of environmental policy statements, how often the natural environment is considered and discussed during decision-making activities, and whether environmental considerations are part of job routines. The organization's managers will be able to discover information about an individual's environmental values when environmental issues are discussed and/or when the individual raises environmental concerns. Concerns usually arise out of cognitive dissonance, when the status quo is different from what an individual desires or expects (Bansal, 2003). Neither party has complete information about the other party, but information is available to both the individual and the organization's membership vis-à-vis the other's environmental values.

Figure 4.1 shows the various pairings of an individual and an organization with regard to environmental values. This two-by-two matrix shows four different conceptual outcomes. I discuss each below. It is important to note several limitations to the conceptual model. First, one might expect to find values to be somewhere in the middle of the continuum, not at the extremes. Second, values are not the only factor influencing environmental behaviour. As discussed above, other dispositional and contextual factors might influence the dependent variable. For instance other organizational issues that affect expectancies related to outcomes may affect behavioural intent. Third, in practice there is never perfect alignment between individual and organizational values. Bansal's (2003) work showed how individual values and organizational values sometimes mesh and at other times do not. Her work highlighted that for their ideas to be supported, individuals often need to 'sell' their environmental ideas as aligning with another non-environmental core value of the organization (for example 'saves resources' would be a good selling point to a company with the core values of cost reduction). I will discuss issues 'selling' under situation B (from Figure 4.1) below. Finally, in situations B and C there is a mismatch between individual and organizational value systems. Hoffman (1993: 10) asserted that without congruence between an individual's value systems and that of the group, 'a dysfunctional employee/ employer relationship develops which may threaten to undermine organizational efficiency'. This conclusion is in keeping with the values

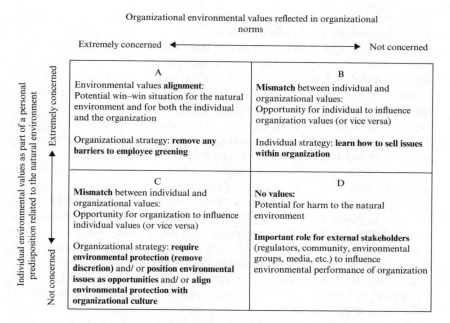

Organizational environmental values reflected in organizational norms

Extremely concerned ←——————————————————→ Not concerned

Individual environmental values as part of a personal predisposition related to the natural environment

Extremely concerned ↑ Not concerned ↓

A	B
Environmental values **alignment**: Potential win–win situation for the natural environment and for both the individual and the organization Organizational strategy: **remove any barriers to employee greening**	**Mismatch** between individual and organizational values: Opportunity for individual to influence organization values (or vice versa) Individual strategy: **learn how to sell issues within organization**
C	**D**
Mismatch between individual and organizational values: Opportunity for organization to influence individual values (or vice versa) Organizational strategy: **require environmental protection (remove discretion)** and/ or **position environmental issues as opportunities** and/ or **align environmental protection with organizational culture**	**No values:** Potential for harm to the natural environment **Important role for external stakeholders** (regulators, community, environmental groups, media, etc.) to influence environmental performance of organization

Figure 4.1   Conceptual framework: individual and organizational environmental values

congruence literature, which would predict less worker satisfaction and lower worker performance (Chatman, 1991; Schneider, 1987). These mismatches are undesirable from a basic business performance perspective, but nevertheless they sometimes exist.

Situation A: Potential Win–Win Situation Due to Values Alignment

In situation A, the individual and the organization share concern for the natural environment. In this situation we would expect there to be an opportunity for synergies that enhance environmental protection and/or sustainable development within the organization. Applying results from previous psychology and organizational behaviour research to this conceptual situation, we would expect a more satisfied employee who has more organizational commitment and who is less likely to leave the organization (Chatman, 1991; Schneider, 1987; Valentine et al., 2002). Thus the employee will be happier if he or she exercises his or her environmental values in the workplace, and the organization can benefit from the employee's ideas and actions that enhance its environmental performance. This is potentially a win–win situation.

The research question we can derive from situation A is: How can both parties take advantage of the opportunity presented from their aligned environmental values? Bansal (2003) and Killmer and Ramus (forthcoming) argue that most tasks associated with corporate greening are discretionary. Killmer and Ramus note that personal predisposition and organizational environmental norms are particularly salient when employees are engaged in discretionary tasks, or what are called extra-role behaviours (Katz and Kahn, 1978; Van Dyne et al., 1995). Indeed two of the four factors in Killmer and Ramus's behaviour intent model by definition are in place in situation A: personal predisposition and organizational norms that support environmental actions. What is not clear is whether other variables are in place, such as supervisory behaviour or self-efficacy related to specific tasks and desired outcomes. Employees generally are more motivated when they perceive support from their supervisors (Conger and Kanungo, 1988; Kanter, 1983). Empirical research by Ramus and Steger (2000) showed that second-party support, demonstrated through both behaviour and providing organizational resources, is an important factor influencing employee motivation to try environmental initiatives in companies. Second-party support from responsible managers in the organization can add to the synergistic effect found when individual and organizational values are aligned; conversely, it can become a serious barrier to individual environmentally responsible behaviours when it is absent (Ramus, 2001, 2003; Ramus and Steger, 2000).

Barriers to employee motivation may be present, related to self-efficacy and expectancy surrounding both the task and the desired outcome. For example the employee may need training to develop the skills and knowledge necessary to successfully complete tasks related to environmental protection and sustainability. When faced with a situation like A in Figure 4.1, organizations and individuals have it in their best interest to remove barriers to environmental motivation in order to take advantage of their mutual concern for the natural environment.

Situation B: Values Mismatch of High Individual and Low Organizational Concern

In this situation, the organization is missing values oriented toward protecting the natural environment, but the individual is concerned about the natural environment. The individual may ask himself or herself, 'How can I improve the environmental performance of this organization if nobody seems to care about the natural environment?' Here the 'issues selling' literature helps us to understand how an individual might be successful in promoting environmental change even when the organization does not (yet) value environmental protection. Issues selling theory explains how organizations, which are bombarded with numerous issues, choose the issues to which they will respond (Dutton et al., 2001). According to Dutton and colleagues, the issue seller needs to understand the social relationships relevant to the issue; the behaviours that are acceptable in their organization; and the organization's goals, plans and priorities. Bansal (2003) used this theory to show that in the case of environmental issues, most issues sellers needed to find a way to align the issue with the organization's core values in order for the issue to make it onto the organizational agenda. If environmental concerns are low on the organization's agenda and are not part of the core values, as is the case in situation B, then from Bansal's research we can see that the issue seller must find other core values with which to align their environmental issue. Indeed Crane (2000: 688) stated that 'the likelihood of successful selling generally relied on protagonists' abilities to manage new, uncontroversial understandings' of the environmental issue. Andersson and Bateman's (2000) work on environmental championing showed that environmental issue sellers who engaged in more environmental scanning, framed and presented the issue effectively, and used influence tactics within the organization, were those who were most successful. From this research we see that employees in situation B, where there are no (or few) organizational rewards and many obstacles to corporate greening, must be highly skilful at selling or championing an environmental issue and must also have a serious commitment to promoting environmental change. Promoting organizational change in such an environment would not be easy, yet we can find examples of successes even in organizations with little or no environmental commitment (Crane, 2000).

Situation C: Values Mismatch of Low Individual and High Organizational Concern

In this situation, the individual is missing a personal predisposition toward protecting the natural environment, but the organization is concerned about the natural environment. Manager(s) in the organization may ask themselves, 'How can we motivate someone without intrinsic motivation to protect the natural environment?' Below I discuss two ways that an organization might answer this question: first, by making a weak situation strong, and second, by reframing environmental issues as opportunities.

From Mischel's work (1973), we can see the potential benefits for the organization of creating a strong situation around environmental protection tasks. Employees might be encouraged to support environmental initiatives through such measures as communicating organizational commitment to implementing an environmental policy aimed at sustainable development; putting management and reward systems in place that reinforce environmentally responsible behaviour; demonstrating clear social norms through top management behaviour; and ensuring supervisory behaviours that encourage environmental initiatives. Ramus's (1997) and Ramus and Steger's (2000) work suggested the usefulness of creating an environmental learning organization, including supporting employee environmental activities through environmental and human resource policies, supervisory behaviours and availability of resources. The corporate environmental management literature suggests the use of human resource management tools to reinforce individual environmental behaviour (Callenbach et al., 1993; Dechant and Altman, 1994; Egri and Hornal, 2002; Milliman and Clair, 1996; Ramus and Steger, 2000; Russo and Fouts, 1997; Starik and Rands, 1995; Wehrmeyer, 1996). In situation C, it might be necessary to change environmental tasks from discretionary to routine or even mandatory.

Another way to transform environmental issues from lower to higher priority for organizational members is to reframe the issues from threats to opportunities (Sharma, 2000; Sharma et al., 1999). Sharma (2000) showed that managerial interpretations of environmental issues changed when the framing of these issues changed. From his research, Sharma (2000: 691) suggested that 'strategic leaders need to legitimate environmental issues as an integral part of the corporate identity while allowing managers time and resources they can apply at their discretion to creative problem solving'. Howard-Grenville and Hoffman (2003: 70) make a similar point, arguing that social issues such as environmental protection need to be 'aligned with the organization's core culture because culture guides both *what* issues get attended to and *how* they get acted upon'. Organizational culture is a set of shared meanings or beliefs that individuals have in the organizational setting. By creating a shared meaning around protecting the natural environment, an organization will be more successful in engaging its people in environmental activities. Thus when faced with situation C, an organization is more likely to benefit from the creative problem-solving from its people if it signals that it sees environmental issues as key business opportunities and aligns environmental issues with the organization's culture.

Situation D: Neither Individual nor Organization Holds Strong Environmental Values

From situation D, the question from the perspective of those outside the organization who care about the natural environment is, How can we motivate this organization to protect the natural environment? In this situation there is little chance of environmental protection in the absence of outside pressure by external stakeholder groups, including regulatory stakeholders, community stakeholders and the media.

Organizations will engage those stakeholders who have the most power, legitimacy and urgency (Mitchell et al., 1997). One might assume that government regulators would tend to have all three of these when an organization risks being out of compliance with environmental laws. Recent stakeholder research however shows that the media have greater salience and influence over firms with low levels of environmental commitment. Henriques and Sadorsky (1999) showed that managers in firms with proactive environmental commitment profiles (top management support, environmental training and reporting, and so on) are much more likely to see regulatory, community and organizational stakeholders as important than those firms with reactive environmental commitment profiles (no top management commitment, no environmental training and reporting, and so on), which instead care more about the media. Henriques and Sadorsky (1999: 95–6) stated that 'reactive firms appear to be more concerned about being caught doing something wrong by a reporter than about being caught by a regulator'. As such, the media might be the most important stakeholder in terms of creating pressure for environmental laggards to come into compliance with environmental laws and to move toward greater environmental protection.

Adding More Contextual Variables

This two-by-two model is a simplification of reality because it discusses the dynamics at one point in time and includes only two sets of variables instead of the entire list in Table 4.1. Nevertheless from this model we have been able to discuss how organizational and individual strategies change depending on the situation each party faces relative to the other's values. Over time, the organization or the individual may succeed in influencing the values of the other party, but as was noted above, values are relatively stable over time.

Space limitations do not permit me to go through the exercise of adding all the variables in Table 4.1, but one can imagine from the discussion of Figure 4.1 that when people and organizations face different situations related to the different variables, then different strategies for motivating change are more or less appropriate. In a dynamic model, as one variable in the model shifts, this then affects the strategies of the other party.

SOME RESEARCH QUESTIONS

From the above exposition of contextual and dispositional variables and discussion of the influence of values on individual environmental motivation in an organizational setting, we can derive a number of research questions and areas for a research agenda. The list below is suggestive but by no means exhaustive.

General Questions

Three general questions emerge from this research:

1. What is the relative importance of each of the different variables when all are taken together?
2. If individual values are key, then who has the most power to shift the values or affect the actions of others? Is it supervisors, team members, organizational leaders, individual employees, family members or friends, community members or other stakeholders?
3. If organizational values are highly important (as the literature suggests), then who has the most power to shift these values – external or internal stakeholders? What are the implications for individual actions in organizational settings? To answer these questions, one must first recognize the difference between different levels of employees (for example, management versus non-management employees).

Along with these general questions, more specific issues might be raised in future research, as discussed below.

Levels of Analysis

I discuss individual motivation in this chapter, developing a set of factors that apply to different levels of employees within organizations. I believe however that different levels of employees may be influenced by these variables in different ways. Top management, board members and the CEO will be influenced by organizational context, self-efficacy beliefs and their own personal predisposition, and they also have greater power to lead change in many organizations. Given this, future studies need to be explicit about the level of employee being studied (for example line manager, CEO or worker on the line). For instance future research could measure the effects of the different variables on different types of employees within the same organization, or it could look at the same level of employee across similar types of organizations. In this way we could begin to understand how important the different factors are to motivation across the organizational hierarchy.

Context

Some corporate environmental management research makes it appear that researchers are comparing incomparable situations or organizations and trying to draw broad conclusions. I have argued in this chapter that context influences individual environmental behaviours, and I have delineated which variables might be the main influences. The argument that context matters is in keeping with Johns (2001: 32), who asserted that 'context often operates in such a way as to provide constraints on or opportunities for behavior and attitudes in organizational settings . . . [and] serve[s] as a main effect on organizational behavior and/or moderator of relationships'. If context is a main effect on organizational behaviour (or even a moderator of relationships), then we need to control for different organizational contexts in our research. Ideally we should control for contextual factors when we can, by measuring them and making them an important part of the research question. Rousseau and Fried (2001: 1) tell us that contextualizing research involves 'linking observations to a set of facts, events, or points of view', which may include in our case demographic variables, internal policies, leadership, supervisor and team member behaviours and values systems, and external environmental factors. Where we cannot control for contextual variables, we should at the very least be explicit and describe the context in which we have done our research so that other researchers know whether they are comparing a similar or a different context.

Strength of the Situation

How important is the strength of the situation in determining employee willingness to behave in an environmentally responsible manner? One way to answer this question is to develop a set of measures of situational strength and use them consistently in empirical studies of individual environmental motivation in different organizations.

Environmental Change Management

One should not ignore the importance of organizational systems that either reinforce or obstruct environmental change. Reinforcement theory (Skinner, 1966, 1969, 1974) argues that if new employee behaviours are desired by the company, then management processes and measuring procedures (setting targets, measuring performance, and granting financial and non-financial rewards) must be consistent with the behaviour that employees are asked to embrace. Measuring situational strength by controlling for consistent use of environmental management systems, management processes (both human resource management and supervisory or top management behaviour) and measurement procedures would allow us to study the likelihood of success in environmental change efforts in an organizational setting.

CONCLUSION

The purpose of this chapter was to use the psychology and organizational behaviour literatures to help set a research agenda surrounding individual motivation to perform environmental actions in business organizations. I discussed the importance of contextual and dispositional variables in studying individual motivation to perform environmental tasks in organizational settings. Next I illustrated how individual and organizational values influence the strategies that an environmentally concerned individual or organization might most appropriately adopt in a given situation. I then developed a model showing how the interaction of individual and organizational predispositions toward environmental concerns results in various situations that either support or create barriers to environmental protection. Finally I suggested research questions and approaches that scholars might adopt in order to better understand individual motivation related to environmental actions in business organizations. My hope is that this chapter will inspire future scholarship at the crossroads between corporate environmental management, psychology and organizational behaviour.

NOTES

1. The author thanks John Antonakis, Alberto Aragón-Correa, Andrew Hoffman, Annette Killmer, Sanjay Sharma and A.J. Sobczak for their comments and suggestions.
2. Environmental protection and environmental sustainability are appreciably different constructs, but for our purposes here we are concerned with any environmental action by an individual that improves the environmental performance of the organization. Some of these environmental actions may do more than protect the natural environment. Indeed some of them may help the organization move toward the illusive goal of sustainable development.
3. See articles in two special issues of the *Journal of Social Issues*, 'Psychology and the promotion of a sustainable future' (McKenzie-Mohr and Oskamp, 1995) and 'Promoting environmentalism' (Zelezny and Schultz, 2000), for reviews of variables influencing individual environmental behaviour.
4. Even where there is a high level of environmental concern and people claim to value the natural environment, people may not lower their consumption of natural resources.

For example people in developed countries often say they are environmentalists, but at the same time they purchase non-fuel efficient vehicles such as SUVs (sports utility vehicles). Thus their expressed environmental values do not completely determine their behaviour.

5. The employee may or may not have selected employment in this firm because he or she perceived the organization to hold core values in alignment with his or her own values concerning the natural environment. Conversely, the firm may or may not have selected the candidate because it perceived that the environmental values of the individual aligned with the organization's environmental values. The framework works independently of a conscious values-congruence choice on the part of either the organization or the individual.

REFERENCES

Ajzen, Icek and Martin Fishbein (1973), 'Attitudinal and normative variables as predictors of specific behaviors', *Journal of Personality and Social Psychology*, **27**, 41–57.

Andersson, Lynne M. and Thomas S. Bateman (2000), 'Individual environmental initiative: championing natural environmental issues in US business organizations', *Academy of Management Journal*, **43**, 548–70.

Aragón-Correa, Juan Alberto, Fernando Matias-Reche and Maria Eugenia Senise-Barrio (2003), 'Managerial discretion and corporate commitment to the natural environment', *Journal of Business Research*, **5870**, 1–12.

Bandura, Albert (1977), 'Self-efficacy: toward a unifying theory of behavioral change', *Psychological Review*, **84**(2), 191–215.

Bandura, Albert (1986), *Social Foundations of Thought and Action: A Social Cognitive Theory*, Englewood Cliffs, NJ: Prentice-Hall.

Bandura, Albert and Robert Wood (1989), 'Effect of perceived controllability and performance standards on self-regulation of complex decision making', *Journal of Personality and Social Psychology*, **56**, 805–14.

Bansal, Pratima (2003), 'From issues to actions: the importance of individual concerns and organizational values in responding to natural environmental issues', *Organization Science*, **14**(5), 510–27.

Behling, Orlando and Frederick A. Starke (1973), 'The postulates of expectancy theory', *Academy of Management Journal*, **16**(3), 373–88.

Callenbach, E., F. Capra, L. Goldman, R. Lutz and S. Marburg (1993), *EcoManagment: The Ellwood Guide to Ecological Auditing and Sustainable Business*, San Francisco, CA: Berrett Koehler.

Chatman, Jennifer (1991), 'Matching people and organizations: selection and socialization in public accounting firms', *Administrative Science Quarterly*, **36**, 459–84.

Conger, Jay A. and Rabindra N. Kanungo (1988), 'The empowerment process: integrating theory and practice, *Academy of Management Review*, **13**(3), 471–82.

Cordano, Mark and Irene Hanson Frieze (2000), 'Pollution reduction preferences of US environmental managers: applying Ajzen's theory of planned behavior', *Academy of Management Journal*, **43**(3), 627–41.

Crane, Andrew (2000), 'Corporate greening as amoralization', *Organization Studies*, **21**(4), 673–96.

Dechant, K. and B. Altman (1994), 'Environmental leadership: from compliance to competitive advantage', *Academy of Management Executive*, **8**(3), 7–27.

Delmas, Magali (2002), 'The diffusion of environmental management standards in Europe and in the United States: an institutional perspective', *Policy Sciences*, **35**(1), 91–119.

Dormann, Jurgen and Chad Holliday (2002), *Innovation, Technology, Sustainability, and Society*, Geneva: World Business Council for Sustainable Development.

Dutton, J.E., S.J. Ashford, R.M. O'Neill and K.A. Lawrence (2001), 'Moves that matter: issues selling and organizational change', *Academy of Management Journal*, **44**, 716–36.

Egri, Carolyn P. and Susan Herman (2000), 'Leadership in the North American environmental sector: values, leadership styles, and contexts of environmental leaders and their organizations', *Academy of Management Journal*, **43**(4), 571–604.

Egri, Carolyn P. and Robert C. Hornal (2002), 'Strategic environmental human resources management and organizational performance: an exploratory study of the Canadian manufacturing sector', in Sanjay Sharma and Mark Starik (eds), *Research in Corporate Sustainability: The Evolving Theory and Practice of Organizations in the Natural Environment*, Cheltenham, UK and Northampton, MA: Edward Elgar, 205–36.

Fineman, Stephan (1996), 'Emotional subtexts in corporate greening', *Organization Studies*, **17**(3), 479–500.

Fineman, Stephan (1998), 'The natural environment, organization and ethics', in M. Parker (ed.), *Ethics and Organizations*, London: Sage, 238–52.

Fishbein, Martin (1963), 'An investigation of the relationship between beliefs about an object and the attitude toward that object', *Human Relations*, **16**, 233–40.

Fishbein, Martin and Icek Ajzen (1975), *Belief, Attitude, Intention, and Behavior: An Introduction to Theory and Research*, Reading, MA: Addison-Wesley.

Graham, J.W. and W.C. Havlick (1999), *Corporate Environmental Policies*, Lanham, MD: Scarecrow Press.

Henriques, Irene and Perry Sadorsky (1999), 'The relationship between environmental commitment and managerial perceptions of stakeholder importance', *Academy of Management Journal*, **42**, 87–99.

Hines, J.M., H.R. Hungerford and A.N. Tomera (1987), 'Analysis and synthesis of research on responsible environmental behavior: a meta-analysis', *Journal of Environmental Education*, **18**, 1–8.

Hoffman, Andrew J. (1993), 'The importance of fit between individual values and organizational culture in the greening of industry', *Business Strategy and the Environment*, **2**(4), 10–18.

Hoffman, Andrew J. (2003), 'Reconciling professional and personal value systems: the spiritually motivated manager as organizational entrepreneur', in Robert A. Giacalone and Carole L. Jurkiewicz (eds), *Handbook of Workplace Spirituality and Organizational Performance*, Armonk, NY and London: M.E. Sharpe, 193–208.

Hostager, Todd J., Thomas C. Neil, Ronald L. Decker and Richard D. Lorentz (1998), 'Seeing environmental opportunities: effects of intrapreneurial ability, efficacy, motivation, and desirability', *Journal of Organizational Change Management*, **11**(1), 11–25.

Howard-Grenville, Jennifer A. and Andrew J. Hoffman (2003), 'The importance of cultural framing to the success of social initiatives in business', *Academy of Management Executive*, **17**(2), 70–84.

Johns, Gary (2001), 'In praise of context', *Journal of Organizational Behavior*, **22**, 31–42.
Kanter, Ruth M. (1983), *The Change Masters*, New York: Simon & Schuster.
Katz, Daniel and Robert L. Kahn (1978), *The Social Psychology of Organizations* (2nd edn), New York: Wiley.
Killmer, Annette and Catherine A. Ramus (2004), 'Motivation theory revisited: a theoretical framework for peripheral tasks', *Rivista di Politica Economica*, January–February, no. 1–11.
McKenzie-Mohr, Doug, Lisa Sara Nemiroff, Laurie Beers and Serge Desmarais (1995), 'Determinants of responsible environmental behavior', *Journal of Social Issues*, **51**(4), 139–56.
McKenzie-Mohr, Doug and Stuart Oskamp (eds) (1995), 'Psychology and the promotion of a sustainable future', *Journal of Social Issues*, Special issue, **51**(4).
Milgrom, Paul and John Roberts (1992), *Economics, Organization, and Management*, Englewood Cliffs, NJ: Prentice-Hall.
Milliman, J. and J. Clair (1996), 'Best environmental HRM practices in the US', in W. Wehrmeyer (ed.), *Greening People: Human Resources and Environmental Management*, Sheffield: Greenleaf.
Mischel, Walter (1968), *Personality and Assessment*, New York: Wiley.
Mischel, Walter (1973), 'Toward a cognitive learning reconceptualization of personality', *Psychological Review*, **80**(4), 252–83.
Mitchell, Ronald K., Bradley R. Agle and Donna J. Wood (1997), 'Toward a theory of stakeholder identification and salience: defining the principle of who and what really counts', *Academy of Management Review*, **22**, 853–86.
Post, James E. and Barbara W. Altman (1994), 'Managing the environmental change process: barriers and opportunities', *Journal of Organizational Change Management*, **7**(4), 64–84.
Ramus, Catherine A. (1997), 'Employee empowerment at GE Plastics Europe: an example of a successful environmental change process', *Corporate Environmental Strategy*, **4**(3), 38–47.
Ramus, Catherine A. (2001), 'Organization support for employees: encouraging creative ideas for environmental sustainability', *California Management Review*, **43**(3), 85–105.
Ramus, Catherine A. (2002), 'Encouraging innovative environmental actions: what companies and managers must do', *Journal of World Business*, **37**(2), 151–64.
Ramus, Catherine A. (2003), *Employee Environmental Innovation in Firms: Organizational and Managerial Factors*, Hampshire, UK and Burlington, VT: Ashgate Publishing.
Ramus, Catherine A. and Ivan Montiel (2004), 'Corporate environmental policies: an empirical study of commitment and implementation', *15th Annual Meeting of the International Association for Business and Society*. Jackson Hole, WY: International Association for Business and Society.
Ramus, Catherine A. and Ulrich Steger (2000), 'The roles of supervisory support behaviors and environmental policy in employee "ecoinitiatives" at leading-edge European companies', *Academy of Management Journal*, **43**(4), 605–26.
Rands, Gordon (1990), 'Environmental attitudes, behaviors, and decision making: implications for management education and development', in W.M. Hoffman, R. Frederick and E.S. Petry (eds), *The Corporation, Ethics, and the Environment*, Westport, CT: Quorum Books, 269–86.

Rokeach, M. (1968), *Beliefs, Attitudes, and Values: A Theory of Organization and Change*, San Francisco: Jossey-Bass.

Rokeach, M. (1973), *The Nature of Human Values*, New York: Free Press.

Rokeach, M. (1979), 'From individual to institutional values: with special reference to the values of science', in M. Rokeach (ed.), *Understanding Human Values: Individual and Societal*, New York: Free Press, 47–70.

Roper Starch Worldwide (1995), 'The environmental two step: looking forward, moving backward', survey conducted for the *New York Times Mirror Magazine* National Environmental Forum, May.

Rousseau, Denise M. and Yitzhak Fried (2001), 'Location, location, location: contextualizing organizational research', *Journal of Organizational Behavior*, **22**(1), 1–13.

Russo, Michael V. and Paul A. Fouts (1997), 'A resource-based perspective on corporate environmental performance and profitability', *Academy of Management Journal*, **40**, 534–59.

Schein, E.H. (1985), *Organizational Culture and Leadership*, San Francisco, CA: Jossey-Bass.

Schneider, Benjamin (1987), 'The people make the place', *Personnel Psychology*, **14**, 437–53.

Schwartz, S.H. (1992), 'Universals in the content and structure of values: theoretical advances and empirical tests in 20 countries', in M.P. Zanna (ed.), *Advances in Experimental Social Psychology*, Orlando, FL: Academic Press, 1–65.

Shamir, Boas (1991), 'Meaning, self and motivation in organizations', *Organization Studies*, **12**(3), 405–24.

Sharma, Sanjay (2000), 'Managerial interpretations and organizational context as predictors of corporate choice of environmental strategy', *Academy of Management Journal*, **43**, 681–97.

Sharma, Sanjay, Amy L. Pablo and Harrie Vredenburg (1999), 'Corporate environmental responsiveness strategies: the importance of issue interpretation and organizational context', *Journal of Applied Behavioral Science*, **35**(1), 87–108.

Sivek, D.J. and H.R. Hungerford (1990), 'Predictors of responsible behavior in members of three Wisconsin conservation organizations', *Journal of Environmental Education*, **21**, 35–40.

Skinner, B.F. (1966), *The Behavior of Organisms: An Experimental Analysis*, New York: Appleton-Century-Crofts.

Skinner, B.F. (1969), *Contingencies of Reinforcement*, New York: Appleton-Century-Crofts.

Skinner, B.F. (1974), *About Behaviorism*, New York: Knopf.

Starik, Mark and Gordon Rands (1995), 'Weaving an integrated web: multilevel and multisystem perspectives of ecologically sustainable organizations', *Academy of Management Review*, **20**(4), 908–36.

Steger, Ulrich (2000), 'Environmental management systems: empirical evidence and further perspectives', *European Management Journal*, **18**(1), 23–37.

Stern, Paul C. (1992), 'Psychological dimensions of global environmental change', in M.R. Rosenzweig and L.W. Porter (eds), *Annual Review of Psychology*, **43**, 269–302.

Stern, Paul C. and Thomas Dietz (1994), 'The value basis of environmental concern', *Journal of Social Issues*, **50**(3), 65–84.

Thomas, Kenneth W. and Betty A. Velthouse (1990), 'Cognitive elements of empowerment: an "interpretative" model of intrinsic task motivation', *Academy of Management Review*, **15**(4), 666–81.

Valentine, Sean, Lynn Godkin and Margaret Lucero (2002), 'Ethical context, organizational commitment, and person–organization fit', *Journal of Business Ethics*, **41**, 349–60.

Van Dyne, Linn, L.L. Cummings and J. McLean Parks (1995), 'Extrarole behaviors: in pursuit of construct and definitional clarity', in L.L. Cummings and B.M. Staw (eds), *Research in Organizational Behavior*, **17**, 215–85.

Vroom, Victor H. (1964), *Work and Motivation*, New York: Wiley.

Walker, Lawrence R. and Kenneth W. Thomas (1982), 'Beyond expectancy theory: an integrative motivational model from health care', *Academy of Management Review*, **7**(2), 187–94.

Wehrmeyer, W. (ed.) (1996), *Greening People: Human Resources and Environment Management*, Sheffield: Greenleaf.

Zelezny, Lynnette C. and P. Wesley Schultz (eds) (2000), 'Promoting environmentalism', *Journal of Social Issues*, Special issue, **56**(3), 365–555.

5. Small firms and natural environment: a resource-based view of the importance, antecedents, implications and future challenges of the relationship[1]

J. Alberto Aragón-Correa and Fernando Matías-Reche

The resource-based view (Barney, 1991; Conner, 1991; Rumelt, 1984; Wernerfelt, 1984) has been widely used to show that advanced environmental practices positively affect financial performance through the generation of organizational capabilities that are competitively valuable for firms (for example Christmann, 2000; Judge and Douglas, 1998; Marcus and Geffen, 1998; Russo and Fouts, 1997; Sharma and Vredenburg, 1998). Recent works urge not only more analysis of the implications of corporate environmental strategies for performance, but also more attention to factors influencing firms' opportunities to implement advanced approaches to the natural environment (Aragón-Correa et al., 2004; Aragón-Correa and Sharma, 2003; Buysse and Verbeke, 2003; Gilley et al., 2000; Starik and Marcus, 2000).

Firm size has often shown a statistically significant effect as a control variable in studies on corporate environmental strategies (for example Aragón-Correa, 1998; Buysse and Verbeke, 2003; Russo and Fouts, 1997; Sharma, 2000); however these results and most of the previous works on organizations and natural environment included only big companies in their samples, often the biggest ones in the industries of interest (Flannery and May, 2000, and Dean et al., 1998; Dean et al., 2000 are exceptions). Small and medium-sized enterprises (SMEs) have been advised to avoid strategic leadership and to wage guerrilla attacks (Chen and Hambrick, 1995), and although these prescriptions have not been grounded in empirical findings from environmental research, scholars seem to have accepted these ideas and assumed that SMEs' lack of resources prevents them from implementing advanced environmental strategies and that environmental initiatives reduce their profitability. Therefore it is not clear from the extant literature whether the central findings in larger firm contexts related to the relationship between profitability and advanced environmental approaches are applicable to SMEs.

Arguments to justify the exclusion of SMEs from previous environmental works have included their presumed lack of interest in anything beyond regulatory compliance (Greening and Gray, 1994; Russo and Fouts, 1997; Sharma and Vredenburg, 1998), the low degree of public interest in SMEs (Scott, 1990), and the difficulties of obtaining data from SMEs (Aragón-Correa, 1998; Rutherfoord et al., 2000). None of these arguments justifies lack of analysis considering that SMEs comprise over 95 per cent of US and European businesses (US Small Business Administration Office, 1998; European Commission, 1999), accounting for approximately 47 per cent of the gross domestic product in the United States and 55 per cent in Europe (Karmel and Bryon, 2002). Additionally Smith and Kemp (1998) estimated that SMEs produce 70 per cent of all the pollution; Marshall (1998) indicated that 60 per cent of carbon emissions from world industry can be attributed to SMEs; and Hillary (2000) estimated that the sum total of SMEs' environmental impacts outweighs the combined environmental impact of large firms.

Debate continues between those who think that small firms can be analysed with the same theories as large firms (Meyer and Heppart, 2000) and those who think that unique aspects of small firms necessitate specific theories (Venkatraman, 1997). However there is broad agreement that research specifically focused on SMEs is necessary (for example Dean et al., 1998; Okada and Sawai, 1999; Way, 2002) and previous research on environmental aspects of organizations may have overlooked much of the behaviour of these firms. Strategic differences between big and small firms, the scope of SMEs' impacts on economies and on the natural environment, and the absence of previous analysis all suggest the importance of giving detailed attention to the issue of the strategic behaviour of SMEs regarding natural environment.

This study tries to reach a better understanding of at least three questions: What corporate environmental strategies might SMEs develop? (Are they really unable to implement advanced environmental strategies?) Which internal factors might determine their environmental actions? (Are resources the only relevant factors?) Finally, could SME performance improve as a consequence of some form of environmental management? (Or is it correct that SMEs, in contrast to big firms, cannot obtain any advantages from advanced environmental strategies, but can only incur costs?) We highlight the potential of a resource-based view of environmental strategies and delimitate how this view is useful for better understanding of SMEs' potential to develop advanced environmental approaches. These arguments have relevant implications for practitioners and policy-makers because we open profitable opportunities of preventive and advanced environmental approaches for SMEs.

STRATEGY AND SMALL AND MEDIUM-SIZED ENTERPRISES

Delimitation of Small and Medium-sized Enterprises

The European Commission and the US Small Business Administration use similar criteria to define SMEs, however there are many others working definitions that differ from these official delimitation and also some differences between European and American views. In any case, the key benchmarking variables usually include: number of employees, turnover, total assets and independence of the enterprise (Karmel and Bryon, 2002).

European Commission states that a SME is a company that has: fewer than 250 employees; either an annual turnover not exceeding €40 million, or an annual balance sheet total not exceeding €27 million;[2] and is independent (less than 25 per cent of the capital or voting rights are owned by one enterprises, or jointly by several enterprises, falling outside the definitions of an SME). The European government distinguishes between 'micro' (fewer than ten employees), 'small' (fewer than 50), and 'medium-sized' (fewer than 250) enterprises. The US Small Business Administration defines SMEs dependent upon the industrial sector in which the company operates. It determines varying threshold for SMEs that generally encompass fewer than 500 employees and a turnover of less than €5 million, but ranging from 100 to 1500 employees and turnover in the range of €1.5 million to €20.5 million.

SMEs' literature has usually included firms that are not far off these official thresholds. Sometimes organizational scholars have preferred criteria based on a share of the market. However it is also common to find empirical papers which do not make a clear delimitation of their samples of 'small firms'.

Strategic Management Literature and Small Firms

Despite the widespread recognition of the important roles that SMEs play in economies, relatively little formal research has been done on competitive strategies for SMEs. The lack of research is especially important compared with the efforts devoted to big firms, and the importance of SMEs in terms of percentage of firms and GDP contribution is far from being reflected in the attention devoted by researchers in terms of scholars' attention or papers. SMEs have often become marginalized as a residual class of firms that failed to become big, occupy secondary labour markets and niches, and frequently use old-fashioned managerial approaches (Scranton, 1999: 19).

Many of the first works were focused on showing the presence or the absence of strategic analysis and planning practices in SMEs (for example Sexton and Van Auken, 1985; Shuman et al., 1985). Subsequently, the focus of research shifted toward demonstrating how different strategies affect SMEs' performance (for example Bracker et al., 1988; Piest, 1994; Risseeuw and Masurel, 1994).

Early studies from the PIMS database (for example Boston Consulting Group, 1974; Strategic Planning Institute, 1977) reinforced the idea that large firms possessed numerous advantages over smaller firms and espoused the virtue of growth-oriented strategies. Afterward researchers came to realize that certain advantages might also accrue to smaller firms (for example Woo, 1987; Woo and Cooper, 1981). Various authors recognized the main importance of the focus strategy (Porter, 1980) to SMEs (for example Brown, 1995; Carroll, 1984; Kao, 1981). Most of these works state that small businesses which succeeded worked as flexible firms producing specialty products or services for niche markets. Therefore rather than competing with large firms, they coexisted by differentiating their products from those of their larger competitors, and specially focusing on rapidly changing regional and seasonal markets, and very particular demands. There are various ways used to develop these niches (Lescure, 1999): the exploitation of technological specialization, batch production designed to supply those segments of the markets that mass-producers could not meet, and subcontracting markets. All these works seem to imply that the niching strategy is the only competitive strategy option available to SMEs, given their lack of resources (Lee et al., 1999).

A Resource-based View of SMEs' Competitive Advantage

Although the majority of the works have usually highlighted the importance of the SMEs' lack of resources (for example D'Amboise and Muldowney, 1988; Eden et al., 1997), some of them have also proposed some valuable resources linked to SMEs such as internally generated funds and simple capital structure (financial resources), or the entrepreneurship of the founders and managers (Rangone, 1999; Yu, 2001). Our interest here will be an analysis of potential SMEs' capabilities.

Flexibility has probably been the SMEs' characteristic most widely cited (for example Chen and Hambrick, 1995; Fiegenbaum and Karnani,

1991; Yu, 2001). Although a comprehensive analysis of small firms' flexibility from the capabilities perspectives is still lacking, it is possible to obtain some clear guidelines about its importance (Yu, 2001: 89). For instance, flexibility allows SMEs to reinforce their capability of managing external relationships by obtaining critical resources to survive via inter-firm relationships (such as subcontracting), personal relationships or new market opportunities (Hendry et al., 1995: 5; Conner and Prahalad, 1996: 487).

Some scholars have also analysed the entrepreneurial capability and innovativeness of small firms (for example Hitt et al., 1991; Woo, 1987). However given that the human resources of SMEs consist of a small number of employees, these features and the future of the firm rest heavily on the manager-founder-entrepeneur's vision. The SME's capabilities, and especially the firm's entrepreneurial skills, are therefore specially influenced by the owner-manager's experiences and socio-economic background (Merz and Sauber, 1995; Miller et al., 1988). In any case, organizational capabilities of shared vision or proactivity may especially help managers so inclined to expand organizational capabilities (or managerial skills) to the whole firm. In fact, SMEs' inertia (lack of flexibility) may be largely associated with owners, who try to use the same knowledge and their previous experiences to solve all kinds of problems (Yu, 2001: 189).

Additionally, SMEs may be distinguished from large firms in terms of the diffuseness of interaction among departments, better personal links, more unified culture and stronger identity. All these features permit easier communications (Kogut and Zander, 1996) and more flexible access to information required to respond to task demands, but also may induce problems of emotional interdependencies (Lawrence and Lorsch, 1967).

Therefore the traditional argument has been that SMEs need specific strategies to compete successfully in an industry due to the lack of resources. However the specific prescriptions for SMEs have varied widely, ranging from being innovative and proactive to being conservative and avoiding direct confrontation (Chen and Hambrick, 1995). The consideration (or not) of the ability of many SMEs to retain certain capabilities (even in a greater degree than bigger firms) may be one of the main reasons for these previous (and contradictory) prescriptions. We would like then to take the approach of making specific predictions related to the natural environment for the different capabilities associated with small firms. We want to highlight that different skills are associated to each SME; however we have tried to find some commonalties in order to make our predictions for their corporate environmental strategies.

CORPORATE ENVIRONMENTAL STRATEGIES AND SMALL FIRMS

A Resource-based View of Corporate Environmental Strategies

Many researchers have developed typologies of corporate postures toward the natural environment (for example Hart, 1995; Greeno, 1994; Roome, 1992). Buysse and Verbeke (2003) drew on Hart's (1995) typology and, building on the resource-based view, showed three patterns of corporate environmental strategy: (1) a reactive environmental strategy, whereby only a few resources are committed, and product and process improvements are only made to conform to legal requirements; (2) a pollution prevention strategy characterized by specific environmental activities allowing firms regulatory compliance plus some extra reduction of environmental liabilities when the latter simultaneously implies less cost (for example saving electricity); and (3) an environmental leader strategy, whereby products and processes are voluntarily designed to prevent their environmental burdens during their entire life cycles.

Despite the differences between the various classifications, they all place firms' environmental strategies along a continuum ranging from merely aiming to meet legal requirements to environmental proactivity. Reactive strategies are compliance and pollution control (end of pipe). Proactive environmental strategies – including eco-efficiency, pollution prevention and environmental leadership – are voluntarily designed to avoid environmental impacts by dealing with their sources (Aragón-Correa, 1998; Buysse and Verbeke, 2003; Sharma, 2000; Sharma and Vredenburg, 1998). Several authors (for example Christmann, 2000; Hart, 1995; Judge and Douglas, 1998) have identified proactive environmental strategies as a firm capability because they are organizational abilities to coordinate heterogeneous resources (for instance human resources, technology and raw materials) (Amit and Schoemaker, 1993; Grant, 1991) in order to reduce environmental impacts and simultaneously maintain or increase firm competitiveness. The most proactive environmental strategies have been characterized as dynamic capabilities that rely on a systematic pattern of capabilities, but the implementation of less proactive practices does not usually require such a systematic approach (Aragón-Correa and Sharma, 2003). A dynamic capability consists of a set of complex but identifiable processes allowing a firm to generate new and creative strategies, enabling it to adapt to changes in the general business environment, and offering more important opportunities to obtain competitive advantage than more basic capabilities (Eisenhardt and Martin, 2000; Teece et al., 1997).

For instance saving money by simply reducing consumption of natural resources (Schmidheiny, 1992; WBCSD, 1997) can be characterized as a limited – not a dynamic – capability focused on specific practices. This strategy is usually implemented step by step, often beginning with simple activities (Lehni, 2000). Each step consists of simple activities intended to positively and simultaneously affect the natural environment and the firm's performance. These activities have usually been labelled 'eco-efficient' practices (for example OECD, 1998; WBCSD, 1997).

In contrast, the most proactive environmental strategies fit the idea of a dynamic capability. A corporate environmental strategy of leadership affects the entire firm and demands a systematic implementation effort (Marcus and Geffen, 1998; Russo and Fouts, 1997). This strategy is related to specific strategic features (Aragón-Correa, 1998) and promotes a strong interest in intangible assets and capabilities as positive outputs (Russo and Fouts, 1997; Sharma and Vredenburg, 1998).

Specific Aspects for Small Firms' Environmental Strategies

Strategic management researchers have long debated the strategic advantages and disadvantages associated with large firm size. Large firms can exploit patents and scale economies in research and development and in their operations (Woo and Cooper, 1981), acquire market share via breadth of product lines and exert bargaining power over suppliers and customers (Scherer and Ross, 1990), and control extensive slack resources (Sharma, 2000). However small firms are usually described as possessing capabilities such as fast decision-making (Chen and Hambrick, 1995), flexibility (Fiegebaum and Karnani, 1991), and entrepreneurial leaders (Hitt et al., 1991; Woo, 1987).

Addressing the natural environment, Sharma (2000) showed that the more discretion managers have in managing the business–natural environment interface, the greater the likelihood of their interpreting environmental issues as opportunities. In studies of large firms, the largest have been observed as having the most proactive environmental activities (Aragón-Correa, 1998; Russo and Fouts, 1997; Sharma, 2000). Scholars have consequently argued that because proactive environmental strategies require accumulation of, and interaction among, resources such as physical assets, technologies and people (Ramus and Steger, 2000; Russo and Fouts, 1997; Sharma, 2000; Shrivastava, 1995), SMEs' lesser resources might prevent them from making environmental advances (for example Greening and Gray, 1994; Russo and Fouts, 1997).

However systematic research focused on SMEs' environmental strategies has been absent from previous literature. Descriptive works on SMEs have often highlighted their poor rate of environmental commitment, describing them as usually only interested in complying with environmental regulations (for example Rutherfoord et al., 2000; Schaper, 2002; Williamson and Lynch-Wood, 2001). On the other hand, authors have also described multiple cases of SMEs' successfully implementing proactive environmental strategies around the world (for example Carlson-Skalak, 2000; Hillary, 2000). Analysing these cases, we find some SMEs showing features coinciding with the most advanced practices of big firms, and many of them implementing programmes to reduce the environmental impacts of activities or processes when they simultaneously obtain cost reductions. Our first interest is to highlight that SMEs' environmental strategies may be varied. Our descriptive proposition is:

Proposition 1. SMEs will exhibit a variety of reactive and proactive corporate environmental strategies ranging from compliance to leadership.

ANTECEDENTS AND PERFORMANCE IMPLICATIONS OF SMEs' ENVIRONMENTAL STRATEGIES

The Influence of Organizational Capabilities on Environmental Approaches

Like all organizational capabilities (Grant, 1991), environmental capabilities demand a complex integration of previous capabilities (Aragón-Correa and Sharma, 2003; Hart, 1995; Marcus and Geffen, 1998). Seeking arguments supporting a relationship between SMEs' environmental strategies and organizational capabilities (and not only resources), we chose to focus on three specific capabilities for our analysis: shared vision, stakeholder management and strategic proactivity. These three capabilities have been among the most analysed in the previous literature, and previous works have clearly stated the importance of one or several of them (for example Aragón-Correa, 1998; Aragón-Correa and Sharma, 2003; Christmann, 2000; Marcus and Geffen, 1998; Russo and Fouts, 1997; Sharma and Vredenburg, 1998). It is out of our scope here to cover all relevant organizational capabilities, but we try to offer a first step toward determining if organizational capabilities have influence on the corporate environmental strategies of SMEs.

Shared vision
The organizational capability of shared vision exists when an organization's members have collective values and beliefs about its objectives and

mission (Oswald et al., 1994). Goal clarity and shared responsibility for organizational objectives are two basic characteristics of shared vision and positively affect organizational learning and employee creativity in the environmental area (Ramus and Steger, 2000).

It is important to note that the capability of shared vision does not just mean that employees know their managers' objectives; rather, shared vision entails a shared feeling that the firm's objectives are important and appropriate and that all of its members may contribute to defining them. Compared to large firms, SMEs may have fewer restrictions and more opportunities for direct communication and shared experiences among organization members (O'Gorman and Doran, 1999). However SMEs' managers have been shown to have difficulty developing clear objectives and communicating with subordinates owing to lack of resources (including time) and unprofessional management (Smeltzer and Fann, 1989; Way, 2002), and most of them lack interest in analysis that employees might offer, in setting precise objectives, and in reaching consensus among managers and employees (Merz and Sauber, 1995).

Hart (1995) proposed that firms having a demonstrated capability of shared vision will be able to accumulate the skills necessary for proactive environmental strategies more quickly than firms without such a capability, because these strategies depend 'upon tacit skill development through employee involvement' (Hart, 1995: 999). Research on corporate environmental changes presents arguments for the importance of employee support for environmental efforts (Barret and Murphy, 1996; Ruiz-Quintanilla et al., 1996; Wehrmeyer and Parker, 1996). A few studies have begun to show empirical evidence supporting these arguments for big firms (for example Andersson and Bateman, 2000; Ramus and Steger, 2000).

In any case, the importance of shared vision for the process of change seems to be high for SMEs and larger organizations. For example Raymond et al. (1998) showed that organizational support is positively associated with opportunities to implement business process re-engineering in SMEs. Therefore:

Proposition 2. The capability of shared vision will positively influence the development of proactive environmental strategies for SMEs.

Stakeholder management

Stakeholder pressures (especially those from consumers and government) have often been cited as factors contributing to environmental advances of firms (for example Cordano and Frieze, 2000; Henriques and Sadorsky, 1999; Miles et al., 1999), and managers' perceptions of stakeholders' interests influences different aspects of corporate ecological responsiveness (Bansal and Roth, 2000).

Sharma and Vredenburg (1998) showed the importance of the capability of stakeholder integration for evaluating the requirements and implications of environmentally proactive strategies. They specifically defined this capability as 'the ability to establish trust-based collaborative relationships with a wide variety of stakeholders, especially those with noneconomic goals' (1998: 735). Henriques and Sadorsky (1999) showed that environmentally proactive firms usually view all their stakeholders as important, and actively manage their environmental worries.

Environmental stakeholders often target larger firms (and not necessarily the worst polluters), because these firms are often the most likely to develop advances in order to avoid damage to their reputations (Greve, 1989). Large firms are also the best able to influence stakeholders' views of their environmental impacts through public relations and media campaigns. Small firms may enjoy a degree of anonymity and therefore might be able to avoid making some environmental efforts, if they were so inclined (Dean et al., 2000). However those SMEs interested in proactive environmental approaches need to pay careful attention to their stakeholders' interests. Although their small size makes them flexible responders to changes in the general business environment, small firms are also seriously challenged by unfavourable and hostile environments (Merz and Sauber, 1995). Less likely than large firms to have access to media or publicity, capability of stakeholder management for SMEs relies on an organizational ability to be sensitive and collaborative to the preferences of relevant external groups (such as neighbours or institutions). Understanding and managing social worries and engaging trust-based relationships may expand SMEs' resources for environmental advances through environmental coalitions and alliances, voluntary collaborations, governmental grants and free consulting.

Flannery and May's (2000) results are especially useful for better understanding the importance of stakeholders for environmental approaches of SMEs. They used a sample of 139 SMEs in the US metal-finishing industry to show that managers' decision intentions concerning the treatment of hazardous wastewater were influenced positively by 'their assessment of support from important others'. Therefore:

Proposition 3. The capability of stakeholder management will positively influence the development of proactive environmental strategies for SMEs.

Strategic proactivity
Aragón-Correa (1998) drew on Miles and Snow's (1978) typology to define strategic proactivity as a firm's ability to initiate changes in its strategic

policies regarding entrepreneurial, engineering and administrative activity rather than to react to events. Strategic proactivity involves taking the initiative in an effort to shape the general business environment to one's own advantage (Chen and Hambrick, 1995). Different authors have proposed 'proactiveness' as a key dimension (with innovation and risk-taking) of an entrepreneurial orientation (Covin and Slevin, 1990; Lumpkin and Dess, 1996; Miller, 1987), and Stopfor and Baden-Fuller (1994) showed that all these dimensions help firms to gain new capabilities. In data on 105 large firms in different Spanish economic sectors, Aragón-Correa (1998) showed that strategic proactivity encouraged adoption of proactive natural environmental postures. Although previous empirical research regarding the influence of strategic proactivity on environmental approaches has been mainly based on large companies, some evidence shows the importance of strategic proactivity for small firms. For example Dean et al. (1998) showed that environmental regulation of specific activities or sectors tends to discourage SMEs' presence but attracts specific kinds of proactive SMEs. This circumstance is especially interesting considering that small firms often show a greater propensity for action than their larger rivals (Chen and Hambrick, 1995). Therefore:

Proposition 4. The capability of strategic proactivity will positively influence the development of proactive environmental strategies for SMEs.

The Influence of Environmental Approaches on SMEs' Performance

The positive relationship found between proactive environmental strategies and the performance of large firms (for example Klassen and Whybark, 1999; Judge and Douglas, 1998; Russo and Fouts, 1997) has been explained as a result of mutual influence between these corporate environmental strategies and capabilities (Christmann, 2000; Hart, 1995; Majumdar and Marcus, 2001; Russo and Fouts, 1997; Sharma and Vredenburg, 1998). The most proactive strategies for managing the interface between a business and its natural environment have the characteristics of a dynamic capability that enables an organization to align itself with changes in its general business environment (Aragón-Correa and Sharma, 2003). An environmental leadership strategy has been shown to be associated with lower costs, improved reputation and generation of new organizational capabilities (Christmann, 2000; Gilley et al. 2000; Hart, 1995; Sharma and Vredenburg, 1998). Other scholars have also noted that eco-efficient practices reduce environmental impacts and simultaneously provide firms with competitive advantage through reduction of costs and addition of net value (Lehni, 2000; WBCSD, 2001).

Although researchers have extensively examined the influence of an environmental approach on big firms' performance, studies of small firms' environmental approaches have used different dependent variables. For example Flannery and May (2000) investigated the influences shaping environmentally ethical decision intentions, and Dean et al. (1998, 2000) estimated the effect of environmental regulations on the formation of small US manufacturing establishments. An assumption in descriptive works is that legislative pressures are the only way to generate environmental advances among small firms because environmental activities do not generate positive implications for SMEs' performance (Rutherfoord et al., 2000). However Miles et al. (1999) emphasized that the relationship between financial performance and adoption of environmental standards for SMEs needed further analysis. In any case, they stated that 'it is reasonable to expect that competent management and a more proactive stance on environmental issues will be rewarded in the small business sector as well' (Miles et al., 1999: 120). We also assume that implications of a proactive environmental strategy for the generation of capabilities and the difficulty many SMEs might have in developing and using such a strategy may generate an excellent competitive opportunity for SMEs. Therefore:

Proposition 5. Proactive environmental strategies will positively influence the financial performance of SMEs.

DISCUSSION, CONCLUSIONS AND FUTURE RESEARCH

Our propositions state an unexplored view of SMEs as organizations with the potential to develop proactive environmental strategies in their industries. Different groups of SMEs with reactive and proactive environmental strategies (leadership, pollution prevention and eco-efficiency) may be delimitated. We propose that SMEs' capabilities positively influence their proactive environmental strategies, and that the most modern preventive practices were positively related to SMEs' performance.

Our research offers ways to contribute to the resource-based view in a small firm context, drawing on the importance of organizational capabilities for generating competitive strategies in organizations (Amit and Schoemaker, 1993; Grant, 1991). Our propositions state that the organizational capabilities of stakeholder management, shared vision and strategic proactivity positively, significantly and simultaneously influence the dimensions of proactive environmental strategies. We suggest that possessing resources is a necessary but not a sufficient condition for developing a competitive strategy of environmental proactivity. These circumstances complement the typical assumption that SMEs lack proactive environmental strategies owing to scarcity of resources.

Furthermore our propositions have stated that the SMEs' capabilities promoting development of environmentally proactive approaches coincide with those found for large companies in previous research (for example Marcus and Geffen, 1998; Sharma and Vredenburg, 1998). Although researchers concerned with organizational size have sometimes stated that what applies to large firms may not apply to small ones, some recent works (Flannery and May, 2000; Raymond et al., 1998) show similar relationships for large and small firms. Traditional arguments may be refitted from the perspective of capabilities: large and small firms often require the same capabilities in order to develop more complex capabilities; however large and small firms might have different chances to generate some of these capabilities.

We also state a positive and significant relationship between modern preventive practices and performance. This idea is also consistent with results obtained for larger firms (for example Judge and Douglas, 1998; Russo and Fouts, 1997), and a proactive environmental strategy may be an appropriate alternative for both small and large firms. The potential of considering the most proactive environmental strategies as dynamic capabilities (Aragón-Correa and Sharma, 2003) is indirectly reinforced by these propositions.

However we would like to highlight that our propositions do not guarantee a positive influence of the implementation of eco-efficient practices on performance. Eco-efficient practices are usually defined as any legal practice to save costs and simultaneously improve the natural environment, and they have often been suggested for small firms and beginners. However practices so delimitated might indirectly negatively affect performance by preventing the generation of organizational capabilities (for example by deterring innovation). Viewed from a resource-based perspective, this idea helps to differentiate between a capability that is specific to a particular function and time, and a global dynamic capability as a means to systematically integrate environment and firm. Limited eco-efficient behaviours may resemble those of many SMEs that develop isolated environmental measures. A more global and systematic eco-efficient approach (Lehni, 2000) might yield different effects on performance than the type of eco-efficiency studied here, requiring for example formal and precise specification of employee participation and provision of performance-contingent rewards (Pawar and Eastman, 1997).

External conditions are also relevant to the development of environmental capabilities (Aragón-Correa and Sharma, 2003), and they should be integrated in future research for SMEs. In any case, more research attention should be paid to the environmental approaches of SMEs in the future. Although previous works have shown that larger firms are often environmentally more proactive than smaller ones, paradoxically many of the capabilities needed to develop proactive environmental approaches may be fostered by certain features of small firms. These advantageous features include aspects such as few levels of hierarchy and high flexibility (Fiegenbaum and Karnani, 1991); low response time (Chen and Hambrick, 1995); and proactiveness and a tendency to take calculated risks (Hitt et al., 1991; Woo, 1987). Future work confirming that SMEs are in fact at a resource disadvantage (but not at a capability disadvantage) when it comes to environmental advances would imply important consequences for government programmes and practitioners.

NOTES

1. Spanish Ministry of Science and Research (Project SEC 2003-07755) and Fundación CentrA partially supported this research.
2. Both the European Commission (1999) and the US Small Business Administration (1998) adjust the thresholds for turnover and balance sheet on a regular basis. At this time, the European Commission is considering modifying substantially upwards the balance sheet threshold.

REFERENCES

Amit, R. and P.J. Schoemaker (1993), 'Strategic assets and organizational rent', *Strategic Management Journal*, **14**, 33–45.
Andersson, L.M. and T.S. Bateman (2000), 'Individual environmental initiative: championing natural environmental issues in US business organizations', *Academy of Management Journal*, **43**, 548–70.
Aragón-Correa, J.A. (1998), 'Strategic proactivity and firm approach to the natural environment', *Academy of Management Journal*, **41**, 556–67.
Aragón-Correa, J.A., F. Matías Reche and M.E. Senise-Barrio (2004), 'Managerial discretion and corporate commitment to the natural environment', *Journal of Business Research*, **57**, 964–75.
Aragón-Correa, J.A. and S. Sharma (2003), 'A contingent resource-based view of proactive corporate environmental strategy', *Academy of Management Review*, **28**, 71–88.
Bansal, P. and K. Roth (2000), 'Why companies go green: a model of ecological responsiveness', *Academy of Management Journal*, **43**, 717–36.
Barney, J.B. (1991), 'Firm resources and sustained competitive advantage', *Journal of Management*, **17**, 99–120.
Barret, S. and D. Murphy (1996), 'Managing corporate environmental policy: a process of complex change', in W. Wehrmeyer (ed.), *Greening People*, Sheffield: Greenleaf, 75–98.

Boston Consulting Group (1974), *Perspectives on Experience*, Boston, MA: Boston Consulting Group.

Bracker, J.S., B.W. Keats and J.N. Pearson (1988), 'Planning a financial performance among small firms in a growth industry', *Strategic Management Journal*, **9**, 591–603.

Brown, R. (1995), *Marketing for Small Firms*, London: Holt, Rinehart & Winston.

Buysse, K. and A. Verbeke (2003), 'Proactive environmental strategies: a stakeholder management perspective', *Strategic Management Journal*, **24**, 453–70.

Carlson-Skalak, S. (2000), 'E Media's Global zero: design for environment in a small firm', *Interfaces*, **30**, 66–83.

Carroll, G.R. (1984), 'The specialist strategy', *California Management Review*, **26**(3), 126–37.

Chen, M. and D.C. Hambrick (1995), 'Speed, stealth, and selective attack: how small firms differ from large firms in competitive behavior', *Academy of Management Journal*, **38**, 453–82.

Christmann, P. (2000), 'Effects of "best practices" of environmental management on cost advantage: the role of complementary assets', *Academy of Management Journal*, **43**, 663–80.

Conner, K. (1991), 'An historical comparison of resource-based logic and five schools of thought within industrial organization economies: do we have a new theory of the firm here?', *Journal of Management*, **17**, 121–54.

Conner, R.K. and C.K. Prahalad (1996), 'A resource-based theory of the firm: knowledge versus opportunism', *Organizational Science*, **7**, 477–501.

Cordano, M. and I.H. Frieze (2000), 'Pollution reduction preferences of US environmental managers: applying Ajzen's theory of planned behavior', *Academy of Management Journal*, **43**, 627–41.

Covin, J.G. and D.P. Slevin (1990), 'New venture strategic posture, structure and performance: an industry life cycle analysis', *Journal of Business Venturing*, **5**, 123–35.

D'Amboise, G. and M. Muldowney (1988), 'Management theory for small business: attempts and requirements', *Academy of Management Review*, **13**, 226–40.

Dean, T.J., R.L. Brown and C.E. Bamford (1998), 'Differences in large and small firm responses to environmental context: strategic implications from a comparative analysis of business formations', *Strategic Management Journal*, **19**, 709–28.

Dean, T.J., R.L. Brown and V. Stango (2000), 'Environmental regulation as a barrier to the formation of small manufacturing establishments: a longitudinal examination', *Journal of Environmental Economics and Management*, **40**, 56–75.

Eden, L., E. Levitas and R.J. Martinez (1997), 'The production, transfer and spillover of technology: comparing large and small multinationals as technology producers', *Small Business Economics*, **9**, 53–66.

Eisenhardt, K.M. and J.A. Martin (2000), 'Dynamic capabilities: what are they?', *Strategic Management Journal*, **21**, 1105–21.

European Commission (1999), *The European Observatory for SMEs Fifth Annual Report 1997*, Brussels: European Network for SME Research.

Fiegenbaum, A. and A. Karnani (1991), 'Output flexibility: a competitive advantage for small firms', *Strategic Management Journal*, **12**, 101–14.

Flannery, B.L. and D.R. May (2000), 'Environmental ethical decision making in the US metal-finishing industry', *Academy of Management Journal*, **43**, 642–62.

Gilley, K.M., D.L. Worrell, W.N. Davidson and A. El-Jelly (2000), 'Corporate environmental initiatives and anticipated firm performance: the differential effects of process-driven versus product-driven greening initiatives', *Journal of Management*, **26**, 1199–1216.

Grant, R.M. (1991), 'The resource-based theory of competitive advantage: implications for strategy formulation', *California Management Review*, **33**, 114–35.

Greening, D.W. and B. Gray (1994), 'Testing a model of organizational response to social and political issues', *Academy of Management Journal*, **37**, 467–98.

Greeno, J.L. (1994), 'Corporate environmental excellence and stewardship', in R.V. Kolluru (ed.), *Environmental Strategies Handbook: A Guide to Effective Policies and Practices*, New York: McGraw Hill, 43–66.

Greve, M.S. (1989), 'Environmentalism and bounty hunting', *Public Interest*, Fall, 15–19.

Hart, S.L. (1995), 'A natural-resource-based view of the firm', *Academy of Management Review*, **20**, 874–907.

Hendry, C., M.B. Arthur and A.M. Jones (1995), *Strategy Through People: Adaptation and Learning in the Small–Medium Enterprise*, London: Routledge.

Henriques, I. and P. Sadorsky (1999), 'The relationship between environmental commitment and managerial perceptions of stakeholder importance', *Academy of Management Journal*, **42**, 87–99.

Hillary, R. (2000), *Small and Medium-sized Enterprises and the Environment*, Sheffield: Greenleaf.

Hitt, M.A., R.E. Hoskisson and J.S. Harrison (1991), 'Strategic competitiveness in the 1990s: challenges and opportunities for US executives', *Academy of Management Executive*, **5**, 7–22.

Judge, W.Q. and T.J. Douglas (1998), 'Performance implications of incorporating natural environmental issues into the strategic planning process: an empirical assessment', *Journal of Management Studies*, **35**, 241–62.

Kao, R.W.Y. (1981), *Small Business Management: A Strategic Emphasis*, Holt: Rinehart & Winston.

Karmel, S.M. and J. Bryon (2002), *A Comparison of Small and Medium Sized Enterprises in Europe and in the USA*, London and New York: Routledge.

Killmer, Annette and Catherine A. Ramus (2004), 'Motivation theory revisited: a theoretical framework for peripheral tasks', Rivista di Politica Economica, (1–11) January–February.

Klassen, R.D. and D.C. Whybark (1999), 'The impact of environmental technologies on manufacturing performance', *Academy of Management Journal*, **42**, 599–615.

Kogut, B. and U. Zander (1996), 'What firms do? Coordination, identity, and learning', *Organization Science*, **7**, 502–19.

Lawrence, P.R. and J.W. Lorsch (1967), *Organization and Environment: Managing Differentiation and Integration*, Boston, MA: Harvard University Press.

Lee, K.S., G.H. Lim and S.J. Tan (1999), 'Dealing with resource disadvantage: generic strategies for SMEs', *Small Business Economics*, **12**, 299–311.

Lehni, M. (2000), *Eco-efficiency: Creating More Value with Less Impact*, Geneva: World Business Center for Sustainable Development.

Lescure, M. (1999), 'Small- and medium-size industrial enterprises in France', in K. Odaka and M. Sawai (eds), *Small Firms, Large Concerns*, Oxford: Oxford University Press.

Lumpkin, G.T. and G.G. Dess (1996), 'Clarifying the entrepreneurial orientation construct and linking it to performance', *Academy of Management Review*, **21**, 135–72.

Majumdar, S.K. and A.A. Marcus (2001), 'Rules versus discretion: the productivity consequences of flexible regulation', *Academy of Management Journal*, **44**, 170–79.

Marcus, A.A. and D. Geffen (1998), 'The dialectics of competency acquisition: pollution prevention in electric generation', *Strategic Management Journal*, **19**, 1145–68.

Lord Marshall (1998), *Economic Instruments and the Business Use of Energy*, London: Stationery Office.

Merz, G.R. and M.H. Sauber (1995), 'Profiles of managerial activities in small firms', *Strategic Management Journal*, **16**, 551–64.

Meyer, G.D. and K.A. Heppart (2000), *Entrepreneurship as Strategy: Competing on the Entrepreneurial Edge*, Thousand Oaks, CA: Sage.

Miles, M.P., L.S. Munilla and T. McClurg (1999), 'The impact of ISO 14 000 environmental management standards on small and medium sized enterprises', *Journal of Quality Management*, **4**, 11–122.

Miles, R. and C. Snow (1978), *Organizational Strategy, Structure and Process*, New York: McGraw Hill.

Miller, D. (1987), 'The structural and environmental correlates of business strategy', *Strategic Management Journal*, **8**, 55–76.

Miller, D., C. Droge and J.M. Toulouse (1988), 'Strategic process and content as mediators between organizational context and structure', *Academy of Management Journal*, **31**, 544–69.

O'Gorman, C. and R. Doran (1999), 'Mission statements in small and medium-sized businesses', *Journal of Small Business Management*, **37**, 59–66.

OECD (1998), *Eco-efficiency*, Paris: OECD Publications.

Okada, K. and M. Sawai (1999), *Small Firms, Large Concerns*, New York: Oxford University Press.

Oswald, S.L., K.W. Mossholder and S.G. Harris (1994), 'Vision salience and strategic involvement: implications for psychological attachment to organization and job', *Strategic Management Journal*, **15**, 477–89.

Pawar, B.S. and K.K. Eastman (1997), 'The nature and implications of contextual influences on transformational leadership: a conceptual examination', *Academy of Management Review*, **22**, 80–109.

Piest, B. (1994), 'Planning comprehensiveness and strategy in SMEs', *Small Business Economics*, **6**, 387–95.

Porter, M. (1980), *Competitive Strategy*, New York: Free Press.

Ramus, C.A. and U. Steger (2000), 'The roles of supervisory support behaviors and environmental policy in employee "ecoinitiatives" at leading-edge European companies', *Academy of Management Journal*, **43**, 605–26.

Rangone, A. (1999), 'A resource-based approach to strategy analysis in small–medium sized enterprises', *Small Business Economics*, **12**, 233–48.

Raymond, L., F. Bergeron and S. Rivard (1998), 'Determinants of business process reengineering success in small and large enterprises: an empirical study in the Canadian context', *Journal of Small Business Management*, **36**, 72–85.

Risseeuw, P. and E. Masurel (1994), 'The role of planning in small firms: empirical evidence from a service industry', *Small Business Economics*, **6**, 313–22.

Roome, N. (1992), 'Developing environmental management strategies', *Business Strategy and the Environment*, **1**, 11–24.

Ruiz-Quintanilla, S.A., J. Bunge, A. Freeman-Gallant and E. Cohen-Rosenthal (1996), 'Employee participation in pollution reduction: a socio-technical perspective', *Business Strategy and the Environment*, **5**, 137–44.

Rumelt, R. (1984), 'Toward a strategic theory of the firm', in R. Lamb (ed.), *Competitive Strategic Management*, Englewood Cliffs, NJ: Prentice Hall, 556–70.

Russo, M.V. and P.A. Fouts (1997), 'A resource-based perspective on corporate environmental performance and profitability', *Academy of Management Journal*, **40**, 534–59.

Rutherfoord, R., R.A. Blackburn and L.J. Spence (2000), 'Environmental management and the small firm: an international comparison', *International Journal of Entrepreneurial Behaviour and Research*, **6**, 310–25.

Schaper, M. (2002), 'Small firms and environmental management: predictors of green purchasing in Western Australian pharmacies', *International Small Business Journal*, **20**, 235–51.

Scherer, F.M. and D. Ross (1990), *Industrial Market Structure and Economic Performance*, Boston, MA: Houghton Mifflin.

Schmidheiny, S. (1992), *Changing Course: A Global Business Perspective on Development and the Environment*, Cambridge, MA: MIT Press.

Scott, W.R. (1990), *Ideology and the New Social Movements*, London: Unwin Hyman.

Scranton, P. (1999), 'Moving outside manufacturing: research perspectives on small business in twentieth-century America', in K. Odaka and M. Sawai (eds), *Small Firms, Large Concerns*, Oxford: Oxford University Press.

Sexton, D.L. and P.M. Van Auken (1985), 'A longitudinal study of small business strategic planning', *Journal of Small Business Management*, **23**(1), 7–16.

Sharma, S. (2000), 'Managerial interpretations and organizational context as predictors of corporate choice of environmental strategy', *Academy of Management Journal*, **43**, 681–97.

Sharma, S. and H. Vredenburg (1998), 'Proactive corporate environmental strategy and the development of competitively valuable organizational capabilities', *Strategic Management Journal*, **19**, 729–53.

Shrivastava, P. (1995), 'Environmental technologies and competitive advantage', *Strategic Management Journal*, **16**, 183–200.

Shuman, J.C., J.J. Shaw and G. Sussman (1985), 'Strategic planning in smaller rapid growth companies', *Long Range Planning*, **18**, 48–53.

Smeltzer, L.R. and G.L. Fann (1989), 'Comparison of managerial communication patterns in small, entrepreneurial organizations and large, mature organizations', *Group and Organization Studies*, **14**, 198–215.

Smith, M.A. and R. Kemp (1998), *Small Firms and the Environment 1998: A Grounded Report*, Birmingham: Groundwork.

Starik, M. and A.A. Marcus (2000), 'Introduction to the special research forum on the management of organizations in the natural environment: a field emerging from multiple paths, with many challenges ahead', *Academy of Management Journal*, **43**, 539–46.

Stopfor, J. and C. Baden-Fuller (1994), *Creating Corporate Entrepreneurship*, *Strategic Management Journal*, **15**, 521–36.

Strategic Planning Institute (1977), *Selected Findings from the PIMS Program*, Cambridge, MA: Strategic Planning Institute.

Teece, D.J., G. Pisano and A. Shuen (1997), 'Dynamic capabilities and strategic management', *Strategic Management Journal*, **18**, 509–33.

US Small Business Administration Office (1998), *1997 Small Business Economics Indicators*, Washington, DC: US Small Business Administration Office.

Venkatraman, S. (1997), 'The distinctive domain of entrepreneurship research', in
J.A. Katz (ed.), *Advances in Entrepreneurship, Firm Emergence, and Growth*,
Greenwich: JAI Press, Vol. 3, 119–38.

Way, S.A. (2002), 'High performance work systems and intermediate indicators of
firm performance within the US small business sector', *Journal of Management*,
28, 765–85.

WBCSD (1997), *Eco-efficient Leadership for Improved Economic and Environmental Performance*, Geneva: World Business Center for Sustainable Development.

WBCSD (2001), *The Business Case for Sustainable Development: Making a
Difference toward the Johannesburg Summit 2002 and Beyond*, Geneva: World
Business Center for Sustainable Development.

Wehrmeyer, W. and K.T. Parker (1996), 'Identification and relevance of environmental corporate cultures as part of a coherent environmental policy', in
W. Wehrmeyer (ed.), *Greening People*, Sheffield: Greenleaf, 163–84.

Wernerfelt, B. (1984), 'A resource-based view of the firm', *Strategic Management
Journal*, **5**, 171–80.

Williamson, D. and G. Lynch-Wood (2001), 'A new paradigm for SME environmental practice', *TQM Magazine*, **13**, 424–32.

Woo, C.Y. (1987), 'Path analysis of the relationship between market share, business-level conduct and risk', *Strategic Management Journal*, **8**, 149–68.

Woo, C.Y. and A.C. Cooper (1981), 'Strategies of effective low share business',
Strategic Management Journal, **2**, 301–18.

Yu, T.F.L. (2001), 'Toward a capabilities perspective of the small firm', *International
Journal of Management Reviews*, **3**, 185–97.

6. Greening service organizations: environmental management practices and performance[1]

George I. Kassinis and Andreas C. Soteriou

Strict regulations, stakeholder pressures and increased awareness of the environmental consequences of their operations has led many firms to re-evaluate the way they do business. This shift in firm attitudes and practices has been followed by research that, among other things, has examined and debated the relationship between firm environmental strategies and performance. Such research suggests that profitable firms tend to have high environmental performance although the nature of this relationship is not fully understood yet (King and Lenox, 2001a; Klassen and McLaughlin, 1996). Moreover other studies point to the positive performance implications of investing in pollution prevention technologies (King and Lenox, 2002; Klassen and Whybark, 1999a).

The majority of such studies have focused on manufacturing firms (Angell and Klassen, 1999; Klassen, 1993; Klassen and Whybark, 1999b). In the context of services, the relationship between environmental management practices and performance, the topic of this chapter, has only recently attracted the attention of researchers (Foster et al., 2000; Goodman, 2000). Examples of service firms that either focus on pollution prevention or adopt environmental management systems (such as ISO 14001) include Wal-Mart (McInerney and White, 1995), the Hyatt Regency (Enz and Siguaw, 1999) and Scandic hotels (Goodman, 2000), and various hospitals (Messelbeck and Whaley, 1999).

The sheer size of the service economy's contribution to gross domestic product adds to the importance of exploring environmental issues in services. Today this contribution exceeds 70 per cent in the US and other industrialized countries, while more than 80 per cent of US employment is in the service sector (Fitzsimmons and Fitzsimmons, 2000; Salzman, 2000). As such, the service economy 'merits consideration both as a source of environmental harm and as a potential instrument to reduce environmental impacts' (Salzman, 2000: 26). Specifically, while on the one hand one may expect 'an environmental bonus from the substitution of services and knowledge for material intensive [manufacturing] activities', on the other 'the information revolution and rise of services [may] have a net negative impact because [services] increase overall economic activity and . . . resource consumption' (Salzman, 2000: 26). Indeed the distinctive characteristics of services vis-à-vis goods (that is the intangibility, perishability and simultaneous production and consumption of services) (Sasser et al., 1978) may present different challenges in deciphering the relationship between environmental practices and performance in services compared to manufacturing. In practice we know little about the environmental impacts of most service operations, how they can be managed, and what impact the environmental practices service firms adopt have on performance.

In this chapter we explore the nature of the relationship between environmental management practices and performance in the context of services. Specifically, we investigate whether the use of such practices by a service firm is positively related to performance through the mediating effect of enhanced customer satisfaction and loyalty. In doing so, we build on Heskett et al.'s (1994) service profit chain framework. We argue that environmental practices are a component of a service firm's operations and as such a component of what Heskett et al. (1994) term the 'front end' of the service profit chain. Specifically, then, we examine the impact of environmental practices on the 'external portion of the service profit chain' and use structural equation modelling to test the hypotheses we develop with data from the hospitality industry in Europe. Our decision to focus on the aforementioned constructs is supported by literature that links customer satisfaction and loyalty to financial performance (Anderson et al., 1997; Rust et al., 1995).

The chapter is organized as follows. In the second section, we discuss the theoretical background and develop our hypotheses. In the third section, we describe our empirical study that focuses on the hospitality industry in Europe and present our methodology and results. In the fourth section, we discuss our findings, provide directions for future research, and conclude.

THEORETICAL BACKGROUND AND HYPOTHESES

Service Operations and Environmental Management

Regulations, rising costs, awareness of the ecological effects of business activities, and stakeholder pressures have forced firms to re-evaluate their strategic approach towards the natural environment (Elkington, 1994;

Rugman and Verbeke, 1998). In light of this, researchers have argued that the effective integration of environmental management practices into firm operations presents numerous benefits including lower costs and enhanced efficiencies (Hart, 1995; Russo and Fouts, 1997), competitive advantages through product or service differentiation (green products or services), and better servicing of niche markets (customers demanding ecologically friendly products and services) (Shrivastava, 1995). Other benefits include an improved image and enhanced loyalty of key stakeholders (Goodman, 2000; Rondinelli and Vastag, 1996).

More specifically, a growing literature examines the competitiveness effects of environmental strategies in manufacturing. Most empirical studies focus on the relationship between environmental performance and financial performance (Dowell et al., 2000; King and Lenox, 2001a; Klassen and McLaughlin, 1996; Russo and Fouts, 1997) and find a positive correlation between the two. A smaller number of studies focus on the relationship between the implementation of environmental practices and performance and suggest that 'green' firms may also be more efficient and innovative (King and Lenox, 2001b; Porter and van der Linde, 1995). Others however argue that corporate environmental programmes generate unrecoverable costs, divert resources from other productive investments and are therefore unsustainable (Walley and Whitehead, 1994). Finally, some studies report mixed results (Christmann, 2000; King and Lenox, 2002). Clearly the debate on the aforementioned relationships continues.

Recently the importance of the natural environment has been addressed in the context of services in general (Grove et al., 1996; Foster et al., 2000; Salzman, 2000) and in the case of the hospitality industry in particular (Enz and Siguaw, 1999; Goodman, 2000; Halme, 2001; Schendler, 2001). The latter provide evidence of the positive performance implications of environmental management measures including cost reductions, resource savings, customer retention and loyalty, and improved employee morale. The generalizability of these results however is limited by the case study or anecdotal nature of the evidence they are based on. Therefore there is a need for further empirical work to examine the relationship between environmental practices and firm performance – such as the one described in this chapter.

In their effort to implement successful environmental practices, service firms face a number of unique challenges that result from the distinctive characteristics of services vis-à-vis goods (Fitzsimmons and Fitzsimmons, 2000; Lovelock, 1996). Here we focus on the consequences of one such characteristic that is likely to have a major impact on environmental management efforts, namely the presence of the customer in the system and the resulting simultaneity of service production and consumption. Researchers

(Chase, 1981; Chase and Tansik, 1983) have identified the impact of customer involvement on the service operating system as one of the most important service idiosyncrasies affecting service performance – especially in high-contact service systems, such as hotels and banks, where customer involvement is typically high.

While true that most services require some direct or indirect customer involvement (Chase and Tansik, 1983; Lovelock, 1996), the physical presence of the customer and his role as co-producer in high-contact service systems create numerous challenges for managers (Soteriou and Chase, 1998). Foster et al. (2000) assert that customer involvement holds potential for influencing environmental actions. Often certain environmental activities are hidden from the customer as they take place in the back office. In restaurants for example, waste disposal or recycling may take place out of customer view. In high-contact systems however, such activities also take place in the front office. An environmentally conscious customer may thus not only apply pressure on management to change company policy (Salzman, 2000) but may also be involved, as co-producer, in a firm's environmental practices such as for example energy and water savings practices in the case of hotels. The challenge and at the same time the opportunity for such high-contact service firms is to meet customer demand and manage customer involvement without compromising the quality of services they provide (Goodman, 2000; Schendler, 2001) in order to meet their overall strategic and financial objectives.

Another particularity of services vis-à-vis manufacturing, which results from the presence of an environmentally sensitive customer in the system, is the more limited choice of available environmental technologies. This is significant because such a choice has important implications for firm operations (Klassen and Whybark, 1999b). For example unlike manufacturers who can choose between pollution control (filters, proper treatment and so on) and pollution preventive solutions (source reduction, reusing and recycling programmes) for the majority of manufacturing operations, most services – especially those of a high-contact nature where environmental activities also take place in the front office – are not given the luxury of a wide spectrum of options. Instead more often than not these choices are limited to pollution prevention – with end-of-pipe measures available for use only in back-office operations.

Pollution prevention is however challenging in its own right. Although fewer resources are wasted and both efficiency and effectiveness are improved through pollution prevention – always compared with pollution control measures – 'pollution prevention typically requires direct modification of critical components of a product or process' (Klassen and Whybark, 1999b: 608). This is unlike the case of pollution control where investment can often be made with minimal disruption to current operations. The above is in line with research on service failsafing (Chase and Stewart, 1994) that focuses on designing 'foolproof' services and avoiding potential fail points. Consider for example the case of a hotel: its environmental actions need to take the form of source reduction, reuse and recycling programmes. Given the presence of the customer in the service system, few if any end-of-pipe solutions – which are widespread in manufacturing – exist. Although such lack of flexibility may be more costly in the short run and may force firms to consider more advanced forms of environmental management, available evidence from manufacturing shows that it is pollution prevention technologies that can potentially lead to performance gains in the long run (King and Lenox, 2002).

Other related service characteristics, such as service simultaneity – the simultaneous production and consumption of services – also present challenges for environmentally minded firms. Since production and consumption occur simultaneously in services, firms may have to consider more advanced forms of environmental management, such as product stewardship. Hart (1995) discusses product stewardship strategies that consider the product's life-cycle costs, including the consumption of the product. Given service simultaneity though, disentangling product stewardship from more conventional forms of environmental management (such as pollution prevention) becomes extremely difficult. This introduces additional challenges and complexities in crafting a service firm's environmental management strategy.

Customer Satisfaction, Loyalty, and Performance

Satisfying the needs and desires of the consumer is among the most fundamental notions of the marketing concept. Among various definitions a popular definition positions customer satisfaction as an evaluation of the perceived discrepancy between prior expectations – or some other norm of performance – and the actual performance as perceived after the consumption of a good or service by a customer (Oliver, 1993). Cumulative satisfaction, defined as a customer's overall experience to date with a product or service (Johnson and Fornell, 1991; Johnson et al., 1995), is thought to be a fundamental indicator of the firm's past, current and future performance, and it is what motivates a firm's investment in customer satisfaction (Anderson et al., 1994).

The literature (for example Heskett et al., 1994, 1997) suggests that customer satisfaction is positively related to the concept of customer loyalty. Specifically, the marketing literature suggests that customer loyalty can be defined in two distinct ways. First, loyalty can be defined as an attitude: different feelings create an individual's overall attachment to a product (the individual's purely cognitive degree of loyalty) (Hallowell, 1996). The second definition is behavioural. Examples of loyalty behaviour include continuing to purchase services from the same supplier and increasing the scale and/or scope of the relationship or the act of recommendation (Oliver, 1999; Yi, 1991).

Loyalty behaviours, including relationship continuance, increased scale or scope of relationship, and recommendation (word-of-mouth advertising) result from customers' beliefs that the quantity of value received from one supplier is greater than that available from other suppliers. Loyalty in one or more of the forms noted above increases profits through enhanced revenues, reduced costs to acquire customers, lower customer–price sensitivity, and decreased costs to serve customers familiar with a firm's service delivery system (Reichheld and Sasser, 1990). A number of recent studies examine the cognitive, affective and conative antecedents of customer loyalty as well as its consequences (Oliver, 1999; Dick and Basu, 1994).

The linkages between satisfaction, loyalty and performance constitute the 'external' portion of the service profit chain framework – discussed in more detail in the next section – and remain the focus of recent research (Fournier and Mick, 1999; Froehle et al., 2000). Earlier efforts utilized the PIMS database to establish a relationship between satisfaction, market share and profitability (Buzzell and Gale, 1987). Reichheld and Sasser (1990) introduced the concept of loyalty into the picture and argued that loyalty is the primary driver of profitability. Overall, there is a general consensus in the literature that improvements in satisfaction lead to higher revenues, reduced future transaction costs and higher profitability – all through improved customer loyalty (Bolton and Drew, 1991; Boulding et al., 1993; Heskett et al., 1994; Reichheld and Sasser, 1990; Schneider and Bowen, 1993; Rust et al., 1995; Zeithaml et al., 1990).

Service–profit Chain and Environmental Practices

Heskett et al.'s (1994) service–profit chain framework links service operations, employee assessments and customer assessments to a firm's profitability and growth (Kamakura et al., 2002). Simply, the service–profit chain describes relationships between market performance (revenue growth and profitability), customer loyalty and customer satisfaction (the external portion of the chain) on the one hand, and employee satisfaction, loyalty and productivity (the internal portion or the 'front end' of the chain) on the other (Heskett et al., 1994). Specifically, it is argued that profitability and revenue growth are stimulated by customer loyalty. The latter is a direct result of customer satisfaction, which is influenced by the value of services provided to customers. Such value – created by satisfied, loyal and productive employees – is a function not only of costs to the customer but also of the results achieved for the customer. Moreover it is based both on perceptions of the way a service is delivered and initial customer expectations. It must finally be noted that the internal quality of the working environment – high-quality support services and policies – enables employees to deliver results to the customer and drives employee satisfaction (Heskett et al., 1994).

In fact, employee involvement in process improvements emerges as a key capability associated with a firm's environmental responsiveness. Environmental performance improvements (such as waste minimization) may result from employee involvement practices or team projects (Hanna et al., 2000; May and Flannery, 1995). Moreover reported examples link employee involvement in such efforts with employee satisfaction and loyalty. Specifically, Enz and Siguaw (1999: 76) report that all four operations named as environmental best practice champions in a Cornell University study of best practices in the US lodging industry indicated that such practices had a positive impact on employee morale (and thus satisfaction) and enhanced the staff's pride in the hotel. Similar results are reported by Goodman (2000) in the case of Scandic hotels.

In this chapter we argue that the service profit chain framework can be used to examine the relationship between the implementation of environmental practices – a component of a firm's operations (Angell and Klassen, 1999; Hanna et al., 2000) – and performance. Specifically, in such a context, environmental practices are placed within the 'front end' of the service profit chain, which Heskett et al. (1994: 166) term 'operating strategy and service delivery system'. Therefore they are arguably built into service design and as such might impact upon customer satisfaction and loyalty, and through them firm performance. Such argumentation is in line with recent literature which argues that the environment must be integrated with management's efforts to address the concerns of all stakeholders – with the overarching objective of such efforts being the enhancement of the value offered to the customer (Angell and Klassen, 1999: 594). More specifically, environmental practices are integrated within the service concept and alter both its structural and managerial elements, including its service delivery, service encounter, quality and information dimensions (Fitzsimmons and Fitzsimmons, 2000: 84–5). For example Scandic's stated priorities included communicating its environmental values and strategy and increasing the participation of employees and customers alike (through education and training) in the hotel chain's environmental activities. Moreover with respect to information, Scandic's new $25 million information system monitored and measured

three environmental performance factors (out of eight key factors moni-
tored) (Goodman, 2000: 206–7).

Overall, then, in this chapter we test whether higher levels of use of environmental management practices in services lead to higher levels of market
performance through the mediating effect of customer satisfaction and
loyalty. In essence, we test the impact of environmental practices on the
external portion of the service profit chain. Figure 6.1 outlines the hypothesized relationships.

Based on the discussion of the second section, we present the following
four hypotheses:

*Hypothesis 1. Higher levels of use of environmental management practices
lead to higher levels of customer satisfaction.*

*Hypothesis 2. Higher levels of customer satisfaction lead to higher levels of
customer loyalty.*

*Hypothesis 3. Higher levels of customer loyalty lead to higher levels of
market performance.*

*Hypothesis 4. Higher levels of use of environmental management practices
lead to higher levels of market performance.*

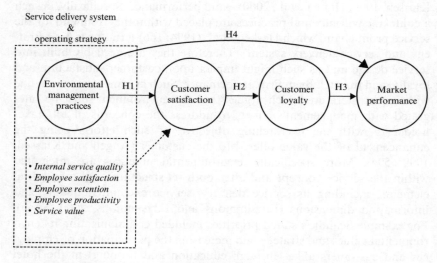

*Figure 6.1   Environmental management practices and the service–profit
chain*

THE EMPIRICAL STUDY

Data Collection and Sample

We collected data on the hotel industry in countries of the European Union (EU). The hospitality industry is the world's largest industry, with 120 million employees and revenues exceeding \$3.8 trillion worldwide. In Europe, the industry accounts on average for more than 10 per cent of the local GDPs. Issues related to environmental management and sustainability have been gaining increasing attention in this industry (Anguera et al., 2000; Enz and Siguaw, 1999; Goodman, 2000).

Our target population included hotels in the countries of Austria, France, Germany, Greece, Italy, Portugal, Spain and the United Kingdom (selected as the EU's top tourist destinations with more than 10 million tourist arrivals per year) along with Cyprus, Malta and Monaco (included because the hospitality industry accounted for a significantly higher percentage of their GDP and employment than the EU average). These countries are all major tourist destinations and accounted for approximately 60 per cent of Europe's 380 million tourists in 1999 – with France and Spain being the number one and two tourist destinations in the world respectively (WTO, 2000). The sampling frame was drawn from the *1999 Official Hotel Guide* (*Official Hotel Guide*, 1999). We focused on high-end hotels (listed as superior deluxe, deluxe, moderate deluxe, superior first class and first class) since environmental practices – being service winners (Fitzsimmons and Fitzsimmons, 2000) – are most likely found in high-end establishments. In fact most case studies reported in the literature support this assumption (Enz and Siguaw, 1999; Goodman, 2000; Schendler, 2001). Moreover the homogeneous clientele of such hotels (for example with respect to income) is more likely to exert similar pressures on them to improve their environmental performance. Also our examination of the hotel industry reveals that most high-end hotels are of medium size. Hotels in our sample were no exception. As such our sample is also homogeneous with respect to hotel size.

A pilot study was first conducted, which consisted of (1) a series of in-depth interviews with hotel managers, and (2) a mail survey, during which a survey instrument was sent to 50 randomly selected hotels in the above countries. Upon completion of the pilot study, the survey instrument (discussed below) was finalized and sent to senior executives of an additional 1238 hotels in the same countries. No problems were observed due to the fact that the questionnaire was in English, given that our population consisted of well-educated senior executives in an industry where the use of the English language is extensive. No biases were observed among respondents from English and non-English speaking countries. Data were collected in the period May–September 1999. The response rate was 8.4 per cent and resulted in a total sample of 104 completed questionnaires. Non-response bias was further assessed by examining differences between response and non-response characteristics with respect to size and type of hotel. No significant differences were found ($p < 0.05$).

In addition we tested for common method bias, which could pose problems for survey research that relies on self-reported data – especially if the same person reports on both: dependent and independent variables. One important concern in such cases is that common method bias may artificially inflate observed relationships between variables. We employed several procedures to avoid common method variance or to estimate its extent. First, the dependent variables were placed after the independent variables in the survey to diminish, if not avoid, the effects of consistency artifacts. Second, Harman's single factor test was performed (Harman, 1967; Podsakoff and Organ, 1986). If common method variance existed, a single factor would emerge from a factor analysis of all questionnaire measurement items, or one general factor that accounted for most of the variance would result. The factor analysis revealed four factors with eigenvalues greater than 1.0 that accounted for 72.2 per cent of the total variance. The first factor only accounted for 30.4 per cent of the variance. These results suggested that common method variance was not a serious problem in our study.

Measures

The survey items used in the survey instrument were drawn from the relevant literatures and finalized based on the results of our pilot study, as shown in the discussion that follows. Where indicated, factor analysis was used (principal components analysis with varimax rotation) in order to assess the dimensionality of our constructs. Scale items and reliabilities along with all survey items are shown in Appendix.

Market performance

Measures of performance used were growth in profits, growth in revenues and market share. Managers were asked to assess how well their hotels performed relative to their competitors with respect to these measures at the time of the survey. A seven-point Likert-type scale was used (worst in industry, 1; about the same, 4; best in industry, 7). Such self-reported measures of performance relative to competitors' performance have been used extensively and successfully in the literature (Dess and Robinson, 1984).

Environmental management practices

Measures for hotel environmental management practices were drawn from studies reported in the literature that dealt with such issues in the hospitality industry (Enz and Siguaw, 1999; Goodman, 2000) and were finalized during the pilot study we conducted. We also consulted the International Hotel and Restaurant Association – a global network of independent and chain operators, national associations, suppliers and educational centres in the hotel and restaurant industry in 147 countries – which presents an annual global environmental award (sponsored by American Express TRS) in collaboration with the United Nations Environment Program. The measures were finalized through factor analysis of the relevant survey items. As shown in the Appendix, measures considered included energy saving, recycling and water saving practices. Managers were asked to rate the degree of use of a specific practice ('not used at all', 1; 'widely used', 7) in their hotel.

Customer satisfaction and loyalty

Managers were asked to rate the degree of agreement or disagreement with statements relating to customer satisfaction and loyalty levels, on whether customers' expectations were exceeded, and on whether customer retention rates were improving using a seven-point scale ('strongly agree', 1; 'strongly disagree', 7). Schneider and Bowen (1993) report high positive correlations between self-reported and customer-reported measures of customer satisfaction. Moreover survey respondents have extensive knowledge to answer such questions, given the level of sophistication of the hotels in our sample and information acquired through independent market research studies or from tourist operators.

METHODOLOGY, ANALYSIS AND RESULTS

Structural Equation Modeling (SEM) (Jöreskog, 1970) was used to simultaneously test a measurement and a structural model to investigate our hypotheses. SEM implicitly asserts a covariance structure whose concordance with the observed covariance based on the data can be tested. One of the unique features of SEM is the ability to provide parameter estimates for relationships among unobserved variables (that is the latent variables).

All indicators used in the study, along with the corresponding constructs and cronbach alpha values are shown in the Appendix. The resulting correlation matrix is shown in Table 6.1.

A confirmatory factor analysis using the principal components method with varimax rotation was used to further verify the dimensionality of our

Table 6.1 Descriptive statistics and correlations

Variable	Mean	SD	ENV1	ENV2	ENV3	CS1	CS2	LOY1	LOY2	PERF1	PERF2	PERF3
ENV1	6	1.414	1									
ENV2	6.25	1.061	0.461**	1								
ENV3	5.5	2.121	0.348**	0.181	1							
CS1	5.5	0.707	0.252*	0.259**	0.212*	1						
CS2	5	0.707	0.253*	0.325**	0.295**	0.767**	1					
LOY1	5	1.414	0.220*	0.163	0.255**	0.474**	0.548**	1				
LOY2	4.5	3.535	0.077	0.221*	0.218*	0.254**	0.328**	0.569**	1			
PERF1	4	0.710	−0.067	−0.012	0.151	0.099	0.165	0.139	0.345**	1		
PERF2	3	0.707	0.091	0.125	0.191	0.193*	0.288**	0.166	0.310**	0.750**	1	
PERF3	3	1.414	0.015	0.046	0.104	0.132	0.193	0.161	0.224**	0.409**	0.448**	1

Note: **$p < 0.01$.
      *$p < 0.05$.

Table 6.2   Rotated factor loadings for the four structural factors

Variables	Factor 1	Factor 2	Factor 3	Factor 4
ENV1	−0.09	0.08	**0.820**	0.215
ENV2	−0.01	0.214	**0.738**	−0.06
ENV3	0.193	−0.08	**0.607**	0.124
CS1	0.05	**0.921**	0.147	0.125
CS2	0.173	**0.890**	0.241	0.01
PERF1	**0.901**	0.01	−0.03	0.02
PERF2	**0.885**	0.115	0.160	0.02
PERF3	**0.656**	0.113	−0.03	0.229
LOY1	0.03	−0.04	0.154	**0.879**
LOY2	0.195	0.195	0.07	**0.827**
Eigenvalue	3.040	1.804	1.366	1.014
Cumulative proportion of total variance explained	30.401	48.439	62.096	72.232

Table 6.3   Goodness of fit summary results

Fit Indices/Statistics	Model A	Model B
Degrees of freedom	32	31
χ^2	40.008	35.426
χ^2/df	1.25	1.14
p-value (Overall model)	0.156	0.267
Bentler-Bonett non-normed fit index	0.97	0.98
Comparative fit index	0.98	0.98
GFI	0.93	0.94
RMSEA	0.05	0.04

constructs. The results, which are shown in Table 6.2, suggest that the fit to a four-factor model was reasonably good.

Two SEM models were constructed as shown in Figure 6.2 and Tables 6.3 to 6.5. In addition to the hypothesized relationships between customer satisfaction, loyalty and performance, Model A includes the direct relationship of environmental management practices (EMP) on customer satisfaction (CS), as suggested in Hypothesis 1. Model B further includes a direct relationship between EMP and performance as suggested in Hypothesis 4. The overall validity of the models was assessed using a multiple-fit criteria approach, as shown in Table 6.3. More specifically, the χ^2 value of the models is 40.008 (d.f. = 32) and 35.426 (d.f. = 31)

Model A: Environmental management practices (EMP), customer satisfaction, loyalty and performance – no direct link between EMP and performance

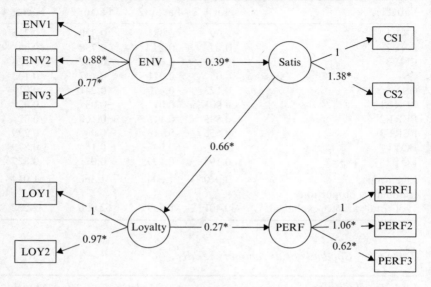

Model B: Environmental management practices (EMP), customer satisfaction, loyalty and performance – with direct link between EMP and performance

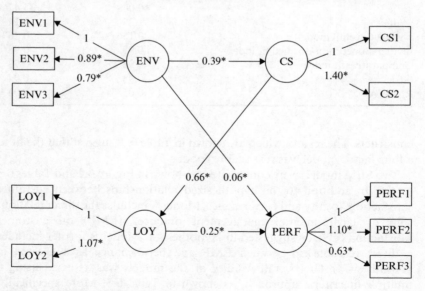

Figure 6.2   Estimated SEM models

Table 6.4   Measurement model results

Model A: Environmental management practices (EMP), customer satisfaction,
loyalty and performance: no direct link between EMP and performance

Indicator	Construct	Parameter estimate	Std error	t-value
ENV1	Env. mgt. practices	1	N/A	N/A
ENV2	Env. mgt. practices	0.875	0.236	3.712
ENV3	Env. mgt. practices	0.774	0.239	3.24
CS1	Satisfaction	1	N/A	N/A
CS2	Satisfaction	1.383	0.169	8.170
LOY1	Loyalty	1	N/A	N/A
LOY2	Loyalty	0.974	0.193	5.056
PERF1	Performance	1	N/A	N/A
PERF2	Performance	1.064	0.161	6.621
PERF3	Performance	0.623	0.126	4.935

Model B: Environmental management practices (EMP), customer satisfaction,
loyalty and performance: with a direct link between EMP and
performance

Indicator	Construct	Parameter estimate	Std error	t-value
ENV1	Env. mgt. practices	1	N/A	N/A
ENV2	Env. mgt. practices	0.893	0.239	3.727
ENV3	Env. mgt. practices	0.790	0.243	3.254
CS1	Satisfaction	1	N/A	N/A
CS2	Satisfaction	1.402	0.192	7.306
LOY1	Loyalty	1	N/A	N/A
LOY2	Loyalty	1.070	0.184	5.801
PERF1	Performance	1	N/A	N/A
PERF2	Performance	1.096	0.161	6.800
PERF3	Performance	0.628	0.127	4.933

Note: In order to define the measurement scales for the constructs, one of the links from
the indicator to the construct has to be set equal to one (Bentler, 1989). Consequently, for
these links the standard errors and t-values have been marked as 'N/A' (not applicable).

respectively, which corresponds to a significance level greater than 0.10 for
both models. Such values are much higher than the minimum threshold
of 0.05, a value required for an adequate fit of the overall model (Bagozzi
and Yi, 1988; Bentler, 1989). We must note that the overall χ^2 statistic provides a test of whether the sample covariance matrix is equivalent to the

Table 6.5   Structural model results

Model A: Environmental management practices (EMP), customer satisfaction,
loyalty and performance: no direct link between EMP and performance

(Predicted sign)	Regression from	Coefficient to	Parameter estimate	Std error	t-value
H1 (+)	Env. mgt practices	Satisfaction	0.388	0.123	3.147
H2 (+)	Satisfaction	Loyalty	0.687	0.116	5.938
H3 (+)	Loyalty	Performance	0.272	0.110	2.465

Model B: Environmental management practices (EMP), customer satisfaction,
loyalty and performance: with a direct link between EMP and
performance

(Predicted sign)	Regression from	Coefficient to	Parameter estimate	Std error	t-value
H1 (+)	Env. mgt practices	Satisfaction	0.395	0.127	3.121
H2 (+)	Satisfaction	Loyalty	0.662	0.137	4.815
H3 (+)	Loyalty	Performance	0.250	0.094	2.645
H4 (+)	Env. mgt practices	Performance	0.056	0.098	0.574

model-implied covariance matrix, within sampling error. A feature of this test is that the proposed model represents the null hypothesis in the test, not the alternative – thus the aim of the researcher is not to reject the null hypothesis. A 'good' value for the χ^2, then, is one that is associated with a 'large' p-value (typical rules of thumb look for p-values larger than 0.05 or 0.10 (Rigdon, 1998: 268–9). As shown in Table 6.3 the ratio of χ^2 to the degrees of freedom is also less than four to one, the maximum value for models of adequate fit (Matsueda, 1982). The values of the root mean square error of approximation (RMSEA) – the value of the discrepancy per degree of freedom – are also less than the maximum recommended value of 0.08 (Steiger, 1990). Table 6.3 also presents the values of representative indices typically examined in SEM, including the goodness of fit index (GFI), the non-normed fit index (NNFI) and the comparative fit index (CFI), which is also the preferred index to be used in models of small sample sizes. All indices examined exceed the minimum criteria of 0.90 reported in the literature, lending support to the overall validity of the conceptual models.

The results from the measurement models are shown in Table 6.4, suggesting that all indicators loaded on the corresponding constructs. Finally, Table 6.5 and Figure 6.2 present the results from the structural models. These lend support to Hypotheses 1, 2 and 3 suggesting a positive relationship between environmental practices and customer satisfaction, between customer satisfaction and loyalty, and finally between loyalty and performance. With the exception of the direct link between environmental practices and performance, all links are statistically significant ($p < 0.05$). Interestingly, Hypothesis 4 is not supported by our data. This finding emphasizes the importance of environmental management practices towards customer loyalty and firm performance, results that are achieved in the hospitality industry through the improvement of customer satisfaction.

DISCUSSION AND CONCLUDING REMARKS

In this chapter we argue and empirically demonstrate that the degree of use of environmental management practices in the hotel industry is positively related to market performance, through the mediating effect of customer satisfaction and loyalty. Specifically, our results lend support to Hypotheses 1, 2 and 3 suggesting a positive relationship between environmental practices and customer satisfaction, between customer satisfaction and loyalty, and between loyalty and performance. These findings are supported by literature which suggests that performance gains associated with the adoption of environmental practices are related to cost reductions, resource savings, opportunities for innovation, customer retention and loyalty, and improved employee morale. In addition our results are backed by the service management and marketing literatures, which show that improvements in satisfaction lead to higher revenues and reduced future transaction costs through improved customer loyalty.

One would expect a positive direct link between environmental practices and performance, as outlined in Hypothesis 4. However our data do not lend support to this hypothesis. The service profit chain framework may help explain, at least in part, this non-finding. As discussed earlier, in such a context, service operations influence firm performance through enhanced customer satisfaction and loyalty. Moreover as we argued, environmental practices can be incorporated within the service profit chain and may impact upon customer satisfaction, loyalty and subsequently performance. In addition to such an explanation, other research (Christmann, 2000) also reports no evidence of a direct relationship between the implementation of environmental practices and performance. On the contrary Christmann finds that such a relationship exists through the mediating effect of complementary assets. In general the characteristics of services vis-à-vis goods may explain, in part, the lack of a direct relationship between environmental practices and performance. Moreover such findings emphasize the importance of environmental practices towards customer loyalty and performance – results that are achieved in the hospitality industry through the improvement of customer satisfaction. While our results point to the importance of environmental practices vis-à-vis customer satisfaction in services, future research clearly needs to further investigate this relationship.

Overall, the chapter makes two contributions. First, it conceptually develops and empirically tests the relationship between the adoption of environmental management practices and market performance in the context of services. So far, existing work has been very limited and largely based on anecdotal or case study evidence. Second, by examining the mediating effect of customer satisfaction and loyalty on the relationship between environmental practices and market performance, the chapter establishes that the use of such practices is positively related to higher levels of customer satisfaction and, eventually, higher levels of performance – through enhanced customer loyalty. The significance of these mediating effects and their positive relationship with performance is especially noteworthy given rising consumer awareness, both in Europe and the United States, where consumers demand increased corporate environmental responsibility – in services and in manufacturing alike.

The service profit chain provided a framework within which to test the relationships outlined above. The intention of our work was not to assess the service profit chain fully, but rather to incorporate environmental practices as an important dimension within the framework. In fact future work needs to assess fully the greening of the service profit chain – both in the hospitality industry and in other service contexts – paying explicit attention to firm characteristics such as size. Such an effort has significant data requirements. As Loveman (1998: 19) points out, 'the main impediment to more comprehensive empirical testing' of the service profit chain 'has been the absence of large sample data spanning all (or even most) of the service profit chain components'. Despite such difficulties, some research on the assessment of the service profit chain, or parts of it, has been conducted (Kamakura et al., 2002; Soteriou and Zenios, 1999).

Venues for future research are in part related to this study's limitations. Specifically, future research needs to investigate further the nature of the relationship between environmental practices and customer satisfaction and loyalty in services, using more refined measures of the latter. Questions to be addressed may focus on the way or the mechanisms through which environmental practices enhance customer satisfaction and loyalty. Given the critical role of employees in this context, a full assessment of the service profit chain needs to establish how employee satisfaction and loyalty are enhanced when firms are environmentally proactive, and how employee satisfaction and loyalty impact upon customer satisfaction and loyalty, and through them market performance. In this context, one can look for example at employee environmental training or employee involvement in continuous environmental progress.

Overall, a systematic assessment of the effectiveness of service firm environmental practices is needed in future work, that is an evaluation of their outcomes in terms of reduced environmental loads produced or cost savings achieved. Moreover the use of finer measures of environmental practices (compared to those used in our study) that cover the entire value chain of service activities needs to be considered. These may include: (1) a distinction between front- and back-office measures; (2) an examination of finer measures of resource savings programmes (such as energy management measures in hotels); (3) an assessment of housekeeping and maintenance practices that reduce impacts, waste and costs (Schendler, 2001); (4) a consideration of environmentally responsible practices in the design and construction of facilities (that is the construction of 'green' rooms with a longer average life (Goodman, 2000; Schendler, 2001)) and (5) an evaluation of the use of environmental information systems that allow customized reporting, sharing of information among managers and also provide a benchmarking system (Goodman, 2000). One may also consider issues related to suppliers. Examples that appear in case studies point to the importance of supplier–service provider collaboration to achieve environmental innovations that reduce the production of waste and the introduction of environmental considerations in the selection of goods provided. Finally, future research needs to examine the use of practices such as information provision and elicitation of customer involvement in a hotel's environmental efforts.

Our findings shed only some light on the importance of environmental management practices and their impact on performance, in services. They do however point to the vast potential for future research regarding this relationship, which is amplified by the dominant presence of the service sector in the global economy.

NOTE

1. This chapter is a substantially updated version of a study published in *Production and Operations Management* see Kassinis and Soteriou (2003).

REFERENCES

Anderson, E.W., C. Fornell and D.R. Lehmann (1994), 'Customer satisfaction, market share, and profitability: findings from Sweden', *Journal of Marketing*, **58**(3), 53–66.

134   *Corporate environmental strategy and competitive advantage*

Anderson, E.W., C. Fornell and R.T. Rust (1997), 'Customer satisfaction, productivity and profitability: differences between goods and services', *Marketing Science*, **16**(2), 129–45.
Angell, L.C. and R.D. Klassen (1999), 'Integrating environmental issues into the mainstream: an agenda for research in operations management', *Journal of Operations Management*, **17**(5), 575–98.
Anguera, N., S. Ayuso and P. Fullana (2000), 'Implementation of EMSs in seasonal hotels', in *ISO 14001: Case Studies and Practical Experiences*, R. Hillary (ed.), Sheffield: Greenleaf Publishing, 162–72.
Bagozzi, R.P. and Y. Yi (1988), 'On the evaluation of structural equation models', *Journal of Academy of Marketing Science*, **16**(1), 74–94.
Bentler, P.M. (1989), 'EQS: Structural Equations Program Manual', handbook for version 3.0, BMDP Statistical Software Inc., Los Angeles.
Bolton, R.N. and J.H. Drew (1991), 'A multistage model of customers' assessment of service quality and value', *Journal of Consumer Research*, **17**(4), 375–84.
Boulding, W., A. Kalra, R. Staelin and V.A. Zeithaml (1993), 'A dynamic process model of service quality: from expectations to behavioral intentions', *Journal of Marketing Research*, **30**(1), 7–27.
Buzzell, R.D. and B.T. Gale (1987), *The PIMS Principles*, New York: Free Press.
Chase, R.B. (1981), 'The customer contact approach to services: theoretical bases and practical extensions', *Operations Research*, **21**(4), 698–705.
Chase, R.B. and D.M. Stewart (1994), 'Make your service fail-safe', *Sloan Management Review*, **35**(3), 35–44.
Chase, R.B. and D.A. Tansik (1983), 'The customer conduct model for organizational design', *Management Science*, **29**(9), 1037–50.
Christmann, P. (2000), 'Effects of "best practices" of environmental management on cost advantage: the role of complementary assets', *Academy of Management Journal*, **43**(4), 663–80.
Dess, G.G. and R.B. Robinson (1984), 'Measuring organizational performance in the absence of objective measures: the case of privately-held firm and conglomerate business unit', *Strategic Management Journal*, **5**(3), 265–73.
Dick, A.S. and K. Basu (1994), 'Customer loyalty: toward an integrated conceptual framework', *Journal of the Academy of Marketing Science*, **22**(2), 99–114.
Dowell, G.S., S. Hart and B. Yeung (2000), 'Do corporate global environmental standards create or destroy value?', *Management Science*, **46**(8), 1059–74.
Elkington, J. (1994), 'Towards the sustainable corporation: win–win business strategies for sustainable development', *California Management Review*, **36**(2), 90–100.
Enz, C.A. and J.A. Siguaw (1999), 'Best hotel environmental practices', *Cornell Hotel and Restaurant Administration Quarterly*, **40**(5), 72–7.
Fitzsimmons, J.A. and M.J. Fitzsimmons (2000), *Service Management: Operations, Strategy and Information Technology*, 3rd edn, Boston, MA: Irwin/McGraw-Hill.
Foster, S.T., S.E. Sampson and S.C. Dunn (2000), 'The impact of customer contact on environmental initiatives for service firms', *International Journal of Operations and Production Management*, **20**(2), 187–203.
Fournier, S. and D.G. Mick (1999), 'Rediscovering satisfaction', *Journal of Marketing*, **63**(4), 5–23.
Froehle, C.M., A.V. Roth, R.B. Chase and C.A. Voss (2000), 'Antecedents of new service development effectiveness: an exploratory examination of strategic operations choices', *Journal of Service Research*, **3**(1), 3–17.

Goodman, A. (2000), 'Implementing sustainability in service operations in Scandic Hotels', *Interfaces*, **30**(3), 202–14.

Grove, S., R.P. Fisk, G.M. Pickett and N. Kangun (1996), 'Going green in the service sector: social responsibility issues, implications and implementation', *European Journal of Marketing*, **30**(5), 56–66.

Hallowell, R. (1996), 'The relationships of customer satisfaction, customer loyalty, and profitability: an empirical study', *International Journal of Service Industry Management*, **7**(4), 27–42.

Halme, M. (2001), 'Learning for sustainable development in tourism networks', *Business Strategy and the Environment*, **10**(2), 100–114.

Hanna, M.D., W.R. Newman and P. Johnson (2000), 'Linking operational and environmental improvement through employee involvement', *International Journal of Operations and Production Management*, **20**(2), 148–65.

Harman, H.H. (1967), *Modern Factor Analysis*, Chicago, IL: University of Chicago Press.

Hart, S.L. (1995), 'A natural resource-based view of the firm', *Academy of Management Review*, **20**(4), 986–1014.

Heskett, J.L., T.O. Jones, G.W. Loveman, W.E. Sasser Jr. and L.A. Schlesinger (1994), 'Putting the service–profit chain to work', *Harvard Business Review*, **72**(2), 164–75.

Heskett, J.L., W.E. Sasser and L.A. Schlesinger (1997), *The Service Profit Chain*, New York: Free Press.

Johnson, M.D., E.W. Anderson and C. Fornell (1995), 'Rational and adaptive performance expectations in a customer satisfaction framework', *Journal of Consumer Research*, **21**(4), 695–707.

Johnson, M.D. and C. Fornell (1991), 'A framework for comparing customer satisfaction across individuals and product categories', *Journal of Economic Psychology*, **12**(2), 267–86.

Jöreskog, K.G. (1970), 'A general method for analysis of covariance structures', *Biometrica*, **57**, 239–51.

Kamakura, W.A., V. Mittal, F. de Rosa and J.A. Mazzon (2002), 'Assessing the service–profit chain', *Marketing Science*, **21**(3), 294–317.

Kassinis, G.I. and A.C. Soteriou (2003), 'Greening the service profit chain: the impact of environmental management practices', *Production and Operations Management*, **12**(3), 386–403.

King, A.A. and M.J. Lenox (2001a), 'Does it really pay to be green? An empirical study of firm environmental and financial performance', *Journal of Industrial Ecology*, **5**(1), 105–16.

King, A.A. and M.J. Lenox (2001b), 'Lean and green? An empirical examination of the relationship between lean production and environmental performance', *Production and Operations Management*, **10**(3), 244–56.

King, A.A. and M.J. Lenox (2002), 'Exploring the locus of profitable pollution reduction', *Management Science*, **48**(2), 289–99.

Klassen, R.D. (1993), 'The integration of environmental issues into manufacturing', *Production and Inventory Management Journal*, **34**(1), 82–8.

Klassen, R.D. and C.P. McLaughlin (1996), 'The impact of environmental management on firm performance', *Management Science*, **42**(8), 1199–214.

Klassen, R.D. and D.C. Whybark (1999a), 'The impact of environmental technologies on manufacturing performance', *Academy of Management Journal*, **42**(6), 599–615.

Klassen, R.D. and D.C. Whybark (1999b), 'Environmental management in opera-
    tions: the selection of environmental technologies', *Decision Sciences*, **30**(3),
    601–31.
Lovelock, C.H. (1996), *Services Marketing*, Upper Saddle River, NJ: Prentice Hall.
Loveman, G.W. (1998), 'Employee satisfaction, customer loyalty and financial per-
    formance', *Journal of Service Research*, **1**(1), 18–31.
Matsueda, R.L. (1982), 'Testing control theory and differential association: a causal
    modeling approach', *American Sociological Review*, **47**(4), 489–504.
May, D.R. and B.L. Flannery (1995), 'Cutting waste with employee involvement
    teams', *Business Horizons*, **38**(5), 28–38.
McInerney, F. and S. White (1995), *The Total Quality Corporation*, New York:
    Truman Tally Books.
Messelbeck, J. and M. Whaley (1999), 'Greening the health care supply chain: trig-
    gers of change, models for success', *Corporate Environmental Strategy*, **6**(1),
    38–45.
Official Hotel Guide (1999), vol 3, Richmond, BC: Reed Travel Group.
Oliver, R. (1993), 'Cognitive, affective, and attribute bases of the satisfaction
    response', *Journal of Consumer Research*, **20**(3), 418–30.
Oliver, R. (1999), 'Whence consumer loyalty?', *Journal of Marketing*, **63**(4), 33–44.
Podsakoff, P.M. and D.W. Organ (1986), 'Self-reports in organizational research:
    problems and prospects', *Journal of Management*, **12**(4), 531–44.
Porter, M.E. and C. van der Linde (1995), 'Toward a new conception of the envir-
    onment–competitiveness relationship', *Journal of Economic Perspectives*, **9**(4),
    97–118.
Reichheld, F.F. and W.E. Sasser (1990), 'Zero defections: quality comes to services',
    Harvard Business Review, **68**(5), 105–11.
Rigdon, E.E. (1998), 'Structural equation modeling', in G. Marcoulides (ed.),
    Modern Methods for Business Research, Mahwah, NJ: Lawrence Erlbaum,
    251–94.
Rondinelli, D.A. and G. Vastag (1996), 'International environmental standards and
    corporate policies: an integrative framework', *California Management Review*,
    39(1), 106–22.
Rugman, A.M. and A. Verbeke (1998), 'Corporate strategies and environmental
    regulations: an organizing framework', *Strategic Management Journal*, **19**(4),
    363–75.
Russo, M.V. and P.A. Fouts (1997), 'A resource–based perspective on corporate
    environmental performance and profitability', *Academy of Management Journal*,
    40(3), 534–59.
Rust, R.T., A.J. Zahorik and T.L. Keiningham (1995), 'Return on quality (ROQ):
    making service quality financially accountable', *Journal of Marketing*, **59**(2),
    58–70.
Salzman, J. (2000), 'Environmental protection beyond the smokestack: addressing
    the impact of the service economy', *Corporate Environmental Strategy*, **7**(1),
    20–37.
Sasser, W.E., R.P. Olsen and D.D. Wyckoff (1978), *Management of Service
    Operations*, Boston, MA: Allyn & Bacon.
Schendler, A. (2001), 'Trouble in paradise: the rough road to sustainability in
    Aspen', *Corporate Environmental Strategy*, **8**(4), 293–9.
Schneider, B. and D.E. Bowen (1993), 'The service organization: human manage-
    ment is crucial', *Organizational Dynamics*, **21**(4), 39–52.

Shrivastava, P. (1995), 'The role of corporations in achieving ecological sustainability', *Academy of Management Review*, **20**(4), 936–60.

Soteriou, A.C. and R.B. Chase (1998), 'Linking the customer contact model to service quality', *Journal of Operations Management*, **16**(4), 495–508.

Soteriou, A.C. and S.A. Zenios (1999), 'Operations, quality and profitability in the provision of banking services', *Management Science*, **45**(9), 1221–38.

Steiger, J.H. (1990), 'Structural model evaluation and modification: an internal estimation approach', *Multivariate Behavioral Research*, **25**, 173–80.

Walley, N. and B. Whitehead (1994), 'It's not easy being green', *Harvard Business Review*, **72**(3), 46–52.

World Tourism Organization (WTO) (1999), *Yearbook of Tourism Statistics*, Madrid: WTO Department of Statistics and Economic Measurement of Tourism.

Yi, Y. (1991), 'A critical review of customer satisfaction', in V.A. Zeithaml (ed.), *Review of Marketing*, Chicago, IL: American Marketing Association.

Zeithaml V.A., A. Parasuraman and L.L. Berry (1990), *Delivering Quality Service: Balancing Customer Perceptions and Expectations*, New York, Free Press.

APPENDIX

Survey Items, Constructs and Cronbach Alpha Coefficients of Measures

Environmental Management Practices (ENV)*** ($\alpha = 0.681$)
1. Use of energy saving measures
2. Use of recycling practices
3. Use of water saving measures

Customer Satisfaction (CS)** ($\alpha = 0.861$)
1. Overall customer satisfaction levels
2. Customers stated expectations are exceeded

Customer Loyalty (LOY)** ($\alpha = 0.708$)
1. Overall customer loyalty levels
2. Customer retention rates have been improving

Market Performance (PERF)* ($\alpha = 0.772$)
1. Growth in profits relative to industry average
2. Growth in revenues relative to industry average
3. Market share relative to industry average

Notes:
*   Managers were asked to assess how well their hotels performed relative to their competitors at the time of the survey using a seven-point scale ('worst in industry', 1; 'about the same', 4; 'best in industry', 7).

**   Managers were asked to rate the degree of agreement or disagreement with statements relating to customer satisfaction and loyalty levels ('strongly agree', 1; 'strongly disagree', 7).

***   Managers were asked to rate the degree of use of a specific practice ('not used at all', 1; 'widely used', 7).

7. Environmental innovation in the hotel industry of the Balearic Islands

Rafel Crespí-Cladera and
Francina Orfila-Sintes

Technological innovation and environmental features are basic for a tourism destination to be competitive in today's market (Hassan, 2000; Huybers and Bennet, 2000). A business strategy to meet current preferences within the tourist market in a competitive international setting must consider the environmental quality provided, and this competitive setting also involves the seasonal nature of tourism demand, greater and more sophisticated service demands, a sensitivity to environmentally friendly consumption, and changes in mediation procedures as well. This chapter studies the determinants for decisions made in environmental management innovation by hotel service companies.

The maintenance and improvement of competitiveness in tourism are intrinsically linked to the conservation of the environment, which is a fundamental tourism resource since it figures among the main attractions for tourists. However the tourism activity contributes to the deterioration of the very resource on which it depends (Llull Gilet, 2001). This deterioration may result ultimately in the decline of the destination (Butler, 1980) and significant unrecoverable losses in the competitiveness of the tourism industry. This decline is exacerbated by two factors: 1) the environment deteriorates rapidly to the extent that it is impossible to recover or repair, and 2) the environment displays the characteristics and externalities of public goods that prevent its socially optimal use.

This chapter studies how tourism companies introduce technological improvements in the management of environmental quality, and analyses which are the determinants – incentives and obstacles – for their adoption in the hotel industry. Indeed the tourism sector includes activities in food service, leisure, transportation and hotel room services. In order to be rigorous in analysing environmental innovation, we focus solely on one of the many tourism activities (Alvarez-Gil et al., 2001; Font, 2002), one that includes a homogenous set of companies in terms of production function (input, products and available technology) and competitive setting. We take hotel companies as our object of study because of their homogeneity and their relative weight in total tourism revenue. In this sense, the Balearic Islands present an adequate background for the study.

Company incentives for the decision to innovate in environmental management have the characteristics of the 'prisoner's dilemma'. The environmental investments undertaken by hotel service companies provide some collective benefits consistent with environmental conservation of the destination and the improvement of the associated tourist product. Thus the industry as a whole, in which the competitors and the tourist destination are included, benefits from the individual decisions for the betterment and conservation of this public good. This circumstance is an obstacle to innovation in environmental management. In spite of this, we can observe that hotels undertake environmental innovations, producing positive externalities for the whole tourism industry in the destination area, including for their direct competitors. In a different way, González and León (2001) interpret this situation as a strategic opportunity that does not require the intervention of public administration. This behaviour could be explained by hypothesizing that some benefits exist in terms of a competitive advantage.

In the second section, the chapter takes on a description of tourism activity, as well as the importance of the environment in the competitiveness of tourism companies. The third section presents the theoretical framework and the model to test. The fourth section introduces the methodology and sample characteristics, and the fifth section includes the results and their analysis. A final section discusses the results obtained and conclusions drawn.

TOURIST ACTIVITY AND THE ENVIRONMENT

In the year 2000, stimulated by the strength of the economy and the special events put on for the celebration of the new millenium, the tourism sector grew on a worldwide scale at the greatest rate of the decade and almost at twice the rate of 1999: 7.4 per cent. While tourism income increased 4.5 per cent, the number of international arrivals reached a record 699 million, with a 50 million increase in international arrivals recorded annually for the most important destinations, such as Spain or the United States. Europe as a destination, which represents 58 per cent of international tourism, grew by 6.1 per cent. All regions of the world took in more tourists, with the greatest growth occurring once again in the Far East and the Pacific: 14.7 per cent. Consequently although Europe and America were the main receiving areas of tourism, their shares in the world total demonstrate a declining tendency. Spain ranked third as a destination on a worldwide scale with 6.9 per cent of the international arrivals, and occupied second place in the ranking of tourism income: $31 billion, which accounted for 6.5 per cent of total tourism income (WTO, 2001).

The evolution of the tourism sector has consolidated it as one of the most relevant sectors quantitatively in world economies. This quantitative relevance, which points to the solid situation of the sector, also implies that destinations are facing ever greater global competition. Huybers and Bennett (2000) find that a competitive setting is characterized as much for its quantitative as for its qualitative increase in supply, in which an ever greater number and variety of alternative destinations are available for the demand. Thus tourism competitiveness depends on the adequate response to the requirements of the market and to the innovations of the competition, and on a permanent incorporation of the opportunities provided by technological development (Okumus and Hemmington, 1998). Along these lines, Mihalič (1999) highlights the environmental awareness of the present tourism market, and Hassan (2000) argues that tourism competitiveness has to be based on a model of environmentally sustainable tourism development that takes into account the ever greater demand for environmentally friendly products and services. Furthermore, González and León (2001) argue for the importance of managing the environmental attributes of the tourist product. Our conjecture about individual firms' incentives for undertaking environmental innovation is that the current market demand for environmentally friendly products pressures firms into innovation in environmental management as a factor of competitiveness. There is evidence to suggest that tourists take environment quality into account in their decisions to choose destinations, and in their satisfaction as visitors. (Llull Gilet, 2001). This demand for environmental features therefore increases the ability to pay for products with lower environmental impact (Hassan, 2000; Mihalič, 1999; Stabler and Goodball, 1997). In addition the difficulties of traditional price competition make the environmental differentiation of the tourism product, especially for hotels, one of the possible new competitive strategies (Huybers and Bennett, 2000).

Moreover environmental management innovation usually involves productive and management efficiency improvements (González and León, 2001; Mihalič, 1999) that determine profitability in the hotel business (Sheldon, 1983).

Nevertheless in the study of environmental management it is important to be centred on one sector, because no matter how many environmental strategies can be applied, companies differ according to the industry to which they belong. Prior studies on environmental management show that greater robustness exists from results when they focus on one single process of the industry (Alvarez-Gil et al., 2001) and that environmental impact differs between subsectors of tourism activity (Font, 2002).

Of all tourism activity, hotels stand out as a central link in the rendering of other tourism services. A geographic area becomes a tourist destination to the extent that there is an offer of hotel rooms to satisfy the basic need of lodging the tourist at his destination. Seventy-one per cent of tourists whose destination is Spain opt to stay in hotels (Instituto de Estudios Turísticos, 2001), and a similar figure is found in the Balearic Islands (*La Despesa Turística*, 2000).

ENVIRONMENTAL MANAGEMENT INNOVATION IN THE HOTEL BUSINESS

Theoretical Framework

The study of innovation in the hotel business includes differential characteristics, of which its service nature primarily stands out. The characteristics that typify services have implications in the definition of technological innovation that are considered in the second European survey on innovation,[1] which focuses on the service sector (OECD, 1997), which is based on the Oslo Manual (1997). The basic differential aspect is the consideration of technological innovation both if new knowledge and technologies used are developed internally, and if they are integrated from outside the firm. In fact empirical studies on innovation in services show that, with the exception of some sectors based on new knowledge (for example in communication and information technology), innovation takes place mainly by way of the acquisition of equipment, materials and components provided by suppliers in the manufacturing sector and other services (Barras, 1986; Sirilli and Evangelista, 1998). We are dealing then with sectors dominated by suppliers (Pavitt, 1984).

Some changes in firm organization, such as the implementation of quality standards, are not technological innovations unless they are directly related to the introduction of new or significantly improved services. Nevertheless if the implementation for example of a quality standard that improves the rendering of a service is obtained, then it is considered to be an innovation.

Consequently, to account for the business innovation, the information from public databases – aggregate data on R&D, patents and so on – are of no use. When innovating, the hotel trade does not assign significant resources for generating new knowledge, nor does it typically give rise to the registration of patents (Hjalager, 2002). Neither is the information about management of environmental quality that hotels are obliged to make public representative. Thus the necessary information to detect environmental management innovation in the hotel business comes from the hotels, the premises in which the service is rendered.

Environmental management innovation is the introduction of or improvement in the systems of management and assurance of environmental quality. Energy and water savings, even though they may improve environmental quality performance, are not explicitly considered since they are decisions about quality and efficiency. The management of environmental quality is not necessarily restricted to systems since there is no standardized and fully accepted system for environmental management in tourism (Font, 2002). Besides, potential competitive implications arise when such management is effective to the extent that the market perceives it. Thus environmental innovation signals a proactive environmental strategy, which is correlated positively to the competitiveness of organizations (Aragón-Correa and Sharma, 2003). The characteristics of the hotel industry allow us to introduce a set of variables that may explain the decision for innovation in environmental management. For instance hotel affiliation makes it possible to consider governance structure or organization in groups (Jones, 1999). Some hotels operate independently while others belong to a local or international hotel chain, or simply belong to a more diversified business group. The incentives for executives to promote environmental innovations depend on the organizational structure and on the governance configuration of the activity. Hotels managed by owners differ from those that have specialized managers who run the company by renting or leasing assets. Other hotels are managed through professional management contracts or even franchises.

The Determinants of Environmental Innovation

Sirilli and Evangelista (1998) observe that differences in organizational structure of productive units affect innovative behaviour. Calveras (2003) models the behaviour of hotels operating in single and in multiple markets and concludes that belonging to a hotel chain yields greater benefits for managing environmental quality proactively. One of the factors of environmental management is the vision, ethics and philosophy that drive executive decisions (Foster et al., 2000). To the extent that signalling the market is costly, hotel chains are in a better position than single hotels in promoting the values or corporate culture of the firm. Consequently the expected benefits and gains from promoting their environmental sensitivity may be greater for hotel chains than for single hotels.

Economies of scale considerations in terms of knowledge transmission and the fulfilment of the minimum legal requirements (Ingram and Baum, 1997) also lead us to formulate the following hypothesis:

Hypothesis 1: Hotels that belong to a chain have greater incentives for the decision to innovate in environmental management than those that operate independently.

In the hotel industry, the specialization of managing hotels is frequent. Teams of executives run hotels in a professional way even though they are not the hotel owners. These management contracts between hotel owners and managers influence the incentives to innovate on environmental issues depending on the time period over which rewards appear. However by mediating a contract to run the business, there is a risk in the contract due to potential losses associated with specific investments that would appear in case of a breach or due to the greater costs faced when renegotiating. Under a management contract, the adoption of measures of environmental innovation would take place only in the case of expected economic profitability in the short term (Mihalič, 1999). Besides, the attitude and perceptions of managers are essential factors in proactive environmental strategy that involves the adoption of environmental innovations (Aragón-Correa and Sharma, 2003). Consequently what is proposed is that when the owner carries out the role of management, a greater tendency may exist for innovation in environmental management. These arguments lead us to formulate the following hypothesis:

Hypothesis 2: Hotels managed by the owners have more incentives for the decision to innovate in environmental management.

The size of the productive unit is relevant, to the extent that economies of scale explain strategic decisions. For a relevant decision, innovation depends on the size of the production unit (Cohen and Levin, 1989) because size affects implementation and profitability. Empirically, this influence may be positive (the effect on economies of scale from innovative activities) or negative (the lack of flexibility in the introduction of changes), so that it becomes interesting to study the influence more deeply. For environmental innovations, a positive size effect is added to economies of scale (Alvarez-Gil et al., 2001). Large companies receive greater pressure from the stakeholders because of their greater environmental impact. Large companies have greater resources available for investment on indivisible assets such as systems of environmental quality management. Large companies have formal structures in their organization that encompass the most formal environmental management. Finally, bearing in mind that in the hotel industry the size of the hotel is positively correlated with the quality level (Chung and Kalnins, 2001), both effects are considered in the following hypothesis:

Hypothesis 3: The size of the hotel positively affects the decision for innovation in environmental management.

An important characteristic of the hotel activity is the particular way it combines fixed assets (basically buildings, facilities and machinery) with human resources (Saleh and Ryan, 1992). This structure implies elevated fixed costs in the industry (Tisdell, 2000) that, when combined with the frequent seasonal demand of sun and beach vacation destinations, make it more profitable for some hotels to close down rather than stay open in mid- and/or low season. The tourist destination of the Balearic Islands is still characterized by an elevated specialization in the sun and beach tourist segment typical of the summer season. In the year 2000, the high season (June to September) accounted for 58.3 per cent of the tourism, the midseason (April, May and October) for 29.6 per cent, and the low season (November to March) for 12.1 per cent (*La Despesa Turística*, 2000). Those hotels that stay open for longer periods show a greater involvement in meeting tourist preferences and greater interest and effort in maintaining a policy of good relations with stakeholders (Hjalager, 1998), and they avoid the problems that cause environmental impact (Foster et al., 2000). Such hotels consequently would not behave like 'free-riders' with respect to the environment. Likewise, staying open for longer periods would involve a greater accumulation of knowledge resources that favour technological innovation as a whole (Dewar and Dutton, 1986). These arguments lead us to formulate the following hypothesis:

Hypothesis 4: The intensity in the use of hotels positively influences the decision for innovation in environmental management.

The segment of the target market helps us to identify the positioning of the hotels in a competitive market. We use a proxy for this concept via the enlargement of the set of services on offer, which is relevant due to the importance of tour operators in the commercialization of hotel beds. The tourism market in the European countries where tour operators commercialize is characterized by a growing demand for quality in the environmental attributes of the tourism product (González and León, 2001; Mihalič, 1999). Also, Stabler and Goodball (1997) detect a greater willingness to pay for those tourist products with lesser environmental impact. Enlarging the set of services on offer is also motivated by economies of scale that include such environmentally friendly services. These arguments allow us to formulate the following hypothesis:

Hypothesis 5: The enlargement of the set of services on offer by the hotel will positively influence the decision for innovation in environmental management.

There are several ways of contracting hotel beds. For example, beds may be booked through tour operators, travel agents, reservation centres, and directly by the client. Each channel applies different pressures and assumes different negotiation capabilities, which reflect clients' environmental anxieties. Stakeholder pressure is one of the most important factors influencing environmental management (Aragón-Correa and Sharma, 2003; Bansal and Roth, 2000; Henriques and Sardosky, 1999). Tour operators represent the main stakeholder of the tourism contracting activity (Alvarez-Gil et al., 2001), with strong negotiating power. One significant implication of the characteristic elevated fixed costs from the process of rendering hotel services is that the occupancy rate required to reach the break-even point or acceptable profitability is high (Tisdell, 2000). This conditions the business objective toward maintaining occupancy levels even at the expense of pricing policies, since production can not be warehoused for subsequent sale. In fact while Llull Gilet (2001) finds that tour operators and desk clients are the second most influential stakeholders for the perception that the hotel trade affects the environment, Medina-Muñoz et al. (2003) find that one of the most tour operator-controlled aspects of hotel supply is environmental management. The Balearic Islands have significant inflows of German tourists who have a greater concern for the quality of the environment as compared to tourists coming from other destinations, Hjalager (1998). Tour operators from these countries of origin express consumer preferences and influence via their negotiation power, exerting pressure toward more sustainable concepts of business and destination management. The statistics from regional authorities show this considerable dependence of the Balearic tourism industry on European tour operators, who extend their negotiation power to prices, physical hotel characteristics and environmental features. Accordingly we formulate the following hypothesis:

Hypothesis 6: The contracting of beds through tour operators positively influences the decision for innovation in environmental management.

The model of hotels' environmentally innovative behaviour formed by these six hypotheses can be verified, though some of them not directly, by an econometric analysis of data concerning a representative sample from the hotel companies in the Balearic Islands, an internationally recognized tourist destination (Instituto de Estudios Turísticos, 2001), whose economy strongly depends on the rendering of tourist services.

DATA AND METHODOLOGY

Data

The relevant universe for this study is formed by all the hotels that operate in the Balearic Islands. In the year 2000, the official census of tourism companies from the Tourism Council listed 1586 hotels after excluding tourist apartments and those classified in the 'Other' category. Tourist apartments are excluded because of the differences in types of services they provide and in regulatory schemes. Those in the 'Other' category are excluded because they represent a mere 0.5 per cent of the total population and are heterogeneous in their operations and in the packages of services offered. Distinguished among the 1586 hotels then are guest houses (*pensiones*), boarding houses (*hostales*), residences, aparthotels and hotels.

The universe has been segmented according to three differentiating characteristics: the geographic location (the island in the Balearics), the category that every hotel displays and the capacity in available beds. Thus by a simple random process, we have a sample selection of the 331 hotels that comprise a representative sample for the aforementioned segments at the 5 per cent significance level. The sample selection process is complemented by a controlled process of random substitution for the non-respondents in the same segment, maintaining the desired 331 observations.

Pollsters trained to the task carried out direct and personal interviews in which the managers of the 331 selected hotels responded to a survey specifically produced to detect the innovative endeavours adopted, and also to gather information on variables that potentially impinge upon these. The definitive design that was used was formerly tested by way of a pilot trial.

Measurement of the Variables

The endogenous variable, environmental management innovation, has been obtained by classifying hotels according to their innovative behaviour in systems of environmental quality management over the previous two-year period. When the activity has not changed, is contracted out, or is rendered by the central services of the company on which the hotel depends, it is deemed that the hotel has not innovated in its environmental management, and the variable takes on a value of 0. Conversely, when systems of environmental quality management have been introduced for the first time or when such management has been renovated or improved, the variable takes on the value of 1.

The variable *INDEP* reflects the fact that a hotel operates in the market independently or by forming part of a hotel chain or business group. *INDEP* takes on the value of 1 when the hotel operates in the market independently, and the value of 0 in any other case.

The diversity of the hotel management is computed by the variable *OWNERMGD*. *OWNERMGD* takes on the value of 1 if the management is carried out by the hotel owner(s), and it is 0 if it is carried out through a contract. This contract may be for management or for property asset leasing.

The size of the productive unit has been accounted for by the number of beds that each hotel offers, even though what counts in industrial sectors is the number of workers. This is because size as measured by number of beds is the habitual practice in studies of hotel activity (Chung and Kalnins, 2001) and is the most suitable.[2] Since the untransformed variable takes on values between eight and 1743 beds, the natural logarithm – *BEDSNLG* – has been used for the number of beds on offer with the aim of avoiding problems of heteroscedasticity.

The intensity of utilization of assets has been quantified by the number of months per year that each hotel stays open, that is the annual open-for-business period. The majority of the sample hotels remain open for six months, so the number of operating months ranges from four to 12 months. The variable name used is *NMONTHS*.

The variable *SERVSET* measures the set of services variation. *SERVSET* takes on the value of 1 when the set of services has expanded and the value of 0 in the baseline data case, that is when the service set has remained the same or has been reduced.

The variable *TOUROPS* takes into consideration the presence of tour operators as the most usual channel of commercialization in the contracting of beds for every hotel. *TOUROPS* takes on the value of 1 when clients contract by engaging this intermediary, without excluding the possibility that they also use other contracting alternatives. This variable takes on the value of 0 when there has been no recourse to tour operators in the commercialization of beds on offer, which will be the baseline data case.

Data Analysis

The empirical verification of the hypotheses set forth will allow us to establish which factors are the ones that increase the probability of environmental management innovation in the hotel industry.

Since the endogenous variable is binary, the estimation is carried out by way of discrete selection, as with a PROBIT model, explaining the decision

Table 7.1 Descriptive statistics and correlation matrix

Variable	Average	Std dev.	1	2	3	4	5	6
1. INDEP	0.66465	0.4728266	1.0000					
2. OWNERMGD	0.71903	0.4501518	0.2109***	1.0000				
3. BEDSNLG	4.8033	1.0893	−0.5452***	−0.1400**	1.0000			
4. NMONTHS	8.287	2.4112	0.0209	−0.1209**	−0.0052	1.0000		
5. SERVSET	0.32326	0.4684302	−0.2479***	−0.0997*	0.3267***	0.1054*	1.0000	
6. TOUROPS	0.8006	0.400151	−0.2904***	−0.0596	0.5099***	−0.2105***	0.1833***	1.0000

Note: N = 331; *p < 0.1; **p < 0.05; ***p < 0.01.

to innovate in environmental management when confronting the group of above-mentioned explanatory variables. What follows is the general break-down of the model that is subject to empirical verification:

$$ENV_j = h(INDEP_j, OWNERMGD_j, BEDSNLG_j, NMONTHS_j,$$
$$SERVSET_j, TOUROPS_j) + \varepsilon_j$$

where the subscript j refers to the hotel. In the formula *INDEP* is the variable of independent hotels, *OWNERMGD* is the variable of owner management, *BEDSNLG* is the hotel size, *NMONTHS* is the intensity of asset utilization, *SERVSET* is the variable for the expansion of services on offer, *TOUROPS* is the variable that takes in the presence of tour operators among the forms of contracting beds, and ε_j is a random shock whose differences between the alternatives of innovation or no innovation $(\varepsilon_1 - \varepsilon_0)$ are independent and equally distributed along a normal standard distribution curve.

RESULTS

The estimated PROBIT model (Table 7.2) appears to be useful in explaining the environmentally innovative behaviour of hotels since the combined effect of the explanatory variables on the dependent variable is statistically significant (Prob > chi^2 = 0). The results obtained empirically support the effects argued from Hypotheses 1 to 5 and show no significance for the relevance of tour operators in explaining environmental innovations (Hypothesis 6).

The results substantiate that hotels that operate independently in the market and do not belong to any chain or business group have a lower propensity to innovate in environmental management. This means that belonging to a hotel chain or a business group is a factor that increases the probability that a hotel will decide to innovate in its environmental management. Others factors that increase this probability are the non-separation of hotel ownership and managing firm, large hotel size, greater intensity in the utilization of hotels as measured by the number of operating months per year, and the expansion of the set of services on offer. Conversely, the lack of significance of the estimated coefficient for the pressure of tour operators rejects Hypothesis 6. A comparison of our results with those of Alvarez-Gil et al. (2001) and those of González and León (2001) is possible to the extent that their explained variables, indicators of environmental practices and of measures that reduce environmental impact, respectively, are proxies of environmental innovation. Both papers take into consideration the effects of belonging to a hotel chain and of

Table 7.2   Model of environmentally innovative behaviour

Value and sign of the estimated coefficients, standard errors, and statistical significance (*significant at 10%; **significant at 5%; ***significant at 1%)

Variable	Coefficient	Std error
Constant	−3.3876***	0.7245
H1. *INDEP*	−0.5307**	0.2128
H2.*OWNERMGD*	0.3943*	0.2059
H3.*BEDSNLG*	0.2450**	0.1170
H4.*NMONTHS*	0.0939**	0.0391
H5.*SERVSET*	0.6316***	0.1876
H6.*TOUROPS*	0.1645	0.3315
No. observations		331
Test of combined significance		0.0000
LR chi^2(7)		57.40
Pseudo-R^2		0.1907
% correct predictions		83.08

greater size, finding them – just as we do – to be determining factors in the implementation of environmental measures. The expansion of the set of services on offer in hotels that target a segment of the market which values qualitative aspects, among which is found environmental conservation, denotes a strategic orientation toward customer satisfaction, and this is also a determining factor according to González and León (2001). The intensity of asset utilization, that is keeping the hotel open for a longer annual period, represents involvement in the environmental conservation of the destination more than in the reduction of costs that González and León (2001) find.

This estimated probit model furnishes relevant data about which variables influence the probability that a hotel decides to innovate in its environmental management, and in which direction – towards increase or decrease. Nevertheless the estimated coefficients do not quantify their impact on the endogenous variable. The calculation of the marginal effects of the estimated coefficients (Table 7.3) reveals the increase (decrease) in the expected probability of the endogenous variable upon changing the exogenous variables from their average values. Thus changing the open-ended variables infinitesimally and changing the binary variables discretely allows for comparison among them.

The changes in the expected probability of environmental management innovation derived from changes in the average values of its determinants

Table 7.3   Marginal effects: change in the expected probability of the
endogenous variable upon changing each exogenous variable

(*significant at 10%; **significant at 5%; ***significant at 1%)

Variable	Marginal effect	Std error
H1.*INDEP*	−0.1185**	0.0518
H2.*OWNERMGD*	0.0721*	0.0344
H3.*BEDSNLG*	0.0495**	0.0235
H4.*NMONTHS*	0.0190**	0.0078
H5.*SERVSET*	0.1447***	0.0474
H6.*TOUROPS*	0.0314	0.0593

will be comparable quantitatively when the scale of measurement of the determinants is the same. In this case, we will be able to gauge the marginal effects of the binary variables and comment on the effects of the others individually. For the variable *BEDSNLG*, a marginal effect of 0.0495 is obtained, which means that by increasing the average size by 1 per cent, the expected probability of environmental management innovation would increase by 5 per cent. On the other hand, upon increasing the period per year that hotels stay open by 1 per cent, the probability of carrying out environmental innovation would increase by 1.90 per cent. The other determinants, binary variables that are significantly explanatory, can be ordered from greater to lesser marginal effect: expansion of the set of services on offer, belonging to a hotel chain or business group, and management carried out by the owner. The marginal effect of −0.1185 for the variable *INDEP* means that if a hotel which operates independently in the market went on to form part of a hotel chain or a business conglomerate, then the expected probability that it decides to innovate in environmental management would increase by almost 12 per cent.

It is worth pointing out the robustness of these results, since alternative estimations of the model lead to the same results. This permits us to conclude that, given the existing correlation between size and category of each hotel, the variable *BEDSNLG* takes in the influence of the category on the endogenous variable, yielding consistent estimators.

DISCUSSION AND CONCLUSIONS

In this chapter, we have analysed the factors which increase the probability that a hotel innovates in its environmental quality management. In the preservation and improvement in the competitiveness of a tourism destination, decisions are intrinsically linked to conservation of the environment because it is a fundamental tourist resource, which in turn deteriorates with tourism production. Also, starting out from the circumstance of the prisoner's dilemma in which hotels find themselves when considering whether or not to invest in the management of environmental quality, we adopt a perspective that allows us to study this decision globally by means of an analysis of the factors that stimulate such a decision.

The development of the theoretical framework reveals the two opposing forces that interact in the environmentally innovative behaviour of hotels, making a study of the determinants of this behaviour relevant. The empirical verification of the proposed model of the determinants for the environmental decision has been carried out with data from the survey of the managers of a representative sample from the universe of Balearic hotels. The valuation of the econometric model that best fits the characteristics of the variables allows us to come to the following conclusions.

The positive impact of belonging to a chain or business group can be due to various motives. Dependent hotels have to offer a level of quality, image and reputation in accordance with that of the chain or group to which they belong. The quality, image and reputation of the chain – positively related to environmental management – entail greater investment, but greater profitability as well, by including all the hotels of the chain, and because of the economies of scale obtained. Hotel chains may be more involved in the development of a tourism destination as compared to an independent hotel because they could conceivably suffer a greater loss accumulated across their hotels in the case of the destination's decline (Calveras, 2003). Belonging to a hotel chain furnishes management know-how and an information flow capable of incorporating other elements, intangible assets, that impinge on the results of competition in the market (Ingram and Baum, 1997).

The positive influence of owner management may be attributed to a greater uncertainty in the costs and in a possible break in negotiations that are implicitly tied to management contracts and the leasing of property assets. This uncertainty and the smaller temporal horizon that is available for recovering investments discourage the dedication of resources to the improvement of environmental management that involves more costs than benefits, or whose positive consequences come about in the long term (Alvarez-Gil et al., 2001; Mihalič, 1999). Moreover owners and executives make up, in the Balearic Islands, the stakeholders who create pressure for the management of environmental quality (Bansal and Roth, 2000; Henriques and Sardosky, 1999).

The positive effect that size imprints on environmental innovation coincides with the theoretical line of argument (Alvarez-Gil et al., 2001) and with the empirical evidence contributed by works that have recently studied the implementation of environmental practices and of environmental impact reduction measures in the hotel trade (Alvarez-Gil et al., 2001; González and León, 2001). The positive significance of the intensity of asset utilization, as measured by the number of months per year that the hotel stays open for business, may be due to the notion that, given the characteristic seasonal nature of the tourist activity in the Balearic Islands, this variable is related to the level of concern and responsibility taken on for environmental conservation of the destination (González and León, 2001). The managers of hotels that stay open for more months will be more involved in the competitiveness of the destination, which is the basis for a model of environmentally sustainable tourism development (Hassan, 2000) and which encourages the diminishing of environmental impact (Foster et al., 2000).

The expansion of the set of services rendered by a hotel affects the application of systems of environmental management positively, by taking in an orientation toward a segment of the market that values qualitative aspects such as environmental conservation (González and León, 2001; Mihalič, 1999), even to the point where that segment of the market presents a greater willingness to pay (Stabler and Goodball, 1997). Bear in mind that the ever greater demand for products and services that are environmentally friendly is also the basis for a model of environmentally sustainable tourism development (Hassan, 2000). Along these lines, this effect of the expansion of the set of services on offer shows that the appreciation for quality is a competitive variable to prioritize in a setting like the current one.

Recourse to tour operators in the commercialization of beds could not be confirmed as constituting a determining factor for the decision to innovate in environmental management. However the theoretical argument about the pressure exerted by these stakeholders in the environmental behaviour of hotels (Alvarez-Gil et al., 2001; Medina-Muñoz et al., 2003) and the empirical verification of their influence on the Balearic tourism industry (Hjalager, 1998) make the empirical results found here somewhat surprising.

The discussion of the results obtained allows us to draw the conclusion that the model of environmental behaviour proposed is of use in the determination of factors that increase the expected probability hotels will innovate in the management of environmental quality. In this sense we find empirical support for accepting that belonging to a hotel chain or business conglomerate, that management carried out by the owner, that size as measured in beds, that the intensity of asset utilization, and that the expansion of the set of services are all factors which impinge positively upon innovation in environmental management.

NOTES

1. According to the Community Innovation Survey II, technological innovation refers to the implementation of new or significantly improved services and/or the implementation of new or significantly improved methods of rendering them. New or significantly improved services are those whose characteristics and manners of use are completely new or significantly improved in terms of quality, features or technologies utilized. The adoption of a rendering method that is characterized by significantly better performance is also a technological innovation.
2. The available data on the number of employees are not as accurate as those on the number of beds. The number of beds on offer in each hotel is a datum that is available and that does not vary in the short term. Besides, with its dependence on the characteristic seasonal nature of sun and beach tourism, which is the majority in the Balearic Islands, what is found is that the hiring of employees is recorded by companies that do not necessarily correspond to the target unit of the study, the hotel. Furthermore, given the objectives of the study, the operational size of the hotel allows us to avoid units of a superior order, such as those of the legally registered entity.

REFERENCES

Alvarez-Gil M.J., J. Burgos-Jiménez and J.J. Céspedes-Lorente (2001), 'An analysis of environmental management, organizational context and performance of Spanish hotels', *Omega*, **29**, 457–71.

Aragón Correa, J.A. and S. Sharma (2003), 'A contingent resource-based view of proactive corporate environmental strategy', *Academy of Management Review*, **28**(1), 71–88.

Bansal, P. and K. Roth (2000), 'Why companies go green: a model of ecological responsiveness', *Academy of Management Journal*, **43**(4), 717–36.

Barras, R. (1986), 'Towards a theory of innovation in services', *Research Policy*, **15**,161–73.

Butler, R.W. (1980), 'The concept of a tourist-area cycle of evolution and implications for management', *Canadian Geographer*, **24**, 5–12.

Calveras, A. (2003), 'Incentives of international and local hotel chains to invest in environmental quality', *Tourism Economics*, **9**(3), 297–306.

Chung, W. and A. Kalnins (2001), 'Agglomeration effects and performance: a test of the Texas lodging industry', *Strategic Management Journal*, **22**, 969–88.

Cohen, W.M. and R.C. Levin (1989), 'Empirical studies of innovation and market structure', in R. Schmalensee and R.D. Willig (eds), *Handbook of Industrial Organization*, Amsterdam: Elsevier Science Publishers, 1060–1107.

La Despesa Turística (2000), publication of the regional government, Palma, Mallorca: Conselleria d'Economia, Comerç i Indústria i Conselleria de Turisme.

Dewar, R.D. and J.E. Dutton (1986), 'The adoption of radical and incremental innovations: an empirical analysis', *Management Science*, **32**(11), 1422–33.

Font, X. (2002), 'Environmental certification in tourism and hospitality: progress, process and prospects', *Tourism Management*, **23**, 197–205.

Foster, S.T., S.E. Sampson and S.C. Dunn (2000), 'The impact of customer contact on environmental initiatives for service firms', *International Journal of Operations and Production Management*, **20** (2), 187–203.

González, M. and C.J. León (2001), 'The adoption of environmental innovations in the hotel industry of Gran Canaria', *Tourism Economics*, **7**(2), 177–90.

Hassan, S.S. (2000), 'Determinants of market competitiveness in a environmentally sustainable tourism industry', *Journal of Travel Research*, **38**(3), 239–45.

Henriques, I. and P. Sardosky (1999), 'The relationship between environmental commitment and managerial perceptions of stakeholders importance', *Academy of Management Journal*, **42**(1), 87–99.

Hjalager, A.M. (1998), 'Environmental regulation of tourism: impact on business innovation', *Progress in Tourism and Hospitality*, **4**, 17–30.

Hjalager, A.M. (2002), 'Repairing innovation defectiveness in tourism', *Tourism Management*, **23** (5), 465–74.

Huybers, T. and J. Bennett (2000), 'Impact of the environment on holiday destination choices of prospective UK tourists: implications for Tropical North Queensland', *Tourism Economics*, **6**(1), 21–46.

Ingram, P. and J. Baum (1997), 'Chain affiliation and the failure of Manhattan hotels, 1898–1980', *Administrative Science Quarterly*, **42**, 68–102.

Instituto de Estudios Turísticos. Secretaría General de Turismo (2001), *Evolución del Turismo en España Año 2000*, Ministerio de Comercio y Turismo, Madrid.

Jones, P. (1999), 'Multi-unit management in the hospitality industry: a late twentieth century problem', *International Journal of Contemporary Hospitality Management*, **11**(4), 155–64.

Llull Gilet, A. (2001), *Contabilidad medioambiental y desarrollo sostenible en el sector turístico*, Tesis Doctoral, Universitat de les Illes Balears.

Medina-Múñoz, R.D., D.R. Medina-Múñoz and J.M. García-Falcón (2003), 'Understanding European tour operators' control on accommodation companies: empirical evidence', *Tourism Management*, **24**(2), 135–47.

Mihalič, T. (1999), 'Environmental management of a tourist destination: a factor of tourism competitiveness', *Tourism Management*, **21**, 65–78.

Okumus, F. and N. Hemmington (1998), 'Management of the change process in hotel companies: an investigation at unit level', *Hospitality Management*, **17**, 363–74.

Organisation for Economic Co-operation and Development (OECD) (1997), *The Measurement of Scientific and Technological Activities. Proposed Guidelines for Collecting and Interpreting Technological Innovation Data*, Community Innovation Survey II, based on the Oslo Manual guidelines for innovation data analysis, Paris: OECD.

Pavitt, K. (1984), 'Sectoral patterns of technical change: towards a taxonomy and a theory', *Research Policy*, **13**, 343–73.

Saleh, F. and C. Ryan (1992), 'Client perceptions of hotels: a multi-attribute approach', *Tourism Management*, June, 163–8.

Sheldon, P.J. (1983), 'The impact of technology on the hotel industry', *Tourism Management*, **4**(4), 269–78.

Sirilli, G. and R. Evangelista (1998), 'Technological innovation in services and manufacturing: results from Italian surveys', *Research Policy*, **27**, 881–99.

Stabler, M.J. and B. Goodball (1997), 'Environmental awareness, action and performance in the Guernsey hospitality sector', *Tourism Management*, **18**(1), 19–33.

Tisdell, C. (ed.) (2000), *The Economics of Tourism*, Cheltenham, UK and Northampton, MA: Edward Elgar Publishing.

World Tourism Organization (WTO) (2001), *Tourism Highlights 2000*, Madrid: WTO.

8. Environmental management, quality management and firm performance: a review of empirical studies

Enrique Claver-Cortés, José F. Molina-Azorín, Juan J. Tarí-Guilló and María D. López-Gamero

Environmental management has assumed an important role in firm strategy (Aragón-Correa, 1998; Throop et al., 1993). Environmental management and quality management are business practices increasingly introduced into firms, very often complementarily (Karapetrovic and Willborn, 1998; Wilkinson and Dale, 1999). In fact quality management offers a striking parallelism with environmental management (Klassen and McLaughlin, 1996; Kleiner, 1991). As happens with quality, a long-term goal of environmental management consists in moving towards a proactive stance, incorporating environmental issues into product design, technology-related decisions, the entire manufacturing process and customer service.

Another similarity between both management systems lies in the relevance they have for the firm's competitive position. Porter's (1980) distinction between cost and differentiation advantages provides a useful framework where these effects can be highlighted. In this sense, both competitive positions can be improved through quality management (Belohlav, 1993; Grant, 2002) and environmental management (Karagozoglu and Lindell, 2000; Klassen and McLaughlin, 1996; Shrivastava and Hart, 1994).

However the results obtained in the empirical studies that have analysed the impact of quality management and environmental management on firm performance are so far inconclusive. In some studies, a positive influence of environmental variables on firm performance has been verified. In others, that relationship could not be found. The same happens with studies dealing with the impact of quality management on firm performance.

The aim of this chapter is to do a thorough review of these quantitative empirical studies. For each management practice, we will examine the firms under analysis, the quality and environmental measures applied, the performance measures, the type of analysis and, finally, the results obtained. Additionally an attempt will be made to identify several implications and suggestions derived from checking the similarities and differences between both sets of studies. This can provide guidelines for future research, introducing some new, relevant ideas about the integration of both management systems and their influence on firm performance.

In this respect our contribution materializes in an integrating model of cause–effect relationships between quality management, environmental management and financial or economic performance. An analysis of these aspects can therefore benefit future empirical research.

A number of definitions must be established first. Quality management can be defined as a holistic management philosophy that focuses on the maintenance and continuous improvement in all the functions of an organization seeking to meet or exceed customer requirements (Flynn et al., 1994; Kaynak, 2003). The output of quality management is quality performance, whose indicators can be, among others, product or service quality, productivity, cost of scrap and rework, conformance to specifications or company reputation (Curkovic et al., 2000; Kaynak, 2003). Environmental management encompasses the firm's technical and organizational activities meant to reduce environmental impacts and minimize their effects on the natural environment (Cramer, 1998; Sharfman et al., 1997). The output of environmental management is environmental performance, a term that refers to the effects and impacts of the firm's activities and products on the natural environment. Some measures of environmental performance can be the consumption of resources or the generation of waste and emissions (James, 1994; Klassen and Whybark, 1999).

The rest of this chapter will be organized as follows. The next section will present an overview of empirical studies on the relationship between quality management and firm performance. After that, we will review studies on the environmental management–firm performance link. The discussion section offers comments on some similarities and differences between these two linkages, from which a model with several variables and relationships will be prepared. Finally, the last section will provide some conclusions.

QUALITY MANAGEMENT AND FIRM PERFORMANCE

Quality can be applied at all firm levels, often showing that costs can be reduced and differentiation levels can be increased (Belohlav, 1993; Grant, 2002). This idea suggests that total quality management (TQM) may have positive effects on performance. According to the theory about quality management, TQM has a positive impact on performance. Deming (1982) points out that higher quality implies lower costs and increased productivity, which in turn gives the firm a greater market share and better competitiveness levels. Likewise the European Foundation for Quality Management model mentions a relationship between quality management factors and firm performance.

Therefore both the practice of many firms and the literature have referred to the positive effects of TQM. Nevertheless this relationship did not start to be academically and empirically analysed until the 1990s. Various authors have analysed this linkage, reaching disparate conclusions. In several empirical studies, a connection was found between quality management practices and improved performance (Easton and Jarrell, 1998; Powell, 1995; Taylor and Wright, 2003), while according to others this does not always hold true (Boje and Winsor, 1993; Spector and Beer, 1994; Taylor and Wright, 2003).

In this sense we must highlight two groups of works. On the one hand are the empirical studies where a valid and reliable instrument has been developed that can measure quality management (Ahire et al., 1996; Badri et al., 1995; Black and Porter, 1995, 1996; Flynn et al., 1994; Grandzol and Gershon, 1998; Quazi et al., 1998; Saraph et al., 1989). These studies have shown that TQM influences firm performance. On the other hand are those empirical works which sought to answer the following question: Does quality management have a positive impact on performance? In this case, Table 8.1 shows the research work focused on the study of this relationship.

Table 8.1 shows that:

1. The authors have mainly worked with industrial and service firms, the former being more common.
2. The studies focus on TQM and ISO 9000 certification with the aim of analysing the quality variable. A distinction must be made within the first group between those measuring TQM as a single construct, and the rest, which use a set of different constructs. TQM is most commonly seen as a set of factors (such as for example leadership, people management, customer focus, supplier management, planning, process management or continuous improvement). Moreover authors tend to use perceptual measures for these elements.
3. The column of performance variables refers both to quality performance (for example quality product, conformance to specifications, design quality, company reputation) and financial performance (for example revenue growth, profitability, net income to sales, net income to assets). Besides, authors use objective measures, perceptual ones and even sometimes combine both types.

Table 8.1 Summary of quality–firm performance link results

Study	Sample	Quality variables	Performance variables	Main analysis	Major findings
Flynn et al. (1995)	45 manufacturing plants in the United States (US)	8 constructs	3 constructs: perceived quality market outcomes, competitive advantage (perceptual), percentage of items that pass final inspection without requiring rework (objective)	Path analysis	A relationship exists between quality management and perceived quality market outcomes and the percentage of items that pass final inspection without requiring rework. Both measures have a significant impact on competitive advantage
Powell (1995)	54 US manufacturing and service firms	12 factors	2 variables (perceptual): total performance, TQM program performance	Correlation analysis	TQM-performance correlation. However, TQM success critically depends on executive commitment, open organization and employee empowerment
Hendricks and Singhal (1996)	Awards presented by 34 firms	1 construct: winning a quality award	The firm's market value (objective)	Event study	The stock market reacts positively to winning quality award announcements
Hendricks and Singhal (1997)	463 firms that have won a quality award	1 construct: winning a quality award	Financial performance (objective)	Wilcoxon signed-rank test and Mann-Whitney	Implementing effective TQM programs improves firm performance

Study	Sample	Factors/constructs	Performance measures	Method	Findings
Easton and Jarrell (1998)	108 firms from different sectors	1 construct	Financial performance (objective)	Wilcoxon rank-sum, Wilcoxon signed-rank test	The long-term performance of firms implementing TQM improved
Dow et al. (1999)	698 manufacturing firms in Australia and New Zealand	9 factors	1 construct (perceptual)	Structural equation modelling	Three out of nine TQM factors have a significant positive correlation. These are the so-called 'soft factors'
Samson and Terziovski (1999)	1,024 manufacturing firms in Australia and New Zealand	6 factors	1 construct (perceptual): operational performance	Regression analysis	The relationship exists. The category leadership, staff management and customer focus were the strongest significant performance predictors
Curkovic et al. (2000)	57 firms (suppliers to General Motors, Ford and Chrysler)	10 factors	8 quality performance measures (perceptual) and 6 firm performance measures (objective)	Correlation analysis	TQM affects quality performance. Quality management may also have an impact on firm performance
Agus and Sagir (2001)	30 Malaysian manufacturing companies	1 construct	1 latent endogenous construct (objective)	Structural equation model	TQM has an indirect impact on financial performance mediated by competitive advantage
Escrig et al. (2001)	231 Spanish industrial and service firms	1 construct	1 construct: financial results	Structural equation model	TQM impact on firm financial performance

Table 8.1 (continued)

Study	Sample	Quality variables	Performance variables	Main analysis	Major findings
Douglas and Judge (2001)	193 general medical hospitals in the US	1 construct	2 dimensions: perceived financial performance (perceptual), industry-expert-rated measure (objective)	Regression analysis	TQM implementation level affects performance
Rahman (2001)	49 firms in Australia, with and without the ISO 9000 certification	9 factors	1 construct (perceptual)	t-test	No significant differences between the impacts of TQM on performance for firms with and without the ISO 9000 certification
Singels et al. (2001)	192 industrial and service firms in the North of Holland	ISO 9000 certification/ no ISO 9000 certification	5 performance measures (perceptual)	t-test	ISO 9000 certified firms did not outperform those without such a certification
Nicolau and Sellers (2002)	Certified firms (40 quality certificates) on the Spanish Stock Exchange	ISO 9000 certification	The variation in share prices on any given day (objective)	Event study	The stock market responds positively to the award of quality certificates

Author (Year)	Sample	Variable	Performance measure	Method	Findings
Tsekouras et al. (2002)	143 Greek firms (with and without the ISO 9000 certification)	ISO 9000 certification/ no ISO 9000 certification	4 financial measures (objective)	t-test	ISO 9000 adoption has no effects on firm performance
Wayhan et al. (2002)	48 ISO 9000-certified companies in North America	ISO 9000 certification	2 measures (objective)	MANOVA	The relationship between ISO and financial growth does not exist, except for the ROA variable
Lai and Cheng (2003)	304 firms in Hong Kong (productive, construction, service and public sectors)	10 factors	4 dimensions (perceptual)	ANOVA	Companies in the public utility and service sectors outperformed manufacturing and construction firms in terms of both TQM and performance
Kaynak (2003)	214 industrial and service firms in the US	7 constructs	3 dimensions (perceptual)	Structural equation model	TQM has positive effects on firm performance
Merino-Díaz (2003)	965 Spanish manufacturing firms	5 constructs	1 factor (perceptual)	Regression analysis	A relation between TQM and performance does exist. However, human resources variables contribute the most to performance
Terziovski et al. (2003)	400 certified firms in Australia	5 constructs	2 factors (perceptual)	Regression analysis	Quality culture has an effect on business performance. The single factor found to contribute the most to this was customer focus

4. Among the statistical techniques used, correlation analyses, regression analyses, structural models and the analyses of significant differences between groups of companies stand out.
5. Regarding the last column, several studies show that TQM will most probably have a positive impact on firm performance. However the effects of the ISO 9000 standard are not so clear. There are studies according to which the standard does not exert an influence on firm performance, while in others it is concluded that this standard may actually have a slight impact on some financial variable. Therefore TQM can influence performance to a greater extent than the ISO 9000 standard (Zhang, 2000).

In the discussion section, the research works included in Table 8.1 will be compared with those dealing with environmental management.

ENVIRONMENTAL MANAGEMENT AND FIRM PERFORMANCE

The influence of environmental management on firm performance may result from the positive impact on firm costs and differentiation levels. Pollution prevention can allow the firm to save and control costs, input and energy consumption and also to reuse materials through recycling (Greeno and Robinson, 1992; Hart, 1997; Shrivastava, 1995a; Taylor, 1992). Thus eco-efficiency involves producing and delivering goods while at the same time reducing ecological impacts and resource intensity and minimizing energy intensity and dispersion of toxics (Knight, 1995; Schmidheiny, 1992; Starik and Marcus, 2000). In this respect, pollution generation is regarded as a sign of inefficiency (Kleiner, 1991; Porter and Van der Linde, 1995a). As for differentiation, reducing pollution may increase the demand from environmentally sensitive consumers, since the ecological characteristics of the products can become a new competitive argument valued by these 'green' customers (Elkington, 1994). Moreover a firm showing good environmental initiatives can acquire a good ecological reputation (Miles and Covin, 2000; Shrivastava, 1995b).

Therefore through prevention, firms can reach a win–win situation, that is one from which both the firm and the environment will benefit. This idea reflects an approach to the influence exerted by the environment on firm competitiveness and profitability, known in the literature as the 'Porter hypothesis' (Porter and Van der Linde, 1995a, 1995b). Nevertheless this view coexists with a more traditional position that mentions the existence of a trade-off between the natural environment and firm profitability, in such a way that the improvement in the environmental impact caused by a firm will lower its profitability. Along this line of thought, it has been suggested that compliance with environmental regulations will make firms incur significant costs, thus reducing their capacity to compete (Jaffe et al., 1995). Furthermore this traditional view responds to 'Porter hypothesis' supporters' claims saying that although cost savings can easily be obtained with certain simple prevention measures, the most ambitious prevention measures may involve costs that will exceed the potential savings to be derived from them (Walley and Whitehead, 1994). The opposite argument says that the returns of investments in prevention will compensate for the initial costs in the long run (Dechant and Altman, 1994; Greeno and Robinson, 1992; Shrivastava, 1995b).

Despite the anecdotal evidence according to which profits make up for the cost of environmental measures (Schmidheiny, 1992), quantitative empirical studies provide inconclusive results. Table 8.2 shows some works that have empirically analysed the impact of the environment on firm performance.

Table 8.2 shows that:

1. The set of firms and industries is varied. Manufacturing sectors are the most common. Besides, few studies analyse just one industry.
2. The environmental variables used are diverse too. Some studies resort to environmental performance, both positive (emission reduction) and negative (emissions generated); others mention environmental management variables (practices, initiatives, technologies, pollution reduction means or methods, ISO 14001 certification). Therefore this column contains environmental performance and environmental management variables. In addition to this, some studies resort to objective measures, while others use perceptual measures.
3. Regarding performance variables, we can see in this column that studies mainly use financial performance. Moreover some studies apply objective measures (for example accounting performance), while others resort to perceptual measures.
4. As far as the type of analysis used in these studies is concerned, regression analysis prevails. Other analyses identified are the event study methodology, the analysis of differences between groups and the structural equation model.
5. Finally, results also differ, but works where a significant positive relationship between environment and firm performance is obtained are predominant. Moreover with regard to ISO 14001, Melnyk et al. (2003) found that firms having gone through certification experience a greater impact on performance than firms which have not certified their

Table 8.2 Summary of environment–firm performance link results

Study	Sample	Environmental variables	Performance variables	Main analysis	Major findings
Hamilton (1995)	463 US firms	TRI (Toxic Release Inventory) emissions	Returns (stock price reaction)	Event study	Significant negative returns on the day TRI emissions data were first announced
Cohen et al. (1995)	S&P 500 US firms with environmental data available	TRI emissions, oil spills, chemical spills, environmental litigation cases	ROA, return on equity (ROE), total return to common shareholders (Compustat)	Groups, t-test	The group of low-polluting firms had better economic performances (not always at a significant level)
Hart and Ahuja (1996)	127 US firms in SIC listed in S&P 500 with SIC codes below 5000	Emission reductions based on TRI from the IRRC Corporate Environmental Profile data	ROA, ROE, return on sales (ROS) (Compustat)	Regression analysis	Pollution prevention activities have a positive influence on financial performance within 1–2 years. ROE takes longer to be affected
Klassen and McLaughlin (1996)	US firms with environmental awards and crises (several industries)	Environmental awards in the NEXIS database; chemical/oil spills, gas leaks or explosions	Stock market returns (NYSE, AMEX, CRSP)	Event study	Environmental awards (crises) led to significant, positive (negative) changes in market valuation
Russo and Fouts (1997)	243 US firms (several sectors)	Environmental ratings (FRDC): compliance, expenditures, waste reduction	ROA	Regression analysis	Positive and significant impact of environmental performance on ROA

166

Study	Sample	Environmental measure	Performance measure	Method	Results
Cordeiro and Sarkis (1997)	523 US firms in SIC codes 2000-3999	TRI releases that are recovered, treated or recycled on-site	Industry analyst earnings-per-share growth forecasts	Regression analysis	High environmental performance is significantly negative in relation to earnings-per-share growth forecasts
Judge and Douglas (1998)	196 US firms (World Environmental Directory)	Integration of environmental issues into the strategic planning process (perceptual measures)	ROI, earnings growth, sales growth, market share change (percept. meas.)	Structural equation model	Positive and significant impact of environmental issue integration on financial performance
Sharma and Vredenburg (1998)	99 Canadian firms (oil and gas)	Proactive environmental strategy (perceptual measures)	Organizational benefits (perceptual measures)	Regression analysis	Positive and significant influence of proactive practices on organizational capabilities and of the latter on organizational benefits
Edwards (1998)	51 environm. leaders in 8 UK sectors	Assessment of various aspects of each firm's environmental perfor. and management	Return on capital employed (ROCE), ROE	Groups	In several comparisons, environm. high-performing firms perform better (not always at a significant level)
Klassen and Whybark (1999)	69 US firms in the furniture industry	Environmental technology portfolio	Manufacturing performance measures (objective and perceptual)	Regression analysis	Positive and significant impact of environmental technology portfolio on manufacturing performance

Table 8.2 (continued)

Study	Sample	Environmental variables	Performance variables	Main analysis	Major findings
Álvarez et al. (1999)	300 Spanish hotels	Environmental strategy (perceptual measures)	Occupation, profits (perceptual measures)	Groups, ANOVA	Groups with a more consolidated proactive environmental strategy had higher occupation levels (significant) and higher profits (not significant)
Christmann (2000)	88 US chemical companies	Envir. management 'best practices': use of pollution prevention technol. (PPT), innovation of proprietary PPT and early timing	Cost advantage (perceptual measures)	Regression analysis	Only positive and significant effect of proprietary PPT innovation. Capabilities for process innovation are complementary assets that moderate the relationship
Gilley et al. (2000)	71 announcements of corporate environmental initiatives	Two types of environm. initiatives: 39 process-driven and 32 product-driven	Anticipated firm performance (stock returns)	Event study	No significant effect of greening on performance. Different types of environmental initiatives have unique implications
De Burgos and Céspedes (2001)	Data by Judge and Douglas (1998)	Data by Judge and Douglas (1998)	Data by Judge and Douglas (1998)	Data by Judge and Douglas (1998)	Positive but not signif. impact of environm. issue integration on financial perform. Positive and signif. impact of envir. perf. on financial perf

Study	Sample	Environmental variable	Performance variable	Method	Results
King and Lenox (2002)	614 US manufacturing firms (Compustat and TRI)	Total emissions, pollution reduction means or methods (waste generation, waste prevention, waste treatment, waste transfer)	ROA, Tobin's q	Regression analysis	Lower emissions (in t) are significantly associated with higher financial performance (in t+1). Significant and positive relationship of waste prevention with ROA and Tobin's q
Wagner et al. (2002)	37 firms in the European paper industry (Germany, Italy, UK, Holland)	Environmental index integrating SO_2 emissions, NO_x emissions and COD emissions	ROS, ROE and ROCE	Simultaneous equation system	Negative and significant effect of environmental performance on ROCE. No evidence of significant impact of any economic performance variable on environmental performance
Melnyk et al. (2003)	1,222 manufacturing firm managers	State of the environmental management system (EMS): no formal EMS, formal EMS and formal certified EMS. 17 environm. options (environm. perform.)	Ten corporate performance perceptual measures	Regression analysis	Positive and significant impact of EMS state on the ten corporate performance measures. Positive and significant impact of EMS state on environmental options
Cañón and Garcés (2003)	80 ISO 14001 certified plants of 34 Spanish firms	ISO 14001 certification	Stock price	Event study	Negative impact of certification on pioneer, middle-polluting and lower size firms

environmental management system. However Cañón and Garcés (2003) did not find a positive impact of certification on performance.

We will dedicate the next section to introducing some additional considerations through the comparison of quality management and environmental management studies. This will allow us to have a better understanding of the relationship between these systems and performance.

DISCUSSION

Some similarities and differences between both sets of studies have been identified that could help in the analysis of the quality–performance relationship as well as the environment–performance link. Several issues are going to be treated: (1) context factors, (2) time effect, (3) measures and relationships, (4) the role of competitive advantage and firm resources, and (5) the integrated model.

Context Factors

Most studies examine firms from different sectors, which requires the introduction of control variables. The variables most often used in these studies are size and industry. In this respect a contingent approach to the impact of quality management and environmental management on firm performance can be taken into consideration. Thus other context factors exist that might moderate the intensity and direction of those relationships.

Quality studies mention the motivation to be certified (when reasons are internal, the certification can have positive effects on performance) (Singels et al., 2001) and the structural control of procedures, operations and work activities (when a greater emphasis is laid on these aspects, the relationship between TQM and financial performance becomes stronger) (Douglas and Judge, 2001).

In the case of environmental management, an aspect often analysed is the more or less pollutant character of the firms and industries. Hart and Ahuja (1996) found that emission reduction enhances financial performance more for firms with high emission levels. Klassen and McLaughlin (1996) showed that financial markets react more positively to the announcement of a first-time environmental award to a firm operating a cleaner industry. However the market valuation of subsequent awards is not significantly affected by the historical environmental cleanliness (pollution intensity) of the industry, although award recipients in dirtier industries receive a marginally stronger, positive market reaction.

Time Effect

The impact of some quality management or environmental management variables on performance may not be an immediate one. For instance in the field of quality, we must highlight the studies by Easton and Jarrell (1998) and Hendricks and Singhal (1997), who analysed the long-term effects of quality management from the financial results for some years published by the firms, as well as the paper by Wayhan et al. (2002), where the effects of the ISO 9000 standard were analysed by comparing financial performance results before and after obtaining the certification.

As far as environmental management is concerned, Hart and Ahuja (1996) along with King and Lenox (2002) examined the influence of environmental variables on firm performance using measures of the former for a specific year, and measures of the latter for the following years. However Wagner et al. (2002) showed that the environmental performance of a firm in one period is directly linked to its economic performance during that period, since all material and energy flows avoided in the period also avoid some part of the general overhead costs of the period.

Despite that, as Nehrt (1996) explained, some environmental tasks (installing technologies, training workers) take time, and diseconomies for the firm appear when more manpower or money are used to accelerate their completion. A key aspect in this debate is that sometimes we talk about variables more closely connected to environmental performance and, on other occasions, we refer to more general variables and tasks associated with environmental management.

Measures and Relationships

An aspect of particular interest in studies dealing with quality and environment is the conceptual definition of the variables used. The review of research on quality management allows us to check the lack of agreement on performance measures. This variable is mainly considered from several points of view: only quality performance (Dow et al., 1999; Lai and Cheng, 2003), only financial performance (Douglas and Judge, 2001; Easton and Jarrell, 1998; Hendricks and Singhal, 1996, 1997) and studies including both quality performance and financial performance (Curkovic et al., 2000; Kaynak, 2003; Powell, 1995).

These performance measures are varied, as some authors include some items in quality performance and others in different measures like competitive advantage and financial performance. In order to clarify these measures, it is necessary to specify their meanings as well as their relationships. These ideas can explain how TQM factors introduced in an integrated

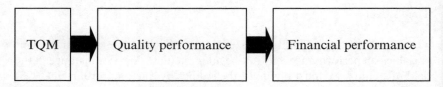

Figure 8.1   Relationship between TQM and financial performance

way may improve the quality performance that will later allow the firm to improve its financial performance (Figure 8.1).

In studies about quality, those we consider 'quality variables' (third column in Table 8.1) include only factors linked to quality management, while the column of 'performance variables' (fourth column) includes both quality performance and financial performance factors. As its name indicates, quality performance can be a quality variable and a performance variable, but we have finally classified it as a performance variable because, in some studies, this was the only existing performance measure and, in all studies, there was always a set of quality management variables that could appear in the column of quality variables.

However in the field of environmental management, the third column of Table 8.2 (environmental variables) contains both environmental management variables (certification, practices, initiatives, technologies) and environmental performance variables (impact of firm activities on the environment, mainly in terms of resource consumption and emission levels), whereas the fourth column of performance variables mainly refers to financial performance. This difference with respect to quality studies lies in the fact that in many works focusing on the environment, the only environmental variable is an environmental performance measure, environmental management variables being non-existent. Nevertheless the variables that always appear are those referring to financial performance, actually the only variables included in the fourth column.

As in quality studies, environmental performance variables, as their name suggests, can be seen as both environmental variables and performance variables. What matters in our view is that quality performance and environmental performance measures are simultaneously outcomes (ends or consequences) of environmental or quality management, and causes (means or methods) to improve financial performance.

From what has just been said, we conclude that one step forward we could take in the field of environmental studies would be to introduce environmental management measures, even to try and build a valid, reliable measurement instrument (Sharma et al., 2003), with the aim of reflecting what could be considered 'Total Environmental Management' (TEM).

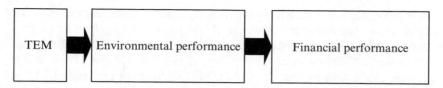

Figure 8.2   Relationship between TEM and financial performance

TQM elements can contribute to building this measurement instrument (Curkovic, 2003). Figure 8.2 shows these relationships in the context of environmental management.

The Role of Competitive Advantage and Firm Resources

Other variables could be added to Figures 8.1 and 8.2 between quality management or environmental management and financial performance. Next, these variables and relationships, which will later appear in an integrated model, are going to be analysed.

Competitive advantage is a variable already considered in some studies on quality (Agus and Sagir, 2001; Flynn et al., 1995) and the environment (Sharma and Vredenburg, 1998; Karagozoglu and Lindell, 2000; Klassen and McLaughlin, 1996). Quality studies for instance show that TQM exerts an influence on financial performance through the creation of competitive advantages. The same would happen with environmental management. A better quality performance or environmental performance can provide competitive advantages which will subsequently improve financial performance. As we have already pointed out, cost and differentiation competitive positions can be improved through quality management and environmental management. However as we said above, the verification of these influences is going to require a conceptual delimitation of each variable so as to establish the cause–effect relationships in the best possible way.

Firm resources are other variables to be considered. Firm resources may play a contingent role both in the quality management–firm performance relationship (Powell, 1995; Escrig et al., 2001) and in the environmental management–firm performance relationship (Christmann, 2000; Hart, 1995; Russo and Fouts, 1997). The resource-based view of the firm (Barney, 1991; Grant, 1991; Wernerfelt, 1984) suggests that competitive advantages and differences in firm performance are primarily the result of resource heterogeneity across firms.

In the area of quality, the cause–effect relationship between TQM and quality performance can be explained through the resource-based view, since the firm develops the resources and capabilities that will allow it to be more efficient, to improve its products and, in short, to achieve competitive advantages. The literature shows that TQM has a positive effect on performance, although some authors believe that soft aspects are the most influential ones (Curkovic et al., 2000; Dow et al., 1999; Merino-Díaz, 2003; Powell, 1995; Samson and Terziovski, 1999). This does not mean that the other TQM factors are not needed. It is necessary to fully implement all the key TQM practices because these factors are interdependent (Douglas and Judge, 2001; Flynn et al., 1994; Hackman and Wageman, 1995; Kaynak, 2003; Saraph et al., 1989). Therefore firms showing a higher level of TQM factor implementation will achieve better TQM results, as is explained in different studies (Easton and Jarrell, 1998; Rahman, 2001; Rao et al., 1999). Similarly ISO 9000 certified firms with a higher quality management level outperform those with a lower level in this field (Claver and Tarí, 2003; Najmi and Kehoe, 2001).

Regarding environmental management, several studies have also resorted to the resource-based view. One of the pioneering studies was the one by Hart (1995), in which were mentioned the key resources and the sources of competitive advantage associated with several environmental strategies. In turn, Shrivastava (1995b) described how environmental technologies may become a strategic resource able to provide inimitable competitive advantages. The study by Russo and Fouts (1997) also deserves a special mention. First, these authors said that the stock of resources will be different depending on whether the firm adopts a control or a prevention approach. Thus in relation to productive capabilities, human resources and organizational capacities, prevention implies a greater productive complexity than control, since better skills, more training and a deeper involvement is required from employees, along with a closer inter-functional coordination. Second, these authors showed that a proactive attitude of the firm towards the environment will probably favour the development of new resources and capabilities that in turn may help to achieve competitive advantages. Sharma and Vredenburg (1998) also insisted on the same idea when they found that certain unique, valuable capabilities emerged among the most proactive firms in the environmental field. Judge and Douglas (1998) highlighted that the integration of environmental aspects into the firm's strategy can become a valuable, rare capability that can hardly be imitated.

Marcus and Geffen (1998) pointed out that, as in the case of TQM, establishing a distinctive competence for managing the physical environment is important, as it can mean less waste, fewer emissions, fewer accidents, lower costs and better integrated systems. Insofar as this competence adds value to customers through product differentiation or lower costs, it also provides competitive advantage. In addition to that, Christmann (2000) indicated that capabilities for process innovation and implementation are complementary assets that moderate the relationship between best practices and cost advantage. Aragón-Correa and Sharma (2003) integrated perspectives found in the literature on contingency, dynamic capabilities and the natural resource-based view with the aim of making a proposal about the way in which dimensions of the competitive environment influence the proactive environmental strategy.

Along the same lines, two additional links can finally be mentioned. On the one hand, resources developed through quality management can be exploited in environmental management. A number of total quality environmental management practices exist that are linked to TQM (Sarkis, 1998). Empowerment, team-based approaches, skill improvements and open communications are TQM elements which can enhance operations and support continuous improvement in operational activities designed for source-reduction programmes (Kitazawa and Sarkis, 2000), and thus for adequate environmental management. This means that TQM can facilitate the adoption of TEM.

On the other hand, according to some studies, firms with a better financial situation are the ones which can more easily adopt a quality management system (Martínez and Martínez, 2003). For this reason, another link of the impact financial performance has on quality management could be established. Similarly in the environmental field, financial performance may influence environmental management (Wagner et al., 2002). Thus a firm with a good financial performance can allocate more resources to prevention-oriented technologies and initiatives.

Integrated Model

Taking into account the above-mentioned relationships, Figure 8.3 shows a set of variables and links between these relationships that would complement the ones established in Figures 8.1 and 8.2. We have introduced both quality management and environmental management in Figure 8.3, as it is quite common for firms to start their way towards continuous improvement through quality management, environmental management being introduced later. In any case, each management practice could be treated on its own.

In an attempt to briefly explain Figure 8.3, and summarizing the ideas contained in the preceding paragraphs, we must say that certain resources and capabilities (R&C) are required in order to implement TQM and TEM practices (1); besides, TQM and TEM can improve quality performance (QP) and environmental performance (EP) respectively, and better QP and EP levels may help to achieve competitive advantages (CA) (2).

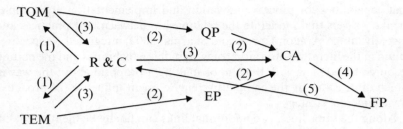

Figure 8.3   Relationships between TQM–TEM and financial performance

Furthermore the introduction of both management systems may develop or improve the firm's resources, which, according to the resource-based view, may help to achieve CA (3) too. Moreover firms that are the earliest to implement TQM will be able to develop some resources and capabilities that will surely come in handy at TEM implementation. Likewise if the firm obtains CA, it will be able to improve its financial performance (FP) (4); and finally, obtaining a high FP implies the availability of financial resources that will surely facilitate the development of other resources and capabilities (5). In other words, firms will be able to use these resources in order to improve TQM and TEM systems (1), relationships being once again maintained.

CONCLUSIONS

This chapter offers a review of some empirical studies that have analysed the impact of quality management and environmental management on firm performance. Through the comparison of both groups of works, we have brought in some ideas that could be useful for future research in the field of environmental management.

We have equally proposed a model of cause–effect relationships between these management systems and firm performance through such parameters as resources and capabilities and competitive advantage. In this sense, the empirical verification of the model is going to require a clear conceptual delimitation of each variable, which would permit the comparison of results coming from different studies.

In our opinion it is also important to continue deepening the analysis of potential time lapses separating the implementation of quality management and/or environmental management and the achievement of financial performance, through longitudinal studies.

Furthermore in the field of environmental management, it would be interesting to continue developing reliable, valid measurement scales as has already been done to a greater extent in the area of TQM. Thus TQM factors can contribute to building such a measurement instrument for environmental management because some elements can be common to implementing both management systems.

Finally, we believe that the resource-based view can play an important role in this type of study. Quality management and environmental management will probably become unique capabilities that can hardly be imitated because of the organizational aspects they involve. Therefore the chance offered by these management systems to improve competitiveness and performance derives from the need to coordinate a set of resources that are heterogeneous and consequently difficult to identify and imitate. In fact the competitive advantage they may generate does not result so much from using certain specific technologies and tangible resources, but rather from the emergence of some tacit, intangible characteristics that have become requirements for the implementation of quality management and environmental management.

REFERENCES

Agus, A. and R. Sagir (2001), 'The structural relationships between total quality management, competitive advantage and bottom line financial performance: an empirical study of Malaysian manufacturing companies', *Total Quality Management*, **12**(7–8), 1018–24.

Ahire, S., D. Golhar and M. Waller (1996), 'Development and validation of TQM implementation constructs', *Decision Sciences*, **27**(1), 23–56.

Álvarez, M., J. de Burgos and J. Céspedes (1999), 'Estrategia medioambiental, contexto organizativo y rendimiento: los establecimientos hoteleros españoles', Working Paper, Carlos III University, Madrid.

Aragón-Correa, J. (1998), 'Strategic proactivity and firm approach to the natural environment', *Academy of Management Journal*, **41**, 556–67.

Aragón-Correa, J. and S. Sharma (2003), 'A contingent resource-based view of proactive corporate environmental strategy', *Academy of Management Review*, **28**, 71–88.

Badri, M., D. Davis and D. Davis (1995), 'A study of measuring the critical factors of quality management', *International Journal of Quality and Reliability Management*, **12**(2), 36–53.

Barney, J. (1991), 'Firm resources and sustained competitive advantage', *Journal of Management*, **17**, 99–120.

Belohlav, J. (1993), 'Developing the quality organization', *Quality Progress*, October, 119–22.

Black, S. and L. Porter (1995), 'An empirical model for total quality management', *Total Quality Management*, **6**(2), 149–64.

Black, S. and L. Porter (1996), 'Identification of the critical factors of TQM', *Decision Sciences*, **27**(1), 1–21.

Boje, D. and R. Winsor (1993), 'The resurrection of Taylorism: total quality management's hidden agenda', *Journal of Organizational Change Management*, **6**(4), 57–70.

Cañón, J. and C. Garcés (2003), 'Repercusión de la certificación medioambiental ISO 14001 en el valor de mercado de las empresas', paper presented at the 13th annual meeting of ACEDE, Salamanca, Spain.

Christmann, P. (2000), 'Effects of "best practices" of environmental management on cost advantage: the role of complementary assets', *Academy of Management Journal*, **43**, 663–80.

Claver, E. and J. Tarí (2003), 'Levels of quality management in certified firms', *Total Quality Management*, **14**(9), 981–98.

Cohen, M., S. Fenn and J. Naimon (1995), 'Environmental and financial performance: are they related?', Working Paper, Vanderbilt University, Nashville.

Cordeiro, J. and J. Sarkis (1997), 'Environmental proactivism and firm performance: evidence from security analyst earnings forecasts', *Business Strategy and the Environment*, **6**, 104–14.

Cramer, J. (1998), 'Environmental management: from "fit" to "stretch" ', *Business Strategy and the Environment*, **7**, 162–72.

Curkovic, S. (2003), 'Environmentally responsible manufacturing: the development and validation of a measurement model', *European Journal of Operational Research*, **146**, 130–55.

Curkovic, S., S. Vickery and C. Droge (2000), 'Quality-related action programs: their impact on quality performance and firm performance', *Decision Sciences*, **31**(4), 885–905.

De Burgos, J. and J. Céspedes (2001), 'La protección ambiental y el resultado. Un análisis crítico de su relación', *Investigaciones Europeas de Dirección y Economía de la Empresa*, **7**(2), 93–108.

Dechant, K. and B. Altman (1994), 'Environmental leadership: from compliance to competitive advantage', *Academy of Management Executive*, **8**(3), 7–27.

Deming, W. (1982), *Quality, Productivity and Competitive Position*, Cambridge, MA: MIT Center for Advanced Engineering.

Douglas, T. and W. Judge (2001), 'Total quality management implementation and competitive advantage: the role of structural control and exploration', *Academy of Management Journal*, **44**(1), 158–69.

Dow, D., D. Samson and S. Ford (1999), 'Exploding the myth: do all quality management practices contribute to superior quality performance?', *Production and Operations Management*, **8**(1), 1–27.

Easton, G. and S. Jarrell (1998), 'The effects of total quality management on corporate performance: an empirical investigation', *Journal of Business*, **71**(2), 253–307.

Edwards, D. (1998), *The Link between Company Environmental and Financial Performance*, London: Earthscan Publications.

Elkington, J. (1994), 'Towards the sustainable corporation: win–win–win business strategies for sustainable development', *California Management Review*, **36**(2), 90–100.

Escrig, A., J. Bou and V. Roca (2001), 'Measuring the relationship between total quality management and sustainable competitive advantage: a resource-based view', *Total Quality Management*, **12**(7–8), 932–8.

Flynn, B., R. Schroeder and S. Sakakibara (1994), 'A framework for quality management research and associated measurement instrument', *Journal of Operations Management*, **11**(4), 339–66.

Flynn, B., R. Schroeder and S. Sakakibara (1995), 'The impact of quality management practices on performance and competitive advantage', *Decision Sciences*, **26**(5), 659–91.

Gilley, K., D. Worrell and A. El-Jelly (2000), 'Corporate environmental initiatives and anticipated firm performance: the differential effects of process-driven versus product-driven greening initiatives', *Journal of Management*, **26**, 1199–1216.

Grandzol, J. and M. Gershon (1998), 'A survey instrument for standardizing TQM modelling research', *International Journal of Quality Science*, **3**(1), 80–105.

Grant, R. (1991), 'The resource-based theory of competitive advantage: implications for strategy formulation', *California Management Review*, **33**(3), 114–35.

Grant, R. (2002), *Contemporary Strategy Analysis. Concepts, Techniques, Applications*, Cambridge, MA: Blackwell.

Greeno, J. and S. Robinson (1992), 'Rethinking corporate environmental management', *Columbia Journal of World Business*, Autumn–Winter, 222–32.

Hackman, J. and R. Wageman (1995), 'Total quality management: empirical, conceptual, and practical issues', *Administrative Science Quarterly*, **40**(2), 309–41.

Hamilton, J. (1995), 'Pollution as news: media and stock market reactions to the Toxics Release Inventory Data', *Journal of Environmental Economics and Management*, **28**, 98–113.

Hart, S. (1995), 'A natural-resource-based view of the firm', *Academy of Management Review*, **20**, 986–1014.

Hart, S. (1997), 'Beyond greening: strategies for a sustainable world', *Harvard Business Review*, **75**(1), 66–76.

Hart, S. and G. Ahuja (1996), 'Does it pay to be green? An empirical examination of the relationship between emission reduction and firm performance', *Business Strategy and the Environment*, **5**(1), 30–37.

Hendricks, K. and V. Singhal (1996), 'Quality awards and the market value of the firm: an empirical investigation', *Management Science*, **42**(3), 415–36.

Hendricks, K. and V. Singhal (1997), 'Does implementing and effective TQM program actually improve operating performance? Empirical evidence from firms that have won quality awards', *Management Science*, **43**(9), 1258–74.

Jaffe, A., S. Peterson, P. Portney and R. Stavins (1995), 'Environmental regulation and the competitiveness of US manufacturing: what does the evidence tell us?', *Journal of Economic Literature*, **33**(1), 132–63.

James, P. (1994), 'Business environmental performance measurement', *Business Strategy and the Environment*, **3**, 59–67.

Judge, W. and T. Douglas (1998), 'Performance implications of incorporating natural environmental issues into the strategic planning process: an empirical assessment', *Journal of Management Studies*, **35**(2), 241–62.

Karagozoglu, N. and M. Lindell (2000), 'Environmental management: testing the win–win model', *Journal of Environmental Planning and Management*, **43**, 817–29.

Karapetrovic, S. and W. Willborn (1998), 'Integration of quality and environmental management systems', *TQM Magazine*, **10**, 204–13.

Kaynak, H. (2003), 'The relationship between total quality management practices and their effects on firm performance', *Journal of Operations Management*, **21**(4), 405–35.

King, A. and M. Lenox (2002), 'Exploring the locus of profitable pollution reduction', *Management Science*, **48**, 289–99.
Kitazawa, S. and J. Sarkis (2000), 'The relationship between ISO 14001 and continuous source reduction programs', *International Journal of Operations and Production Management*, **20**(2), 225–48.
Klassen, R. and C. McLaughlin (1996), 'The impact of environmental management on firm performance', *Management Science*, **42**, 1199–1214.
Klassen, R. and D. Whybark (1999), 'The impact of environmental technologies on manufacturing performance', *Academy of Management Journal*, **42**, 599–615.
Kleiner, A. (1991), 'What does it mean to be green?', *Harvard Business Review*, **69**(4), 38–47.
Knight, C. (1995), 'Pollution prevention, technology challenges, and competitive advantage in the process industries', *Total Quality Environmental Management*, Autumn, 87–92.
Lai, K. and T. Cheng (2003), 'Initiatives and outcomes of quality management implementation across industries', *Omega*, **31**(2), 141–54.
Marcus, A. and D. Geffen (1998), 'The dialectics of competency acquisition: pollution prevention in electric generation', *Strategic Management Journal*, **19**, 1145–68.
Martínez, A. and M. Martínez (2003), 'Análisis de los posibles efectos de ISO 9000 en los resultados de empresas industriales', paper presented at the XIII annual meeting of ACEDE, Salamanca, Spain.
Melnyk, S., R. Sroufe and R. Calantone (2003), 'Assessing the impact of environmental management systems on corporate and environmental performance', *Journal of Operations Management*, **21**, 329–51.
Merino-Díaz, J. (2003), 'Quality management practices and operational performance: empirical evidence for Spanish industry', *International Journal of Production Research*, **41**(12), 2763–86.
Miles, M. and J. Covin (2000), 'Environmental marketing: a source of reputational, competitive, and financial advantage', *Journal of Business Ethics*, **23**, 299–311.
Najmi, M. and D. Kehoe (2001), 'The role of performance measurement systems in promoting quality development beyond ISO 9000', *International Journal of Operations and Production Management*, **21**(1/2), 159–72.
Nehrt, C. (1996), 'Timing and intensity effects of environmental investments', *Strategic Management Journal*, **17**, 535–47.
Nicolau, J. and R. Sellers (2002), 'The stock market's reaction to quality certification: empirical evidence from Spain', *European Journal of Operational Research*, **142**(3), 632–41.
Porter, M. (1980), *Competitive Strategy*, New York: Free Press.
Porter, M. and C. Van der Linde (1995a), 'Green and competitive: ending the stalemate', *Harvard Business Review*, **73**(5), 120–34.
Porter, M. and C. Van der Linde (1995b), 'Towards a new conception of the environment–competitiveness relationship', *Journal of Economic Perspectives*, **9**(4), 97–118.
Powell, T. (1995), 'Total quality management as competitive advantage: a review and empirical study', *Strategic Management Journal*, **16**(1), 15–37.
Quazi, H., J. Jemangin, L. Kit and C. Kian (1998), 'Critical factors in quality management and guidelines for self-assessment: the case of Singapore', *Total Quality Management*, **9**(1), 35–55.

Rahman, S. (2001), 'A comparative study of TQM practice and organisational performance of SMEs with and without ISO 9000 certification', *International Journal of Quality and Reliability Management*, **18**(1), 35–49.

Rao S., T. Raghunathan and L. Solis (1999), 'The best commonly followed practices in the human resource dimension of quality management in new industrializing countries: the case of China, India and Mexico', *International Journal of Quality and Reliability Management*, **16**(3), 215–25.

Russo, M. and P. Fouts (1997), 'A resource-based perspective on corporate environmental performance and profitability', *Academy of Management Journal*, **40**, 534–59.

Samson, D. and M. Terziovski (1999), 'The relationship between total quality management practices and operational performance', *Journal of Operations Management*, **17**(4), 393–409.

Saraph, J., P. Benson and R. Schroeder (1989), 'An instrument for measuring the critical factors of quality management', *Decision Sciences*, **20**(4), 810–29.

Sarkis, J. (1998), 'Evaluating environmentally conscious business practices', *European Journal of Operational Research*, **107**, 159–74.

Schmidheiny, S. (1992), *Changing Course: A Global Business Perspective on Development and the Environment*, Cambridge, MA: MIT Press.

Sharfman, M., R. Ellington and M. Meo (1997), 'The next step in becoming "green": life-cycle oriented environmental management', *Business Horizons* (May–June), 13–22.

Sharma, S., J. Aragón-Correa and A. Rueda (2003), 'Gestión medioambiental proactiva: validación de un instrumento de medida', paper presented at the 13th annual meeting of ACEDE, Salamanca, Spain.

Sharma, S. and H. Vredenburg (1998), 'Proactive corporate environmental strategy and the development of competitively valuable organizational capabilities', *Strategic Management Journal*, **19**(8), 729–53.

Shrivastava, P. (1995a), 'The role of corporations in achieving ecological sustainability', *Academy of Management Review*, **20**, 936–60.

Shrivastava, P. (1995b), 'Environmental technologies and competitive advantage', *Strategic Management Journal*, **16** (Summer Special Issue), 183–200.

Shrivastava, P. and S. Hart (1994), 'Greening organizations – 2000', *International Journal of Public Administration*, **17**, 607–35.

Singels, J., G. Ruël and H. van de Water (2001), 'ISO 9000 series. Certification and performance', *International Journal of Quality and Reliability Management*, **18**(1), 62–75.

Spector, B. and M. Beer (1994), 'Beyond TQM programmes', *Journal of Organizational Change Management*, **7**(2), 63–70.

Starik, M. and A. Marcus (2000), 'Introduction to the Special Research Forum on the Management of Organizations in the Natural Environment: a field emerging from multiple paths, with many challenges ahead', *Academy of Management Journal*, **43**, 539–46.

Taylor, S. (1992), 'Green management: the next competitive weapon', *Futures*, September, 669–80.

Taylor, W. and G. Wright (2003), 'A longitudinal study of TQM implementation: factors influencing success and failure', *Omega*, **31**(2), 97–111.

Terziovski, M., D. Power and A. Sohal (2003), 'The longitudinal effects of the ISO 9000 certification process on business performance', *European Journal of Operational Research*, **146**(3), 580–95.

Throop, G., M. Starik and G. Rands (1993), 'Sustainable strategy in a greening world: integrating the natural environment into strategic management', *Advances in Strategic Management*, **9**, 63–92.

Tsekouras, K., E. Dimara and D. Skuras (2002), 'Adoption of a quality assurance scheme and its effect on firm performance: a study of Greek firms implementing ISO 9000', *Total Quality Management*, **13**(6), 827–41.

Wagner, M., N. Van Phu, T. Azomahou and W. Wehrmeyer (2002), 'The relationship between the environmental and economic performance of firms: an empirical analysis of the European paper industry', *Corporate Social-Responsibility and Environmental Management*, **9**, 133–46.

Walley, N. and B. Whitehead (1994), 'It's not easy being green', *Harvard Business Review*, **72**(3), 46–52.

Wayhan, V., E. Kirche and B. Khumawala (2002), 'ISO 9000 certification: the financial performance implications', *Total Quality Management*, **13**(2), 217–31.

Wernerfelt, B. (1984), 'A resource-based view of the firm', *Strategic Management Journal*, **5**, 171–80.

Wilkinson, G. and B. Dale (1999), 'Integrated management systems: an examination of the concept and theory', *TQM Magazine*, **11**, 95–104.

Zhang, Z. (2000), 'Developing a model for quality management methods and evaluating their effects on business performance', *Total Quality Management*, **11**(1), 129–37.

9. Competitive effects from eco-manufacturing strategy: influencing factors[1]

Jesús Ángel del Brío, Esteban Fernández and Beatriz Junquera

In the last few years companies have been forced to introduce more and more advanced environmental practices. According to Klassen's (2000a) classification, these practices include the implementation of: (1) pollution-control practices – remediation and end-of-pipe pollution controls; (2) pollution prevention practices – the use of materials, processes or practices that reduce or eliminate the creation of pollutants or waste at source; and (3) management system practices – programmes directed at increasing external stakeholder involvement in operations, formalized procedures for evaluating environmental impact during capital decision-making, employee training for spill prevention and waste reduction, the establishment of an environmental department, and procedures for encouraging cross-functional integration of environmental issues and so on.

These practices contribute to better environmental performance. However firms are increasingly concerned about the possible negative influence of these kinds of practices on their competitiveness (Walley and Whitehead, 1994). In fact companies that are not aware of the competitive advantage they can gain from environmental practices will not be willing to embrace environmental innovation after they have exceeded the levels set by legislation.

However environmental practices do not have to have a negative effect on competitiveness. The implementation of these practices can in fact lead to both negative and positive competitive effects. Maxwell et al.'s work (1997) shows how negative and positive competitive effects meet simultaneously in several companies: Volvo, Polaroid and Procter & Gamble. It shows that environmental pressures can threaten the long-term survival of the companies in question. Nevertheless this chapter does show that if environmental practices are well thought out, they can lead to a number of business advantages, including higher quality, reduced costs, improved environmental image and access to new markets.

Maxwell et al.'s work (1997) is only one example. Environmental practices can have a negative effect on many competitive aspects. However it has now been pointed out that some environmental practices can also lead to: (1) improved environmental performance, and (2) simultaneous improvements in other business performance indicators (process/product/operational innovations, cost reductions, a better corporate image, greater employee motivation and so on). A research stream starts from the assumption that the same environmental practices that internalize the negative environmental effects may simultaneously benefit the company, generating positive effects that are internally and privately accumulated within it. This line includes works from Hart (1995), Porter and van der Linde (1995), Russo and Fouts (1997), Sharma and Vredenburg (1998) and Christmann (2000) to name a few. This is the predominant position among researchers (Russo and Fouts, 1997), following the resource-based view. They follow Hart's argument (1995) that social demands, as part of the business environment, can encourage companies to try to develop unique resources when they expect that it will have a valuable and inimitable effect on their performance. This argument explains why Russo and Fouts (1997) find a positive relationship between environmental performance and competitiveness.

Nevertheless it is not easy to achieve positive competitive effects from environmental practices. A relatively recent approach, which gained in popularity as environmental practices became ever more complex, regards them as being closely linked to decisions that affect other departments, particularly manufacturing, rather than seeing it as being an independent, autonomous field (Porter and van der Linde, 1995). This kind of approach is justified because: (1) manufacturing activities normally have the greatest impact on the natural environment in a company (Klassen and Angell, 1998; Klassen, 2000a); (2) more competitive opportunities can be derived from environmental practices if they are carried out within a comprehensive framework (Angell and Klassen, 1999); and (3) environmental practices lead to greater manufacturing strengths and sustainable competitive advantages (Newman and Hanna, 1996).

The objective of this chapter is to conduct an empirical analysis of the competitive effects that can be derived from environmental practices and the conditions that determine the nature of these competitive effects. We will consider the strategic integration of environmental practices, particularly the role of manufacturing strategy. The main focus of this chapter will be to throw some light on the factors that make it possible to gain competitive advantages from environmental practices. Likewise, future research will be based on the negative competitive effects that come from environmental practices and how these are produced. This research will be used to find solutions to these losses in competitiveness. A sample of ISO 14001-certified industrial factories in Spain will be analysed.

BACKGROUND AND HYPOTHESIS FORMULATION

The theoretical model presented in Figure 9.1 represents a central argument that the organization as a whole is responsible for competitive effects derived from the environmental practices of a company: (1) environmental situation and objectives influence competitive effects from environmental practices; and (2) decisions that affect other departments, particularly manufacturing, likewise influence competitive effects from environmental practices.

Positive and negative competitive effects are brought about through environmental practices, and we have made a thorough review of the literature to find the most relevant examples. On the one hand, the literature agrees almost unanimously that firms with different environmental objectives and qualitatively different environmental performance differ in the effects of environmental practices on competitiveness (Hart, 1995; Russo and Fouts, 1997; Angell and Klassen, 1999; Handfield et al., 2001). In the same way, the literature acknowledges that the approach of manufacturing strategy and the strategic integration of environmental practices influence their competitive effects (Newman and Hanna, 1996; Klassen and Angell, 1998; Angell and Klassen, 1999; Klassen, 2000a). In this chapter, we analyse how these factors influence competitive effects brought about by environmental practices. Based on the analysis of the available literature, the following hypotheses have been deduced and are then subjected to empirical contrast.

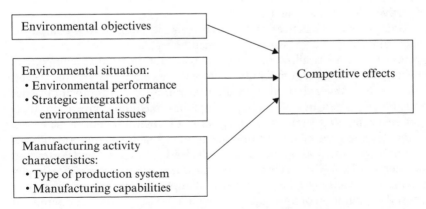

Figure 9.1   Theoretical model: eco-manufacturing strategy

The Company's Environmental Objective

The environmental objective is not one-dimensional (Dooley and Fryxell, 1999). The first dimension of the environmental objective is always to comply with environmental legislation. Brío et al. (2002) find that environmental legislation is particularly effective in the first stages of environmental concern. Second, incident prevention is also an environmental objective. Companies differ depending on the environmental issues they deal with (their probability of causing environmental damage and the seriousness of that damage). However these differences include not only those influenced by the natural environment, but also those resulting from the social environment in which the company operates. So the public's reaction to environmental damage is often shaped more by the public's perceptions of the facts than the facts themselves (Juhasz et al., 1993). This difference explains much of the debate that takes place between managers and engineers and the rest of the population after incidents that have damaged the natural environment. The 'experts' and the public often perceive and evaluate the same facts differently because their knowledge of the facts, perceptions of damage and 'social' environments are different. So a third environmental objective is to avoid damage to the corporate image. Natural environment protection, despite other business priorities, also forms an additional dimension of environmental objectives: corporate citizenship (Marsden and Andriof, 1997). Another dimension of the environmental objective relates to the consequences on internal operations of the company (integration of environmental issues), including the materials, technologies and human resources used in the production systems. Market requirements derived from consumers lead to a new dimension of the environmental objective: 'green products' (Chen, 2001). Another dimension of the environmental objective is 'environmental leadership'.

Some of these objectives only intend to avoid damage to a company's image and the problems with environmental regulators. However another group of objectives allow the companies to obtain positive competitive effects from their environmental practices (Newman and Hanna, 1996). These include those derived from the integration of environmental issues and the characteristics of leading companies, including 'green' products and environmental leadership. Integration of environmental issues leads to the development of unique organizational capabilities that are difficult to imitate (Grant, 1991), and, as a result, leads to innovation (Porter and van der Linde, 1995). Trying to introduce new environmentally friendly products or changes to the environmental impact of existing products may boost the reputation of an organization (Gilley et al., 2000). Environmental leading companies can also improve their innovative capabilities because of first-mover advantages (Nehrt, 1996). As a result, factories with more advanced environmental objectives may achieve a better corporate image and more innovation from their environmental practices. The following hypothesis has therefore been put forward:

Hypothesis 1. Only factories that have prioritized advanced environmental objectives achieve more positive competitive effects (better image and more innovation) from their environmental practices.

Environmental Performance and Strategic Integration

Ilinitch et al. (1998) show how environmental performance is multidimensional. They identify four conceptual dimensions of corporate environmental performance: (1) organizational systems – organizational processes, including environmental audit programmes, environmental mission statements and so on; (2) stakeholder relations – the interaction between the company and its various external constituencies; (3) regulatory compliance – the degree to which companies meet legislation; and (4) environmental impact or environmental efficiency – negative economic and environmental externalities generated in business. Some papers point out that negative competitive effects occur when environmental performance improves. For example it may lead to higher costs (Brennan et al., 1994; Das et al., 2000). Likewise, the quality of some products sometimes suffers, at least during the first stage of the implementation of environmental practices (Carnahan and Thurston, 1998). Nevertheless other papers have suggested that certain environmental performance dimensions can generate positive competitive effects (Aragón-Correa and Sharma, 2003). For example product quality may increase as a result of ecological considerations being applied to their design (Brennan et al., 1994). In short, the main aim of some environmental practices is to improve environmental performance only as regards legislation compliance. They prevent waste and emissions (already produced) from generating negative effects on the natural environment. This is achieved thanks to specialist technologies to fight pollution (usually quite expensive and unproductive, because they do not generate value) (Andersson and Wolff, 1996). These approaches are therefore a constraint for a company (Angell and Klassen, 1999), so their influence on competitiveness is negative: they reduce the company's innovative capability (Porter and van der Linde, 1995). Nevertheless when the main aim of environmental practices in a factory is to avoid the production of this kind of waste and emissions – environmental impact decrease or improved environmental efficiency – consumers may perceive their products as being of a higher quality and of better corporate image. Simultaneously they may lead a company to product innovation and to new market penetration (Azzone and Noci, 1998). As a result, more environmental efficiency leads to higher quality, corporate image improvement, more innovation and new market penetration. We have therefore put forward the following two hypotheses regarding environmental performance:

Hypothesis 2a. Improved environmental performance in terms of legislation compliance leads to negative competitive effects (innovation decrease).

Hypothesis 2b. Leadership in the most advanced dimensions of environmental performance (environmental efficiency) leads to positive competitive effects (higher quality, image improvement and more innovation).

A firm can respond in various ways to any individual issue, but it would seem that a coordinated, company-wide approach is called for, since avoiding one environmental problem can be enough to seriously hurt a whole company (Corbett and Wassenhove, 1993). Banerjee (2001) distinguishes four levels of strategic integration of environmental issues. The first level (enterprise strategy) examines the role played by the company within society and describes its basic mission. In environmental terms, protection should be the fundamental mission to be integrated at this level. The second level (corporate strategy) determines the type of business a company should become involved in to achieve the aims of its business strategy. Decisions about products, technological development and the company's business portfolio are taken at this level. From an environmental perspective, it would include everything related to developing markets and green products, cleaner technologies and integrating green business portfolios. The third level (competitive strategy) includes locating additional organizational resources to achieve competitive advantage and integrating different business functions. In terms of environmental protection, the use of recycled materials could be a viable environmental competitive strategy. The fourth level (functional strategy) involves planning operative procedures for different functions such as marketing, manufacturing and R&D. 'Green' marketing practices and design-for-environment (DfE) are only two examples from an environmental point of view.

In general, integrating the natural environment into competitive strategy and into manufacturing strategy also enables companies to improve environmental performance. This has been suggested by Hart (1995) and Burgos and Céspedes (2001), and found empirically by Florida (1996), Newman and Hanna (1996) and Angell and Klassen (1999). Integrating environmental practices into competitive strategy and manufacturing strategy likewise leads to positive competitive effects because of socially complex environmental skills derived from environmental practices (Hart, 1995). A lot of competitive effects are derived from knowledge-based capabilities. Sometimes synergies develop between different types of capabilities, synergies that develop better when they are joined together (Langlois and Robertson, 1995). This can also take place between environmental capabilities and other capabilities in the company. This means that the strategic integration of environmental practices can make it easier to allocate the necessary resources for sustainable development more quickly than other companies that do not have this capability. Sroufe et al. (2000) find that formal and cross-functional integration of environmental practices makes product innovation easier. In short, the strategic integration of environmental issues may lead to innovation. We can therefore derive the following hypothesis:

Hypothesis 3. The strategic integration of environmental practices allows a factory to achieve more positive competitive effects from its environmental practices, particularly innovation.

Manufacturing Characteristics

Literature has revealed that different types of production systems have different requirements for environmental practices. Newman and Hanna (1996) recognize that different production systems – dedicated and general purpose processes – have different environmental order-winning criteria.[2] They also point out that in different ways, both kinds of production systems can lead to a beneficial environmental position, and in all of them the most advanced environmental practices can lead to positive competitive effects. The just-in-time production system, in particular, has been acknowledged to have distinct complementarities with the most advanced environmental actions: some empirical papers have found synergies between some lean and environmental practices (King and Lenox, 2001; Rothenberg et al., 2001). The just-in-time production system is enabled by, and helps to develop, process improvement capabilities (Womack et al., 1990). Lower inventory levels require workers to be more cognizant of change in the production process (MacDuffie, 1995). Once workers have developed such awareness, teaching them additional related skills may be more innovative. This means that innovative capabilities may improve when new environmental practices are implemented in just-in-time factories. The following hypothesis has therefore been put forward:

Hypothesis 4. Just-in-time factories lead to more positive competitive effects from their environmental practices, particularly innovation.

The traditional strategic school of thought considers that classic manufacturing objectives are incompatible (trade-offs)[3] with environmental objectives (Azzone and Noci, 1998; Das et al., 2000; Guide, 2000; Kitazawa and Sarkis, 2000; Klassen, 2000a). However these trade-offs have varied through time (Skinner, 1996). Moreover displacing the production frontier towards the right (by modifying technologies) means that several objectives can be targeted at one and the same time (Clark, 1996). Something similar occurs in the relationship between manufacturing objectives and environmental performance (Florida, 1996; Curkovic et al., 2000; Hanna et al., 2000; Theyel, 2000). In this way, different environmental and manufacturing objectives can improve at the same time (Porter and van der Linde, 1995; Shrivastava, 1995; Klassen and Angell, 1998; Angell and Klassen 1999; Klassen, 2000b). For example several authors show that experience in quality provides synergies with environmental issues (Kitazawa and Sarkis, 2000; Klassen, 2000a). Klassen and Angell (1998) suggest that manufacturing flexibility, by enabling efficient adaptation to change and uncertainty, can support environmental practices. Tu et al. (2001) find that product customization supports innovation. There are therefore synergies between environmental and classic manufacturing objectives.

Following Penrose's (1959) arguments, manufacturing objectives in which the company takes competitive advantage over its competitors are called manufacturing capabilities.[4] Manufacturing capabilities constitute a great competitive strength, since as they develop slowly they cannot be changed quickly, and as a result they are difficult to imitate (Levinthal and March, 1993). In Mahoney and Pandian's terminology (1992), idiosyncratic bilateral synergies are generated. Manufacturing capabilities are knowledge based, so their historical development allows them to accumulate more resources if their initial stock is greater (mass efficiencies) (Dierickx and Cool, 1989). The greater the mass efficiencies, the greater the company's ability to generate new knowledge, taking advantage of the synergies from different kinds of capabilities (Kogut and Zander, 1992). New knowledge is able to displace the production frontier upward. This displacement of the production frontier may lead to better environmental performance and to positive competitive effects. As a result, as manufacturing capabilities are accumulated by a firm, positive competitive effects from environmental practices are easier to achieve. The following hypotheses are therefore put forward:

Hypothesis 5a. Manufacturing capabilities for quality lead to positive competitive effects (improvement of product and corporate image, product quality and relationships with internal and external stakeholders) as a consequence of the implementation of environmental practices.

Hypothesis 5b. Manufacturing capabilities for flexibility reduce costs as a consequence of the implementation of environmental practices.

Hypothesis 5c. Manufacturing capabilities for product customization improve factories' innovative capability as a consequence of the implementation of environmental practices.

RESEARCH METHODOLOGY

Sample

For the purposes of the study, all factories with International Standard Organization 14001 (ISO 14001) or Eco-Management and Audit Scheme (EMAS) registration (or both) dedicated to industrial activities were taken as the study population (those whose main activity was identified in the category of services were therefore excluded).

We then contacted the certification agencies – Asociación Española de Normalización y Certificación (AENOR), Laboratori General D'Assaigs i Investigació (LGAI), Bureau Veritas Quality International (BVQI), Det Norske Veritas (DNV), Entidad de Certificación y Aseguramiento, S.A. (ECA), Systems and Services Certification-International Certification Services (SGS-ICS), Lloyd's, Cámara de Madrid and Instituto Valenciano de Certificación (IVAC) – and we created a database including all the factories that were certified as of April 2003. Our database was completed with information (with respect to activity, location, telephone number, fax, email, employees and turnover) taken from the Dun & Bradstreet electronic database, from the factories' websites and from telephone calls.

The initial database included a total of 1542 factories. Seventy-four of them decided not to participate from the very beginning, which gave us a total of 1468 factories. We later eliminated the services factories, given that the questionnaire did not fit their circumstances. This left us with a total of 1023 remaining factories that were eligible to carry out the study. The questionnaires were sent out and received between the months of June and September 2003. The final design of the questionnaire covered: (1) general aspects, (2) environmental objectives and performance, (3) manufacturing capabilities, and (4) competitive effects.

During the design phase of the questionnaire, a series of different actions supported the validity of the instrument and the items included in it. First of all, we undertook a comprehensive review of the literature. We also took advantage of the accumulated experience in a previous case analysis when developing the approach to the work and in elaborating the questionnaire.

A third action was based on the precision used in defining the questionnaire items, which enables us to reduce ambiguity. Once the questionnaire was drafted, it underwent a pretest phase, during which we conducted personal interviews with three people who were in charge of the environmental department at different certified plants. Their suggestions enabled us to decrease further the ambiguity of the questions and their interpretation.

We should also point out that the letter asked that the person most closely involved in environmental issues be the one to answer the questionnaire. Although possible job titles were proposed, it was added that any other person the company felt was best informed with respect to these issues should be the one to complete the questionnaire. A letter that offered an in-depth explanation of the reasons for performing the study and its objectives accompanied the questionnaire.

One hundred and twenty-three valid questionnaires were received, representing a 12.02 per cent[5] response rate. The sample representativity and distribution of the factories by sectors and sizes can be seen in Table 9.1. The average size of the factories was approximately 789 workers.

Table 9.1   Comparison of sample distribution and population by size and by sectors

	Size				
	Population			Sample	
Workers	Number	%		Number	%
0–249	687	67.16		79	64.75
250–499	141	13.78		15	12.3
500–999	98	9.58		15	12.3
More than 1,000	97	9.48	13	10.65	

	Industrial Sector				
	Population			Sample	
Sector	Number	%		Number	%
Food	104	10.17		12	9.8
Chemical	233	22.78		36	29.5
Energy	42	4.11		6	4.9
Construction	147	14.37		14	11.5
Automotion	103	10.07		12	9.8
Electronics	114	11.14		12	9.8
Materials	162	15.83		17	13.9
Machinery	118	11.53		13	10.7

Table 9.2   Logistic regression for sample representativeness

Variables	B	Degrees of freedom	Signification
Sector equation			
Chemical	1.540	1	0.215
Energy	0.222	1	0.638
Construction	0.025	1	0.873
Automotion	0.829	1	0.362
Electronics	0.376	1	0.540
Materials	0.541	1	0.462
Machinery	0.786	1	0.375
Size equation			
Size	1.941	1	0.164

Two logit analyses were performed following Osterman's method (1994) in order to evaluate the sample representativity more reliably than a mere description. The dependent variable in both cases was the probability of response. The independent variables were, in the first case, factory size (as measured by the number of employees) and, in the second case, sector (as measured by means of as many dummy variables as the number of sectors minus one, which has been used as the basis for the study).[6] The results confirmed the lack of signification, since none of the independent variables – the number of workers in the first analysis or the dummy variables representative of the industrial sector in the case of the second analysis (Table 9.2 shows that none of the variables is introduced in the equation) – fit the equation. Therefore the aforementioned results confirm the lack of sample bias based on these variables.[7]

Measures

We now present the measures used in the study. Following recommendations by Malhotra and Grover (1998) internal consistency (or reliability) of the items has initially been carried out for each case through assessment of Cronbach's Alpha. Factor analysis using items from multiple measures in the research model has been used to establish construct validity.

Importance of the environmental objective in recent years
We used the construct developed by Vastag et al. (1996) for environmental objectives in a company. However we thought that this construct was

Table 9.3   Factor loadings of traditional environmental objectives in recent years

Items	TRADOBJ
Legislation compliance	0.853
Incident prevention	0.888
To avoid damage to corporate image	0.719
Cronbach's Alpha	0.761
Eigenvalue	2.034
Percentage of variance explained	67.80

Table 9.4   Factor loadings of advanced environmental objectives in recent years

Items	ADVOBJ
Corporate citizenship	0.678
Integration of environmental issues	0.783
'Green' products	0.747
Environmental leadership	0.792
Cronbach's Alpha	0.768
Eigenvalue	2.259
Percentage of variance explained	56.481

incomplete at the present time, so we added some additional items and rated each of them on a five-point scale: 1 if the objective was considered of little importance and 5 if it was considered of great importance. We looked at two dimensions of the environmental objective: (1) traditional objectives – legislation compliance, incident prevention and to avoid damage to corporate image – (*TRADOBJ*), and (2) advanced objectives – corporate citizenship, integration of environmental issues, 'green' products and environmental leadership – (*ADVOBJ*). Internal consistency of the answers was examined by Cronbach's Alpha. Construct validity was tested by factor analysis. Both factor analyses revealed that both constructs were a measure of a single variable. Tables 9.3 and 9.4 show the main results.

Strategic integration of the environmental practices
Respondents were asked to choose the answer that best fitted the situation of their factory from among the proposals elaborated by Newman and

Hanna (1996): (1) environmental reactors, (2) environmental benchmarkers, (3) environmental integrators, and (4) environmental innovators.[8] We then elaborated a dyadic variable, with a value of 0 if the factories were identified as being in one of the first two stages (low degree of integration) and 1 if it was considered to be in one of the last two stages (high level of integration) (*BENCH*). Unlike the other companies, this last group integrates environmental practices with those of other functions in the company.

Environmental performance
As environmental performance is multidimensional, we built constructs based on Ilinitch et al.'s (1998) paper. Nevertheless North American and Spanish public policies are different. So we also considered Aragón-Correa's work (1998) and we modified the construct according to this idea. As a result, we looked at four dimensions of environmental performance: (1) organizational systems – written environmental policy, top management committee responsibility, management incentives, information from top management, personnel assigned at least half-time and environmental audit – (*PERORSY*), (2) stakeholder relations – total quality environmental management (TQEM), active environmentalist stakeholders, Design for Environment (DfE), Coalition of Environmentally Responsible Economies (CERES), voluntary industry principles and communication of public investments and expenditures – (*PERSKRL*), (3) legislation compliance – environmental fines and environmental proceedings against the company – (*PERENVCOM*), and (4) economic and environmental impact (environmental efficiency) – waste, spills and emissions, insurance expenditures, legal expenses and standard compliance – (*PERENVEFF*). For each dimension, a five-point scale was used: 1 if the issue considered was much worse in the factory analysed than in its competitors and 5 if it was much better. Internal consistency of the answers was examined by Cronbach's Alpha. Construct validity was tested by factor analysis. Four factor analyses – one for each dimension considered part of the environmental performance – revealed that each construct was a measure of a single variable. Tables 9.5, 9.6, 9.7 and 9.8 show the main results.

Type of production system
The questionnaire included a question that asked the respondents to choose the type of production system that best described their factory from amongst the following choices: unit project production system, workshop, batches, mass, just-in-time and continuous production system. We created a total of five dummy variables (as many as the types of production systems listed minus one, which was taken as the basis for analysis: the continuous production system).

Table 9.5   Factor loadings of organizational systems as measures of environmental performance

Items	PERORSY
Written environmental policy	0.802
Top management committee responsibility	0.896
Management incentives	0.517
Information from top management	0.887
Personnel assigned at least half-time	0.775
Environmental audit	0.855
Cronbach's Alpha	0.881
Eigenvalue	3.833
Percentage of variance explained	63.88

Table 9.6   Factor loadings of stakeholder relations as a measure of environmental performance

Items	PERSKRL
TQEM	0.666
Active environmentalist stakeholders	0.449
DfE	0.609
CERES	0.609
Voluntary industry principles	0.546
Communication of public investments and expenditures	0.484
Cronbach's Alpha	0.861
Eigenvalue	3.363
Percentage of variance explained	56.058

Table 9.7   Factor loadings of environmental efficiency as a measure of environmental performance

Items	PERENVEFF
Waste, spills and emissions	0.563
Insurance expenditures	0.687
Legal expenses	0.743
Standard compliance	0.704
Cronbach's Alpha	0.839
Eigenvalue	2.698
Percentage of variance explained	67.451

Table 9.8 *Factor loadings of legislation compliance as a measure of environmental performance*

Items	PERENVCOM
Environmental fines	0.965
Environmental proceedings against the company	0.965
Cronbach's Alpha	0.974
Eigenvalue	1.930
Percentage of variance explained	96.514

Manufacturing capabilities

We developed constructs based on works by Kim and Arnold (1996), Vastag et al. (1996), Das et al. (2000) and Baldwin and Lin (2002). We looked at five manufacturing capabilities: (1) quality – customer service, rate of defects, functional quality, duration and reliability, correct manufacturing and reliable delivery – (*MCQUALITY*), (2) flexibility – design flexibility, volume flexibility, mix flexibility and broad product line – (*MCFLEX*), (3) efficiency – manufacturing cost, work productivity, use of machinery and level of inventories – (*MCEFF*), (4) lead time – process implementation time, operation time and lead time – (*MCLEADT*), and (5) product customization – after-sales service, customization, client retention, safety report and new product cycle – (*MCCUSTOM*). For each dimension, a five-point scale was used: 1 if the issue considered was much worse in the factory analysed than in its competitors, and 5 if it was much better. Internal consistency of the answers was examined by Cronbach's Alpha. Construct validity was tested by factor analysis. Five factor analyses – one for each dimension of the manufacturing capabilities – revealed that each construct was a measure of a single variable. Tables 9.9, 9.10, 9.11, 9.12 and 9.13 show the main results.

Competitive effects

We developed constructs based on works by Sharma and Vredenburg (1998), Hanna et al. (2000), Baldwin and Lin (2002), Rao (2002) and Melnyk et al. (2003). We looked at three competitive effects: (1) quality, image and relationships with internal and external stakeholders – product quality, market share, employee morale, working conditions, workers' skills, consumer satisfaction, product image, corporate image and relations with ecologists and environmental regulators – (*CEQUALITY*), (2) innovation and growth – process innovations, product innovations and penetration in international markets – (*CEINNGR*), and (3) efficiency – consumption of

Table 9.9   Factor loadings of quality as a measure of manufacturing capabilities

Items	MCQUALITY
Customer service	0.568
Rate of defects	0.836
Functional quality	0.846
Duration and reliability	0.880
Correct manufacturing	0.866
Reliable delivery	0.687
Cronbach's Alpha	0.878
Eigenvalue	3.731
Percentage of variance explained	62.19

Table 9.10   Factor loadings of flexibility as a measure of manufacturing capabilities

Items	MCFLEX
Design flexibility	0.871
Volume flexibility	0.873
Mix flexibility	0.864
Broad product line	0.791
Cronbach's Alpha	0.874
Eigenvalue	2.894
Percentage of variance explained	72.35

Table 9.11   Factor loadings of efficiency as a measure of manufacturing capabilities

Items	MCEFF
Manufacturing cost	0.781
Work productivity	0.786
Use of machinery	0.877
Level of inventories	0.697
Cronbach's Alpha	0.800
Eigenvalue	2.481
Percentage of variance explained	62.03

Table 9.12   Factor loadings of lead time as a measure of manufacturing capabilities

Items	MCLEADT
Process implementation time	0.930
Operation time	0.917
Lead time	0.704
Cronbach's Alpha	0.820
Eigenvalue	2.202
Percentage of variance explained	73.39

Table 9.13   Factor loadings of product customization as a measure of manufacturing capabilities

Items	MCCUSTOM
After sales service	0.816
Customization	0.725
Client retention	0.813
Safety report	0.684
New product cycle	0.772
Cronbach's Alpha	0.824
Eigenvalue	2.916
Percentage of variance explained	58.322

raw materials and use of equipment – (*CEEFF*). For each dimension, a five-point scale was used: 1 if with regard to the question considered, the company's environmental practices had got worse, and 5 if they had got better.[9] Internal consistency of the answers was examined by Cronbach's Alpha. Construct validity was tested by factor analyses. Three factor analyses – one for each competitive effect considered – revealed that each construct was a measure of a single variable. Tables 9.14, 9.15 and 9.16 show the main results.

RESULTS AND DISCUSSION

We will now present the results of our empirical work along with a discussion of the results. Table 9.17 summarizes the main results. Regression models were tested according to the hypotheses presented above.

Table 9.14   Factor loadings of quality, image and external–internal stakeholder relations as measures of competitive effects

Items	CEQUALITY
Product quality	0.697
Market share	0.642
Employee morale	0.705
Working conditions	0.793
Workers' skills	0.744
Consumer satisfaction	0.805
Product image	0.842
Corporate image	0.833
Relations with ecologists and environmental regulators	0.747
Cronbach's Alpha	0.907
Eigenvalue	5.188
Percentage of variance explained	57.64

Table 9.15   Factor loadings of innovation and growth as measures of competitive effects

Items	CEINNGR
Process innovations	0.898
Product innovations	0.896
Penetration in international markets	0.823
Cronbach's Alpha	0.854
Eigenvalue	2.285
Percentage of variance explained	76.18

Table 9.16   Factor loadings of efficiency as measures of competitive effects

Items	CEEFF
Consumption of raw materials	*0.854*
Use of equipment	*0.854*
Cronbach's Alpha	0.642
Eigenvalue	1.458
Percentage of variance explained	72.877

Table 9.17   *Summary of main results*

Dependent variables	Significative independent variables	Explained variance (%)
Quality, image, and relation with external and internal stakeholders	Positive competitive effects:	
	● Advanced environmental objectives	19.9
	● Environmental efficiency	5.4
	● Manufacturing capabilities for quality	14.4
Innovation and international growth	Positive competitive effects:	
	● Advanced environmental objectives	17.1
	● Strategic integration of environmental issues	3.9
	● Environmental efficiency	2.4
	● Just-in-time production system	2.3
	● Manufacturing capabilities for product customization	11.6
	Negative competitive effects:	
	● Legislation compliance	3.8
Efficiency	Positive competitive effects:	
	● Manufacturing capabilities for manufacturing flexibility	6.5

Influence of the Environmental Objective

The approach with respect to environmental objectives influences competitive effects (Table 9.18). The relationships were found to be statistically significant at $p < 0.0001$. Advanced environmental objectives of the companies appeared to explain around 20 per cent of the improvement of quality, corporate image and the companies' relations with internal and external stakeholders from environmental practices and around 18 per cent of the improvement of innovation and international market penetration. Hypothesis 1 was therefore validated.

Influence of the Environmental Performance and its Strategic Integration

The influence of the various dimensions of environmental performance is shown in Table 9.19. All of the relationships were found to be statistically significant at $p < 0.05$. The level of environmental efficiency with regard to competitors appeared to explain around 6 per cent of the improvement of quality, corporate image and the companies' relations with internal and

Table 9.18   Regression equations: influence of the environmental objective

Variables	Unstd b	Beta (B)	t-value	p (one-tailed)
Dependent variable: CEQUALITY				
ADVOBJ	0.453	0.453	5.595	0.000
	(0.081)			
Constant	$-1.661*10^{-18}$		0.000	1.000
	(0.081)			
R^2	0.206			
Adjusted R^2	0.199			
F-statistic	31.302			
Probability of F	0.000			
N	123			
Dependent variable: CEINNGR				
ADVOBJ	0.422	0.422	5.117	0.000
	(0.082)			
Constant	$-8.34*10^{-17}$		0.000	1.000
	(0.082)			
R^2	0.178			
Adjusted R^2	0.171			
F-statistic	26.181			
Probability of F	0.000			
N	123			

external stakeholders from environmental practices and around 3 per cent of the improvement of innovation and international market penetration. Hypothesis 2b was therefore validated.

The level of legislation compliance regarding competitors appeared to explain around 4 per cent of the decrease in innovation and international market penetration as a consequence of environmental practices. Hypothesis 2a was therefore validated.

The strategic integration of environmental issues appeared to explain around 4 per cent of the improvement of innovation and international market penetration as a consequence of environmental practices. Hypothesis 3 was therefore validated.

Influence of Manufacturing Characteristics and Capabilities

The influence of the various manufacturing characteristics is shown in Table 9.20. All of the relationships were found to be statistically significant at $p < 0.05$. The just-in-time production system appeared to explain around

*Table 9.19   Regression equations: environmental performance and
integration into manufacturing strategy*

Variables	Unstd b	Beta (B)	t-value	p (one-tailed)
Dependent variable: CEQUALITY				
PERENVEFF	0.249	0.249	2.831	0.005
	(0.088)			
Constant	$6.046*10^{-18}$		0.000	1.000
	(0.088)			
R^2	0.062			
Adjusted R^2	0.054			
F-statistic	8.014			
Probability of F	0.005			
N	123			
Dependent variable: CEINNGR*				
PERENVCOM	−0.280	−0.280	−3.137	0.002
	(0.089)			
BENCH	0.399	0.200	2.315	0.022
	(0.172)			
PERENVEFF	0.183	0.183	2.041	0.043
	(0.089)			
Constant	−0.195		−1.623	0.107
	(0.120)			
R^2	0.123			
Adjusted R^2	0.101			
F-statistic	5.576			
Probability of F	0.001			
N	123			

Notes: * Data diagnostics tests for collinearity indicated no violations of this regression assumption in Tables 9.19 and 9.20.

3 per cent of the improvement of innovation and international market penetration. Hypothesis 4 was therefore validated.

Manufacturing capabilities for quality appeared to explain around 15 per cent of the improvement of quality, corporate image and the companies' relations with internal and external stakeholders from environmental practices. Manufacturing capabilities for product customization appeared to explain around 12 per cent of the improvement of innovation and international market penetration. Manufacturing capabilities for manufacturing flexibility appeared to explain around 7 per cent of the improvement of process efficiency from environmental practices. Hypotheses 5a, 5b and 5c were therefore validated.

Table 9.20   Regression equations: manufacturing capabilities and production system characteristics

Variables	Unstd b	Beta (B)	t-value	p (one-tailed)
Dependent variable: CEQUALITY				
MCQUALITY	0.391	0.389	4.592	0.000
	(0.085)			
Constant	−0.018		−0.210	0.834
	(0.084)			
R^2	0.152			
Adjusted R^2	0.144			
F-statistic	21.090			
Probability of F	0.000			
N	123			
Dependent variable: CEINNGR				
MCCUSTOM	0.339	0.342	4.007	0.000
	(0.085)			
JIT	0.469	0.172	2.015	0.046
	(0.233)			
Constant	−0.105		−1.164	0.247
	(0.090)			
R^2	0.153			
Adjusted R^2	0.139			
F-statistic	10.573			
Probability of F	0.000			
N	123			
Dependent variable: CEEFF				
MCFLEX	−0.269	−0.270	−3.041	0.003
	(0.088)			
Constant	−0.002		−0.025	0.980
	(0.087)			
R^2	0.073			
Adjusted R^2	0.065			
F-statistic	9.245			
Probability of F	0.003			
N	123			

CONCLUSIONS AND FUTURE RESEARCH

Previous works have enabled us to conclude that different kinds of factors condition the positive and/or negative competitive effects derived from environmental practices. However none of these works has so far examined the type of competitive effects, or to what degree each factor in fact exerted its influence. This is the objective of the present study of a group of Spanish ISO 14001-certified factories.

This chapter addresses the debate regarding the role of environmental practices in competitiveness. The main conclusion is that environmental practices may lead to positive competitive effects in several circumstances. We have found some of them. Corporate and product image, relationships with external and internal stakeholders and product quality improve as a consequence of the implementation of environmental practices in factories: (1) with advanced environmental objectives, (2) that are leaders in environmental efficiency, and (3) with manufacturing capabilities for quality. Innovation and international growth improve as a consequence of the implementation of environmental practices in factories: (1) with advanced environmental objectives, (2) with strategically integrated environmental issues, (3) that are leaders in environmental efficiency, (4) with the just-in-time production system, and (5) with manufacturing capabilities for product customization. Nevertheless innovation and international growth worsen in leading factories in legislation compliance. Finally, efficiency improves in factories with manufacturing capabilities for manufacturing flexibility.

However a lot still remains to be done. Among other issues, we are a long way from fully accounting for the variance of this diversity of potential organizational effects that arise as a consequence of environmental practices. The kind of environmental leadership and top management perceptions of environmental practices (a constraint versus an opportunity) may influence their competitive effects. Environmental organizational peculiarities (organizational culture and environmental human resource policies) can likewise affect competitive effects from environmental practices. Several manufacturing decisions (supplier relationships, quality and organization of innovative activities in the factory) may also influence competitive effects from environmental practices. All of them will be the main aim of our future research. In this work we have only studied the situation as it stands in certified factories, which naturally leads to limitations. These include differences due to the bias typical in this population, in favour of large size. Other limitations are likewise a consequence of the better environmental development in certified companies. We will be dealing with all of these concerns in future studies.

NOTES

1. This work has been financed by the Spanish Ministerio de Ciencia y Tecnología (SEC2003-05238).

2. Reasons why a customer purchases from a particular manufacturer.
3. The traditional research stream of strategic management argues that classic manufacturing objectives are incompatible. Such claims are based on the concept of trade-off (Skinner, 1969) whereby any facility that has a production system conforming to the production frontier is incapable of simultaneously improving two or more objectives, so it must therefore prioritize one of them.
4. Also manufacturing competencies (Hayes and Wheelwright, 1979).
5. Before sending out the questionnaire, we phoned the person in charge of environmental issues to inform them that they would be receiving it shortly. In addition, this letter also stated the firm commitment to continue sending information of interest regarding issues related to the factory's environmental practices. At the same time as the questionnaire was sent out, two additional documents were provided to the respondents. Finally, we made a commitment to the factories that participated in the study to send them the report containing the global results of this study. We used all of these incentives in an attempt to improve the response rate, which tends to be rather low when conducting studies in Spanish factories, especially if the studies concern the analysis of environmental issues (Brío et al., 2002).
6. The food industry was taken as a basis. If any of the other variables representative of the different sectors was representative, it would mean that the probability of companies from that sector responding is significantly different from that of companies in the food industry.
7. This allowed us to support the study's external validity.
8. The questionnaire included a detailed description of each one in accordance with the characteristics assigned by Newman and Hanna (1996) for each of the stages.
9. Except for the items that appear in italics in Table 9.16, which are interpreted in the opposite sense.

REFERENCES

Andersson, Tommy and Rolf Wolff (1996), 'Ecology as a challenge for management research', *Scandinavian Journal of Management*, **12**, 223–31.
Angell, Linda C. and Ronald D. Klassen (1999), 'Integrating environmental issues into the mainstream: an agenda for research in operations management', *Journal of Operations Management*, **11**, 63–76.
Aragón-Correa, Juan A. (1998), 'Strategic proactivity and firm approach to the natural environment', *Academy of Management Journal*, **41**, 556–67.
Aragón-Correa, Juan A. and Sanjay Sharma (2003), 'A contingent resource-based view of proactive corporate environmental strategy', *Academy of Management Review*, **28**, 71–88.
Azzone, Giovanni and Giuliano Noci (1998), 'Seeing ecology and "green" innovations as a source of chance', *Journal of Organizational Change Management*, **11**, 94–111.
Baldwin, John and Zhengxi Lin (2002), 'Impediments to advanced technology adoption for Canadian manufacturers', *Research Policy*, **31**, 1–18.
Banerjee, Subhrabrata B. (2001), 'Managerial perceptions of corporate environmentalism: Interpretations from industry and strategic implications for organizations', *Journal of Management Studies*, **38**, 489–513.
Brennan, Louis, Surendra M. Gupta and Karim N. Taleb (1994), 'Operations planning issues in an assembly/disassembly environment', *International Journal of Operations and Production Management*, **14**, 57–67.

Brío, Jesús A. del, Esteban Fernández and Beatriz Junquera (2002), 'The role of the Environmental regulators in the promotion of the environmental activity in Spanish industrial companies', *Ecological Economics*, **40**, 279–94.

Burgos, Jerónimo de and José Céspedes (2001), 'Environmental performance as an operations perspective', *International Journal of Operations and Production Management*, **21**, 1553–72.

Carnahan, James and Deborah Thurston (1998), 'Trade-off modelling for product and manufacturing product design for the environment', *Journal of Industrial Ecology*, **2**, 79–92.

Chen, Chialin (2001), 'Design for the environment: a quality-based model for green product development', *Management Science*, **47**, 250–63.

Christmann, Petra (2000), 'Effects of the "best practices" of environmental management on cost advantage: the role of complementary assets', *Academy of Management Journal*, **43**, 663–80.

Clark, Kim B. (1996), 'Competing through manufacturing and the new manufacturing paradigm: Is manufacturing strategy passé?', *Production and Operations Management*, **5**, 42–57.

Corbett, Charles J. and Luk N. Van Wassenhove (1993), 'The green fee: internalizing and operationalizing environmental issues', *California Management Review*, **35**, 116–35.

Curkovic, Sime, Steve A. Melnyk, Robert B. Handfield and Roger Calantone (2000), 'Investigating the linkage between TQM and environmentally responsible manufacturing', *IEEE Transactions on Engineering Management*, **47**, 444–64.

Das, Sanchoy K., Pradeep Yedlarajiah and Raj Narendra (2000), 'An approach for estimating the end-of-life product disassembly effort and cost', *International Journal of Production Research*, **38**, 657–73.

Dierickx, Ingerman and Karel Cool (1989), 'Asset stock accumulation and sustainability of competitive advantage', *Management Science*, **32**, 1504–14.

Dooley, Robert and Fryxell, Gerald (1999), 'Are conglomerates less environmentally responsible? An empirical examination of diversification strategy and subsidiary pollution in the US chemical industry', *Journal of Business Ethics*, **21**, 1–4.

Florida, Richard (1996), 'Lean and green: the move to environmentally conscious manufacturing', *California Management Review*, **39**, 80–105.

Gilley, K. Matthew, Dan L. Worrell, Wallace N. Davidson III and Abuzar El-Jelly (2000), 'Corporate environmental initiatives and anticipated firm performance: the differential effects of process-drive versus product-driven greening initiatives', *Journal of Management*, **26**, 1199–1216.

Grant, Robert M. (1991), 'The resource-based theory of competitive advantage: Implications for strategy formulation', *California Management Review*, **33**, 114–35.

Guide, V. Daniel R. (2000), 'Production planning and control for remanufacturing: Industry practice and research needs', *Journal of Operations Management*, **18**, 467–83.

Handfield, Robert B., Steve A. Melnyk, Roger G. Calantone and Sime Curkovic (2001), 'Integrating environmental concern into the design process: the gap between theory and practice', *IEEE Transactions on Engineering Management*, **18**, 189–208.

Hanna, Mark D., W. Rocky Newman and Pamela Johnson (2000), 'Linking operational and environmental improvement through employee involvement', *International Journal of Operations and Production Management*, **20**, 148–65.

208 *Corporate environmental strategy and competitive advantage*

Hart, Stuart L. (1995), 'A natural resource-based view of the firm', *Academy of Management Review*, **20**, 986–1014.

Hayes, Robert H. and Steven C. Wheelwright (1979), 'Link manufacturing process and product life cycles', *Harvard Business Review*, January–February, 133–140.

Ilinitch, Anne Y., Naomi S. Soderstrom and Tom E. Thomas (1998), 'Measuring corporate environmental performance', *Journal of Accounting and Public Policy*, **17**, 383–408.

Juhasz, Judit, Anne Vari and Jamps Tolgyesi (1993), 'Environmental conflict and political changes: public perception on low level radioactive waste management in Hungary', in Anne Vari and Pal Tamas (eds), *Environment and Democratic Transition*, Boston, MA: Kluwer.

Kim, Jay S. and Peter Arnold (1996), 'Operationalizing manufacturing strategy. An exploratory study of constructs and linkage', *International Journal of Operations and Production Management*, **16**, 45–73.

King, Andrew A. and Michael J. Lenox (2001), 'Lean and green? An empirical examination of the relationship between lean production and environmental performance', *Production and Operations Management*, **10**, 244–56.

Kitazawa, Shinici and Joseph Sarkis (2000), 'The relationship between ISO 14001 and continuous source reduction programs', *International Journal of Operations and Production Management*, **20**, 225–48.

Klassen, Ronald D. (2000a), 'Exploring the linkage between investment in manufacturing and environmental technologies', *International Journal of Operations and Production Management*, **20**, 127–47.

Klassen, Ronald D. (2000b), 'Just in Time manufacturing and pollution prevention generate mutual benefits in the furniture industry', *Interfaces*, **30**, 95–106.

Klassen, Ronald D. and Linda C. Angell (1998), 'An international comparison of environmental management in operations: the impact of manufacturing flexibility in the US and Germany', *Journal of Operations Management*, **16**, 177–94.

Kogut, Bruce and Udo Zander (1992), 'Knowledge of the firm, combinative capabilities, and the replication of the technology', *Organization Science*, **3**, 383–97.

Langlois, Richard N. and Paul L. Robertson (1995), *Firms, Markets and Economic Change*, London: Routledge.

Levinthal, Daniel A. and James G. March (1993), 'The myopia of learning', *Strategic Management Journal*, **14**, 95–112.

MacDuffie, John P. (1995), 'Human resource bundles and manufacturing performance: Organizational logic and flexible production systems in the world auto industry', *Industrial and Labor Relations Review*, **48**, 197.

Mahoney, Joseph T. and J. Rajendran Pandian (1992), 'The resource-based view within the conversation of strategic management', *Strategic Management Journal*, **13**, 363–80.

Malhotra, Manoj K. and Varun Grover (1998), 'An assessment of survey research in POM: from constructs to theory', *Journal of Operations Management*, **16**, 407–25.

Marsden, Chris and Jörg Andriof (1997), 'Understanding corporate citizenship and how to influence it', Working Paper, BP Corporate Citizenship Unit, Coventry: Warwick Business School.

Maxwell, James, Sandra Rothenberg, Forrest Briscoe and Alfred Marcus (1997), 'Green schemes: corporate environmental strategies and their implementation', *California Management Review*, **39**, 118–34.

Melnyk, Steve A., Robert P. Sroufe and Roger Calantone (2003), 'Assessing the impact of environmental management systems on corporate and environmental performance', *Journal of Operations Management*, **21**, 329–51.

Nehrt, Chad (1996), 'Timing and intensity effects of environmental investments', *Strategic Management Journal*, **17**, 537–47.

Newman, W. Rocky and Mark D. Hanna (1996), 'An empirical exploration of the relationship between manufacturing strategy and environmental management: two complementary models', *International Journal of Operations and Production Management*, **16**, 69–87.

Osterman, Paul (1994), 'How common is workplace transformation and how can we explain who adopts it?', *Industrial and Labor Relations Review*, **20**, 986–1014.

Penrose, Edith T. (1959), *The Theory of the Growth of the Firm*, New York: John Wiley.

Porter, Michael E. and Claas van der Linde (1995), 'Green and competitive: ending the stalemate', *Harvard Business Review*, September–October, 120–37.

Rao, Purba (2002), 'Greening the supply chain: a new initiative in South East Asia', *International Journal of Operations and Production Management*, **22**, 632–55.

Rothenberg, Sandra, Fritz K. Pil and James Maxwell (2001), 'Lean, green and the quest for superior environmental performance', *Prodution and Operations Management*, **10**, 228–43.

Russo, Michael V. and Paul A. Fouts (1997), 'A resource-based perspective on corporate environmental performance and profitability', *Academy of Management Journal*, **40**, 534–59.

Sharma, Sanjay and Harrie Vredenburg (1998), 'Proactive corporate environmental strategy and the development of competitively valuable organizational capabilities', *Strategic Management Journal*, **19**, 729–53.

Shrivastava, Paul (1995), 'The role of corporations in achieving ecological sustainability', *Academy of Management Review*, **20**, 936–60.

Skinner, Wichham (1969), 'Manufacturing: Missing link in corporate strategy', *Harvard Business Review*, May–June, 136–45.

Skinner, W. (1996), 'Manufacturing strategy on the S curve,' *Production and Operations Management,* **5**(1), 3–14.

Sroufe, Robert, Sime Curkovic, Frank Montabon and Steven A. Melnyk (2000), 'The new product design process and design for environment', *International Journal of Operations and Production Management*, **20**, 267–91.

Theyel, Gregory (2000), 'Management practices for environmental innovation and performance', *International Journal of Operations and Production Management*, **20**, 249–66.

Tu, Quiang, Mark A. Vonderembse and T.S. Ragu-Nathan (2001), 'The impact of time-based manufacturing practices on mass customisation and value to consumer', *Journal of Operations Management*, **19**, 201–17.

Vastag, Gyula, Sandor Kerekes and Dennis A. Rondinelli (1996), 'Evaluation of corporate environmental management approaches: a framework and application', *International Journal of Production Economics*, **43**, 193–211.

Walley, Noah and Bradley Whitehead (1994), 'It's not easy being green', *Harvard Business Review*, **72**, 46–52.

Womack, James P., Daniel T. Jones and Daniel Roos (1990), *The Machine that Changed the World*, New York: Rawson Associates.

10. The firm–nature relationship: past experiences and future challenges

John P. Ulhøi and Henning Madsen

According to orthodox economic theory, economic agents seek to maximize their profit through socio-economic activities. A well-known example of the latter is the manufacturer who produces goods demanded by the marketplace. Economic theory also recognizes that positive and/or negative spillovers from such activities may influence third party interests. Such effects are traditionally perceived as 'external' economies, that is economic effects outside dyadic economic relationships and activities, and are normally referred to as externalities.

The problem of externality goes back to the late nineteenth century, when Alfred Marshall (1920), with his seminal contribution *Principles of Economics*, introduced the phenomenon of external economies. The explicit focus on and interest in the environmental problem was taken up by Arthur C. Pigou (*The Economics of Welfare*, 1920), who is normally seen as the first economist to introduce a taxation approach to handling externalities, for example environmental negative effects. His contribution can also be seen as a clear attack on the free market, which left unregulated cannot guarantee social welfare, since social and economic interests often collide. As argued by Lowe and Lewis (1980), the existence of externalities is a major rationale for the regulation of the use of certain resources and of the manufacture of some goods. Where some of the costs of an action fall upon third parties, there is a potential allocative advantage derived from any intervention which tends to make the principals of the action act as if all costs were borne by themselves. The same applies, they argued, to any external benefits arising from an activity.

The problem of externality has often been associated with the problem of property rights (Baumol and Oates, 1979). This is probably because collectively held assets, for example biodiversity or fresh air, do not fit well into economic logic based on efficiency, effectiveness and private ownership of assets. Without well-defined property rights, too much time will be spent by economic agents in protecting the collectively held good from overuse. A controversial, albeit very influential, contribution to this problem was published by Coase (1960). This contribution was to be seen as an attempt to extend 'the invisible hand' by creating the possibility for bilateral negotiations between the polluter and the polluted, where the former (in the case of negative externality effects) could 'bribe' the affected party to accept the spillover. This marked the introduction of the idea that it should be possible to define 'licenses to pollute'. However apart from the moral dimensions of such solutions, the included assumption of zero transaction costs is almost tantamount to assuming that environmental problems do not exist in the first place. In consequence, the Coase theorem was increasingly replaced by a focus on economic regulation (and to some extent various incentive schemes), which became the dominating approach up to the early 1990s. This development was fuelled by the growing environmental movement and some of its classical texts (Carson, 1962; Boulding, 1966; Hardin, 1968; Georgescu-Roegen, 1971; Meadows et al., 1972), which convincingly argued for the need for action against increasing environmental degradation.

In response there have been two dominating approaches to environmental protection: (1) permissions and standards (direct regulation of behaviour), and (2) environmental taxation (indirect regulation of behaviour), where the latter is typically seen as an economic approach. OECD (1989) has identified the following economic tools: (1) charges; (2) subsidies, for example in the form of favourable loans or tax deductions; (3) return deposit, for example on bottles; (4) the creation of new markets; (5) the polluter-pays principle. However earlier OECD studies (1980, 1989) identify a number of barriers to economic tools, for example fear of unwanted effects of distribution and administrative problems.

Environmental instruments can be called economic insofar as they affect estimates of the costs and benefits of alternative actions, and affect decision-making and behaviour in such a way that alternatives are chosen which lead to an environmentally more desirable result. Economic instruments, as opposed to direct regulations, leave actors free to respond to certain stimuli in a way of their own choosing (OECD, 1989). Among other things, economic instruments are characterized by being based on economic incentives to innovate in order to prevent unnecessary environmental costs, and by giving manufacturers a choice when faced with environmental problems. Since the early 1990s however there has been an increasing focus on self-regulative approaches, that is approaches based on voluntarism on behalf of the polluter (the manufacturer). This chapter recognizes that one of the potentially most critical constraints on present economic development is the balance between nature's waste assimilation capacity and the rate of socio-economic transformation of natural-based inputs, especially the time period during which such transformations take place. The constraints, or limits, set by this critical and essential biophysical–socio-economic relationship, that is the relationship between the production of waste and the capacity of the natural environment to 'absorb' it, are what the Brundtland Report (WCED, 1987) defines as the constraints of sustainable development. In plain language, this can be translated into rates of harvesting and waste production which do not exceed natural or managed yields and/or assimilation capacities.

The chapter is organized in the following way. The following section briefly identifies the key elements in the development of the integrated environmental management system approach. In continuation of this a following section describes the methods used in the empirical studies, in which we have identified key points of relevance to the ongoing discussion on self-regulative greening activities taking place in many countries around the world. This is followed by a section including the analyses of the findings. Having analysed the results, the chapter then discusses progress with regard to the issue of 'sufficiency' and identifies some of the remaining challenges that need to be addressed. In closing, the chapter concludes and addresses the implications for research, managers and other policy-makers.

THE SELF-REGULATIVE APPROACH TO THE ENVIRONMENTAL PROBLEM

The aim of the earliest studies of the relationship between corporate management and the physical environment was to determine whether, and to what extent, the environmental dimension was included in the firm's management function. These seminal studies, which date back to the mid-1970s (Wheelwright, 1973; Gladwin, 1977), clearly show that corporate interest in the environment was spurred both by the growing pressure of public opinion and by legislation. In the 1970s, only a handful of companies had incorporated environmental aspects into their value base and goal-setting activities.

Apart from some international initiatives (such as the CERES Principles, issued in 1990 by the Coalition of Environmentally Responsible Economies; the ICC Business Charter for Sustainable Development, issued by the International Chamber of Commerce in 1991; the Keidenren Global Environmental Charter, issued by Japan Federation of Economic Organisations in 1991), the most influential and generally accepted approach to voluntary self-regulation is the integrated environmental management system (EMS). Such systems are highly structured frameworks for the environmental policy and strategy of the firm and for assigning related goals, roles and responsibilities.

In addition to these guidelines, an increasing number of normative recipes on the art of environmental and resource management have also emerged (cf. Sandgrove, 1992; Gilbert, 1993; Stead and Stead, 1992; Ulhøi, 1993; Taylor, 1994; Welford, 1995). The list is far from exhaustive however, and as can be expected, varies widely in quality. The increasing popularity of the field has produced a variety of normative literature which tends to favour a 'quick-fix' approach to corporate environmental management and to include almost anything in the concept of environmental management, for example even traditional resource-optimization (for example Schmidheiny, 1992; Hopfenbeck, 1993; Nemerov, 1995; DeSimone et al., 1997).

However there is empirical evidence to suggest an unfortunate discrepancy between what is said (at the intentional level of managers) and what is actually done at the practical level (Madsen and Ulhøi, 1996), arguing that the real situation is a little less green than the asserted situation. Claims about being green appear too often in commercials, typically of the type where the manufacturer launches a whole new series of washing powder under the name of 'Greeny', alongside other dubious claims of the 'this-product-removes-your-wrinkles' type. This is not only unfortunate from an environmental point of view however; what is more important is that such deceit damages other manufacturers who seriously attempt to implement constructive and useful environmental initiatives. Too often, what the consumer actually buys is far from what the commercials promised. Recycled packaging will often need virgin materials and additional energy to be recycled. Green consumerism is often marketed as a 'license to increase consumption' while at the same time inviting the consumer to become an environmentally 'concerned citizen', thus redirecting attention from structural and institutional obstacles or from asking whether increasing consumption is actually possible in a sustainable world.

The willingness of some manufacturers to exploit the green label epitomizes the very worst and most deceitful characteristics of the free market economy. In contrast to the few who are genuinely changing business practices, process and products, a lot of manufacturers are quick to jump on the green bandwagon in a cynical exploitation of the latest market fad; compare for example the variety of products marketed as 'green this and green that' without objective documentation for the asserted environmental qualities. Recent contributions to the field of environmental management have begun critically to challenge the rhetoric of much of the debate (Welford, 1997; Beder, 2001).

As argued by Dadd and Carothers (1991), green consuming is still consuming. This is a fundamental paradox, and one that cannot continue to be swept under the carpet in discussions of how to realize an environmentally more sustainable future. The answer to the environmental problem seems to be not just to consume appropriately but, more importantly, to consume less. Up to now, the most widely adopted environmental management systems (EMS) have been the EU's standard EMAS and ISO 14000 schemes, the latter replacing the original BS7750. The EMS approach has, among other things, been criticized for the failure of mechanistic approaches in developing appropriate organizational structures which, through lack of cross-functional relationships and the building of trust, may doom an environmental programme (Hunt and Auster, 1990). Companies are also aware of this, though some observers argue that much of companies' environmental rhetoric represents ill-concealed attempts to control the direction, if not the content, of the debate or dialogue on environment and sustainability with their stakeholders (Welford, 1997). An illuminating chapter by Newton and Harte (1997) describes how the environmental debate has become the victim of such 'green evangelism'.

Any evaluation of the rate of adoption of corporate environmental management, including its potential impact on the competitive position of a company, must be based on the key elements involved in the adoption process. A primary concern must therefore be the drivers which encourage management to take the environmental challenge seriously and introduce corporate environmental management into their company. What can actually be studied here is the influence of various stakeholders on initiatives designed to improve the environmental performance of the company. Here it should be stressed that when information is collected from companies it actually represents managers' perceptions of such influences. As described in Madsen and Ulhøi (2001), these stakeholders can be categorized into three groups: stakeholders with a direct influence on the companies' decision process, stakeholders with whom the companies have a market-based relation, and stakeholders with only a very indirect and limited influence. Keeping these categories in mind may help in interpreting the potential impact of the various stakeholders on the competitive position.

Real-life companies, however, do not carry out their business activities in a vacuum. As described by Freeman (1984), they are embedded in a cobweb of stakeholders representing different and often conflicting interests. It has even been hypothesized that adopting stakeholder principles and practices results in better economic performance (Donaldson and Preston, 1995). And companies' impact on the environment has actually been recognized by most of the important stakeholders, such as consumers, regulators, politicians and NGOs (Madsen and Ulhøi, 2001).

The academic community is increasingly recognizing that traditional stakeholders are now being joined by new actors espousing values that represent the natural environment (Welford, 1995; Fineman and Clarke, 1996). Engaging stakeholders, in other words, supports current self-regulation policies (Petts et al., 1999) and presents new learning opportunities (Ulhøi and Rikhardsson, 1997).

But does stakeholder influence have derived effects? One might expect that the influence of various stakeholders and the general public debate would make companies more aware of their own environmental impact. It could also be expected that the combination of stakeholder influence and awareness of own impact would lead to initiatives aimed at reducing companies' environmental impact. And such initiatives would clearly have a positive effect. These four main topics (stakeholder influence, own impact, initiatives and improvements) have formed the basis for a number of research questions in a series of surveys of Danish industrial companies over the last decade. The following two sections present the research design and results of these surveys.

RESEARCH DESIGN

There have been frequent surveys of the adoption of corporate environmental management in Danish industry over the last decade. The survey instrument used is a structured questionnaire based primarily on the four topics mentioned in the second section. In addition to a pilot survey in 1994, three full-scale surveys have been carried out every four years: one in late 1995, another in late 1999, and a third in 2003.

In all three surveys, a sample of industrial companies with more than ten employees was randomly selected from an electronic database. The sample size was set at nearly 600 companies, which represents almost 10 per cent of the companies in the population. A few companies were later excluded from the sample to avoid overlap with previous surveys, thereby reducing the sample size to approximately 550 companies.

Initial contact with the sampled companies was made by means of a telephonic pre-notification procedure, the purpose of which was to identify the person in the companies responsible for environmental matters and obtain his or her agreement to participate in the survey as well as to complete and return the questionnaire. During this stage, some respondents refused to participate in the survey, mainly due to lack of time. This refusal reduced the sample size further, but normally around 500 questionnaires were sent out.

After a single reminder had been sent out, the number of completed questionnaires usually returned in the surveys was approximately 300, that is a response rate of approximately 60 per cent in relation to the number of questionnaires sent out and approximately 55 per cent in relation to the original sample size. Although a few of the returned questionnaires had to be rejected for various reasons, this must be considered a quite satisfactory result regarding the validity of the analyses. For each of the four basic topics in the questionnaire a scale was constructed based on the items identified for each topic from the theory of environmental management and published guidelines (see Table 10.1). Responses could be given on a five-point Likert scale, so that questions could be answered by expressing either the degree of agreement or disagreement, or the level of perceived impact or influence.

Various statistical techniques were used to analyse the collected information, ranging from simple frequency tabulations, calculation of averages

Table 10.1   Items constituting the scales for the four main topics

1. Stakeholders	2. Impact areas	3. Areas for initiatives and improvements
• Employer and Industrial Associations • Distributors • Owners/ Shareholders • Business Networks • Unions • Financial Institutions • Consumer Organizations • R&D Institutions • International Regulations • Competitors • Customers • Suppliers • Local Regulations • Employees • Environmental Organizations • National Regulations • Press & Media	• Extraction of raw materials • Suppliers production process • The company's own production process • The company's total logistic • Use of the company's products • Discharge of the company's products • Recycling of the company's products	• Protection of soil • Reduction of solid waste • Reduction of fluid waste • Reduction of discharges • Reduction of water consumption • Reduction of air born emissions • Reduction of noise • Reduction of energy consumption • Reduction in or substitution of raw materials • Reduction in auxiliary materials • Substitution of environmental harmful materials • Improvements in the working environment (the internal environment) • Waste sorting at the source • Recycling of left over from production • Reception of left over from customers • Reception of worn out products • Initiatives in R&D • Initiatives in total logistics

and simple pair-wise comparisons, to more advanced techniques like factor analysis and profile analysis (a multivariate analysis of variance). The latter techniques made it possible to identify underlying structures in the information as well as differences in responses to the same topic in two surveys. As a rule, a 5 per cent level of significance was set for the pair-wise comparisons or when testing the three basic hypotheses in the profile analysis (parallel profiles, coincident profiles and level profiles). Any significant differences identified in a profile analysis were further evaluated by means of simultaneous confidence intervals based on the Bonferroni principle, using a similar level of significance. This allows the individual items causing the differences to be identified.

For the purpose of this chapter, analyses only include data from the two recent full-scale surveys. There are two main reasons for excluding the 1995 survey. First, in an attempt to cover the situation in Danish companies in general, it included all kinds of companies. This implies that industrial companies only constitute half of the sample and thus half of the returned questionnaires. Second, the questionnaire underwent a major revision and restructuring process between 1995 and 1999, based on the experiences from the 1995 survey. This implies that a full comparison between 1995 on one hand and 1999 and 2003 on the other is not always possible. However the questionnaire used in the 1999 and 2003 surveys is identical, allowing for a full comparison.

RESULTS

The General Trend

The fact that the scales for the four basic topics mentioned in section 2 (see Table 10.1) include a different number of items makes it difficult to get a general impression of the development. To overcome this hurdle and facilitate an overall evaluation, the information from each of the items in the four basic topics has been transformed into a single index ranging from 0 to 10 (see Figure 10.1).

As can be seen from Figure 10.1, the general trend is characterized by a fairly low level of involvement, fluctuating between 3.5 and 4.5 compared with the maximum value of 10. Although there was a slight decreasing tendency from 1999 to 2003, there are no major differences. This is confirmed by a profile analysis, that is the profiles are not only parallel but coincident too. However the profiles are not level, due to the difference between perceived stakeholder influence and own impact on the one hand and reported initiatives and improvements on the other. A pair-wise comparison confirms

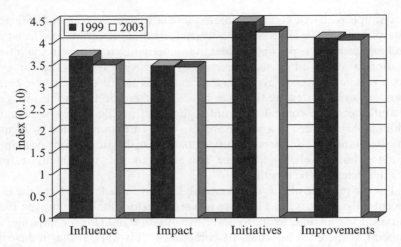

*Figure 10.1   The general trend in the development of perceived stakeholder
influence, perceived own impact, reported initiatives and
reported improvements*

that this difference is significant. Thus the level of reported initiatives and
improvements is significantly higher than the level of perceived stakeholder
influence and own impact. This result is valid in 1999 as well as 2003.
However a more diversified impression of the development would require
detailed analyses of each of the four basic topics.

Perceived Stakeholder Influence

As described in Madsen and Ulhøi (2001), by means of a factor analysis
the perceived influence from the stakeholders mentioned in the questionnaire (see the first column of Table 10.1) can be categorized into three
groups: (1) stakeholders with a direct influence on the companies' decision
process; (2) stakeholders with whom the companies have a market-based
relation; and (3) stakeholders with only a very indirect and limited influence. Except for minor repositioning of individual stakeholders, this grouping can be observed in both surveys.

   Stakeholders with a direct influence on the companies' decision process
(owners and shareholders, employees and various regulators) seem to have
the highest perceived influence as regards environmental initiatives (see
Figure 10.2). However with a level of around 3 to 3.5 on the applied five-
point scale, this is still only moderate. Those stakeholders perceived to have
the highest influence are local regulators, and owners and shareholders.

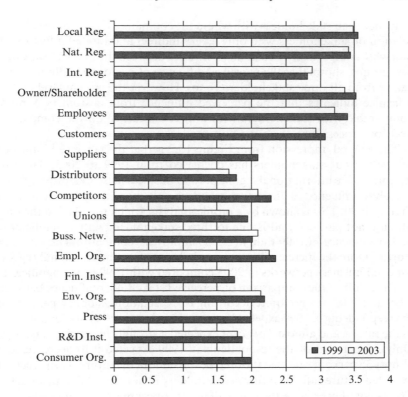

*Figure 10.2   Development in perceived influence from a range of
stakeholders to take initiatives related to the environment
(average responses – originally measured on a 5-point Likert
scale ranging from 1 = no influence to 5 = very high
influence)*

The perceived influence of the remaining two stakeholder groups is low,
ranging from 1.5 to 2.5 (see Figure 10.2). The only exception is customers,
where the level is around the same as in the first group.

Taking employees as being representative of the group of stakeholders
with a direct influence on the companies' decision process and competitors
as being representative of stakeholders with whom the companies have a
market-based relation, as well as stakeholders with only a very indirect and
limited influence, a pair-wise comparison shows that there is a very significant difference in the perceived influence from the first group compared with
the other two groups. In other words, stakeholders with a direct influence
on the companies' decision process have a significantly higher perceived

influence than stakeholders with whom the companies have a market-based relation or stakeholders with only a very indirect and limited influence. A pair-wise comparison of customers, who are between the first and the other two groups, shows that the perceived influence of customers differs significantly from all three stakeholder groups. However the critical level of significance indicates that the perceived influence from customers is more comparable with stakeholders with a direct influence on the companies' decision process than the other two categories.

The general impression from Figure 10.2 is that the perceived influence of the various stakeholders has decreased from 1999 to 2003. The two exceptions are international regulators and business networks, although the perceived influence of these two groups is only marginally higher in 2003 than in 1999. This is shown by a profile analysis, which reveals that the profiles are not parallel, and is due to three stakeholders with a significantly higher influence in 1999 than in 2003: employees, competitors and unions. Furthermore the increase in perceived influence from international regulators and business networks in 2003 compared with 1999 is not significant.

The result of the comparison of perceived stakeholder influence between 1999 and 2003 was not quite according to expectations, since 56 per cent of the respondents in 1999 expected a general increase in stakeholder influence in the future, and almost 7 per cent expected a strongly increasing tendency. Only 2.5 per cent of the respondents in 1999 expected it to decrease, and almost 35 per cent said that it would be the same in the future. The perceived expected future influence from stakeholders is not that different in 2003. This is possibly because the respondents have become a bit more realistic as a result of the experiences gained since 1999. In 2003, half of the respondents expect future influence from stakeholders to be equivalent to the present situation. But 45 per cent still expect it to increase, whereas 5 per cent now expect it to decrease.

Perceived Own Influence

The items included in the scale concerning companies' perception of their own environmental impact can be seen in column 2 of Table 10.1. The responses indicate that a grouping into two groups seems appropriate: issues related to production itself (extraction of raw materials, suppliers' production process, the company's own production process and logistics related to the production process) and issues related to the use, discharge or reuse of the products.

However as can be seen from Figure 10.3, the perception of all these 'own impacts' is generally at a medium to low level, ranging from 2 to 2.75 on the applied five-point Likert scale. In general the perceived 'own impact' from

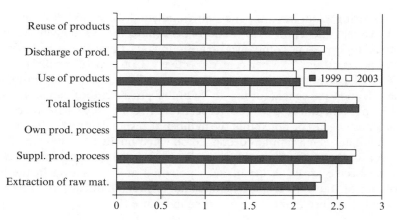

Figure 10.3   The respondents' perception of the environmental impact from their own company due to its business activities (average responses – originally measured on a 5-point Likert scale ranging from 1 = no impact to 5 = very high impact)

the production process is slightly higher than the perceived impact from use, discharge or reuse of the products. Even if the difference in level between the two groups is only marginal, a significant difference can be observed when comparing the most extreme results: perception of the impact from total logistics and impact due to the use of the products. So it seems reasonable to conclude that companies consider issues related to the production process to have a larger environmental impact than the use, reuse and discharge of the products.

There are some differences when comparing 1999 and 2003, as can be seen from Figure 10.3, but they seem only to be marginal. This is confirmed by a profile analysis, which shows that the profiles are both parallel and coincident. Thus the perception of the companies' own environmental impact in 2003 does not differ significantly from the situation in 1999.

Initiatives Taken

The next question is the extent to which perceived stakeholder influence and the perception of the companies' own impact on the environment has led to initiatives to reduce this impact. Among the more general initiatives is the publication of a separate environmental report, inclusion of environmental issues in the annual report, or certification according to a recognized scheme. All situations show a rise in activity from 1999 to 2003. With regard to reporting about the companies' environmental status, 15.2 per cent published a separate report in 1999 and 14 per cent included statements in their annual report. Some companies do both. In 2003, these figures had risen to 18.4 per cent and 22.6 per cent respectively. Concerning certification, in 1999 3.4 per cent of the companies reported certification according to EMAS and 9 per cent according to ISO 14000. In 2003, the figures had risen to 3.7 per cent and 18.8 per cent respectively. In contrast to these increasing tendencies, it can be noted that the number of respondents who do not find such initiatives relevant has decreased only marginally from 1999 to 2003.

But to what extent have the general initiatives led to actual initiatives in more specific areas? A list of such potential areas is shown in the last column of Table 10.1, and respondents' answers about where initiatives actually have been taken are presented in Figure 10.4.

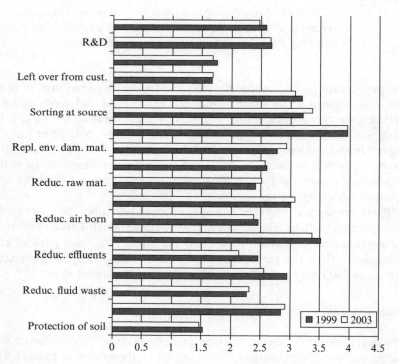

Figure 10.4   Reported level of initiatives on environmental issues within a number of areas (average responses – originally measured on a 5-point Likert scale ranging from 1 = no relevance to 5 = initiatives taken on a larger scale)

It is not possible to identify any unambiguous grouping in the potential areas mentioned in Table 10.1. However there is a tendency for initiatives which imply cost reductions to form one group, and initiatives concerning the collection and destruction of leftover or worn-out products from customers to form another. The remaining areas do not fall into any stable grouping, but split up into different groups with different contents from survey to survey. The results in Figure 10.4 indicate that whereas cost-reducing initiatives are frequently taken, or at least considered, initiatives in many of the other areas are hardly taken or even considered relevant.

More specifically, the areas where most initiatives are reported are in energy reduction and the introduction of waste sorting at source, as well as reuse of leftovers from production, followed by reduction of noise, water consumption and solid waste. However the most frequently mentioned initiative concerns improvements in the working environment. This may be due to a compulsory statutory health and safety regulation scheme for Danish industrial companies. Even though the focus is on the working environment however, it also results in a derived reduction in the companies' environmental impact.

The most frequently reported initiatives all have a clear cost-reducing consequence, as well as a reduction in the environmental impact. For the remaining areas, involvement in initiatives must generally be characterized as moderate to low.

Comparing the situation in 1999 with 2003, a varying pattern emerges. In some areas, more initiatives have been taken in 2003 than in 1999, while in other areas the opposite is true. A profile analysis confirms this impression, but only two significant differences can be identified: reduction of water consumption and effluents. Both are more frequently reported in 1999 than in 2003. In the remaining areas, there are no significant differences between 1999 and 2003.

Improvements Achieved

Have the initiatives led to any improvements? Apparently, according to Figure 10.5, which shows the actual improvements due to initiatives in the areas mentioned in Figure 10.4.

However while a comparison of Figures 10.4 and 10.5 seems to show an identical pattern, the level of improvements achieved is lower than the level of initiatives taken. In other words there is a clear relationship between where initiatives have been taken and where improvements have been achieved.

This observation is confirmed by a profile analysis of initiatives versus improvements for each of the two surveys. The results of these analyses are

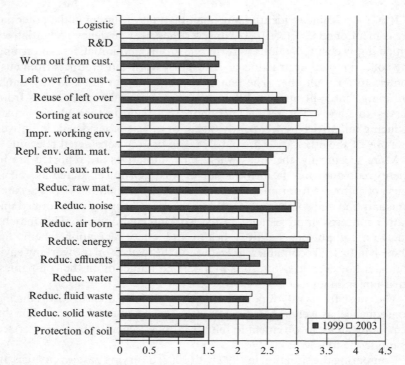

Figure 10.5   Reported level of improvements achieved within a number
of areas (average responses – originally measured on a
5-point Likert scale ranging from 1 – no relevance to
5 = improvements achieved on a larger scale)

almost identical. In 1999, the profiles are parallel but definitely not coincident ($\alpha_k = 0.016$). The profiles are parallel in 2003 too, but they are also coincident, though only just ($\alpha_k = 0.054$). There are a number of significant contrasts in both analyses, though they are not powerful enough in 2003 to reject the hypothesis of coincident profiles. These contrasts confirm that the level of initiatives is generally higher than the level of achieved results. In both surveys there are significant contrasts for improvements of the working environment, reuse of leftovers from production, R&D and total logistics. In 1999 there is also a significant contrast in relation to reduction of energy consumption.

A comparison of the level of improvements achieved in 1999 and 2003 produces a result similar to the situation described above concerning initiatives taken. In some areas, more results have been achieved in 2003 than in 1999, while in other areas the reverse is true. However a profile analysis identifies only two significant differences, going in different directions. Thus in 1999 more results were achieved in reducing water consumption than in 2003. But in 2003 more results were achieved in sorting waste at source than in 1999. The remaining areas do not differ significantly from 1999 to 2003.

DISCUSSION

Respondents may exaggerate somewhat when judging their own performance, not because they intentionally do this, but because they may be influenced by their own seriously meant intention of performing at a certain level. In order to deal with such a potential bias, it would be necessary to check each participating company to see whether the respondent's statement agrees with actual performance. This is not only very time-consuming and expensive, but is also likely to generate resistance to participating in the study in the first place. This study (like most other studies in the field) is therefore entirely based on the self-perception of the respondent. This means that the results reported in the previous section may give a too-optimistic impression of the situation.

As regards stakeholder influence, the development between 1999 and 2003 is interesting, since it is in contrast to expectations expressed in 1999. As mentioned in the previous section, the general response in 1999 regarding expected future stakeholder influence was that an increase could be expected (Madsen and Ulhøi, 2001). But the perception in 2003 does not seem to confirm this expectation. On the contrary, the perceived influence of most of the stakeholders mentioned in the questionnaire seemed to have decreased. One explanation could be that managers always believe that they are under the increasing influence of various stakeholders.

Surprisingly it is not competitive challenges but legislation that still seems to be one of the major drivers of environmental-related initiatives. This has been reported in several surveys over the years (see for example Fineman and Clarke, 1996; Ulhøi et al., 1996; Madsen and Ulhøi, 1996). But two positive aspects can be identified as well. The first is that the perceived influence of customers is at a relatively high level. This could indicate an increasing market-based influence, even if it has decreased from 1999 to 2003. The second is the high level of perceived influence of local regulations. This may be a regional phenomenon however, since environmental control functions in Denmark are normally handled by local authorities (city or county). Recently these authorities have taken a more proactive attitude, rejecting the traditional control function and adopting a more dialogue-based contact with companies.

This new approach is in line with the rationale of stakeholder management (see for example Madsen and Ulhøi, 2001) and the call for more flexibility in regulations (Porter and van der Linde, 1995). Moreover the presence of a statutory health and safety scheme, which is compulsory for many industrial companies, may influence perceptions as well. Although this scheme focuses on the working environment, it clearly has derived effects on the natural environment. And it underlines the remark by Donaldson and Preston (1995) that employees are considered an important stakeholder in many European countries. However since it is compulsory, compliance with the statutory health and safety scheme in itself may not result in a competitive advantage. With some caution due to differences in sampling procedure, it is possible to compare trends in environmental initiatives with a similar survey from Switzerland (Baumast and Dyllick, 2001). The stable or declining tendency in environmental initiatives in Danish industry from 1999 to 2003 (see Figure 10.4) is paralleled by the Swiss results, which indicate a decline from 1997 to 2001. However there is insufficient information for a more detailed evaluation of this situation, which may be influenced by the industrial structure and the different stages of adopting EMS in the two countries.

In light of the results and the discussion above, the question is however whether the predominantly self-regulative approach is radical enough to reverse the growing environmental degradation of the planet caused by the process of production and consumption (Ulhøi and Welford, 2000).

It is not so much that self-regulation and the EMS approach are wrong per se, only that relying solely on such approaches is inadequate. What is really required is a paradigm shift that would involve industry accepting its ethical and social responsibilities (Smith, 1993; Shrivastava, 1995; Welford and Gouldson, 1994). However business is unlikely to accept this wider agenda without significant pressure from stakeholders, which at the moment is extremely weak. The roots of any solution aimed at achieving sustainable development, that is to go beyond the idea of replacing existing growth in consumerism with 'green growth', thus lie more in tackling human consciousness than in management systems (Ulhøi and Welford, 2000; Starkey and Welford, 2001) so as to realize that instead of trying to pass on the responsibility for environmental degradation to others such as the manufacturer and/or the legislator, we need to start pointing the finger at ourselves. Growth still remains growth, and by believing that green growth holds the answer to all our environmental problems we are fooling ourselves. By using resources more efficiently and by preventing some problems from occurring, we will win time. However to really get closer to a less unsustainable balance, we need to consider whether infinite material growth is necessary. The eco-modernist agenda is limited because it only looks at the production mode of

- company activities, whereas an emphasis on (both the creation and satisfaction of) consumption may actually be more fruitful. The root cause of much environmental degradation is consumption in the strong economies of the West, and the reason for much of that consumption is that we see it as some sort of substitute for happiness that can no longer be derived from other sources. Spiritual aspects of our consciousness have nevertheless been progressively and systematically relegated to the domain of the subjective, private, individual or even subconscious. To all but a few, they are not perceived as having direct relevance to society.

CONCLUSION

The tool of corporate environmental management has been around for years. But as the results of the surveys presented in this chapter demonstrate, the rate of adoption does not seem to be convincing. Positive trends can be observed, but a breakthrough in reducing the environmental impact of industrial business activities does not seem to be imminent at the moment. One plausible explanation for the recent decrease in corporate greening is that managers generally have to focus on core or bottom line issues. In other words, in addition to environmental issues the general business climate also has to be taken into account. Another reason may be that the fast pace of the first wave of corporate greening resulted in a quick return on investment. That is many companies have already 'picked the low-hanging fruit', and implemented all the environmental initiatives with a fast, straightforward payback potential. The next level of corporate greening activities is likely to require a longer payback period, as it will involve the implementation of more advanced or expensive cleaner technologies and it will be increasingly difficult and expensive to improve waste sorting and treatment. Last but not least, the general mindset of both manufacturers and consumers acts as a major brake on the speed of corporate greening. These two groups often tend to believe that it is possible to 'grow one's way out of the environmental problem' (as long as the growth is 'green'), apparently preferring the material dimensions of life to life's spiritual qualities.

Increasingly, large businesses, their business associations, norm-setters and even governments are asserting that industry has to become more environmentally responsible – through the use of (standardized) environmental management systems (EMS) and corporate environmental management tools (environmental audits, life cycle assessments, reports and so on) – and strive for some ill-defined notion of eco-efficiency. Coming from such powerful players, this naturally carries some weight. The question is however whether it is radical enough to reverse the growing environmental degrad- ation of the planet caused by the processes of production and consumption. As independent researchers, we should not compromise the independence which allows us to critically scrutinize whether we have arrived at an accurate conclusion regarding the contributions of eco-modern activities, values, roles and motives.

If businesses are to make their deeds comply with their words, it will require a fundamental change in ethics. However given the recent ethical crises in the international business community (Enron and Parmalat being just two of the most recent scandals), there is little hope that such change will happen by itself. This therefore makes it all the more important to consider which new institutional settings and incentive schemes might bring about such a development. In order to move towards a sustainable future, we also need to go beyond seeing the environment in sterile scientific terms (with the sometime addition of a less important social dimension), and rediscover, recognize, appreciate and enjoy the spiritual dimension of ecology.

IMPLICATIONS

This has a number of implications. First, it seems obvious that political initiatives in the form of regulations and so on are still needed, as market forces do not seem to play an influential role. However regulation is normally a stick approach to changing behaviour, which ignores other motivating factors. In other words it preserves the status quo of the competitive situation. A challenge for politicians therefore is to introduce initiatives using the carrot approach, which can really change the attitudes and behaviour of customers and consumers as well as managers. Second, managers need to be increasingly aware of the potentialities for competitiveness in introducing corporate environmental management. Being forced – one way or another – to focus on short-term results eliminates their motivation to introduce more costly initiatives that have a more long-term and lasting effect but which do not pay back immediately. This parallels the observation by Donaldson and Preston (1995) that response to social and ethical considerations is often consistent with long-run increases in profit and value. Clearly, market mechanisms as well as political initiatives play an important role in changing this situation.

Finally, there are implications for research and educational institutions. First, empirical studies (Ulhøi et al., 1996) have reported a lack of interest among top MBA students for environmental management courses from leading European business schools, such as for example INSEAD. In the case of Denmark, most business schools had introduced environmental management courses in the late 1980s and/or early 1990s. However by the end of the 1990s, most of them had closed due to lack of interest among the students. One of the authors of this chapter ran an intensive summer school for the University of Warwick from 1997 until 2001, where it 'died' due to lack of interest among the students. Moreover among the early university adopters of environmental management courses, professors setting up such courses in the same countries have received remarkably little support from their institutions, and even experienced resistance from colleagues (Ulhøi et al., 1996). A major problem here is that attitudes also need to be changed. As regards research, the question is whether corporate environmental management should be considered as a separate discipline. Obviously, after the emergence of environmental management in the 1970s, efforts were focused on developing the contents of this topic. This justified a separation from other topics. But is it still realistic to consider it as a separate topic, or should it be integrated into other managerial disciplines? To achieve the optimal advantages of corporate environmental management, it seems more logical to integrate it into other managerial disciplines.

Recognizing that the eco-efficiency or EMS approach is not enough has at least two overall implications. First, such an approach does not take us very far towards achieving sustainable development. Second, and more worryingly, it is perhaps because the proponents of eco-modernism (who are powerful) overstate the possible achievements of eco-modernist approaches, that they can obstruct the additional changes required. In other words, people in powerful positions who tell us that environmental management systems and associated tools will take us down the road of sustainable development create so much inertia that we will only go as far along the road as the industrial lobbyists tell us.

REFERENCES

Baumast, A. and T. Dyllick (2001), 'Umweltmanagement-Barometer Schweiz – Erste Ergebnisse zur Befragungsrunde 2001', in A. Baumast and T. Dyllick (eds), 'Umweltmanagement-Barometer 2001', IWÖ-Diskussionsbeitrag no. 93, Institut für Wirtschaft und Ökologie, Universität St Gallen, St Gallen, CH, 35–44.

Baumol, W.J. and W.E. Oates (1979), *Economics, Environmental Policy and the Quality of Life*, Englewood Cliffs, NJ: Prentice-Hall.

Beder, S. (2001), 'Global spin', in, R. Starkey and R. Welford (eds), *Business and Sustainable Development*, London: Earthscan, 242–67.

Boulding, K.E. (1966), 'The economics of the coming spaceship earth', in H. Jarret (ed.), *Environmental Quality in a Growing Economy*, Baltimore, MD: Johns Hopkins University Press.

Carson, R. (1962), *Silent Spring*, Boston, MA: Houghton Mifflin.

Coase, R. (1960/77), 'The problem of social cost' (first published in 1960), in R. Dorfman and N.S. Dorfman, *Economics of the Environment. Selected Readings*, 2nd edn, New York: W.W. Norton & Company.

Dadd, L. and A. Carothers (1991), 'A bill of goods? Green consuming in perspective', in C. Plant and J. Plant (eds), *Green Business: Hope or Hoax? Towards an Authentic Strategy for Restoring Earth*, Philadelphia, PA: New Society Publishers.

DeSimone, L.D. and F. Popoff with the World Business Council for Sustainable Development (1997), *Eco-efficiency: The Business Link to Sustainable Development*, Cambridge, MA: MIT Press.

Donaldson, T. and L.E. Preston (1995), 'The stakeholder theory of the corporation: concepts, evidence, and implications', *Academy of Management Review*, **20**(1), 65–91.

Fineman, S. and K. Clarke (1996), 'Green stakeholders: industry interpretations and response', *Journal of Management Studies*, **33**(6), 715–30.

Freeman, R.E. (1984), *Strategic Management: A Stakeholder Approach*, Boston, MA: Pitman.

Georgescu-Roegen, N. (1971), *The Entropy Law and the Economic Process*, Cambridge, MA: Harvard University Press.

Gilbert, M.J. (1993), *Achieving Environmental Management Standards: A-Step-by-Step Guide to Meeting BS7750*, London: Pitman Publications.

Gladwin, T.N. (1977), *Environment, Planning and the Multinational Corporation*, Greenwich, CT: Jai Press.

Hardin, G. (1968), 'The tragedy of the commons', *Science*, **162**, 1243–48.

Hopfenbeck, W. (1993), *The Green Management Revolution*, New York: Prentice-Hall.

Hunt, C.B. and E.R. Auster (1990), Proactive Environmental Management: Avoiding the Toxic Trap, *Sloan Management Review*, Winter, pp. 7–18.

Lowe, J. and D. Lewis (1980), *The Economics of Environmental Management*, Oxford: Philip Allan Publishers.

Madsen, H. and J.P. Ulhøi (2001), 'Integrating environmental and stakeholder management', *Business Strategy and the Environment*, **10**(2), 77–88.

Marshall, A. (1920), *Principles of Economics*, 8th edn, London: Macmillan.

Meadows, D.H., D.L. Meadows, J. Randers and W.W. Behrens III (1972), *The Limits to Growth*, New York: Universe Books.

Nemerov, N.L. (1995), *Zero Pollution Industry*, New York: John Wiley & Sons.

Newton, T.J. and G. Harte (1997), 'Green business: Technicist Kitsch?' *Journal of Management Studies*, **34**(1), 75–98.

OECD (1980), *Pollution Charges in Practice*, Paris: OECD Publications Service.

OECD (1989), *Economic Instruments for Environmental Protection*, Paris: OECD Publications Service.

Petts, J., A. Herd and C. Horne (1999), 'The climate and culture of environmental compliance within SMEs', *Business Strategy and the Environment*, **8**, 14–30.

Pigou, A. (1920), *The Economics of Welfare*, London: Macmillan & Co.

Porter, M.E. and C. van der Linde (1995), 'Toward a new conception of the environment–competitiveness relationship', *Journal of Economic Perspectives*, **9**(4), 97–118.

Sandgrove, K. (1992), *The Green Manager's Handbook*, Aldershot: Gower.

Shrivastava, P. (1995), 'The role of corporations in achieving ecological sustainability', *Academy of Management Review*, **20**(4), 936–60.

Schmidheiny, S. (1992), *Changing Course*, Cambridge, MA: MIT Press.

Smith, D. (1993), *Business and the Environment: Implications of the New Environmentalism*, London: Paul Chapman.

Starkey, R. and R. Welford (2001), 'Win-ein revisited: a Buddist perspective', in R. Starkey and R. Welford (eds), *Business and Sustainable Development*, London: Earthscan, 351–6.

Stead, W.E. and J.G. Stead (1992), *Management for a Small Planet*, Newbury Park, CA: Sage.

Taylor, B., C. Hutchinson, S. Pollack and R. Tapper (1994). *Environmental Management Handbook*, London: Pitman Publishing.

Ulhøi, J.P. (1993), 'Corporate environmental and resource management: what, why and how?', *International Journal of Management*, **10**, 440–51.

Ulhøi, J.P. (1997), 'Industry and environment: a case study of cleaner technologies in selected European countries', *Journal of Engineering and Technology Management*, **14**(3), 259–70.

Ulhøi, J.P., H. Madsen and P. Rikhardsson (1996), *Training in Environmental Management: Industry and Sustainability*, Luxembourg: Office for Official Publications of the European Communities.

Ulhøi, J.P. and P.M. Rikhardsson (1997), 'A stakeholder learning perspective on corporate environmental management', conference proceedings of *the 13th EGOS Colloquium: Organisational Responses to Radical Environmental Changes*, Budapest University of Economic Sciences, Budapest, 3–5, July.

Ulhøi, J.P. and R.J Welford (2000), 'Exploring corporate eco-modernism: challenging corporate rhetoric and scientific discourses', conference proceedings of *the International Conference of Systems Thinking in Management*, Deakin University, Geelong, Victoria, 8–10 November.

Welford, R. (1997), 'From green to golden: the hijacking of environmentalism', in R. Welford (ed.), *Hijacking Environmentalism*, London: Earthscan Publications, 16–40.

World Commission on Environment and Development (WCED) (1987), *Our Common Future*, Oxford: Oxford University Press.

Welford, R. (1995), *Environmental Strategy and Sustainable Development: The Corporate Challenge of the 21st Century*, London: Routledge.

Welford, R.J. (1997), *Hijacking Environmentalism: Corporate Responses to Sustainable Development*, London: Earthscan.

Welford, R.J. and A. Gouldson (1994), *Environmental Management and Business Strategy*, London: Pitman Publishing.

Wheelwright, S.C. (1973), 'Developing a corporate response to pollution control', *European Business*, **73**, 64–72.

11. The siesta is over: a rude awakening from sustainability myopia

Monika I. Winn and Manfred Kirchgeorg

In this chapter, we contend that the growing number of increasingly extreme natural disasters (such as the tsunami of 2005, storms, floods and droughts) puts us on the verge of a radical paradigm shift regarding the relationship between ecological, societal and economic systems – one in which the environment will be assigned drastically higher status. We first trace the brief history and practice of 'corporate environmental management', examine its underlying assumptions regarding the relationship between economic and ecological systems, and characterize it as an 'inside-out' view. Second, we sketch the recent history and present status of the business practice of 'sustainability management', examining underlying assumptions about the relationship between economic, ecological and social systems; while broadened, this paradigm is still characterized by its 'inside-out' view. Third, we develop the main argument of this chapter. Essentially, we predict a figure-ground shift in assumptions, with drastically heightened importance ascribed to the ecological system in ecological, societal and economic system interrelations, which we characterize as an 'outside-in' view. We sketch implications for management practices that are likely to emerge in response to ecological discontinuities and examine implications for sustainability management research.

For years, the concept of the environment in management studies and education signified the economic, political, legal, social and technological context of business. The natural environment was not only conceptually absent, it was also viewed as irrelevant to business practice (for example Gladwin et al., 1995, Shrivastava, 1995a, Purser et al., 1995). If nature was granted consideration at all, it was done through mediating social or economic variables. Environmental pollution for example was viewed as a social or regulatory pressure; natural resources were framed as economic inputs.

Not long ago however a dramatic change occurred. The natural environment emerged as a concept in its own right. Environmental problems and concurrent philosophical and scientific developments brought new perspectives (Dunlap and Van Liere, 1978; Milbrath, 1989), variously referred to as deep ecology or eco-centric views to the previously exclusively technocentric perspective of management studies (Gladwin et al., 1995; Purser et al., 1995). In just over ten years, a lively scholarly debate has flourished and studies of the relationship between the natural environment and business organizations now assert an increasingly legitimate place in mainstream management literature.

A second major change occurred even more recently. The concept of sustainable development and its implications for incorporating ecological, social and financial considerations has been drawing increasing attention by business scholars and managers (Gladwin et al., 1995; Hart, 1995; Hart, 1997; Hart and Milstein, 2003; Starik and Rands, 1995). In fact, acknowledging the relevance of the natural environment and of sustainable development for business is turning some long-established assumptions and management frameworks on their heads. The rise of these concepts has stimulated rich, new and diverse fields of study in business strategy, operations management, organizational theory and other management disciplines. Today, studies of the natural environment and sustainable development are increasingly taking their place in mainstream management journals[1].

While these important and significant changes in the perceptions of managers and scholars are taking hold, the main argument in this chapter focuses on a third, not yet manifest, but we believe imminent development. We argue that business practice and management studies are currently on the verge of yet another radical paradigm shift bound to prompt a fundamental overhaul and radical re-examination of assumptions and worldviews (see Gladwin et al., 1995) about the relationship between business and the environment. We are at the dawn of a third phase of environmental management and practice – one in which natural disasters become a recurrent fact of managerial life. As multinational corporations face increasingly massive ecological discontinuities, new perspectives, firm capabilities and long-term strategies for survival will be required for a new era of management characterized by extreme upheaval, destruction and chaotic change.

With this chapter, we hope to contribute to the literature by drawing the attention of strategy and organization theory scholars to the source of what many expect to be vastly increasing numbers and severity of massive discontinuous ecological changes; by pointing to the need to rapidly develop management practices, capabilities and competencies that enable the survival and adaptability of firms, thus reducing the disruption caused to business and other sectors of society, as well as minimizing associated suffering; and lastly, by offering thoughts for a broadened sustainability management framework, thus advancing the practice and theory of business and sustainability.

Our argument traces three phases of management research related to the environment: corporate environmental management, sustainability management, and management in an era of ecological discontinuities. Each phase is characterized by the emergence of a new concept or paradigm, by associated changes in underlying assumptions and world-views, and by concurrent changes in management practice. 'Corporate environmental management' marks the first phase for which we sketch the emergence of the natural environment as a concept relevant to business and management studies, and its manifestations in practice. For the second and still evolving phase of 'sustainability management', we note a broadened scope, the inclusion of social systems, and an overall systems thinking, along with emerging business practices and concurrent management innovations.

The third phase, which we coin 'management in an era of ecological discontinuities', shifts our attention to the future. We suggest that changes in large-scale ecological system parameters (for example global climate change) are causing more frequent incidents of increasingly severe natural disasters, which in turn prompt radical changes in management thought and practice. Evidence for catastrophic large-system changes is drawn from multiple sources; we then examine underlying assumptions to predict likely changes in management paradigms and practice. We explore implications for management practices effective in the face of natural disasters and ecological discontinuities, and offer new research questions for the study of sustainability management.

THE PAST: THE NATURAL ENVIRONMENT ENTERS MANAGEMENT CONCEPTS AND PRACTICES

In the 1960s and 1970s a host of books examining the state of the environment and major, high-profile disasters such as the Santa Barbara oil spill in 1969, the toxic lagoons in residential areas of the City of Niagara Falls' Love Canal (1978), or the chemical explosions near Seveso, Italy in 1976 galvanized public attention to the environmental damage and risks caused by industry, along with its effects on the health of humans and ecosystems.[2] Earth Day in 1970, publications like Carson's *Silent Spring* (1962) and *Limits to Growth* (Meadows et al., 1972), and the rapidly growing number of environmental interest groups of all shades of green, marked the rise of the environmental movement in general (Dalton and Kuechler, 1990), and of corporate environmentalism in particular (Hoffman, 1997).

Studies of acid rain, air, water and soil pollution, the dispersion of toxic chemicals, and the dying off of species, and their coverage in the media, fuelled a public outcry over the abuse and poisoning of the environment and of communities by industrial practices. While some attention was paid to the cumulative effect of millions of individuals' consumption practices, the brunt of the pressures for change was directed at industry, particularly the chemical industry (Hoffman, 1997). Newly formed governmental agencies, such as the US Environmental Protection Agency in 1970, passed a host of environmental regulations, specifying and punishing harmful practices. Firms suddenly forced to comply with new sets regulations faced the need to create and fund environmental compliance and associated internal capabilities. Many firms added 'the environment' to other compliance functions such as health and safety, effectively increasing their cost of doing business. The 'era of compliance' in the 1970s thus rang in new business practices and gave birth to what was to become 'corporate environmental management'.[3]

While these changes occurred in public perception, regulatory agencies and business practice, a growing philosophical debate developed to capture, categorize and catalyse world-views associated with both old and new views of the relationship between humans (and human organizations) and nature. While different in some aspects, there appeared to be consensus about fundamental dichotomies between the 'old' and the emergent 'new' paradigm, often referred to as the technocentric, egocentric or dominant social paradigm versus the deep ecology, ecocentric or 'new environmental' paradigm. (Dunlap and Van Liere, 1978; Gladwin et al., 1995; Milbrath, 1989; Purser et al., 1995).

Changing Assumptions about Business and the Natural Environment

Driven by public pressure, the recognition that damage to the environment could affect people's health and quality of life, and subsequent regulatory and legal instruments, the fundamental logic underlying these developments can be characterized as an effort to reduce anthropogenic harm to the environment. The natural environment was now explicitly considered, drew the attention of managers, and became part of business decision-making to varying degrees. Even if not ecocentric or 'deep green' (according to deep ecology views, Purser et al., 1995), the old paradigm was significantly altered by incorporating conceptions and considerations of the natural environment, and a paradigm shift occurred. The early assumption, fuelled by the initial compliance era, that businesses must give up profit if tending to the environment, gave way to the discovery of ample opportunities for economic and environmental benefit. Previously ignored, invisible and conceptually absent, the environment was increasingly treated like other components of the firm's business environment, such as the technological or social context in which firms operate. This was a fundamental and we argue paradigmatic change, even though the environmental management paradigm continued to focus firmly on profitability, was instrumental in nature, and had a short-term horizon compared to a more ecocentric approach (Purser et al., 1995).

Underlying the emergence of environmental management practices was the fundamental recognition that the activities of a firm or industry can negatively impact upon the natural environment, and conversely, that changes in the firm's activities can improve on that impact and reduce harm done. Attention was focused on reducing, rather than eliminating, negative impacts of the economic system (of which one's firm is a part) on the ecological system. The latter was viewed as external to and as lying outside of this primary domain of economic action. We characterize this management world-view as an 'inside-out' perspective.

Management Innovation: Corporate Environmental Management

Although the starting point was compliance with regulation, the more proactive firms – those whose reputation had been most under fire – found that they could reduce the costs of compliance by taking a more strategic perspective of the environmental function in the firm; moreover they discovered that reducing waste paid off handsomely and could save them millions of dollars (for examples see DeSimone et al., 1997; Hoffman, 2000). In the 1980s, as industries in many countries began to improve and tighten their production processes in general, as the quality movement made 'continuous improvement' a household term, and as cost reduction became an increasingly important mandate, environmental management was found to be a source of deliberate cost avoidance and advanced strategically 'beyond compliance' (Hart, 1997; Hoffman, 1997; Nattrass and Altomare, 2002). Pollution control was replaced by pollution prevention and waste minimization; voluntary industry standards (for example King and Lenox, 2000) and comprehensive environmental management systems, such as the ISO 14001 standards, began to spread through industries and countries along globalizing supply chains.

The 1990s saw environmental management broaden further, advancing to embrace 'eco-efficiency' (De Simone et al., 1997). As more financial, organizational and intellectual resources were allocated toward environmental management, a flurry of additional management innovations spread through industries. New management practices ranged from the more technical tools, such as environmental impact assessments or full product life cycle assessment, to cross-functional programmes and eventually strategic systems, such as product stewardship, environmental cost accounting or product design for environment (for example Kolluru, 1994; Kirchgeorg, 1998; Thompson, 2003). Bansal and Roth offer additional CEM initiatives and link them to corporate motivations and expected benefits (2000). Often referred to summarily as 'corporate greening' (Shrivastava, 1995b; Winn and Angell, 2000), the innovations and developments in the arena of environmental management over the past three decades have been significant, both at the intra-organizational and the industry level (Lawrence et al., 2001). Yet despite eco-efficiency initiatives and productivity improvements that often also raised environmental performance per unit of production, total environmental performance improvements are more doubtful, particularly when factoring in overall consumption growth (Starik and Rands, 1995).

At the same time as environmental management practices advanced, firms found themselves forced by regulators and pushed by other stakeholders to disclose information about their environmental impact or performance (Heller and Mroczko, 2002), giving rise to another important new management practice, environmental reporting. Responding to pressures from increasingly diverse stakeholders, firms interacted with a widening set of constituents, prompting cross-fertilization of perspectives and exchange of skills and ideas (Hart and Sharma, 2004; Winn, 2001). So in addition to gaining important new capabilities in areas like cost control, tighter management systems and reduced liability, firms also gained from engaging in organizational learning processes and developing beneficial relationships through interactions with diverse stakeholders (Zietsma et al., 2002).

In looking back, and as the growing literature attests, environmental management and its rich arsenal of tools and programmes has become an increasingly accepted and even taken for granted practice (Hoffman, 1999; Lawrence et al., 2001).

THE PRESENT: SUSTAINABLE DEVELOPMENT BROADENS STRATEGIC DOMAINS

The next phase, sustainable development entering strategic management, was predicated by multiple developments. First, the inclusion of more stakeholders and more diverse perspectives continued in the 1990s through to the present, drawing management attention to a widening range of issues. This development can be observed across different country contexts, although the specific constellation of governmental, competitive and societal influences differed by country (for example Branzei and Vertinsky, 2002). Within firms, previously separate internal business functions related to the environment are often increasingly managed in a more integrated fashion, raising environmental management to strategic levels.

And as predicted by Gladwin et al. (1995), Hart (1995) and others, global social issues, like explosive population growth, increasing poverty and widening wealth disparity, have garnered managerial attention over recent years, as have associated business opportunities (Prahalad and Hart, 2001): 'An understanding of the human dimensions of sustainability must encompass the "driving forces" of anthropogenic global environmental change: population change, economic growth, technological change, political and economic institutions, and attitudes and beliefs' (Stern et al., 1992, cited in Gladwin et al., 1995: 878). Finally, the much-discussed trend of the globalization of a 'shrinking world' over recent years, has drawn attention to conditions and dynamics in previously ignored poor and emergent economies (Osland et al., 2002).

The coining of the concept of 'sustainable development' has likely contributed to the launch of this next phase more than any other single event (WECD, 1987). Sustainable development has since acquired the status of a strategic vision in the politics of many countries (Meffert and Kirchgeorg, 1993). Often criticized as vague and nebulous, there have been many efforts over the past decade to capture this vision in operational terms and to generate action guidelines and objectives. The 1990s saw the shaping of national sustainability strategies (see for example the report 'Sustainable Netherlands') intended to adapt production and consumption structures on the basis of scenarios (Buitenkamp et al., 1992). The typical starting point was the original definition proposed in the Brundtland Report: 'Sustainable development is development that meets the needs of the present without compromising the ability of future generations to meet their own needs' (WECD, 1987: 43).[4] As initiatives unfolded in many public sectors, the concept of sustainable development also increasingly entered discussions of corporate environmental management and business strategies, albeit slowly (Gladwin et al., 1995). Along with increasing attention to sustainability came a renewed interest in corporate social responsibility, particularly in Europe. Critiques of the limitations of the economy–ecology dyad stemming from the primary environmental focus of corporate environmental management and evolving ecological sustainability notions have resulted in a slowly expanding view of sustainability: 'Efforts aimed only toward ecological health and integrity, in the absence of efforts to alleviate poverty, stabilize population, and redistribute economic opportunity, may produce trivial results at best' (Gladwin et al., 1995: 879).

Before describing the management innovations associated with this next and currently unfolding phase and examining its underlying assumptions, it may be helpful to briefly review recent critical advances in knowledge on social, economic and ecological systems. Even prior to the landmark publication of the Brundtland Report, relationships between ecological, economic and social systems had become the subject of important scientific studies. Particularly well known are the 'world models' developed in the 1970s by Forrester (1971) and by Meadows et al. (1972). Using simulation models, these researchers attempted to model complex systems interdependencies in order to determine the effects of overuse of the ecological system on the quality of life and survivability of mankind.

Regardless of criticisms of these models, they alerted scientists and the general public to the limited carrying capacity of global ecological systems, and they focused attention on finding ways to reduce the negative impact of economic activity on ecological systems (see also King, 1995; Jennings and Zandbergen, 1995; Starik and Rands, 1995). Pearce and Turner for example developed a set of 'management rules' intended to reduce threats to ecological system dynamics (Pearce and Turner, 1990: 40ff), not unlike the first three system conditions of the Natural Step approach (for example Nattrass and Altomare, 2003). According to Pearce and Turner the sustainable use of natural resources can be ensured when (1) the depletion rate of renewable resources does not exceed their regeneration rate; (2) the amount of toxic and waste materials does not exceed the assimilation capacity of the ecological system; and (3) the depletion of non-renewable resources is smaller or equal to their substitution rate.

Changing Assumptions about Environmental, Social and Economic Sustainability

The work by these authors appears to be driven by the recognition of the threat of irreversible damage to the ecosystem on which human activity depends, a recognition that underpins applications of these findings about system dynamics and vulnerabilities from the natural, biological, systems and ecological sciences to management and management theories. An excellent collection of works applying these ideas to management paradigms and developments in organization theory can be found in a special issue of the *Academy of Management Review*, October 1995. The underlying assumptions are directly relevant for the assumptions guiding sustainability as a strategic management approach (for example 'sustaincentrism' in Gladwin et al., 1995).

First of all, an appreciation and greater understanding of large systems dynamics entered into consideration. Second, we note an increased recognition of the interdependence of social and ecological systems, and a growing attention to the health and viability of social and institutional systems and the necessity for their reduced environmental impacts. Third, and relatedly, there was the belief that production and consumption processes could be and needed to be adapted so as not to disrupt dynamic ecological balances, and to ensure sustained resource availability (Daly, 1991, as cited in Starik and Rands, 1995). As a consequence, the perceived need to reduce negative impacts of economic processes on the natural environment became

more urgent; the underlying assumption was that grave changes in the ecological balance could be prevented by proactive, sector-wide behaviour.

Even though the sense of urgency grew, the implication for management
remained largely the same: to massively reduce negative consequences from
economic or firm activity on the environment. Attention was not paid to
the reverse effects, namely that of massive disruptions or discontinuities in
the ecological system on firms. Nor do we find considerations of such discontinuities in current sustainability management frameworks. Among the
rare exceptions of such works is King's article (1995) on 'ecological surprises' in which he examines characteristics of communities that had successfully avoided ecological system collapse over long periods of time.
Other articles clearly point to the spectre of limited carrying capacity and
the likelihood of impending irreversible changes, but without fully examining the meaning of these (for example Gladwin et al., 1995; Shrivastava,
1995a; Starik and Rands, 1995).

We conclude that in the emerging sustainability management literature,
attention is paid to the impact of economic and social system behaviour on
ecological systems, but virtually none to the impact of ecological balance
disturbances on the economic or social system. As a result, the dominant
perspective for management is still best characterized as an 'inside-out'
view, one in which the primary perspective is to look from the firm (which
itself resides inside the economic system realm) out at the external environment. A difference to the inside-out view identified for the corporate
management paradigm above is that a second 'external' system, the 'social
system', has joined the natural environment, which is similarly viewed as
vis-à-vis and outside the firm's 'own' economic environment. The underlying assumption in this view is that the sustainable firm must manage and
deliberately interact with two 'outside' systems, namely the ecological and
the social realm. We contend that the 'inside-out' view, while expanded in
scope, continues to hold for the sustainability management paradigm.

We detect other changes in assumptions however. The sustainability management approach is characterized by a much greater recognition of the existence of, and need for, a high level of integration. This differs considerably
from the former dichotomies between the ecocentric versus technocentric
approach (Gladwin et al., 1995), which had been manifested in the compromise of incremental impact reductions in the CEM paradigm. A second
change is the broadening of the perceived range of influence and impact by
firms in terms of their geographical scope and types of environmental
impacts, and in terms of attempting to reduce negative social impacts (for
example on economically affected communities) and to accept social obligations (for example improving existing human rights conditions). Third, we
note an explicit mainstreaming of environmental and, to a lesser degree,

Triple bottom line approach

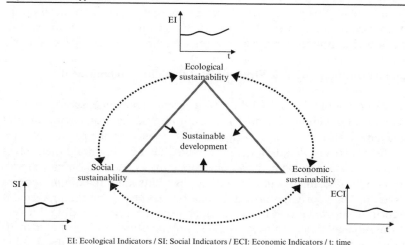

EI: Ecological Indicators / SI: Social Indicators / ECI: Economic Indicators / t: time

Figure 11.1   Balancing ecological, social and economic sustainability

social goals in business practices. Now taking a deliberate systems perspective, environmental, social and ecological systems are increasingly viewed as
interrelated subsystems of a broader, global, system (see for example Gladwin
et al., 1995 or the United Nations Millennium Development Goals).[5]

Overall there is clear recognition that the health and vitality of the
overall system in this paradigm depends on the health of each nested sub-
system, and on a kind of optimized balance between the three major
systems. Figure 11.1 is intended to depict this notion of sustainability, indicating minor variations in representative indicators for each system.
Sustainability management is aimed at achieving that balance by incorporating environmental goals and social objectives, in addition to still primary
economic objectives.

In sum, we characterize the sustainability management approach as
follows. First, it is built on the assumption that each of the three major
systems must be viable and healthy, if the global system planet is to flourish. Second, it assumes that a 'balancing' of these three will attain the goal
of overall global system wellness and its long-term sustainability, thus
requiring an integrated management approach. Third, it views deliberate
interaction, partnering, networking and learning from multiple and
diverse constituents as critical for successfully realizing such an integrated
management approach, for a host of reasons (for example: benefiting from
other perspectives; improved knowledge management; keeping the pulse

of diverse views and thus reducing potential for conflict) (Hart and Sharma, 2004). Sustainable development perspectives rest on the assumption that changing course, that is changing economic and social systems behaviour, is required to prevent irreversible damage to ecological systems.

Management Innovation 2: Strategic Sustainability Management

The development of sustainability strategies in management is much more recent and far behind the now maturing approaches for environmental management (Sharma and Henriques, 2005). Much of the progress comes from firms actively wrestling with the issues, having committed themselves to a path of sustainable business development. Consensus on paradigms, criteria for assessment, minimum requirements and maximum potentials are as yet poorly developed, as can be expected from a management practice (or movement) at this early stage. Advances from leading thinkers in firms, consultancies, think tanks, research institutes and academic institutions at country and even supra-country levels (such as the United Nations or the European Commission)[6] are contributing to the development of sustainability management in practice. Rather than attempting a comprehensive review of the many different efforts, below we examine just two approaches for sustainability management in this chapter, Europe-based The Natural Step, and Stuart Hart's US-based framework for creating sustainable value. Both have gained practical relevance through their acceptance and dissemination in a number of firms.

The challenges of managing in a fashion consistent with the paradigm of sustainable development are huge and, we would argue, mostly exceed current management capabilities available to managers. Such capabilities include *inter alia* a basic level of ecological and social knowledge, along with sustainability-oriented integrated firm strategies, systems, policies and visions. All the insights of effectively managing organizational change are needed, as is a firm grip on current competitive realities in the marketplace. But it does not stop there. To manage toward sustainability means to play in an arena of unprecedented complexity, with consideration of not one, but three major systems (economic, social and ecological), and in the face of globally deepening interrelatedness and interdependence of these, and of nested subsystems. The major systems need to move in some degree of unison toward the common goal of sustainability, yet the many determinants tend to be well outside a manager's discretion. Both growing the knowledge related to sustainable firm management, and building and managing partnerships and effective networks, thus become part and parcel of sustainability management.

As mentioned, many firms are embarking on this challenging path, and find it to be a difficult and sometimes impossible path to pursue. One management framework that has gained considerable support internationally is Sweden's The Natural Step (Bradbury and Clair, 1999; Nattrass and Altomare, 2003; Robert, 1994; Senge and Carstedt, 2001). Its appeal is that it provides non-negotiable system conditions (adding a social dimension to Pearce and Turner's management rules, namely fair and effective resource use), which need to be operationalized by each organization according to its particular competitive circumstance, capability and willingness to change. The Natural Step (TNS) can be adopted by any organization, from businesses to not-for-profit organizations, and from municipalities to entire regions. It is however a very general approach, and as such requires considerable developmental effort by firms, along with sustained personal and organizational commitment, to make it strategically meaningful. Focusing on process and organizational change, TNS leaves the actual definition of strategic objectives largely to individual organizations. Among the many examples of organizations applying TNS are Nike, Starbucks, Ikea and the municipality of Whistler, British Columbia.

Another influential approach is the framework developed by Hart and Milstein (2003). It makes strategic sense of the long list of diverse environmental management tools and programmes, types of stakeholder interaction, and sustainability objectives, placing them into a portfolio of quadrants that vary in degrees of difficulty of implementation, time horizons, innovative capability, risk exposure and potential for long-term growth and value creation. This approach, aptly captured under the term 'creating sustainable value', has a strong tradition in competitive dynamics and the resource-based view of the firm, tying competitive advantage to a firm's stock of resources and capabilities. The portfolio has tremendous practical appeal. It allows firms to assess their progress made and to pinpoint areas of potential market opportunity and capability development. It is firmly rooted in the assumption that competitive advantage and financial viability is a necessary precondition for a sustainable strategy, and helps firms to map their environmental, stakeholder and other sustainability-related initiatives vis-à-vis their strategic sustainability objectives.

Different firms have taken different approaches, as they adjusted their corporate mission and strategy to incorporate sustainable development (see the websites of many major North American or European companies, for example Dow Chemical and Xerox, or Germany's Henkel and Otto). As the concept's three pillars of economic, social and environmental considerations gained acceptance, the challenge grew for business to graduate from the more functionally based, focused environmental management to strategic sustainability management. The new approach had to be strategic, and grounded in competitive dynamics; it had to build on environmental capabilities, and also deliberately incorporate social concerns.

Moreover effectively implementing strategic sustainability management required not only the integration of these three considerations, but also a kind of balance or synthesis between them. The wide range of different approaches reflects both the experimental and emergent nature of inventing new management practices at this early stage. Some firms used dialogues with stakeholders and business organizations to develop extensive indicator catalogues that define their social, ecological and economic goals along with realistic achievement levels.

Meanwhile the term 'triple bottom line' has taken hold in the corporate vocabulary, referencing the need to assess not only financial performance, but also the firm's social and environmental performance (Elkington, 1998). While it is difficult enough to assess and measure environmental performance however, social performance is an even broader, more diverse and somewhat shifting concept, and that much more difficult to measure. Firms are likely to have the least understanding of their social performance, as compared to their financial or even their environmental performance. But even if social performance could be measured reliably, to offer comparisons between firms or industries, the even greater challenge is to assess a firm's integrated 'sustainability performance'.

For both internal management and external disclosure purposes, the need to assess, report on and compare sustainability performance between firms has grown. Efforts to build on the capabilities developed in environmental reporting can be seen in recent efforts to standardize heterogeneous and largely incomparable reporting approaches. A particularly good example are the sustainability indicators developed by the Global Reporting Initiative, which provide guidelines for firms toward worldwide, standardized sustainability reporting (GRI, 2002).

In sum, the advances of strategic sustainability management, though in their infancy, are considerable. One critical question to ask in light of the 'world studies' cited earlier is whether these advances have sufficiently improved on the relationship between firms collectively and their ecological and social environments. In the following section, we offer a partial answer to this question. We now introduce a new development which we believe has the potential to dramatically and radically alter perceptions and management practice.

THE FUTURE: (UN)NATURAL DISASTERS AND MANAGEMENT FOR SURVIVAL

Even if experts continue to argue over the role of human activity as a contributor to climate change and natural catastrophes, natural disasters

Table 11.1   Great natural catastrophes 2001
(4 out of 50 significant events)

Nr	Date (2001)	Region	Event	Fatalities	Economic losses (US$ m)	Insured losses (US$ m)	Effect on GDP
4	13.1	El Salvador	Earthquake, landslides	845	1 500	300	10.6%
5	26.1	India	Earthquake	14 000	4 500	100	0.89%
15	6–12.4	USA	Severe storm, hail	1	2 500	1 900	0.02%
20	5–17.6	USA	Tropical storm Allison	25	6 000	3 500	0.06%

Source: Münchener Rück Topics, 2003.

appear to have increased in number and severity in the past decade. The majority of these disasters are extreme weather events, such as droughts and heatwaves, storms (for example, tornadoes, hurricanes, typhoons), floods and fires. Earthquakes can wreak particularly severe and widespread damage (see Münchener Rück, 2003). As an example, Table 11.1 lists the four great natural catastrophes of 2001 with their associated losses and relative economic impacts on affected countries.

Recent work suggests that especially climate change-related natural disasters are no longer isolated events, but rather indicators of global and local changes in ecological system parameters. Whether anthropogenic (that is 'unnatural') or not, large system changes may bring about not only locally or regionally confined ecological disasters, but also dramatic changes in social and economic system parameters. Figure 11.2 illustrates this relationship.

Support for the existence of such a trend is growing. Certainly, the news and popular media offer no shortage of disasters in the headlines (examples from the summer of 2004 range from coverage of individual hurricanes, massive floods and wildfires, to the movie *The Day After Tomorrow* or *Business Week*'s special report 'Global warming: why business is taking it so seriously' [7] (Carey, 2004). Below are four types of sources supporting our thesis.

First we cite a study reporting increased variability of weather and ocean influences that result in increased natural catastrophes in the region of the South Pacific (Hay, 2002). Particularly severely affected are island and coastal areas, where the entire population faces growing threats to its existence, as do the region's ecosystems. Table 11.2 shows for example that the Fiji islands are subject to increasingly powerful cyclones, which cause

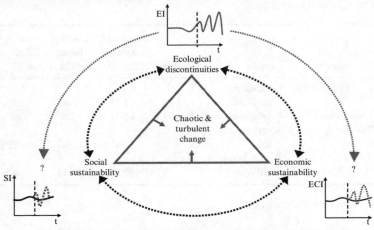

EI: Ecological Indicators / SI: Social Indicators / ECI: Economic Indicators / t: time

Figure 11.2   Effects of ecological discontinuities on sustainable development

Table 11.2   Losses associated with four similar tropical cyclones affecting Fiji

Year	Name of cyclone	Estimated loss (Fiji $ m)
1952	–	0.5
1972	Bebe	6.0
1983	Oscar	30.0
1993	Kina	150.0

Source: Campbell (1999), cited in Hay (2002), p. 4.

increasingly greater, economically quantifiable damage. Hay's study also delineates the use of risk analyses due to abrupt ecological system effects on the socio-economic system (Hay, 2002).[8]

The reinsurance industry provides a second source of evidence. Both their damage statistics and changing policies in this sector support our thesis of growing ecological system swings and anticipated effects on economic and social systems. Analyses of natural catastrophes globally, and the associated massive economic damage, indicate a significant increase in recent decades. According to the Topics GEO 2003 report (Münchener

Table 11.3   Development of natural catastrophes and economic losses
(in US$ bn, 2003 values)

Decade	1950–59	1960–69	1970–79	1980–89	1990–99	Last 10 years
Number of events	20	27	47	63	91	60
Economic losses	42.7	76.7	140.6	217.3	670.4	514.5
Insured losses	–	6.2	13.1	27.4	126.0	83.6

Source: Münchener Rück 2003, p. 15.

Rück, 2003), the number of natural catastrophes rose nearly fivefold, economic losses nearly sixteenfold over the last five decades (see Table 11.3). The hot summer of 2003 in Europe was noted as a particularly extreme case. In its Topics Geo 2003 report, Munich Reinsurance Company states: 'The outstanding event of the past year in Europe was the extreme heat and drought in the summer. Initial climatological analyses indicated that – in statistical terms – the event as a whole was to be expected much more seldom than once in 450 years.' The report also offers a remarkable statement about the relationship between climate extremes and natural catastrophes: 'extreme events which can be traced to climate change will have increasingly grave consequences in the future [including] new types of weather risks and greater loss potentials. . . . Neither human beings, buildings, and infrastructure, nor the agricultural and livestock sectors are prepared for such extremes. . . . we would be well advised to prepare ourselves for dramatic changes' (Münchener Rück, 2003).

A third source in support of our thesis comes from the investor community's growing concern with financial and economic risks of global warming, particularly to pension funds. At the Institutional Investor Summit on Climate Risk (IISCR) held in November 2003 by the US-based Investor Network on Climate Risk (INCR), the state treasurer of California noted the huge risk of global warming to the US economy, which Wall Street has ignored to date. Connecticut's state treasurer meanwhile highlighted the need for companies to 'adequately disclose potential liabilities related to climate risk' (INCR Summary Report, 2003: 4) and the CEO of Swiss Re further supported the need to plan for highly uncertain effects of climate change on business. In his remarks, Harvard scientist Holdren mentions the following unpleasant 'surprises' potentially resulting from climate change:

Large increases in the frequency of highly destructive storms; drastic shifts in ocean current systems that control regional climates (e.g. Gulf stream/Western

Europe); multi-meter sea-level rise, over a period of centuries, from disintegration of West-Antarctic ice sheet; runaway greenhouse effect from decomposition of methane clathrates, drastically increasing the severity of all expected impacts as well as the probability of big surprises. (Holdren, 2003: slide 53).

Investors are urged 'as part of their fiduciary responsibility, to take a range of actions designed to understand and to mitigate investor climate risk' (IISCR Summary Report, 2003: 3).

The fourth source of support for our thesis is a report to the US Pentagon, 'An Abrupt Climate Change Scenario and Its Implications for United States National Security' by Schwartz and Randall (2003), which examines scenarios and impacts of increasing weather extremes due to climate change on the American society. The authors emphasize that it is not the threat from terrorism, but the vulnerability of countries and societies to natural catastrophes and climate change that offers the greatest future challenges to national security. The report highlights regions where natural catastrophes and climate change can reduce the carrying capacity of ecosystems such that the continuation of production and consumption processes is threatened, diminishing or compromising the survival of economic and social systems to such a degree, that potentially entire regions would be no longer inhabitable by people.

The number of studies, reports and initiatives in support of our thesis is growing rapidly. The Canadian Natural Hazards Assessment Project (2004) is one more indicator for the growing attention paid to natural disasters. Concurrently we detect new terminology entering the scientific literature, such as 'abrupt climate change', 'inevitable surprises', 'rapid non-linear climate change' or 'regional vulnerability' (previously introduced to management studies by King, 1995, but largely ignored by organization theorists so far). 'Resilience' in particular has become a widely used term. Resilience denotes an ecosystem's capacity to maintain its normal functions before it reaches threshold levels catapulting it into rapid and discontinuous change with completely uncertain outcomes. Applied to communities' adaptability, the term is also used increasingly to refer to their ability to deal with rapid, discontinuous change from ecological systems.

Attention to more and more extreme ecological events has been particularly strong in those regions of the world that have been subject to extreme weather events for some time (for example, for 50 years in the South Pacific), but also by those industry sectors particularly affected. As mentioned above, increasing natural catastrophes, and associated massive economic and insured losses, have not gone unnoticed by the insurance industry, which is forced to develop global risk-spreading mechanisms, reinsurance and other insurance service modifications to reduce their own exposure. The insurance industry, which is especially concerned about both systematic changes and massive loss events, may in fact serve as an indicator or early warning sector.

Clearly, different economic sectors are likely to be affected differentially. Particularly vulnerable are sectors that rely on relatively narrowly confined temperature and seasonal conditions, such as agriculture, aquaculture, fisheries and forestry, as well as tourism (especially coastal and mountain destinations). Other industries likely to suffer potentially devastating effects are those dependent on, and vulnerable to the disruption of, large-scale infrastructure (energy, automotive and other transportation sectors) and financial markets.

But although some sectors and regions may be affected more and earlier than others by rapid environmental changes, the effects of climate change, extreme weather events and the collapse of season and weather dependent ecosystems will likely be felt broadly. Ecosystem services, such as clean air, seasons needed for proper growing cycles, pollination provided by healthy bee populations, can be disrupted. As Gladwin et al. state: 'how many organizations could exist in the absence of oxygen production, fresh water supply, or fertile soil?' (1995: 875). Perhaps the most important aspect of abrupt and massive ecological discontinuities is that they are difficult to predict and prepare for, that their outcome is highly uncertain, and consequently that they are extremely challenging for business planning.

Changing Assumptions about Ecological Discontinuities

Given the growing attention paid to these developments, we see a strong potential for a drastic change in public and management perspectives. The changes in the physical environment have been observed for some time. The risk of passing thresholds of carrying capacity leading to irreversible collapse of ecosystems or biogeochemical cycles (such as ocean circulation patterns) has been raised by many (earlier, we cited the world models and the *Academy of Management Review 1995* special issue), but to date, their implications have been largely ignored or dismissed. We believe however that the time may be ripe for a fairly sudden figure-ground shift, both in public and subsequently in mainstream management theorists' perspective. Bombarded with scientific panel reports, headlines and greater personal affectedness by severe weather events, and following several years of persistent sensitization by other globally unsettling events to the vulnerability of presumed stable institutions, we suspect that we may soon see a tipping of public opinion about extreme events; we view the reinsurance sectors and the investor communities initiatives as early indicators. The resulting reinterpretation and shifts in attention (Hoffman and Ocasio,

2001) have the potential to trigger a paradigm shift in managerial perceptions and views.

While the outcome of these events remains uncertain, we can examine the more subtle changes in underlying assumptions. Keeping the cited studies in mind, we find that no longer is the endangerment of ecological balances through anthropogenic environmental impacts the main topic. Instead, the threat of massive and unpredictable ecological system discontinuities, manifested in sudden disasters and slower system changes, and their impact on the stability and survivability of socio-economic systems shifts into the centre of consideration. Now attention shifts from the primacy of human organizations and their impact on the environment to the environment as the primary actor; the direction of considered impact reverses, and salient cause–effect relations trace the impact of abrupt ecological system changes on equally dramatic changes in socio-economic system parameters. In contrast to the 'inside-out' view of corporate environmental management and sustainability management, the expected figure-ground reversal can be characterized by its 'outside-in' view.

In the studies cited, the environment is an unpredictable actor that affects socio-economic (as well as ecological) systems in unexpected, 'surprising' and largely unpredictable ways.[9] The assessments of disaster statistics in the reports by Hay, by Randall and Schwartz, by reinsurance experts and by the investor community underscore that dealing with outside-in effects will have increasing salience for economic and social actors in the future. What are the implications for sustainability management? The basic assumptions of incremental improvements inherent in sustainability thinking, along with its objectives of integrating and balancing of economic, ecological and social system viability, offer little guidance for dealing with chaotic change. Under conditions where ecological outside-in effects dominate social actor inside-out effects, the 'balanced system management' underlying sustainability views need to at a minimum be expanded and complemented, and may even need to be substituted by conceptual frameworks fairly new to organization theories, such as 'resilience management' or 'discontinuity management' (Folke et al., 2002).

Applying these perspectives to management, we see a radical departure from the inside-out perspective of environmental management, and its more systems theory-informed cousin from sustainability management. We see a new set of assumptions beginning to shape industry's perspective, one in which ecological systems 'out there' can inflict catastrophes and major damage on social and economic systems. This perspective differs further from the assumptions of sustainability management in that it deals with radical, unpredictable, discontinuous changes or catastrophes of increasingly uncertain outcomes over the long term.

As mentioned earlier, sufficient disturbance of ecological system parameters can cause massive and unpredictable system change (for example mutual effects of global climate changes and changes in ocean circulation patterns affect seasons, habitats, species extinction and biodiversity, to name but a few). While the parameters of a newly evolving system are likely to develop over extended periods of time (Holling, 2001) the resulting type of system is highly uncertain. More important for this chapter's focus on business organizations, the period of adjustment to a new system dynamic is likely to be characterized by highly chaotic conditions for socio-economic actors, causing organizational instability as well as great suffering by humans and other life forms.

We have argued that sustainability management rests on assumptions of balance and integration. In contrast, the new 'ecological discontinuity' management will need to develop capabilities to respond to unpredictable, radical, large-scale changes in the ecological system; these chaotic changes have the potential to unravel local and possibly national social and economic systems, leading to further detrimental effects on ecosystem functioning and parameters (Bossel, 2001; Holling, 2001).

Under these conditions, is it possible to secure the survival of social and economic actors, using the strategic vision of sustainable development? Or do sustainability management frameworks offer guidelines only if we assume that ecological systems are not subject to discontinuous and abrupt, chaotic changes in the near future? We argue that the latter has been the case, and that we are at risk of facing the blinding effect of a 'sustainability myopia'. The current limited vision of sustainability management, under conditions of ecological system discontinuities, is at best ineffective.[10] Holding on to it could not only limit the potential of sustainability management frameworks to leverage their advances to the benefit of social, economic and ecological system stability, but could further reduce the survivability of societal and economic actors.

Management in an Era of Ecological Discontinuities: Survival and Beyond

Recent disasters have sensitized the public, political and economic leaders to the vulnerabilities of socio-economic system functioning. The threat from terrorism has remained particularly pertinent since the events of 11 September 2001, followed by outbreaks of epidemic diseases like SARS, and infrastructure breakdowns like widespread power outages. What these events have in common with the ecological discontinuities subject of this chapter is that they too are large scale, systemic and of a highly destructive and even deadly nature.

In the wake of these events, consulting services assisting business with emergency planning and preparedness have flourished. Euphemistically called business continuity management or BCM (for example www. globalcontinuity.com), considerable attention and resources have been allocated to prepare for and limit damage from man-made and natural disasters.

Dealing with discontinuous change itself is not new to businesses, nor to management studies. Environmental jolts or shocks to firms from their market, economic or technology environments (Meyer, 1982; Tushman and Anderson, 1986) and managing in hyperturbulent environments have been the subject of studies for some time (Meyer et al., 1993). More generally, insights from managing organizational change can provide general direction under conditions of ecological discontinuities and chaotic change. As Huber and Glick state: 'When the environment changes to a state incompatible with the nature of the organization, the organization has available the following strategies: (1) adapting to the changed environment; (2) moving to a different environment; (3) managing the environment into a more compatible state; (4) temporarily relying on slack resources, loose coupling, or other buffers' (1993: 7). We note that none of these works on environmental change however considered the ecology as a potential source of disturbance; rather, jolts are viewed as endogenous to the socio-economic system. Nor does this literature account for disasters, viewing them instead as rare events.

More directly applicable to managing in the face of emergencies are crisis management (for example Mitroff, 1994; Mitroff et al., 1987; Smart and Vertinsky, 1987) and risk management techniques (for example Kotheimer and Coffin, 2003), along with capabilities developed around public sector emergency preparedness. While fairly rudimentary in the organization theory literature, these approaches are geared primarily to dealing with the immediate impacts of disasters, and to mitigating risks and losses. We suggest that (1) this literature needs to be developed much further, and (2) that a longer-term framework is needed which extends past immediate crisis response. Since ecological global systems cannot be affected significantly by actors in the short term, broader adaptive behaviours that secure the survivability of the economy and society become increasingly relevant. Crisis management, risk management and emergency responses need to be supplemented with long-term management for survival.

IMPLICATIONS FOR SUSTAINABILITY MANAGEMENT RESEARCH

The very foundation of sustainable development is that a balancing of ecological, economic and social goals is fundamentally possible and desirable. Our question in this chapter was the following: what strategic guidance can be provided by sustainability management in the face of increasing discontinuities in the ecological system, which subsequently, due to system interdependencies, cause significant discontinuities in the social and ecological system? Can the dawning 'outside-in' view displace sustainability management or thinking? And should it? We argue that both have a place, and that in no way should the learning that has occurred in sustainability management, both by individual firms and by industries collectively, be supplanted by an exclusive focus on managing for ecological discontinuities and chaotic change. Nevertheless the 'balance assumption' implicit in much of sustainability management, that is to dynamically balance ecological, social and economic systems, does not provide adequate or sufficient strategic direction.

Instead the resilience of society in general, and of business organizations in particular vis-à-vis such discontinuities requires special attention in sustainability management and scholarship. We also note that, in the face of overwhelming external events, 'hope' will have to be a critical component in effectively dealing with the challenges ahead. This is where entrepreneurial ingenuity (Cohen and Winn, 2004), opportunity-seeking (Sharma, 2000) and the solution focus of business in general may be able to provide a potent antidote to the real risk of collective resignation.

Holling offers this broadened perspective: 'Sustainability is the capacity to create, test, and maintain adaptive capability. Development is the process of creating, testing, and maintaining opportunity. The phrase that combines the two, "Sustainable Development" therefore refers to the goal of fostering adaptive capabilities while simultaneously creating opportunities' (2001: 399). Here, 'sustainable development' refers not only to the management of relatively constant, stable developmental paths, but must also include an examination of potentially existence-threatening events and conditions, to which only intelligent and courageous adaptation can secure a new growth path.

Important new research questions for management scholars derive from these developments. Perhaps most urgently needed are answers to the question of what capabilities and competences firms can build to enhance their chances for survival under conditions of ecological discontinuities and chaotic change. An examination of how today's corporation, and especially the multinational corporation, is affected may lead to additional research questions. Are some forms of business organizations better equipped for survival than others? And are some better equipped then others, following ecological discontinuities, to minimize subsequent disruptions to ecological and social systems generally, and human suffering specifically? How can work on crisis management, emergency preparedness and risk management be incorporated into sustainability management frameworks?

To find ways to improve the resilience and adaptability of organizations under conditions of chaotic change, future research might draw on previous work on diversity, and look to processes like organizational learning and flexibility (Harvard Business Review, 2001). An expanded understanding of 'sustainability management' also requires continued research to integrate discontinuity, resilience management and risk management. Furthermore the practical mandate of such research is evident; effective survival strategies must include implementation guidelines.

Earlier we asked the question: Are we at risk of 'sustainability myopia'? Our answer is yes. We suggest that 'sustainable development' loses its relevance as a strategic vision if it leads decision-makers to prioritize a 'balance assumption', and causes them to underestimate the existence and potential impact of discontinuous change. Increasingly, organizations and decision-makers must take into account the possibility of extreme impacts by the ecological system on social and economic systems. It is our hope that the predicted figure-ground shift will serve as a gentle awakening from 'sustainability myopia', and that it will occur with sufficient time to prepare, respond and correct trajectories. We argue that an expanded understanding of sustainability management includes consideration of ecological discontinuities and seeks to build capabilities and competencies that strengthen the resilience and adaptability of organizations and their broad communities. Only then can we refer to 'true' sustainability management.

NOTES

1. We cite the creation of new journals as evidence (for example *Organization and Environment; Business Strategy and Environment; Corporate Environmental Strategy*), as well as a growing number of individual articles and special issues on the environment and sustainability in *Academy of Management, Operations Management* and other major management journals.
2. These comments refer primarily to the North American context, although one may find roughly parallel developments in Europe.
3. Examples of country-based differences in regulatory approaches abound, such as the centralized US approach compared to the conciliatory and participatory Canadian approach (see Jennings and Zandbergen, 1995).
4. Reviews of different conceptions of sustainability and critiques of the WCED definition can be found in Gladwin et al. (1995), Jennings and Zandbergen (1995), Starik and Rands (1995), particularly as applicable to business organizations and management theories.
5. Namely: 1. Eradicate extreme poverty and hunger; 2. Achieve universal primary education; 3. Promote gender equality and empower women; 4. Reduce child mortality; 5. Improve maternal health; 6. Combat HIV/AIDS, malaria and other diseases; 7. Ensure environmental sustainability; 8. Develop a global partnership for development (http://www.un.org/millenniumgoals/).
6. A recent example is a proposed European framework for Corporate Social Responsibility (European Communities, 2001).
7. *Business Week* states: 'Many scientists agree on the basics of global warming and the effects on the planet could be dire', and lists these consequences: 1. flooding; 2. ocean disruptions; 3. shifting storm patterns, 4. reduced farm output; 5. animal extinctions, and 6. droughts (16 August 2004: 63).

8. Additional analyses of the impact of changes on ecological systems on socio-economic systems are noted by Folke et al. (2002).
9. In some ways, these developments take us full circle from early predictions of ecological system continuities resulting from anthropogenic interference with the environment, to their actual occurrence. In his monograph *Earth in the Balance*, Al Gore (1992) had high-lighted the threats and scenarios of an ecosystem out of balance, spelled out even more concretely in the report by Schwartz and Randall. While interesting, this coming of age of earlier predictions is not directly relevant for this chapter. Here we focus instead on the changes in managerial perceptions and resulting management practices.
10. The exclusive focus on and critique of sustainability management approaches in this chapter should be seen in the context of the following consideration: the collective ignoring of troubling ecological trends and potential crises has, for several decades, been amazingly persistent on part of most social, institutional and economic actors (and was decried by many authors cited here). We acknowledge this phenomenon; it is not new and it runs through most sectors of society, including management scholars. Our intention in this chapter is to point out that these trends have also been, if not ignored, then not fully developed, by those most closely familiar with them, namely sustainability scholars and managers.

REFERENCES

The Academy of Management Review (1995), 'Special topic forum on ecologically sustainable organizations, **20**(4), 873–1115.

Bansal, P. and K. Roth (2000), 'Why companies go green: a model of ecological responsiveness', *Academy of Management Journal*, **360**, 20.

Bossel, H. (2001), 'Assessing viability and sustainability: a systems-based approach for deriving comprehensive indicator sets', *Conservation Ecology*, **5**(2), 12. Online: http://www.consecol.org/vol5/iss2/art12

Bradbury, H. and J.A. Clair (1999), 'Promoting sustainable organizations with Sweden's natural step', *Academy of Management Executive*, **13**(4), 63–74.

Branzei, O. and I. Vertinsky (2002), 'Eco-sustainability orientation in China and Japan: Differences between proactive and reactive firms', in Sanjay Sharma and Mark Starik (eds), *Research in Corporate Sustainability: The Evolving Theory and Practice of Organizations in the Natural Environment*, Cheltenham, UK and Northampton, USA: Edward Elgar, 85–123.

Buitenkamp, M., H. Venner and T. Wams (eds) (1992), *Sustainable Netherlands*, Amsterdam: Milieudefensivie.

Canadian Natural Hazards Assessment Project (CNHAP) (2004), 'The Meteorological Service of Environment Canada, Critical Infrastructure Protection and Emergency Preparedness, and the Geological Survey of Canada'. Online: www.ocipep.gc.ca/research/natural_haz_e.asp

Carey, John (2004), 'Global warming: why business is taking it so seriously', *Business Week*, 16 August.

Carson, Rachel (1962), *Silent Spring*, Boston, MA: Houghton Mifflin.

Cohen, B. and M.I. Winn (2004), *Market Imperfection, Opportunity and Sustainable Entrepreneurship*, Working paper.

Dalton, Russell J. and Manfred Kuechler (eds) (1990), *Challenging the Political Order: New Social and Political Movements in Western Democracies*, New York: Oxford University Press.

Daly, Herman E. (1991), *Steady-State Economics*, 2nd edn, Washington, DC: Island Press.

De Simone, Livio D., Frank Popoff with the World Business Council for Sustainable Development (1997), *Eco-Efficiency*, Cambridge, MA: MIT Press.

Dunlap, R.E. and K.D. Van Liere (1978), 'The new environmental paradigm', *Journal of Environmental Education*, **9**(4), 10–19.

Elkington, John (1998), *Cannibals with Forks*, Gabriola Island, Canada: New Society Publisher.

European Communities (2001), *Promoting a European Framework for Corporate Social Responsibility: A Green Paper*, Luxembourg: Office for Official Publications of the European Union. Online: http://europa.eu.int/comm/employment_social/soc-dial/csr/greenpaper.htm

Folke, C. et al. (2002), 'Resilience and sustainable development: building adaptive capacity in a world of transformations', scientific background paper on resilience for *The World Summit on Sustainable Development* on behalf of The Environmental Advisory Council to the Swedish Government, Stockholm: Ministry of the Environment.

Forrester, Jay W. (1971), *World Dynamics*, Cambridge, MA: Wright-Allen Pr.

Gladwin, T.N., J.J. Kennelly and T.-S. Krause (1995), 'Shifting paradigms for sustainable development: implications for management theory and research', *Academy of Management Review*, **20**(4), 874–907.

Gore, Albert (1992), *Earth in the Balance: Ecology and Human Spirit*, Boston, MA; New York; London: Mifflin.

Global Reporting Initiative (GRI) (2002), *Sustainability Reporting Guidelines*, Boston, MA: Global Reporting Initiative.

Hart, S.L. (1995), 'A natural-resource-based view of the firm', *Academy of Management Review*, **20**(4), 986–1014.

Hart, S. (1997), 'Beyond greening: strategies for a sustainable world', Harvard Business Review, **75**(1), 66–76.

Hart, S.L. and M.B. Milstein (2003), 'Creating sustainable value', *Academy of Management Executive*, **17**(2), 56–69.

Hart, S.L. and S. Sharma (2004), 'Engaging fringe stakeholders for competitive imagination', *Academy of Management Executive*, **18**(1), 7–18.

Harvard Business Review (ed.) (2001), 'Harvard Business Review on managing diversity', Boston, MA: Harvard Business School Press.

Hay, J. (2002), 'Integrating disaster risk management and adaptation to climate variability and change: needs, benefits and approaches from a South Pacific perspective', Paper presented at the UNDP Expert Group Meeting, Havana.

Heller, Trudy and Jeanne Mroczko (2002), 'Information disclosure in environmental policy and the development of secretly environmentally-friendly products', in Sanjay Sharma and Mark Starik (eds), *Research in Corporate Sustainability: The Evolving Theory and Practice of Organizations in the Natural Environment*, Cheltenham, UK and Northampton, USA: Edward Elgar, 237–55.

Hoffman, Andrew J. (1997), *From Heresy to Dogma: An Institutional History of Corporate Environmentalism*. San Francisco, CA: New Lexington Press.

Holffman, A.J. (1999), 'Institutional evolution and change: environnmentalism and the U.S. chemical industry' *Academy of Management Journal*, **42**(4), 351–71.

Hoffman, A.J. (2000), *Competitive Environmental Strategy*, Washington, DC: Island Press.

Hoffman, A.J. and W. Ocasio (2001), 'Not all events are attended equally: toward a middle-range theory of industry attention to external events', *Organization Science*, **12**(4), 414–34.

Holdren, John P. (2003), 'Risks from global climate change: what do we know? What should we do?' Institutional Investor Summit on Climate Risk (IISCR). Online: http://www.incr.com/summit_JPH_N03b.pdf

Holling, C.S. (2000), 'Theories for sustainable futures', *Conservation Ecology* **4**(2). Online: http://consecol.org/vol4/iss 2/art7

Holling, C.S. (2001), 'Understanding the complexity of economic, ecological, and social systems', *Ecosystems*, **4**, 390–405.

Huber, George P. and W.H. Glick (eds) (1993), *Organizational Change and Redesign*, New York: Oxford University Press.

Investor Network on Climate Risk (INCR) (2003), *Summary Report*, Institutional Investor Summit on Climate Risk (IISCR). Online: http://www.incr.com/summit_ summary_report.pdf

Jennings, P.D. and P.A. Zandbergen (1995), 'Ecologically sustainable organizations: an institutional approach', *Academy of Management Review*, **20**(4), 1015–52.

King, A. (1995), 'Avoiding ecological surprise: lessons from long-standing communities', *Academy of Management Review*, **20**(4), 961–85.

King, A.A. and M.J. Lenox (2000), 'Industry self-regulation without sanctions: the chemical industry's responsible care program', *Academy of Management Journal*, **43**(4), 698–716.

Kirchgeorg, Manfred (1998), *Marktstrategisches Kreislaufmanagement*, Wiesbaden, Germany: Gabler Verlag.

Kolluru, R. (ed.) (1994), *Handbook of Environmental Management*, Englewood Cliffs, NJ: Prentice Hall.

Kotheimer, C.J. and B. Coffin (2003). 'How to justify business continuity management', *Risk Management*, **50**(5), 30–34.

Lawrence, T.B., M.I. Winn and P.D. Jennings (2001), 'The temporal dynamics of institutionalization', *Academy of Management Review*, **26**(4), 624–45.

Meadows, D.H., D.L. Meadows, J. Randers and W.W. Behrens III (1972), *The Limits to Growth*, New York: Universe Books.

Meffert, H. and M. Kirchgeorg (1993), 'Leitbild des Sustainable Development', *Harvard Business Manager*, **2**, 34–45.

Meyer, A.D. (1982), 'Adapting to environmental jolts', *Administrative Science Quarterly*, **27**, 515–37.

Meyer, A.D., J.B. Goes and G.R. Brooks (1993), 'Organizations reacting to hyperturbulence', in George P. Huber and W.H. Glick (eds), *Organizational Change and Redesign*, New York: Oxford University Press, 66–111.

Milbrath, Lester W. (1989), *Envisioning a Sustainable Society*, Albany, NY: State University of New York Press.

Mitroff, I.I. (1994), 'Crisis management and environmentalism: a natural fit', *California Management Review*, **36**(2), 101–13.

Mitroff, I.I., P. Shrivastava and Firdaus E. Udwadia (1987), 'Effective crisis management', *Academy of Management Executive*, **1**(4), 283–92.

Münchener Rück (2003), 'Topics Geo' annual review of natural catastrophes, München.

Nattrass, Brian and Mary Altomare (2002), *Dancing with the Tiger*, Gabriola Island, Canada: New Society Publisher.

Osland, J.S., K.K. Dhanda and K. Yuthas (2002), 'Globalization and environmental sustainability: an analysis of the impact of globalization using the Natural Step framework', in Sanjay Sharma and Mark Starik (eds), *Research in Corporate Sustainability: The Evolving Theory and Practice of Organizations in the Natural*

Environment, Cheltenham, UK and Northampton, USA: Edward Elgar, 85–123.
Pearce, D. and R.K. Turner (1990), *Economics of Natural Resources and the Environment*, New York: Harvester Wheatsheaf.
Prahalad, C.K. and S. Hart (2001), 'The fortune at the bottom of the pyramid', *Strategy and Business*, **26**, 2–14.
Purser, R.E., C. Park and A. Montuori (1995), 'Limits to anthropocentrism: toward an ecocentric organization paradigm?', *Academy of Management Review*, **20**(4), 1053–89.
Robert, Karl-Henrik (1994), *Den Naturliga Utmaningen: The Natural Challenge*, Falun, Sweden: Ekerlids Foerlag.
Schwartz, P. and D. Randall (2003), '*An abrupt climate change scenario and its implications for United States national security*', Confidential report prepared for the Department of Defense, Washington, DC.
Senge, P.M. and G. Carstedt (2001), 'Innovating our way to the next industrial revolution', *Sloan Management Review*, Winter, 24–38.
Sharma, S. (2000), 'Managerial interpretations and organizational context as predictors of corporate choice of environmental strategy', *Academy of Management Journal*, **43**(4), 681–97.
Sharma, S. and I. Henriques (2005), 'Stakeholder influences on sustainability practices in the Canadian forest products industry', *Strategic Management Journal*, **26**(2), 159–80.
Shrivastava, P. (1995a), 'The role of corporations in achieving ecological sustainability', *Academy of Management Review*, **20**(4), 936–60.
Shrivastava, Paul (1995b), *Greening Business: Profiting the Corporation and the Environment*, Cincinnati, OH: Thompson Executive Press.
Smart, C. and I. Vertinsky (1984), 'Strategy and the environment: a study of corporate responses to crisis', *Strategic Management Journal*, **5**, 199–213.
Starik, M. and G.P. Rands (1995), 'Weaving an integrated web: multilevel and multisystem perspectives of ecologically sustainable organizations', *Academy of Management Review*, **20**(4), 908–35.
Stern P.C., O.R. Young and D. Druckman (eds) (1992), *Global Environmental Change: Understanding the Human Dimensions*, Washington, DC: National Academy Press.
Thompson, D. (ed.) (2003), *Tools for Environmental Management*, Gabriola Island, Canada: New Society Publishers.
Tushman, M.L. and P. Anderson (1986), 'Technological discontinuities and organizational environments', *Administrative Science Quarterly*, **31** (3), 439–66.
United Nations Millennium Goals, Online: accessed 18 January, 2005 at www.un.org/millenniumgoals
WECD (ed.) (1987), *Our Common Future*, Oxford: Oxford University Press.
Winn, M.I. (2001), 'Building stakeholder theory with a decision modeling methodology', *Business and Society*, **40**(2), 133–66.
Winn, M.I. and L.C. Angell (2000), 'Toward a process model of corporate greening', *Organization Studies*, **21**(6), 1119–47.
Zietsma, C.E., M.I. Winn, O. Branzei and I. Vertinsky (2002), 'The war of the woods: facilitators and impediments of organizational learning processes', *British Journal of Management*, **13**, 61–74.

12. Sustainable enterprise in clusters of innovation: new directions in corporate sustainability research and practice

Frank Boons and Nigel Roome[1]

The transition to sustainable development can be viewed as a social and industrial experimentation or innovation (Roome, 1998), which cannot be accomplished by any organization acting alone. In Europe this transition is understood to involve a search for innovations that foster competitiveness within the framework of environmental and social sustainability (Roome and Cahill, 2001). This prospective report for the European Commission outlines the need to establish multi-actor platforms that draw on new managerial skills and business capabilities, within reshaped policies for innovation policy to support this transition. The emphasis is on organizations working together on innovation, whereas much empirical research on business and sustainability has been dominated by a focus on the firm. There is an important and growing literature on the role of organizational linkages (Starik and Rands, 1995), partnerships (see for example De Bruijn and Tukker, 2002) and networks in the transition to sustainability (Carley and Christie, 1993; Roome, 2001a). This chapter draws on this systems view of transformation to sustainability to highlight its implications for research and to formulate some of the more relevant research questions that derive from the perspective.

Empirical evidence shows that progress toward more sustainable forms of development involves organizations working toward goals that span their individual interests or actions. These groups or clusters of organizations assume many forms depending on the mix of their individual and shared goals and ambitions, and the extent to which clusters are designed or structured. Clusters can take the form of supply chains, more localized forms of industrial ecology, knowledge networks, technology development, or local or regional partnerships for sustainable development. What is clear is that these clusters are increasingly important in the transition to sustainable development as well as providing a unit in the study of contemporary approaches to sustainable development on which we base our understanding of transition processes.

This chapter provides a conceptual and theoretical background to the study of clusters of innovation for sustainability (CIS). We use this to draw out some key research issues that derive from our chosen approach. In particular the chapter outlines a systems approach to sustainability. It discusses how clusters of innovation for sustainability fit within this perspective and develops a theoretical framework to structure the analysis of the workings of these clusters for sustainability. The chapter closes with a series of research questions and issues.

BACKGROUND: SYSTEMS PERSPECTIVES IN THEORY AND PRACTICE

Sustainable development presents challenges to societies at the local as well as the global level. Despite the continued march of the development process, environmental degradation continues to occur, ecological limits are crossed and social inequalities arise, while access to the opportunities that meet basic needs is unavailable to many. For firms, the challenge of sustainable development arises through the demands of (international and national) governmental and non-governmental organizations and wider society. They ask for the integration of ecological and social concerns with economic choices and actions.

Starik and Rands (1995) discuss ecological sustainability in terms of the web of relationships in which economic actors are embedded. Individual relationships, as well as the totality of relationships, are seen as important in the achievement of sustainable development (Roome, 1998: 9). This web of relationships is observed through concepts such as product chains (Boons, 1995; Hartman and Stafford, 1998), societal functions (Rotmans et al., 2001a, 2001b) industrial ecology (Boons and Baas, 1997) networks (Roome, 2001a). It is also argued that substantial technological and social innovation is necessary as sustainability involves systems change (Vorley and Keeney, 1998).

Systems approaches to the study of organizations are not exclusively concerned with sustainable development. Systems perspectives have also gained ground in the contemporary literature on competitive advantage (Piore and Sabel, 1984; Best, 1990; Porter, 1998) and innovation (Edquist, 1997). Both areas constitute important elements of sustainability. The weight of these ideas suggests that the network or cluster (see also Boons and Baas, 1997; Boons and Berends, 2001) provides a critical unit for analysis if we are to understand and/or foster sustainable development through systems change involving firms as partners in innovation.

This literature attempts to chart the ways in which actors deploy a systems perspective when forming clusters for the purpose of innovation, competitiveness and/or sustainability. It is assumed that clusters with different purposes often work in similar ways, yet specific demands and issues likely shape their purpose. We explore what this means for the goal of sustainable development which links competitiveness to other social and environmental objectives through innovation.

A systems perspective is more important against the backdrop of the processes of globalization. Globalization is envisioned as a system of systems created by interconnections between localities across national borders. Globalization affects sustainability, competitiveness and innovation in many ways. In terms of narrow definition, economic and financial globalization (Roome, 2000) connections are created through:

1. Cross-border flows of raw materials, energy, products and services, waste and emissions, knowledge and information, and 'trade' in financial instruments and derivatives. (Vickery and Casadio, 1996; Gladwin, 1998; Spencer, 2003).
2. Investments and related activities in R&D3[2] (Niosi, 1999; Von Zedtwitz and Gassmann, 2002; Archibugi and Iammarino, 2002), production, distribution and marketing (Ruigrok and van Tulder, 1995) at multiple geographical locations.
3. Global flows of capital (Petrella, 1996).

A broader definition of globalization (Roome, 2000) connects national economic systems and national innovation systems with global concerns about the development process and changes in our social and cultural structure. The spread of knowledge and trade has meant that national economic and innovation systems appear to converge. Moreover the agenda of national economic and innovation systems has become global, in response to economic issues and issues such as global climate change or the development of a hydrogen economy. Globalization can also have a destabilizing effect by linking events and processes in different parts of the world. Multinational corporations are crucial actors in linking such systems.

We see that local networks or systems of actors increasingly have to consider the consequences of their actions on other locations, as well as the consequences for them arising from events or choices in other locations. Moreover globalization has specific, often paradoxical, implications for sustainable development (Roome, 1998), and through that for clusters of innovation for sustainability. For example while it is important to spread knowledge for social betterment and environmental gain, companies and national innovation systems also find it necessary to appropriate knowledge for competitive gain.

DEFINITIONS: CLUSTERS FOR INNOVATION AND SUSTAINABILITY

In this section we define and examine the three central concepts of our chapter – clusters, innovation and sustainability – and their relationships.

Clusters: Actualized Networks or Systems of Actors

The sociological literature on organizations has a long tradition of looking at groups or networks of organizations (Lammers, 1984). This perspective can be summarized using the overarching concept of embeddedness (Granovetter, 1985), which was elaborated by Zukin and DiMaggio (1991: 15–23) into four types: structural, cultural, cognitive and political.

The concept of embeddedness draws on Pfeffer and Salancik's (1978) idea of dependency. Dependency offers an explanation for the actions of organizations grounded in the actions and choices of other actors in networks. This led Wassenberg (1983) to a make critical the distinction between potential and activated networks. A potential network is a theoretical or conceptual construct that defines the web of relationships by reference to some criterion. In contrast, an activated network is the network that functions in practice, based on a real set of relationships.

This distinction makes possible consideration of the extent to which actors that depend on one another are actually involved in joint effort to define or reach some goal. It offers a means to identify whether a gap exists between membership of the potential and actualized networks, whether the gap is seen by any of the actors in the actualized network, and what they then choose to do about it. A gap of this kind was critical in the events that surrounded Ontario Hydro's attempts to develop a more sustainable system of energy development and use in Ontario (Roome and Bergin, 2000).

We define clusters as actualized networks. That is clusters are sets of actors, their strategies, motivations, belief systems and actions, relationships, and the institutions they construct and maintain.

Clusters and Innovation

With this definition of a cluster in mind we now turn to their relationship with innovation. Systems perspectives are increasingly used to study innovation processes, although the concept of a system is used in different ways. Metcalfe (1995) defines a system of innovation as: 'a set of distinct institutions which jointly and individually contributes to the development and diffusion of new technologies and which provides the framework within which governments form and implement policies to influence the innovation process. As such it is a system of interconnected institutions to create, store and transfer the knowledge, skills and artefacts, which define new technologies'. Johnson and Jacobsson (2000) distinguish between national, regional, industry and technological systems.

In this chapter a broader definition of an innovation system is used. An innovation system is taken as consisting of the following elements:

1. Actors – and their capabilities and competencies.
2. Networks – as linkages that provide modes for the transfer of tacit and explicit knowledge.
3. Institutions – as the rules and belief systems that guide actors' behaviour.

The innovation literature increasingly recognizes the role and contribution of clusters of organizations to innovation rather than the role of individual firms. This comes with the increased involvement of end users in the innovation process, the growing number and type of technology-based strategic alliances involving groups of firms and other actors, and the attention given to public–private partnerships in the area of research, technology and development (Smits and Kuhlmann, 2004; Jacobs, 1998; Jacobs and de Man, 1996). Consequently clusters have become an issue in innovation policies throughout the world (OECD, 2001).

The contribution of clusters to innovation for sustainable development has been explicitly recognized in policy advice to the European Commission (Roome and Cahill, 2001). This connection is further developed in the next section.

Clusters and Sustainable Development

The Brundtland Commission defines sustainable development as 'development that meets the needs of the present generation without compromising the ability of future generations to meet their own needs' (WCED, 1987). They also suggest it is 'a process of change in which the exploitation of resources, the direction of investments, the orientation of technological development, and institutional change are all in harmony and enhance both current and future potential to meet human needs and aspirations' (WCED, 1987: 46). There have been numerous explorations and criticisms of these concepts (Daly, 1991).

Starik and Rands (1995: 908) define ecological sustainability in a way that fits the systems perspective. They argue that sustainable development is 'the ability of one or more entities to exist and flourish – either unchanged or in evolved forms – for lengthy time-frames, in such a manner that the existence and flourishing of other collectivities of entities is permitted at related levels and in related systems'.

In practice sustainable development involves integrating social issues, and the limits provided by the ecological carrying capacity of the earth, with economic issues in business choice. Although efforts have been made to calculate the technical limits of the ecological carrying capacity, environmental issues are seen as socially defined and prioritized rather than givens (Hannigan, 1995). Consequently stakeholder inputs in economic and other decision-making provides a basis to ensure that relevant ecological concerns are appropriately addressed. This implies that sustainable development is context dependent and thereby involves local processes or inputs even though responses may have global relevance. Stakeholder involvement is also necessary for the integration of social issues, which are also socially constructed and prioritized.

Context dependency means that when ecological and social aspects are integrated with economic choices it is important to consider the system in question. The governance of business, clusters of firms and other actors, and the economic and social system are central issues in the transition to sustainable development. So too is the choice of the right system level (WCED, 1987).

Work reported by Long and Arnold (1998) on environmental partnerships, the special issue of the journal *Business Strategy and the Environment* on networks, environmental management and sustainable development (Roome, 2001a), and partnership and alliances by De Bruijn and Tukker (2002) provide many examples of clusters for sustainability. They describe actualized systems aiming for sustainability goals. Sustainability goals seem to pose specific problems for clusters because:

1. The need to integrate different perspectives and interests is often a novel mental and collective 'mindset' for many of the actors participating in the cluster.
2. The involvement of different stakeholders in the economic processes of product development, production and marketing calls for new skills of engagement, interaction and governance.
3. The cultural and structural changes implied by the points above requires a process of 'unlearning'; seen as the breaking down of existing cultural (belief systems) and structural (interests and positions of actors) embeddedness as well as learning.

4. Sustainability goals sometimes call for substantial technical innovations.

Types of Sustainability Systems and Clusters

It is argued that clusters have to operate at the 'right' system level. This gives rise to the need to clarify the different types of possible sustainable system. The following types of system are suggested based on an earlier classification by Boons and Baas (1997):

1. Product life cycles: where the boundary of the system is drawn around an industrial ecosystem involving the economic actors (producers as well as consumers) connected by a specific product.
2. Material life cycle: where the boundary is drawn around actors dealing with a specific material. The examples of steel, plastics and platinum described by Frosch and Gallopoulos (1989) illustrate this approach.
3. Geographic area: where the boundary usually includes production but excludes the consumption of end products as there is usually a geographic separation between the production and consumption of the (end) product.
4. Sectoral: where the boundary is drawn round a group of companies that perform similar activities. Here the basic organizing principle is the similarity of activities. Sectoral clusters have less to do with common material and energy flows and more to do with developing an overall approach to sustainability through initiatives such as the Responsible Care Program of the chemical industry.
5. Technological: examples are based on a boundary that includes the joint development or demonstration of more sustainable forms of technology and sets of technologies such as those connected with the hydrogen economy or fuel cell vehicles.

There also appears to be an analytical distinction between conceptually and technologically driven systems. Conceptually driven systems examine the practical application of concepts such as industrial ecology. They do not depend on particular technologies but explore ways to bring about a concept. Technology-driven systems develop where the concern is to apply a technology or set of technologies that are seen as more sustainable. In practice this distinction may be less concrete, but there does seem to be a qualitative difference.

Roome and Cahill's (2001) report for the European Commission on the future for competitive and sustainable manufacturing identified production and consumption systems as an appropriate boundary within which to strive for sustainability. This is concept rather than technology driven.

Each of these types of system involves different actors, potential and actualized networks and institutions. Each system has a different capacity to make contributions to sustainable development. When these systems are actualized as clusters for sustainability, the sustainability component has consequences for all of the elements of the system. We observe that:

1. The set of actors involved in sustainability is broader than for innovation or competitive systems, because social and ecological aspects are taken into account.
2. The cluster needs specific capabilities to deal with the integration of these aspects in member companies and the overall cluster.
3. The complexity of identifying and integrating ecological, economic and social demands means that the support for decisions of the cluster is more complex than in an innovation or competitive system.
4. Institutions need to be designed that allow collective learning around the integration of the three elements to take place.

Actualization of Clusters in Terms of Sustainability

One function performed by clusters for sustainability is the development and enactment of some form of vision (see also Dierkes et al., 2001) for sustainability. The specific nature of this vision, and how it relates to technological development, is examined in this section. The types of system and system boundaries identified above are also related to specific sustainability visions.

Freeman (1997) proposes that (ecological) sustainable development is a specific policy goal for technology development. He sees this goal as longer term, more complex and bound more closely to the interaction between public and private sectors than is the case with most technology development goals. Freeman (1997: 415) identifies the following characteristics of sustainable development as a mission for technology policy. The direction of technological change is subject to the influence of a wide range of actors, government, firms, consumers and societal interests. It involves decentralized control of a large number of actors. Diffusion of the results of technology development is actively encouraged. Emphasis is placed on both incremental and radical innovations that permit a large number of firms to participate. There is also concern to ensure the complementary nature of a diverse set of policies as well as securing coherence with other policy goals.

One obstacle to sustainability is lock-in (David, 1985). Lock-in means that the scope of search processes to find more sustainable solutions is limited once technological developments take given directions. This excludes some options from further consideration. However sustainable development often requires radical breakthroughs (major process and product innovations) that lead to significant reductions in resource use and environmental damage.

Freeman's notion of mission-oriented technology development is taken further with the idea of vision as the development and joint enactment of a future image of sustainability, shared by the actors that make up a cluster.

A vision can be defined as a vague but compelling future state of the system. Such a vision prescribes a future state of the system within which the cluster is actualized, set in terms of the goals desired of that system. This implies that a cluster goes beyond the goals of individual organizations to address the changes required in setting new system goals. System goals involve goals that cannot be reached by individual organizations. This means that individual organizations might willingly contribute to the cluster at one point in time without benefit because they know that in the future they will gain from cluster projects. In this way some actors may have costs without at the same time receiving direct benefits.

The values or principles that drive a vision for sustainability are based on three dimensions and their integration:

1. Economic: resources should be used efficiently and effectively as a basis for competitiveness.
2. Ecological: the carrying capacity of the earth's ecosystem providing limits to what human activities can be sustained.
3. Social equity: the aspiration to meet the basic needs of all, and extending to all the opportunity to satisfy their aspirations for a better life (WCED, 1987: 44).

Elaborating these values, translating them into a vision and acting on them requires the participation of actors in the system. Participation is partly a function of the equity: meeting the needs of all requires their involvement in the process. Setting ecological values requires participation. Participation is also required to undertake the change process that brings about new systems goals.

The suggestion that sustainable development will lead to the reform of present patterns of production and consumption implies that innovation should be radical, and qualitatively different from current practice. This change involves the sectors and regional economic clusters that make up these systems. This does not imply that incremental and efficiency-improving innovations are not part of the process of sustainable development. But they are always steps in a process which aims at more substantial transformations and innovations.

In summary we view clusters as actualized systems of actors, their relationships and institutions; the actors see themselves as part of a system and seek to enhance the performance of the system. They develop a collective vision. Sustainable development provides the direction for enhancing system performance. The direction is conditioned by the selection of a specific system boundary [see our earlier typology, which distinguished products, materials, spatial, sectoral and technological systems]. In addition, that direction is grounded in the need to integrate ecological, economic and social values. This requires specific processes of participation, multi-actor knowledge development and decision-making. Sustainable development requires innovation that affects social, technical, organizational and social concerns. Moreover social and organizational innovations facilitate the process of participation and systemic learning. Clusters of different types require different forms of relationships and institutions in order to sustain the process of sustainable development. Clusters of innovation for sustainability are themselves social innovations.

These characteristics conform to the advice to the European Commission from an expert group on future policies and actions in support of research and development, technology and innovation for sustainable manufacturing in Europe (Roome and Cahill, 2001).

THEORETICAL FRAMEWORK

Given these definitions and distinctions we can now begin to build a theoretical framework for the study of clusters of innovation for sustainability that draws on the basic concepts and definitions outlined above. In particular we see that sustainable development concerns social, organizational and technical change, which requires an explicit account of the dynamics of clusters. Clusters have to be maintained over time and must satisfy certain conditions. We conceptualize these as capabilities, which can be identified at different levels. They affect the functioning of the cluster as a whole, the organizations that contribute to the cluster, managers and others that represent these organizations and manage the cluster and its constituent organizations. In addition, capabilities are needed to integrate these levels. We have also suggested that the processes of globalization have specific influences on clusters of innovation for sustainability. We explore these key issues in this section, and then use this theoretical framework to develop specific questions for research in our final section.

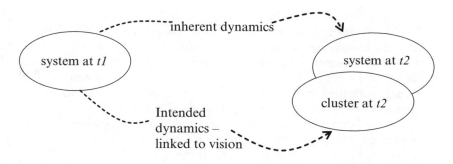

Figure 12.1   Two types of dynamics in CIS

The Dynamics of Cluster of Innovation for Sustainability

Two types of dynamics are discerned in CIS. Inherent dynamics concerns the evolution of a system over time as it progresses more or less left to itself. The second type is intended dynamics – the development of the cluster as intended (or designed) by actors, based on their espoused vision for sustainability. An important issue for research is the way in which these two types of dynamic processes relate to one another.

Inherent Dynamics of Systems

The dynamics of clusters is developed from the metaphor of organizational life cycles involving emergence, growth, maturity and decline. Several authors have analysed the developments of groups of organizations over time (Abernathy and Utterback, 1978; Nooteboom, 1996; Shearman and Burrell, 1987). They see that development moves from knowledge experimentation to more stable technological and systems relationships with incremental improvements in the dominant design or pattern of relationships. This ultimately leads to defensive positions and redundancy of technologies and relationships. The literature on innovation also makes use of the concept of a dominant design, the tendency of innovations to start as path breaking, but gradually become more incremental and efficiency oriented.

Innovation for sustainable development emphasizes radical innovation and implies a starting point for new product life cycles rather than providing for changes in an existing dominant design. Sustainable development questions the technological trajectory or paradigm – the cognitive aspect of dominant designs – pointing to the constraining and organizing principles of beliefs about what is feasible or at least worth attempting.

Similarly Shearman and Burrell (1987) identify different types of social networks in industrial sectors associated with the different phases of the life cycle. Initially such networks provide opportunities as well as barriers to open communication and engagement with new ideas, while later on they make systems more rigid (see also Boons, 1998; Boons and Berends, 2001). Put simply, technological lock-in has a social as well as technological component. Thus the phase in the life cycle of a cluster is an important factor in predicting the type of ecological and social innovations that can be generated. This is also the ground for the perspective in organizational sociology referred to as new institutional theory (DiMaggio and Powell, 1983; see also Alter and Hage, 1992: 68–77).

Intended Dynamics and Actualizing Clusters

In the case of intended dynamics several authors use systems perspectives to develop methods of intervention that seek to actualize systems into clusters.

Checkland (1981) has developed the most general approach. He describes actualizing a system as a process of reflection and action. During the reflection stage, actors discuss a systems view and develop goals and system requirements (what should be the boundary of the system given the system goals, what coordination mechanisms are necessary and so on). This normative vision of the system boundary and other system requirements is developed into separate projects. These are then implemented in an action stage. Individual projects do not necessarily involve the whole system, but they are formulated and evaluated with overarching system goals and performance in mind. The evaluation of individual projects leads into the next cycle, in which there is an adjustment of system goals and requirements, and the formulation of new projects to act out.

Chisholm (1998) has developed an approach which conforms to this general cycle. The empirical base for his work consists of community development projects (focusing on the social dimension of sustainable development). He formulates a number of principles or lessons shown in the box below.

Other authors apply similar principles to the process of sustainable development in contexts ranging from sustainable technological and systems change, local or regional sustainable development, and systems transition. (Vergragt and van der Wel, 1998; Rotmans et al., 2001a, 2001b).

PRINCIPLES FOR SUSTAINABLE DEVELOPMENT AFTER CHISHOLM (1998)

- Using a systems perspective is crucial to the development process
- Recognize that cluster actors and outsiders have difficulties in understanding systems
- The use of action research is crucial
- All actions (projects) need to be designed effectively, which requires interaction among cluster members
- Cluster developers must be flexible, acting on emerging events
- The development of the cluster needs to be integrated into 'normal' activities; they are not separate things
- Grass roots support is essential and needs to be built and maintained
- Appropriate coordination structures need to be developed
- The process of cluster development is disorderly and non-linear
- It takes a system to change a system

The Relationship between Inherent and Intended Dynamics

The methods to promote intended dynamics are not easy in clusters of innovation for sustainability. Implementation is complicated by the inherent dynamics discussed above. Inherent dynamics tend to move systems toward rigidity, in a technological sense (lock-in) as well as a social sense (institutionalization). In the initial phases the system has flexibility that allows for the exchange of ideas and the formation of the new relationships that give shape to a new system. As the new system develops over time, the ideas on which it is based can be exploited more efficiently, through the development of expertise, the standardization of norms, and the development of routines at the organizational and institutional level. Paradoxically this rigidity helps meet the needs of the system (Boons and Berends, 2001), yet lock-in and institutionalization may constrain the innovations necessary for further gains toward sustainable development.

Several authors have suggested that experimentation and stability should not be separated in a phased cycle and that organizations need to develop the capacity to have concurrent flexibility (experimentation) and stability

(Holmqvist, 2003; Roome, 2001b; Boons and Berends, 2001). While some of this work has focused more on organizational and inter-organizational learning, it has application for clusters of innovation for sustainability. It raises some interesting issues about the mechanisms, processes and capabilities used in experimentation and stability and in connecting the two in a concurrent process (Roome, 1999).

Clusters of innovation for sustainability may provide a means by which some actors involved can separate experimentation and the maintenance of organizational stability spatially. Spatial separation may not apply equally to all the actors participating in a cluster. For example multinational companies may engage in clusters of innovation for sustainability to provide 'experimental spaces' where innovations can be tried and tested. This may also apply to the representatives of government ministries, seeking to stimulate innovation for reasons of national competitiveness or sustainability. These actors may participate in more than one cluster. The cluster's work is potentially impacted upon by the motives behind the involvement of actors, the mechanism actors use to link these experiments with their more stable policy-making and strategic activities (such as strategic alliances), the manner and means through which they capture knowledge and experiences, or appropriate, share and deploy that through the organization outside the cluster, and whether knowledge is significant for ecological or social aspects of sustainability or competitiveness.

Local actors might have less potential to separate the arenas for experimentation and stability as well as having fundamentally different goals, motives, approaches toward knowledge and experiences of innovation. This raises issues about the interaction and motives and organization of the actors in the cluster, and the way these aspects interact in the formation of shared goals, visions and actions in the cluster.

This last point is particularly relevant in the context of the effects of globalization of clusters and cluster actors, which we now explore.

Globalization and Clusters of Innovation for Sustainability

Globalization essentially concerns the connectedness between locations, organizations and their activities across national borders. Indeed it is argued that sustainable development is a governance response to the processes of 'broad definition' globalization (Roome, 2000). Consequently when sustainable development is discussed in the context of the forces of narrower economic and cultural globalization it becomes more complex, leaving aside the issues raised by more recent turbulence about global risk and security (Roome, 2001a). Clusters of innovation for sustainability are therefore bound to the forces and processes of globalization.

We recognize that clusters of innovation for sustainability are often formed as a response to calls for sustainable development in the face of global environmental and social change. We also distinguish the following issues for CIS in the face of globalization of trade:

1. Regionally based clusters are linked to each other through global trade as in the case of international or global product chains.
2. Regional clusters (as a basis for competition) seeking global penetration.
3. Regional environmental innovations seeking global 'market niche' penetration as found in the case of sustainable technology pilots and demonstrations.

CIS also act as counterweights to global trade when they are formed as part of:

4. Global regionalism based on notions of more sustainable regional production and consumption systems. This is developing as a strategic response to the threats arising from global trade, the loss of jobs and security issues.

Globalization also specifically pertains to the cross-border development and transfer of knowledge, information and experiences as well as the flows of resources and materials as part of economic globalization and global environmental change.

The transfer and adaptation of knowledge and solutions between local settings is a core issue arising from the work of CIS. Especially as globalization of knowledge for sustainability implies a commitment to the sharing and diffusion of knowledge and technologies that enhance the uptake of responses to meet the challenges of sustainable development in many locations. Clusters of innovation for sustainability are often characterized by the active involvement of national, regional and supra-national organizations from the government, business and research and academic sectors in addition to more local actors. These CIS actors are actively involved in processes that involve the development and capture of knowledge and information about sustainability and its dimensions – economic, social and environmental. However this distinction between commercial and non-commercial interests is not clear cut. The development of commercially viable, more sustainable technologies itself may depend on the widespread development of other enabling technological and social contexts. Commercial interests may then seek to appropriate their own technological knowledge while simultaneously encouraging the diffusion of other technologies on which their technology depends for its wider adoption. What is clear is that these contradictory motives for involvement in clusters can affect the way clusters develop over time, and do influence their functioning.

The activities of a focal CIS may also depend on the prior transfer or introduction of knowledge, information or experiences from another CIS. In other words a focal CIS may draw on knowledge or experiences from outside the boundary of the CIS.

Clusters of innovation for sustainability embrace multiple paradoxes in relation to globalization. These tensions and paradoxes are critical issues in the working of clusters and the involvement of individual actors. They raise issues of relevance to research that concerns the operation and function of clusters.

Capabilities in Clusters of Innovation for Sustainability

The preceding sections show the complexity of sustainable development through innovation in clusters in terms of dynamic issues. These are complex in practice as well as theory. The practical concerns touch on the capabilities needed to manage these processes. In this section we develop our understanding of CIS capabilities. These capabilities are based on tacit knowledge developed in clusters to deal with the complexity in systems change, processes of multi-actor interaction and intervention in systems. We introduce the concept of capabilities before considering how capabilities are discussed in the literature on environmental management and sustainability.

Capabilities are situated at the organizational level. However they connect to the individual level and the cluster level. Organizational CIS capabilities contribute to the fulfilment of functions at the cluster level. At the same time, organizational capabilities are based on the skills or competence of individual managers and others. We use this framework to identify key research questions related to capabilities.

Organizational Capabilities

Research on capability conceptualizes firms as needing resources to undertake activities. These are divided into assets – resources that can be possessed – and capabilities. Capabilities are defined as 'resources that are intangible and tacit; they include the knowledge and skills of the firms' employees as well as organizational routines' (Den Hond, 1996: 54). Capabilities are difficult to teach or to transfer, non-observable in use, and often have a complex and/or systems character (Winter, 1987). Firms cannot possess capabilities; they are either developed or accessed by hiring individuals or groups that have mastered them. Capabilities are acquired through experience and learning. Capabilities need to be maintained and renewed. Capabilities are useful when integrated into the firm's organizational memory as routines.

According to Zahra and George (2002) there are four stages in the process: acquisition, assimilation, transformation and exploitation. Capabilities are developed in 'an interconnected process through which organizations value, absorb and apply externally generated knowledge' (Heugens, 2003: 302).

Environmental (Sustainability) Skills and Competence of Individuals

Several authors have focused on what they call environmental or sustainability capabilities of managers: Den Hond (1996), Clarke and Roome (1995, 1999) and Heugens (2003). To avoid confusion we term these individual skills. The latter two authors specifically relate their ideas to action–learning networks. Clarke and Roome (1995) focus on collaborative relationships in which skills are acquired by individuals through interaction with others around projects ranging from the development of visions to the construction of new technologies. Heugens adds that important skills are developed in adversarial relationships as well as being acquired internally.

Without explicitly defining what these skills are, Heugens refers to them as external stocks of knowledge that are internalized. According to Heugens (2003: 302) there are three types of skills distinguished in the environmental management [sic sustainability] literature:

- Technical skills: redesign of production processes or products to minimize impact upon the natural environment.
- Relational skills: skills that concern the interaction with internal and external stakeholders.
- Sustainability skills: 'capabilities for dealing with economic and ecological problems simultaneously' (Heugens, 2003: 303).

These are defined at the organizational level. Sweet et al. (2003) have developed ideas and conducted empirical research about the skills of individuals who represent organizations in teams or action–learning networks linked to sustainability. They distinguish different styles of information processing and decision-making. These influence the way that managers make choices and work in teams. Styles are based on the need for information and the ability to entertain alternate interpretations or foci. Five styles are identified: decisive (uni-focal/satisficing); flexible (multi-focal/maximizing); hierarchic (uni-focal/maximizing); integrative (multi-focal/maximizing). And a fifth style, systemic, found in individuals with maximizing styles who have an equal predisposition to hierarchic and integrative styles.

The authors argue that all styles can be developed and that each style has strengths and weakness. They conclude that 'certain cognitive styles, based on systemic, integrative or more open styles are required in managing sustainability issues' (Sweet et al., 2003: 275). Their argument is that by its very nature sustainability requires integration, a concern to link sustainable solutions to context and the ability to appreciate systems of relationships. Yet the authors also acknowledge that systemic styles are rare in the population of managers, while Chisholm (1998) has also suggested that systems understanding is difficult to access. Nevertheless these skills are transformed into capabilities within teams or organizations.

Functions of Innovation Systems

In addition to the capabilities in organizations there is a literature on the functions of innovation systems. Functions specify the requirements innovation systems must fulfil to be effective. Smits and Kuhlman (2004) list a number of functions fostered or supported by instruments in innovation policy:

1. The management of interfaces.
2. Building/organizing innovation systems.
3. Providing a platform for learning and experimenting.
4. Providing infrastructure for strategic intelligence.
5. Stimulating demand articulation, strategy and vision development.

Other functions include:

1. Knowledge creation and maintenance, including institutionalization.
2. 'Networking': knowledge diffusion and exchange, including institutionalization.
3. Demand articulation.
4. Regulation/formation of markets, of knowledge consumption.
5. Provision and stimulation of resources for innovation (people and money for science, research, venture capital).
6. Priority-setting with respect to allocation of public and private resources.
7. Alignment of competing interests: provision of arenas/platforms for negotiation.

8.   Facilitation of individual and institutional learning.
9.   Facilitation of behavioural and institutional adaptation and change (creative destruction and prime movers).

In contrast to skills and capabilities, which reside with individuals and organizations, functions are located at the cluster level. Taken together it is possible to consider the capabilities that support and foster the work of clusters of innovation for sustainability.

Capabilities in Clusters of Innovation for Sustainability

These insights can be combined to identify a set of CIS capabilities, which are unique to innovations for sustainability in clusters, or are essential for their effective work. Whether these capabilities, functions and competencies are sufficient and necessary to foster and support the work of CIS over time remains a topic for empirical enquiry.

Roome (2001b: 27–31) describes four sets of capabilities for organizations committed to sustainability: community-building skills, skills in dealing with different language communities, capabilities for dealing with the dynamics of language and meaning, and capabilities related to the development of trust. The capabilities described below are a further operationalization of these categories.

Technical Capabilities

This is knowledge related mainly to diminishing the ecological impact of existing production and consumption processes, and the development of more sustainable products and services. They include technologies such as the exchange of waste streams and utility sharing in regional clusters, reducing the energy impact of a product chain.

Value Integration Capabilities

Sustainability essentially deals with the integration of economic, social and ecological aspects of economic activities that lead to development. A unique aspect of a CIS is the capability to integrate these values, even though they can be contradictory. The capability to integrate requires skills at the individual level (Sweet et al., 2003). It requires routines to integrate information and to inform the decision-making and action of different parts of the organization, at the organizational level. It involves integration of stakeholders (economic, governmental, societal) in the process of building visions and making decisions at the cluster level. This is viewed as a process capability rather than a content capability.

Systems and Boundary Capability

Sustainable development requires actors to select an optimal system boundary when they form clusters and develop goals. For example technology-driven sustainability requires many possible boundaries constructed with different sets of actors depending on how ubiquitous the technology would prove to be. Envisioning the right system level is a process requirement and an individual skill that is translated to the organizational and cluster level. It requires the capability to develop and implement a systems-oriented strategy at each of the levels and to connect those three levels in a coherent way.

Actualization Capability

Actors need to be able to mobilize other actors that are part of the present or future system. We call this the actualization of the selected system. In a regional cluster for instance there will be firms that do not wish to cooperate because sustainability is not their aim. Involving these leaders and laggards requires specific skills.

Trust Capability

Trust needs to be developed in order for actors in a cluster to work together successfully. Many studies have shown this requires substantial effort, given the complex nature of sustainability goals, and the possibility that short-term losses harm the interests of some and that these might only be recouped by gains in the longer term (see for instance, Long and Arnold, 1998).

Regulatory Capability

Clusters have a regulatory part or context: integration of governmental agencies and their policies concerning ecological, social and economic issues has to take place in and around clusters. This may even affect the fiscal system, which may support or constrain innovation possibilities. For regional clusters, the coordination between different levels of governmental agencies (local, regional, national, international) is important.

Unlearning Capability

It is especially important to be able to break existing routines, assumptions, frames of reference and routines when dealing with existing clusters or systems. This relates to the problems of dealing with competing techno-logical systems (see Johnson and Jacobson, 2000: 633; Boons, 1995). And because existing clusters tend to change only in incremental ways (Boons, 1995).

Balancing Capability

Participation in a CIS is challenging to organizations. It brings the possi-bility to experiment in an inter-organizational context but may undermine the need for stability. Balancing this experimentation and stabilizing tendency requires specific capabilities for each organization and for the cluster as a whole.

This leads us to our most pertinent research questions.

RESEARCH ISSUES AND QUESTIONS

Conceptual, theoretical and empirical issues follow our focus on sustain-ability brought about through the designed, or purposeful, interaction of organizations, businesses and other actors, striving for systems innovations through clusters. The approach we advocate is grounded in a systems perspective of organizations, where sustainable development is seen as an innovation process, guided by economic, social and environmental prin-ciples, involving networks of actors in change that affects different contexts. Our approach fits with the empirical observation that actors increasingly work in clusters to accomplish sustainable development goals. These clusters of innovation for sustainability can be viewed as actualized net-works as opposed to the potential networks we would define theoretically. Important research issues arise from the gap between the potential and actualized networks in terms of the inclusion and exclusions of actors, the processes of visioning, and the capacity of an actualized network to accom-plish the innovation and change it sets for itself.

From an analytical point of view we distinguish clusters that are formed to undertake innovations in supply chains, those in sectors, those that promote industrial ecologies, those concerned with technological innova-tions or that contribute to new societal functions (such as mobility and nutrition). Each of these clusters has a qualitatively different scope and focus in terms of the system that is subject to change and the innovations that change requires. Each type of cluster involves different sets of salient actors. However it remains unclear whether these different clusters confront similar or generic issues, and/or have to work through similar processes, in order to bring about innovation for sustainability. This is a critical comparative research question.

We see an analytical and empirical distinction between four key issues. The context within which clusters operate, the 'functions' clusters have to perform in order to bring forward innovations that successfully meet the needs of that, or other, context(s), the capabilities that reside in organizations enabling them to contribute to the work of the cluster, and the skills managers and other individuals bring to the content and process of innovation. In addition, the work of clusters is seen to depend on capabilities to link context, functions, capabilities and skills. There are a series of critical research questions about what functions, capabilities, skills and linking capabilities are required, necessary or sufficient alone or in combination for clusters to work effectively toward sustainability. And how do firms and managers and other organizations contribute to these functions, capabilities and competencies and resolve the issues that might divide organizational members of clusters?

Our perspective has significance in terms of the unit of analysis for research and empirical enquiry. It emphasizes the cluster within a specified system as the unit of analysis. It places importance on the processes of innovation within the cluster, as it develops over time, in relation to cluster participants and their institutional and physical context(s). This raises a number of research questions and issues.

Are clusters of innovation for sustainability different from other clusters of innovation, and if so how? Do different national innovation systems have a different capacity to support innovation for sustainable development? Is innovation for sustainable development seen in different ways, or does it have different meaning and characteristics depending on the national innovation system within which it is embedded? What is the relationship between the demands of economic globalization on companies involved in CIS, the interests of national innovations systems to capitalize on innovations, and the demands on governance of knowledge for sustainability arising from the work of a CIS?

In terms of the dynamics of clusters of innovation for sustainability there are research issues about how visions of desired systems are developed and brought into effect. How do clusters influence the systems they seek to change? More specifically: what is the effect of the fit, or the lack of fit, between the ambition set for system change and the capacity of the actualized network to bring about that change? What are the effects of the motives, strategies and interactions of organizations involved in a cluster on the performance of the cluster? How is the knowledge developed in a cluster collected, diffused, exploited and appropriated by organizations that contribute to the cluster? How are social and technical opportunities for change identified, and their contribution to change assessed and evaluated? How and why do cluster dynamics develop over time? How does the significance of functions, capabilities and skills that provide a basis for the work of a cluster shift over time? What is the evolving relationship between skills, capabilities and functions? How are these developed? How do different organizations and clusters deal with the issue of experimentation and stability? What mechanisms and capabilities are key to maintain the fit between experimentation and stability in the cluster and in the organizations that participate in clusters?

Methodologically many of the questions identified above address issues of how, why and what are the effects of phenomena and processes. These questions are more appropriately studied through comparative and/or longitudinal case studies of clusters than static statistical sampling based on cross-sectional data. Moreover the adoption of a systems perspective presumes that simple cause and effect is less relevant than multiple causality and the contextual fit of solutions. This raises an issue about the relevance of conventional hypothesis testing based on simple causation using statistical analysis or otherwise in the study of cluster processes.

In the same way that systems change to bring about sustainability is perceived to be based on innovation in complex systems, so we take the view that research of these multilevel, multi-organizational, multi-context, dynamic phenomena also obliges fundamental innovation in research methods and the reporting of research. This is no trivial task.

We have begun to address some of the research questions and issues identified above through a research project funded by the NWO, the Dutch Social Science Research Council. This project involves the development of a conceptual and theoretical paper on which this current chapter draws. It also involves a PhD and two post-doctoral projects, which are examining a variety of CIS in local and global contexts and apply the results of research to inquiry through the use of a policy laboratory. We thank the NWO and the Erasmus University Rotterdam and Utrecht University for their support in making this research possible.

NOTES

1. We acknowledge the input of Marko Hekkert, Ruud Smits and Igor Struyf to this chapter.
2. R&D3 stands for Research and Development, Deployment and Demonstration. It refers to strategies, which recognize the importance of combining 'technology push' with

'demand pull' mechanisms to promote the diffusion of emerging technologies (Barreto et al., 2003: 269).

REFERENCES

Abernathy, W. and J. Utterback (1978), 'Patterns of industrial innovation', *Technology Review*, June/July, 40–47.
Alter, C. and J. Hage (1992), *Organizations Working Together*, London: Sage Publications.
Archibugi, D. and S. Iammarino (2002), 'The globalization of technological innovation: definition and evidence', *Review of International Political Economy*, **9**(1), 98–122.
Best, M. (1990), *The New Competition*, Cambridge: Polity Press.
Boons, F. (1995), *Produkten in ketens. Een institutionele analyse van de substitutie van PVC leidingsystemen en melkverpakkingen*, Tilburg: Tilburg University Press.
Boons, F. (1998),'Caught in the web: the dual nature of networks and its consequences', *Business Strategy and the Environment*, **7**(3), 204–12.
Boons, F. and L. Baas (1997), 'Industrial ecology: the problem of coordination', *Journal of Cleaner Production*, **5**, 79–86.
Boons, F.A. and M. Berends (2001), 'Stretching the boundary: the possibilities of flexibility as an organizational capability in industrial ecology', *Business Strategy and the Environment* **10**(2), 115–24.
Carley, M. and I. Christie (1993), *Managing Sustainable Development*, Minneapolis, MN: University of Minnesota Press.
Checkland, P. (1981), *Systems Thinking, Systems Practice*, Chichester: John Wiley & Sons.
Chisholm, R. (1998), *Developing Network Organizations*, Reading, MA: Addison Wesley.
Clarke, S. and N. Roome (1995), 'Management for environmentally sensitive technology: networks for collaboration and learning, *Technology Analysis and Strategic Management*, **7**(2), 191–215.
Clarke, S. and N. Roome (1999), 'Sustainable business: learning action networks as organizational assets', Greening of Industry Network Special Issue of *Business Strategy and the Environment*, **8**(5) 296–310.
Daly, H. (1991), *Steady State Economics*, 2nd edn, Washington, DC: Island Press.
David, P. (1985), 'Clio and the economics of QWERTY', *American Economic Review*, **75**(2), 332–7.
De Bruijn, T. and A. Tukker (2002), *Partnership and Leadership Building Alliances for a Sustainable Future*, Dordrecht: Kluwer.
Den Hond, F. (1996), 'In search of a useful theory of environmental strategy: a case study on recycling of end-of-life vehicles from the capabilities perspective', PhD thesis, Vrije Universiteit Amsterdam.
DiMaggio, P. and W. Powell (1983), 'The iron cage revisited: institutional isomorphism and collective rationality in organisational fields' *American Sociological Review*, **48**, 147–60.
Dierkes, M., L. Marz and C. Teele (2001), 'Technological visions, technological development, and organizational learning', in M. Dierkes, A. Berthoin Antal,

J. Child and I. Nonaka (eds), *Handbook of Organizational Learning and Knowledge*, New York: Oxford University Press, 282–301.

Edquist, C. (ed.) (1997), *Systems of Innovation: Technologies, Institutions and Organizations*, London: Pinter.

Freeman, C. (1997), 'Technology and the environment', in C. Freeman and L. Soete (eds), *The Economics of Industrial Innovation*, 3rd edn, London: Pinter, 413–25.

Frosch, R. and N. Gallopoulos (1989), 'Strategies for manufacturing', *Scientific American*, **261**(3), 144–52.

Gladwin, T. (1998), 'Economic globalisation and ecological sustainability: searching for truth and reconciliation', in N. Roome (ed.), *Sustainability Strategies for Industry. The Future of Corporate Practice*, Washington, DC: Island Press.

Granovetter, M. (1985), 'Economic action and social structure: the problem of embeddedness', *American Journal of Sociology*, **91**, 481–501.

Hannigan, J. (1995), *Environmental Sociology: A Social Constructivist Perspective*, London: Routledge.

Hartman, C.L. and E.R. Stafford (1998), 'Crafting "enviropreneurial" value chain strategies through green alliances', *Business Horizons*, **41**(2), 62–72.

Heugens, P. (2003), 'Capability building through adversarial relationships: a replication and extension of Clarke and Roome (1999)', *Business Strategy and the Environment*, **12**(5), 300–312.

Holmqvist, M. (2003), 'A dynamic model of intra- and interorganizational learning', *Organization Studies*, **24**(1), 95–123.

Jacobs, D. (1998), 'Innovation policies within the framework of internationalization', *Research Policy*, **27**, 711–24.

Jacobs, D. and A. de Man (1996), *Clusters en concurrentiekracht. Naar een nieuwe praktijk in het Nederlandse bedrijfsleven?*, Alphen aan den Rijn: Samsom.

Johnson, A. and S. Jacobsson (2000), 'The emergence of a growth industry: a comparative analysis of the German, Dutch and Swedish wind turbine industry', mimeo, Chalmers University, Sweden.

Lammers, H. (1984), *Organisaties vergelijkenderwijs*, Utrecht: Het Spectrum.

Long, F.J. and M.B. Arnold (1998), *The Power of Environmental Partnerships*, Fort Worth: Dryden Press.

Metcalfe, S. (1995), 'Economic foundations of technology policy', in P. Stoneman (ed.), *Money, Trade and Payments*, Boston, MA: MIT Press.

Niosi, J. (1999), 'The internationalization of industrial R&D: from technology transfer to the learning organization', *Research Policy*, **28**, 107–17.

Nooteboom, B. (1996), 'A dynamic theory of network efficiency', conference paper for the EMOT workshop, 6–8 September, Modena, Italy.

OECD (2001), *Innovative Clusters: Drivers of National Innovation Systems*, Paris: OECD.

Petrella, R. (1996), 'Globalisation and internationalisation: the dynamics of the emerging world order', in R. Boyer and D. Drache (eds), *States Against Markets: the Limits of Globalisation*, London: Routledge.

Piore, M.J. and C.F. Sabel (1984), *The Second Industrial Divide*, New York: Basic Books.

Pfeffer, J. and G. Salancik (1978), *The External Control of Organizations: A Resource Dependency Perspective*, New York: Harper & Row.

Porter, M.E. (1998), 'Clusters and the new economics of competition', *Harvard Business Review*, Nov–Dec, 77–90.

Roome, N. (ed.) (1998), *Sustainability Strategies for Industry: The Future of Corporate Practice*, Washington DC: Island Press.

Roome, N. (1999), 'Global change, sustainable development, the role of business and new governance issues: a vision for the new millennium', *Ökologisches Wirtschaften*, **5–6**, 7–9.

Roome, N. (2000), 'Globalisation and sustainable development: toward a transatlantic agenda', in C. Bonser (ed.), *Security, Trade, and Environmental Policy*, Dordrecht: Kluwer Academic Publishing, 161–86.

Roome N. (ed.) (2001a), 'Networks, environmental management and sustainable development', *Business Strategy and the Environment*, **10**(2), special issue.

Roome N. (2001b), 'Metatextual organizations: innovation and adaptation for global change', inaugural address Erasmus University, 2 February.

Roome, N. and R. Bergin (2000), 'The challenges of sustainable development: lessons from Ontario Hydro', *Corporate Environmental Strategy*, **7**(1), 8–19.

Roome, N. and E. Cahill (2001), 'Sustainable production: challenges and objectives for EU research policy', Report of the Expert Group on Competitive and Sustainable Production and Related Services, DG XII (Research), Brussels: European Commission.

Rotmans, J., R. Kemp and M. van Asselt (2001a), 'Transition management: a promising policy perspective', in M. Decker (ed.), *Interdisciplinarity in Technology Assessment*, Berlin: Springer Verlag, 165–97.

Rotmans, J., R. Kemp and M. van Asselt (2001b), 'More evolution than revolution: transition management in public policy', *Foresight*, **3**(1), 1–17.

Ruigrok, W. and R. van Tulder (1995), *The Logic of International Restructuring*, Routledge: London.

Shearman, C. and G. Burrell (1987), 'The structures of industrial development', *Journal of Management Studies*, **24**(4), 325–45.

Smits, R. and S. Kuhlmann (2004), 'The rise of systemic instruments in innovation policy', *The International Journal of Foresight and Innovation Policy*, **1**(2), 4–32.

Starik, M. and G. Rands (1995), 'Weaving an integrated web: multilevel and multisystem perspectives of ecologically sustainable organizations', *Academy of Management Review*, **20**(4), 908–35.

Sweet, S., N. Roome and P. Sweet (2003), 'Corporate environmental management and sustainable enterprise: the influence of information processing and decision styles', *Business Strategy and the Environment*, **12**(4), 265–77.

Vergragt, P. and M. van der Wel (1998), 'Backcasting: an example of sustainable washing', in N. Roome (ed.), *Sustainability Strategies for Industry: the Future of Corporate Practice*, Washington, DC: Island Press, 171–84.

Vickery, G. and C. Casadio (1996), 'The globalisation of investment and trade', in J. De la Mothe and G. Paquet (eds), *Evolutionary Economics and the New International Political Economy*, London: Pinter.

Von Zedtwitz, M. and O. Gassmann (2002), 'Market versus technology drive in R&D internationalization: four different patterns of managing research and development', *Research Policy*, **31**(4), 569–88.

Vorley, W. and D. Keeney (eds) (1998), *Bugs in the System: Redesigning the Pesticides Industry for Sustainable Agriculture*, London: Earthscan.

Wassenberg, A. (1983), *Netwerken van organisaties*, Meppel: Boom.

WCED (1987), *Our Common Future*, New York: Oxford University Press.

Winter, S. (1987), 'Natural selection and evolution', in J. Eatwell, M. Milgate and P. Newman (eds), *The New Palgrave Dictionary of Economics*, Vol. 3, London: Macmillan, pp. 614–17.

Zahra, S. and G. George (2002), 'Absorptive capacity: a review, reconceptualization and extension', *Academy of Management Review*, **27**(2), 185–203.

Zukin, S. and P. DiMaggio (eds) (1991), *Structures of Capital: The Social Organization of the Economy*, Cambridge: Cambridge University Press.

13. Self-regulation and new institutions: the case of the Green Network in Denmark

Martin Lehmann, Per Christensen and Jesper Møller Larsen

At the 2002 Earth Summit in Johannesburg, it was concluded that public–private partnerships should be one of the pivotal mechanisms of greening. This underlined the shift in regulatory regimes that has been going on for more than a decade. Moving from largely command-and-control measures in the 1970s and 1980s, through cleaner production initiatives and self-regulatory initiatives in the 1990s, the emphasis is increasingly on using the network and partnerships as levers for promoting a greening of industry.

In this chapter, we analyse one of the foremost Danish initiatives in public–private partnerships, namely the Green Network that operates in the county of Vejle. This initiative involves more than 200 companies plus ten public bodies that range from county authorities and municipalities to Arbejdstilsynet (the Danish Working Environment Authority). The Network started in 1994 and has grown in size and importance ever since. Its fundamental aim is providing new forms of cooperation between public authorities and private companies. Initially a major focus was on changing the role of the authorities away from being inspectors towards becoming facilitators or consultants. The vehicle for this was that companies committed themselves to making an 'environmental statement', a seminal form of environmental management system (EMS). Among other things, such statements demanded the active involvement of the authorities, and the process gave the companies a taste for acting proactively. Changing the role of the public authorities and their relationship with companies proved a success. A growing number of companies joined the programme and benefited from the process of making an 'environmental statement' that committed them to making more effective use of resources, lowering costs and improving their relationship with the authorities. At the same time, membership of the Network allowed them to display their 'Green Network Flag', a form of green marketing.

When the Network began, cleaner production and environmental management systems were at the core of the activities that a progressive firm would be expected to undertake. Through the 1990s however the 'environmental landscape' changed profoundly. First, life-cycle thinking and a new emphasis on product-oriented environmental policies increased the responsibilities of companies. Second, a broadening of the concept of environment took place. More correctly, emphasizing sustainability as the goal led to a more holistic stance that included companies taking more social responsibility and introducing triple bottom line measures, that is reporting corporate performance against economic, ecological and social measures. Through all these shifts, the Green Network has maintained a leading role, not only developing new tools for companies but also fostering a spirit of proactivism. This spirit ensures that companies are keenly interested in new developments and are eager to maintain their role as leaders in both their industry and regional contexts.

Herein we outline some of the research we have undertaken on the Green Network case in order to distil some conclusions about how and why it became a success. Moreover some recommendations aimed at other regional and local networks are arrived at, indicating how successful public–private partnerships might be fostered.

THEORY AND PERSPECTIVES

The whole idea of public–private partnerships grew out of the discussion on self-regulation and proactiveness that took place during the 1990s. Thence the role envisaged for industry in the ecological transformation of society changed considerably. This is vividly described by Martin Hajer in *The Politics of Environmental Discourse* (1995). Therein, 'ecological modernisation' is the term that describes the emergence of a new societal paradigm. Inherent in this change is a shift from reactive and passive attitudes in industry. The shift is away from an insistence that pollution prevention is costly and thus minimizes profits, towards a new era where win–win solutions that create profits for greener companies are emphasized. Accompanying this fundamental shift, there are a host of other changes taking place in the relationship between companies and their environments (Gouldson and Murphy, 1998; Mol and Spaargaren, 2000).

In relation to cleaner production measures and environmental management systems (BS 7750, ISO 14001, EMAS), as self-regulation became the order of the day, new relationships between the authorities and companies emerged. This demanded a shift in attitudes from the authorities as their role changed from inspection and policing more towards facilitation and acting as consultants. On the other side of the coin, there was evidently a dramatic increase in the capacities of companies to handle environmental problems in-house and on the shop floor. Such capacities include not only the skills to build and manage certifiable EMSs but also to innovate, initially through cleaner technologies and later via product-oriented initiatives. These innovations often happen within the network of the companies, including suppliers and customers (Håkansson, 1989; Håkansson and Snehota, 1995; Lundvall, 1985). As product innovation occurs moreover, the whole 'product chain' that the company is involved in is affected.

Ecological modernization also means a change in the role of governance. From command-and-control and being solely authority driven, governance becomes reflexive and communicative, that is also developing out of the interactions in the network. Reflexivity in this context means that the various subsystems of society can govern their own activities through the creation of procedures that support autonomy, that is there is a realization that they have an interest in doing something about the problems. Most often, reflexivity is nurtured by a state apparatus putting pressure on the industry through specifying the problems to be addressed and the goals to be achieved. Ultimately however it is more or less left to companies and trade organizations to find appropriate solutions to the problems (Christensen et. al., 1997). Thus EMS, environmental- or eco-labelling, and regional or local networks for enhancing environmental performance can all be viewed as new forms of governance.

Last but not least, the period of ecological modernization is also characterized by a fundamental change in the relationship between companies and their stakeholders. Moving away from the 1970s and 1980s perception of only suppliers and customers as stakeholders, companies had to realize that public authorities and a number of environmental organizations and social movements (Mol and Sonnenfeld, 2000) should be taken into consideration. Again, in the 1970s and 1980s the most important consideration for companies was not to breach environmental regulations or permits. As the extent, character and understanding of environmental problems changed during the 1980s however, it became obvious that companies faced a more diffuse, threatening and volatile atmosphere, where complete neglect of the environment was no longer an acceptable position. Furthermore the demand became that not only should companies take responsibility for their past 'sins' (for example contaminated sites) but also for their product's impact from cradle to grave. Some observers stressed that this was a characteristic feature of all modern societies changing to 'risk societies' (Beck, 1986; Hajer, 1995). Taking this risk into consideration creates a 'reflexive modernization', whereby individuals and companies react by taking various steps that will minimize their own risk.

The existence of this risky environment is strongly conveyed to companies by a number of newly recognized stakeholders: banks, insurance companies, the media and so on. It is also evident in a state apparatus that expects companies to address a wider range of environmental problems: inspectors expect or demand that companies must be preventative, broader in their concept of the environment, and self-regulating. Moreover a number of consultancy firms and technological service institutions, which offer themselves as partners in different projects and networks, also act to convey notions of being 'responsible', 'legitimate', 'accountable' and 'ahead of competitors'.

Out of all these transformations a picture of companies as vulnerable entities exposed to growing pressure from their 'environment' develops. That picture is our point of departure in this chapter. Regional and local networks must be seen as rational ways for small and medium-sized enterprises (SMEs) in particular to respond to the confusing and complex range of demands made on them by their 'environments'.

The literature on networks emphasizes the social content of organizations' relationships (for example Grabher, 1993; Granovetter, 1985), and suggests that networks provide organizations (actors) with access to resources and activities the single organization (or actor) otherwise does not have at its disposal (Håkansson, 1989; Håkansson and Snehota, 1995). The decision to join (and/or leave) the network thus becomes intentional and the network itself is an intended construction, a 'loosely coupled system' (Weick, 1982), where members' common or overlapping goals can be achieved (Boons, 1998), where common problems and risks may be addressed more effectively, or where ideas and concepts can be developed and matured. The precondition for that is however a certain amount of 'trust' and 'reciprocity' in the network relations, and an overcoming of the challenges such as maintaining flexibility and adaptability (Boons and Berends, 2001).

There is no doubt that firms are engaged in a wide range of networks, and both social and strategic factors play a part in the creation and development of networks. In terms of ecological modernization, the network thus combines activities, resources and interactions that traditionally are found in otherwise seemingly distinct contexts, that is relating business, regulatory measures and new forms of knowledge. In such terms, the Green Network may be what Clark and Roome (1995) have coined a learning – action network: 'relationships which lay over and complement formal organisational structures linking individuals together by the flow of knowledge, information, and ideas'. Such networks 'are embedded in the complex of organisational and social relationships, management structures and processes that constitute business and its social context' (Clark and

Roome, 1999: 297), and therefore operate at the core of where a multitude of institutions are imposed on or offer themselves to companies. The inherent challenges that follow are for example to bridge the gaps of differences in culture and 'language' (technical vs. political vs. academic), to maintain momentum, and to develop and evolve.

As the Green Network attempts to reconcile external pressures with the daily life of the organization, dealing with turbulent times and increasing demands on companies to find new ways to create profits and remain legitimate, it takes on many of the characteristics of the 'learning–action network'. However consideration of some institutional issues may additionally help to explain the role such a network has in bringing about changes in organizations' environmental behaviour. Institutional theory describes how organizations respond to pressures from their environment, realigning themselves. These pressures are not only economic or material in nature, but also social and political; that is not only money, but also legitimacy must be considered.

Institutional theory explains how organizations, for example companies or networks of companies, can accommodate the manifold and often conflicting pressures from the environment (Meyer and Scott, 1983; Hoffman, 2001; Hoffman and Ventresca, 2002). The environment is filled with institutions that introduce contagious new ideas, concepts and norms into companies. These institutions come from the 'environment' and are imprinted on the organization by a variety of stakeholders, such as those previously mentioned. The mixture of impressions varies according to each individual setting, but often companies find themselves in an 'institutional field' with very similar impacts. When considering environmental policies and sustainability therefore, this field is not that different from company to company, consisting as it does of regulatory bodies, consumers, consultants, suppliers and NGOs. These stakeholders, through their expectations, put pressure on companies, requiring them to be legitimate, to act according to general norms and to put forward convincing ideas and concepts worthy of imitation.

An environment that is increasingly institutionalized, with a growing number of international organizations (UN, WBCSD, Greenpeace and so on) playing a role, and pressures from the media and the Internet, creates what John Meyer (1994) called a 'rationalized environment' that demands a more or less worldwide uniformity from organizations. This is the order of the day for many companies exposed to environmental demands, whether they come from authorities, NGOs, customers and consumers or the public at large.

Institutions can be seen from different perspectives and be of a variety of types. Richard Scott (1995) divides them into three pillars: regulative, normative and cognitive. These encompass different analytical perspectives, that is ways of looking at institutions, but also different kinds of institutions. Commonly, an 'institution' is a synonym for an organization or association. In a number of theories though, institutions are defined as 'the rules of the game'. Scott's definition goes beyond that however. For him, 'institutions consist of cognitive, normative and regulative structures and activities that provide stability and meaning to social behaviour'. Defined thus, institutions are essentially the way people make sense of and fit into the social world. They are created and modified via interactions between social interest groups by processes of cooperation, competition and conflict. Scott's three pillars of institutions are:

1. Regulative – rules, laws, written codes of behaviour, sanctions.
2. Normative – values, norms, perceived roles.
3. Cognitive – knowledge, thought (ideas), beliefs, models.

The cognitive pillar refers to an individual's subjective construction of reality. The normative pillar, on the other hand, is a group interpretation. Fairly obviously, each of the three pillars acts to influence the others.

Impinging institutional activities demand a company's attention and force it to react. This reaction may either be to reject new ideas, practices and demands, or to take them into the company's bricolage of existing institutions. Adoption of institutions can be, in some instances, very reactive. Though they are seemingly integrated into the organization, they are often decoupled from the everyday activities, particularly from core activities where the products, services, ideas or whatever the company makes are produced. But institutions can also be integrated into the fabric of the organization, becoming an active part of its daily life. Recent institutional theory stresses that this process is not merely passive, piling up institutions inside the organization, but also active because it demands discretion and 'strategizing' (Oliver, 1991), 'translation' (Røvik, 1998) or 'appropriation' (Jamison, 2001) to mould the institutions so that they fit in, that is institutional pressures do not always create uniformity (Milstein et al., 2002).

Røvik has described how companies face an increasing choice of recipes for how to organize themselves, and these must be translated to fit into the actual situation of the company (Røvik, 1998). Some recipes though never become implemented; they are 'spat out' or decoupled from the organization. Others meanwhile are institutionalized as scripts or schemes which companies work according to. After a time more modern or sophisticated recipes are adopted however (Røvik, 1996). This constant flow of recipes or standards is typical of the situation for contemporary companies. What is important for survival is their ability to cope with the flow, siphoning off relevant recipes and incorporating them into their organization and, in due time, dispensing with and replacing them. Inherently this focus on capacity to absorb and translate new recipes is similar to the intentions of much modern theory of learning and innovation (Cohen and Levinthal, 1990; Zollo and Winter, 2002; van den Bosch et al., 2003) although emphasis is not on knowledge per se, but on institutions and the way they are dealt with. In Røvik's work, the absorptive capacity of the company or network can be characterized by five fundamental features (Røvik, 1998: 284).

High absorption capacity is the ability to look for, find and absorb many different recipes at the same time. This depends on the open-mindedness of the organization, its curiosity and its will to embark on new experiences. The capacity to decouple recipes that do not fit in means that those which blur the vision of the organization or which are not compatible with the whole or part of the existing set-up of institutions are excluded. The ability to translate new recipes in a quick and easy way means that the internal costs of so doing are minimized, while weaving the recipes into the fabric of the organization is relatively simple. Another key capacity is the ability to detach old or worn-down institutions in one way or another. The fifth and final defining capacity is the ability to preserve and reactivate older forms of institutional recipes, that is having a reservoir of 'tacit' knowledge that can be reactivated in due course if necessary.

In this chapter, we will use Røvik's five characteristic features of 'absorptive capacity' to evaluate how the Green Network has functioned and to pinpoint the reasons for its success. We will not look at individual organizations but rather at the Network as a form of organizational activity, albeit with loose rather than tight couplings.

Data on the Green Network have been collected through interviews with key persons, observations and participation in meetings and activities over a longer period, as well as via access to documents, including contracts and newsletters.

THE GREEN NETWORK, A STORY OF A DEFEAT

In 1992, the Danish Ministry of Trade and Industry in cooperation with the Ministry for Energy and Environment published a call for proposals for a Danish network to be the international showcase for Danish environmental technology and know-how. The tender was to initiate new ways of strategically addressing a combination of environmental and business issues, that is to condense several otherwise separate activities and normative institutions.

Four regional alliances were proposed by the regions of Herning, Næstved, Odense and Vejle, respectively. The Herning alliance won and is now known as Green City Denmark. The Vejle alliance, at that time known as the Green City Network, lost. Having put several person-years of work into establishing a viable collaboration, the defeat was a huge anticlimax. The general opinion amongst key persons in the alliance however was that the proposal had grasped essential and at the same time innovative forms of cooperation between public and private actors. From the ashes, then, rose the Green Network. A reconstitution towards local aspects rather than national or international markets took place. This included more focus on the environment, rather than the economy and exports, plus an assessment of which elements of the original programme were sustainable and best suited, and which were not. The result was a formalized, regional partnership between local companies, public and private organizations, and public authorities in the county of Vejle and in West Funen. The emphasis was on dialogue, the communication of knowledge, and the exchange of ideas about environmental affairs, founded on the idea that politics, economics and environment can go hand in hand. Four months after the defeat, the Green Network organization was established with six members from local public authorities (O-members) – the municipalities of Fredericia, Horsens, Kolding, Middelfart and Vejle, plus the county of Vejle – and approximately 30 enterprises in the region (V-members). In addition, the structure of the Network allowed for other interested actors from both inside and outside the region to become members (I-members). Originally there were around 15 I-members. As of 2002, newly developed objectives and strategies have made it feasible to include a fourth type of member (K-members) for local municipalities from outside the O-block. The different membership categories (see Table 13.1) present a variety of opportunities for cooperation within the three-pillar approach that activities in the Network are related to, namely an Enterprise–Enterprise pillar, an Enterprise–Authority pillar and an Authority–Authority pillar.

Organization of the Network included the establishment of a General Assembly (to be held once a year), the Board, the Coordination Group, the Secretariat, and a number of other organs associated with specific projects (see Figure 13.1).

An increase in challenges, new objectives and activities has given rise to corresponding changes in the organizational structure. With the increase in membership numbers (see Table 13.2), V-members have also increased their influence on the activities of the Network, resulting in the establishment of the Idea-Forum in 1999 (at the same organizational level as the Coordination Group). Up to that point, activities in the Network

Table 13.1   Outline of tiered membership and corresponding obligations

Type	Description	Obligations
O	O-members consist of a fixed circle of public members, namely Fredericia, Horsens, Kolding, Middelfart and Vejle municipalities, and Vejle County	O-members are obliged to cooperate with and assist the V-members that fall under their environmental jurisdiction in producing an environmental statement
V	V-members are public or private enterprises located in the Green Network region, that is Vejle County and/or Middelfart Municipality	By entering the Green Network, V-members commit themselves to continual improvements in correspondence with the Green Network Mission. Improvements are documented in a joint statement after one or more of the Green Networks manuals. The statement must comply with Green Networks minimum conditions for such (as set by the board)
I	I-members consist of other interested companies, educational institutions, advisers, and so on, who wish to follow the work in Green Networks and have the ability to participate in the activities in the Network. All entities, regardless of geographic location, may become an I-member	No formal obligations, but should be positively working with environmental issues
K	K-members are the remaining, smaller municipalities within Vejle County that are not an O-member (potentially 12 municipalities)	Like O-members, K-members are obliged to cooperate with and assist the V-members that fall under their environmental jurisdiction in producing an environmental statement

were predominantly along the Enterprise–Authority axis or even the Authority–Authority axis. Such activities did not necessarily adhere to the needs and wishes of companies (Larsen, 2002). With the creation of the Idea-Forum, V-members were presented with an enhanced opportunity to establish and implement activities that were relevant for the companies themselves, that is activities that did not necessarily involve public partners.

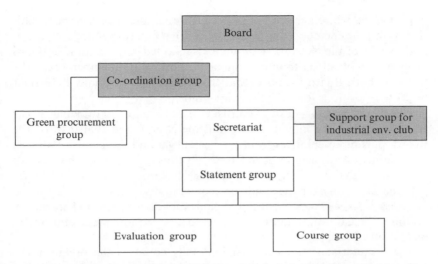

Note: Organizational units with representatives from both the six public authorities and the enterprises are shown as grey. White indicates units that consist only of public members

Figure 13.1   Organogram for the Green Network, 1994

Table 13.2   V-members in the Green Network from 1994 to 2004

Year	1994	1995	1996	1997	1998	1999	2000	2001	2002	2003	2004*
V-members	29	41	57	66	104	133	157	171	178	183	194

Note: * up until June 2004.

Source: Green Network, 2002a, 2004.

Beside the Idea-Forum, three organs have been of particular importance to the development and success of the Network due to their institutionalized role and permanence: the Board, the Coordination Group and the Secretariat.

The Board is – together with the General Assembly – the decision-making body. It consists of 12 members elected at the general assembly: six from enterprises and six from public authorities. In addition to holding the power to make decisions, the Board has an important role in signalling to the Network organization what is important and how to proceed. The Board brings stability and continuity to the organization. The former is reflected in the internal organization of the Board, where the chair and, typically, the vice-chair are both selected from enterprise members. This signals to both members and wider society that enterprises are a vital and leading part of the Network. Continuity is reflected in the continued Board membership of all six founding public authorities (O-members) plus the fact that both Board members and the chairperson normally hold their respective positions for a relatively long time.

The Coordination Group consists of environmental managers or employees from the municipalities and the county, the chairman of the Board, plus representatives from the Secretariat and the Danish Working Environment Authority in Vejle County. It thus integrates the interests of the Board with those of the municipalities. The Group functions as a buffer between ideas for activities and the economic resources available for the Network.[1] As such, by ensuring organizational backing and necessary funding, the Co-ordination Group acts to ensure more successful implementation of activities.

The Secretariat is the web that internally connects the organization. It manages the Network's profile, contacts to members and so on. The Secretariat is represented at the general assembly, at meetings, in activities and so on. It is tasked with ensuring coherence between project goals and activities. At first the Secretariat employed only one person; currently there are 3½ posts. The Secretariat has never had any formal authority to facilitate its functions. Its has however been extremely important because its innovative, dynamic and competent employees have ensured that knowledge, information and decisions have been effectively disseminated from a few key persons to the other members of the Network (Larsen, 2002).

It is also important to stress that the Secretariat is quite an independent organ. Although its staff are situated in the county hall, the Secretariat acts in accordance with the needs and wishes of the Green Network organization. Though employees are most often recruited from within the county administration and still work in the same premises, they have the freedom to relate independently to administrative staff in the county as well as to companies and other partners in the Network. This enhances the bridge-building functions of the Secretariat.

With the diversity of its membership, and commitment – economically as well as politically – from all its actors, the key concepts that underpin the success of the Green Network partnership are mutual respect, maintaining a balance of interests and power, and a commitment to identifying opportunities for development.

we speak the same language. . . . most essential reasons for the success have been the composition of the board and a distinct will to collaborate. . . . It has been very positive to experience the motivation for co-operation . . . (Green Network, 2002b: 6–7; our translation)

The Achilles Heel of the organization seems to be the economic power that public members have. Loss of support from this quarter would surely result in the total collapse of the Network. There is however no sign that support would be withdrawn. The initial motivation for authorities to join the Network has been reinforced by its operation. Moreover the beginning of a transition towards a more dialogue-based way of cooperating is a very promising step for the authorities, as well as other members. Besides gaining useful experience of new forms of cooperation with industry, the authorities have also made dramatic savings in the time and resources used for inspection. In fact they report cost savings of up to 30 per cent (Green Network, 2003a). So although there are some initial costs involved in developing a fruitful dialogue with companies, it pays off in the longer run.

THE ENVIRONMENTAL STATEMENT

From the outset, the fundamental activity in the Green Network was to prepare an environmental statement. This statement forms the basis for cooperation. V-members are obliged to make it on at least a biannual basis and the O-members (and now also K-members) have the obligation to assist them.

The cornerstone in the co-operation was right from the beginning the Environmental Statement Project . . . it [the environmental statement] is now 'only' a stepping stone towards a host of interesting Green Network offers . . . (Green Network, 2003b)

The environmental statement of the companies was pivotal in establishing the Network. At that time, it was rather progressive to compose and make such a statement. It signalled a proactive approach on behalf of firms as well as new and advanced ways of working with the environment from the authorities (see Table 13.3).

In the early 1990s, many efforts were made to develop methods of analysing companies in a more holistic way so that the emphasis would not only be on the abatement and treatment of waste but also on preventative measures. Analysis of the companies' environmental conditions could be expected to result in the adoption of cleaner technologies and, later, establish the basis for establishing an EMS. A lot of different manuals and concepts were in play at that time, many of them being more or less directly

Table 13.3   Major motives for joining the Network

O-members	V-members
The possibility of influencing the behaviour of industries in an environmentally positive way	An expectation of improving the company's reputation
An opportunity to develop and test new ways of cooperation adapted to industries and authorities [in the Network]	A need to document environmental activities carried out at firm-level
The chance to establish a professional network between public authorities in the region	Environmental attitude [management level]
	An opportunity to make cost and resource savings

Source: Vedstesen and Sonne (2000).

translated from US Environmental Protection Agency manuals designed for larger companies (Christensen and Nielsen, 1993). The European Councils Order on EMAS (European Council, 1993) significantly influenced Green Network's translation and adaptation of such concepts. In addition experiences, that is more general guiding principles in terms of environmental management systems, from implementing BS 7750 in a number of Danish companies plus the 1995 Danish Law on Green Accounts (Ministry of Environment and Energy, 1995) influenced the process. Prior to this, Vejle county authorities had actually developed their own seminal model for analysis. This they used when helping companies to take preventative measures and manage their environment in a more systematic way. Given the quantity and diversity of the information available, the creation of a reasonable format for the environmental statement was a major breakthrough. In fact the manual developed was quite simple and well adapted to the needs of SMEs.

The success of the model is directly reflected in the number of statements that have been produced, the corresponding number of certificates issued from Green Network, and the related continuity (see Table 13.4).

In the context of international environmental standards, certification is the guarantee that environmental improvements are made and things are being done 'by the book'. Acceptance of the environmental statement by the Green Network is the corresponding step that guarantees its members have reached a similar level. Companies are then awarded a Green Network Certificate together with a Green Network Flag, which is currently being displayed by 170 companies and 40 public organizations (schools, hospitals and so on) in the region. In addition, the statement serves as the Green

Table 13.4   Number of certificates issued from 1995 to 2002

Year	1995	1996	1997	1998	1999	2000	2001	2002	2003	Total
1st time	8	10	26	25	31	40	31	26	19	216
2nd time			6	10	23	25	23	32	24	143
3rd time					6	8	20	24	16	74
4th time							6	7	17	30
5th time									5	5
Total	8	10	32	35	60	73	80	89	81	468

Note: 1st, 2nd, 3rd, 4th and 5th time refers to the number of certificates a company/organization have received, reflecting the continued efforts of the network members.

Source: Green Network, 2002a, b, c; 2003c, d.

Account that approximately 1200 companies nationwide have to publish. Approximately 30 per cent of Green Network's V-members are covered by this obligation, that is around 50 companies (Clausen, 2003).

Since 1998, V-members that are EMAS registered automatically (that is no additional statement need to be prepared) receive their Green Network certificate. Before a Green Network certificate can be issued to an ISO 14001 certified company or organization however its environmental objectives and an action plan must be published. Rather than applying the normal two-year cycle of the Green Network statement, the revision periods stemming from either international management system may be followed.

Quantitative results are reported in the members' environmental statements; however compiling of overall data was terminated in 2000. Examples of results obtained over the two-year period from setting of goals (1998) to publishing results (2000) include: 80 per cent of companies reported energy savings, one-third of these above 15 per cent; 53 per cent of companies reported water savings, 56 per cent of these above 15 per cent. More recent success stories include a company that has reduced work-related accidents from 11 per year to more than two years without accident; a company that in a five-year period reduced its use of VOCs by 77 per cent; a company within the metal industry that has reduced its energy consumption by 75 per cent. However in recent years, product-oriented improvements, chemical substitutions, Green Procurement and so on have been more predominant activities among the members.

Preparing the statement not only improves the environmental work of the company but also – and equally importantly – functions as an aid to the authorities in developing their differentiated style of inspection. In that sense, preparation of the environmental statement fosters the proactive and reflexive characteristics of the company and authority so that together they can establish adequate governance of the environment.

Once companies have made their first environmental statement – most with assistance by their public counterpart – they are expected to work with the environmental aspects of their production or service. They must revise goals and objectives independently or at least make progress towards doing so unaided. By gradually taking the lead, companies act in a self-regulating manner. Furthermore, as one of the aims of the environmental statement is – just as in ISO 14001 and EMAS – that continuous improvements are mandatory, the company becomes increasingly proactive or 'positive'.[2]

In succeeding in making some companies 'positive', the authorities have the opportunity to focus more on companies that are characterized as being 'passive' or 'neutral'. That is, they can devote more time to those that are not part of the Network, as these tend to be the ones 'lagging behind'.

Working with a differentiated style of inspection makes the job more interesting and rewarding for the inspectors. Recent evaluations show however that the new style of regulation and inspection has as its prerequisite that authority staff are more competent (Christensen et al., 2001). They must be able to function in more 'chaotic' situations where correct answers to the problems are not always given and where the ability to engage in a constructive dialogue is a more important skill than any particular technical proficiency. Although there are these potential difficulties, public authorities want to join the Network. Their expectation is that membership of a formal and professional network will establish a learning environment where competencies and capabilities will be improved (see Table 13.3). Thus networking contributes to the creation of a learning organization.

> Concepts and understandings are changing continuously . . . one of the reasons for the development of the professional network – there is a subject group working with strategic environmental dialogue where you learn from mistakes of others, reflect on processes and concepts etc. (Larsen, 2002: 117; our translation)

THE ACTIVITIES AND THE DEVELOPMENT

Several revisions of the manual have taken place since the first one appeared in 1996. Although the fundamental concept remains more or less the same, the demands of the statement have grown. Companies must still make an environmental statement that covers the activities going on within their fences. However new tools have been developed such that the environmental management of companies can widen in scope (see Table 13.5).

Table 13.5   Significant projects developed in the Green Network in the period after 1997

Project	Short description
LCA-project, 1997	To make the concept of Life-Cycle Assessment operational in the cooperation with V-members for the reduction of environmental strain in relation to their products (not only from the production) The results are presented in an LCA-Manual available to members
Green Purchases, 1997	To strengthen members' environmental activities through more environmentally friendly purchasing. This includes the education of purchasers working for O-members and cooperation between O-members. V- and I-members are to be included in the near future
Environmental Education Network, 1998	To strengthen and focus the educational activities at firm level (V-members) on environmental aspects and at the same time promote network and capacity development to the benefit of, for example, a firms' employees
Environmental Forum Denmark, 1998	Experience and knowledge sharing about public-private partnerships across regions in Denmark. This is achieved through: (1) support to existing environmental networks and promoting co-operation between them; (2) stimulating development of new networks; and (3) being the link between Danish actors in international networks
The Developing Authorities, 1998	One of Green Network's objectives is to develop new and innovative public-private ways of cooperation. In doing so, one of the main issues is to simplify while at the same time strengthen the co-operation between private enterprises and public authorities. The Strategic Environmental Dialogue (Vejle Amt, 1999) is one of the outcomes
Environmental Management in Agriculture, 2001	Green Network received its first agricultural member in 2000. This led to a decision that the environmental statement manual should be published in a version accounting for the special circumstances surrounding the agricultural trade. The manual was ready in 2002
Social Reporting, 2002	Arising from the existing Green Network manual for environmental assessment, this project aims at developing methods and tools that can assist members in reporting on their social responsibilities. In a combination with other reporting initiatives on environment and economics, the project will offer a platform from which to report on sustainability. In addition to the development of tools and methods, the project seeks to continuously educate

Table 13.5   (continued)

Project	Short description
	company and authority representatives in the use of these
Partnership for Trade & Environment, 2003	The partnership is a concrete result of the present and former government's efforts on the Green Market Economy. It is a platform for the work of private companies and public authorities on sustainability. The partnership is intended as a means of strengthening environmental efforts that are market driven. Dialogue, enhancing capabilities, information sharing, coordination between networks, development of existing and new tools and methods are all part of this process

Revision of the manual has been an ongoing process fuelled by three different kinds of pressures: (1) the practical experiences of actors in the Network; (2) increased product-orientation; and (3) present and future legislation on Green Accounts. The latter two pressures arise from the institutionalized environments of the company. Life-cycle assessment (LCA) and cradle-to-grave design in environmental management systems (LCM) are concepts that have been much discussed during the last decade. Although it is not at all clear how all ordinary companies should work in order to achieve LCM, Green Network has succeeded in transforming sometimes rather abstract notions into a handy manual that member companies can work with. The same applies to the long Danish discussion process about how to make a Green Account, as well as to the changes that have been going on in relation to ISO 14001 and EMAS. In all instances, the Green Network has functioned as a receptive body that noted all the changes taking place. Very often at the forefront of events, the Green Network then managed to interpret these changes in an appropriate way, enabling them to be integrated into the practices and daily lives of member organizations. Besides the revisions of the environmental statement, a number of other projects and activities have emerged over the last 10 years – all more or less naturally connected to the environmental statement, either as supportive or supplementary activities. In a certain sense, these activities mirror some of the general developments going on nationally and internationally. Table 13.5 provides an overview of the more significant projects that have been developed within the Network since 1997.

Taken together, these projects can be seen as a number of new institutions created within the Network. These institutions are based on a mixture of regulatory, normative and cognitive influences from the environment. They are moulded and translated into norms, standards and procedures that can be coped with by participating organizations. In the course of this process, Network partners will enhance their skills and improve their grasp of how to work with the environment. In this sense, the method of cooperating makes a good foundation for the learning organization:

> . . . the projects can be seen as dynamos for the enterprises; when these have become familiar with the environmental statement they can take a step forward and help in maintaining the commitment . . .. (Larsen, 2002: 108; our translation)

DISCUSSION

Taking the Green Network as a starting point for analysis demands some additional thoughts on the relationship between a network and a company. Is the Network an organization in its own right? We believe so, because the Green Network acts as a formalized organization. It thus has very much the same degree of organizational complexity as larger companies. Contrary to this, many of the networks that 'network theory' deals with are of a much more informal character (see for example Håkonsson and Waluzsewski, 2002; Lundvall, 1985). Therefore the conclusions that we can draw here may not necessarily apply in those cases.

From the outset, the focus of the Network was on dialogue, exchanging ideas and communicating knowledge among the partners. Fundamentally, the Green Network is based on the now institutionalized idea that economics and environment can go hand in hand. This 'win–win' way of thinking was popular when the Green Network began and, to an extent, retains currency. It was coupled with the idea of a changing role for authority inspectors, who would then come to act more like consultants, working with companies to find economically viable and environmentally sound solutions. Cooperation between companies and authorities is the common value held by all parties in the Network. It is also what fuels the process of translating many of the new ideas emerging from the institutional field into knowledge directly relevant to network members. Deciding what to adopt and developing the tools in joint projects ensures that the translation of processes always takes place in accordance with the basic institutions and attitudes in the Network.

Though the organizational structure seems complicated, the organizational diagram actually reflects the fundamental ideas of balancing powers and establishing room for different voices to be heard. Formal organization thus provides not only a forum for companies to discuss ideas and visions among themselves; it also provides other fora where companies can work closely with the authorities.

Evaluating the five capacities outlined in Røvik's theory demonstrates that they all are present. Regarding the first three capabilities – to absorb, to decouple and to translate – the Green Network has shown a remarkable ability to keep up with trends in the way that notions of ecological modernization have developed. They have been able to keep abreast of all the important developments during the last ten years, absorbing what they find important, and putting aside (decoupling) influences that do not fit into their visions, and programmes or which are not in accordance with their basic views. New influences from the institutional field are quickly translated. The Green Network was among the first organizations to launch new manuals on for example LCA, and how to handle the supply of transport services in the EMS. Moreover the manuals, tools and ways of propagating knowledge (Idea-forum, Green Network Flag, newsletter, website and so on) all have a distinct touch of the 'Green Network way of doing things', that is keep it simple, work together and share knowledge. The Network has succeeded in overcoming a number of the challenges that face 'learning–action networks', that is having facilitated translation and championing the reception of new ideas and recipes.

The last two capacities – getting rid of old institutions and being able eventually to reactivate old ideas again – have only been observed to a limited degree. This is probably because most of this 'digestion' is hidden behind the fact that many of the old scripts and institutions are gradually transformed as the whole set-up of tools and skills develop. In theory however, the Green Network has organized itself in such a way that the capacity for detachment is in place, that is by using project groups that can easily be shut down if a project is no longer necessary, viable or of interest to the members. In addition to developing new ideas and tools, we find that the basic concept – making companies take an overview of their environmental impacts so that they can address problems in a systematic and preventative way – is still at the heart of all Network activities. We also find significant continuity in the people, companies and administrative bodies making up the Network. Not many companies have left the Network, and many key people who eventually leave their companies actually act as ambassadors for the whole idea, either in other companies within the region or by sowing the seeds of the Green Network idea in other regions of the country.

> . . . all projects must provide impact. Even if the project is shut down physically, the experiences gained from it must have been reproduced within the organisation

and continue to live. There is strong focus on this in Green Network. (Green Network, 2003b; our translation)

CONCLUSION

Building networks as public–private partnerships is not a totally new idea. It has been tried in many places around the world, mostly with success. In Denmark, the most successful of the networks is the Green Network in Vejle County, Jutland. This was among the first environmental networks established in Denmark. Its fundamental ideas about creating a sound basis for the environmental work of companies relied heavily on a model of cooperation that soon became institutionalized in the Network. Together with an organizational structure that maintained essential balances between the parties involved, this fundamental institution of cooperation paved the way for success. It created a learning organization with the capacity to absorb new things from its environment and translate them to their own needs.

Many other regional and local successors try to mimic the success of the Green Network (CASA, 2001). Primarily this is done by taking over the manual used, and issuing certificates and flags just as they do in the Green Network. But this adoption of tools and practices is no guarantee of success. Many of the fundamental ways of operating the Green Network are not transferred. Indeed wholesale transfer of for instance institutions is probably not possible. Other regional networks will therefore face the problem of how to establish an organization with some of the same absorptive capacities that have contributed to the success of the Green Network, that is an organization capable of receiving and dealing with all the ideas circulating in the environment of the Network, taking in the most promising and translating them according to their own needs. To do this, not only skilled and enthusiastic people are needed, but also organizational structures that can maintain the correct balances between the different partners involved in the Network.

NOTES:

1. The fee for joining the Green Network is dependant on the type of membership. For O-members it is calculated based on the number of people living in the municipality – currently DKK 2 per resident. For V-and I-members there is a standard fee of DKK 2000. For K-members – other municipalities in the county – the fee is DKK 5000. The county of Vejle is exempted from paying a membership fee, however it is instead providing funding for the posts in the Secretariat.

2.   Vejle Amt (1999). Vejle County works with a differentiated approach to approval and inspection. Three types of attitudes towards environmental management have been identified: negative, neutral and positive, each corresponding to a certain way of approving and inspecting enterprises.

REFERENCES

Barreto, L., A. Makihira and K. Riahi (2003), 'The hydrogen economy in the 21st century: a sustainable developement scenario', *International Journal of Hydrogen Energy*, **28**(3), 267–84.

Beck, Ulrik (1986), *Risikosamfundet: På vej mod en ny modernitet*, Copenhagen: Hans Reitzels Forlag.

Boons, F. (1998), 'Caught in the Web: the dual nature of networks and its consequences', *Business Strategy and the Environment*, **7**(5), 204–12.

Boons, F. and M. Berends (2001), 'Stretching the boundary: the possibilities of flexibility as an organizational capability in industrial ecology', *Business Strategy and the Environment*, **10**(2), 115–24.

CASA (2001), *Regionale Miljønetværk og Grønne Job*, Copenhagen: Den Grønne Jobpulje, Miljøstyrelsen, Miljø- og Energiministeriet.

Christensen, L., O. Busck and B. Bauer (2001), *Differentieret Miljøtilsyn. Miljøprojekt nr. 600*, Copenhagen: Miljøstyrelsen, Miljø- og Energiministeriet.

Christensen, P. and E.H. Nielsen (1993), 'Environmental Audits, Clean Technologies and Environmental Protection in Denmark', *European Environment*, **3**(2), 18–22.

Christensen, P., E.H. Nielsen and A. Remmen (1997), *Environmental Management Programmes: Promoting New Forms of Reflexive Governance in Danish Industry*, 1st European Dialogue Conference on Science for a Sustainable Society. Integrating Natural and Social Sciences. Roskilde University, Denmark, October.

Clark, S.F. and N. Roome (1995), 'Managing for environmentally sensitive technology: networks for collaboration and learning', *Technology Assessment and Strategic Management*, **7**(2), 191–215.

Clark, S. and N. Roome (1999), 'Sustainable business: learning – action networks as organizational assets', *Business Strategy and the Environment*, **8**(5), 296–310.

Clausen, D.B. (2003), Co-ordinator, Green Network Secretariat, Vejle, Denmark.

Cohen, W.M. and D.A. Levinthal (1990), 'Absorptive capacity: a new perspective on learning and innovation', *Administrative Science Quarterly*, **35**(1), 128–52.

European Council (1993), *Council Regulation (EEC) No 1836/93 of 29 June 1993*, Brussels: European Council.

Gouldson, Andrew and Joseph Murphy (1998), *Regulatory Realities: The Implementation and Impact of Industrial Environmental Regulation*, London: Earthscan.

Grabher, Gernot (1993), 'Rediscovering the social in the economics of interfirm relations', in Gernot Grabher (ed.), *The Embedded Firm: On the Socioeconomics of Industrial Networks*, London and New York: Routledge, 1–33.

Granovetter, M. (1985), 'Economic action and social structure: the problem of embeddedness', *American Journal of Sociology*, **91**(3), 481–510.

Green Network (2002a), Green Network Homepage, http://www.greennetwork.dk, accessed May–June 2002.

Green Network (2002b), *Nyhedsbrev Nr. 2 – Juni 2002*, Vejle: Green Network Sekretariatet.
Green Network (2002c), *Nyhedsbrev Nr. 4 – December 2002*, Vejle: Green Network Sekretariatet.
Green Network (2003a), *Projektbeskrivelse vedr: etableringen af et Partnerskab for miljø og erhverv*, Vejle: Green Network Sekretariatet.
Green Network (2003b): Green Network Homepage, http://www.greennetwork.dk, accessed March–June 2003.
Green Network (2003c), *Nyhedsbrev Nr. 3 – August 2003*, Vejle: Green Network Sekretariatet.
Green Network (2003d), *Nyhedsbrev Nr. 5 – December 2003*, Vejle: Green Network Sekretariatet.
Green Network (2004), Green Network Homepage, http://www.greennetwork.dk, accessed July 2004.
Hajer, Martin A. (1995), *The Politics of Environmental Discourse: Ecological Modernization and the Policy Process*, Oxford: Clarendon Press.
Hoffman, Andrew J. (2001), *From Heresy to Dogma*, Stanford, CA: Stanford University Press.
Hoffman, Andrew J. and Marc J. Ventresca (2002), *Organizations, Policy and the Natural Environment. Institutional and Strategic Perspectives*, Stanford, CA: Stanford University Press.
Håkansson, H. (1989), 'Technological innovation through interaction', in Håkan Håkansson (ed.), *Industrial Technological Development: A Network Approach*, London: Routledge, 3–25.
Håkansson, Håkan and Ivan Snehota (1995), *Developing Relationships in Business Networks*, London: Routledge.
Håkansson, Håkan and Alexandra Waluszewski (2002), *Managing Technological Development: IKEA, the Environment and Technology*, London: Routledge.
Jamison, Andrew (2001), *The Making of Green Knowledge: Environmental Politics and Cultural Transformation*, Cambridge: Cambridge University Press.
Larsen, Jesper M. (2002), *Green Networking: Udvikling af Regional Privat-Offentlige Miljøsamarbejder i et Institutionelt Perspektiv*, Aalborg: Aalborg University.
Lundvall, Bengt-Åke (1985), *Product Innovation and User-Producer Interaction*, Aalborg: Aalborg University Press.
Meyer, John W. (1994), 'Rationalized Environments', in Robert Scott and John W. Meyer (eds), *Institutional Environments and Organizations: Structural Complexity and Individualism*, Thousand Oaks, CA: Sage Publications, 28–54.
Meyer, John W. and Robert Scott (1983), *Organizational Environments. Ritual and Rationality*, updated edition 1992, Thousand Oaks, CA: Sage Publications.
Milstein, Mark B., Stuart L. Hart and Anne S. York (2002), 'Coercion breeds variation: the differential impact of isomorphic pressures on environmental strategies', in Andrew J. Hoffman and Marc. J. Ventresca (eds), *Organizations, Policy and the Natural Environment: Institutional and Strategic Perspectives*, Stanford, CA: Stanford University Press, 151–72.
Ministry of Environment and Energy (1995), *Statutory Order from the Ministry of Environment and Energy, No. 975 of December 13 1995, on the Duty of Certain Listed Activities to Draw up Green Accounts*, Copenhagen: Ministry of Environment and Energy, Danish Environmental Protection Agency.
Mol, Arthur P.J. and David A. Sonnenfeld (2000), 'Ecological modernisation around the world: an introduction', in Arthur P.J. Mol and David A. Sonnenfeld (eds),

Ecological Modernisation Around the World: Perspectives and Critical Debates,
London, UK and Portland, US: Frank Cass Publishers, 3–14.

Mol, Arthur P.J. and Gert Spaargaren (2000), 'Ecological modernisation theory in
debate: a review', in Arthur P.J. Mol and David A. Sonnenfeld (eds), *Ecological
Modernisation Around the World: Perspectives and Critical Debates*, London, UK
and Portland, US: Frank Cass Publishers, 17–49.

Oliver, C. (1991), 'Strategic responses to institutional processes', *Academy of
Management Review*, **16**(1), 145–79.

Røvik, Kjell A. (1996), 'Deinstitutionalization and the logic of fashion', in Barbara
Czarniawska and Guje Sévon (eds), *Translating Organizational Change*, Berlin
and New York: Walther de Gruyter, 139–72.

Røvik, Kjell A. (1998), *Moderne organisasjoner: Trender I organisationstenkningen
ved tusenårsskiftet*, Oslo: Fakbokforlaget.

Scott, Robert (1995), *Institutions and Organizations*: Thousand Oaks, CA: Sage
Publications.

Spencer, J.W. (2003), 'Global gatekeeping, representation, and network structure:
a longitudinal analysis of regional and global knowledge diffusiion networks',
Journal of International Bussiness Studies, **34**(5), 428.

van den Bosch, Frans A.J., Raymond van Wijk and Henk W. Volberda (2003),
Absorptive Capacity: Antecedents, Models and Outcomes, Rotterdam: Erasmus
Research Institute of Management.

Vedstesen, Anna M. and Heidi E. Sonne (2000), *Green Network – Et Case-studie af
et Regionalt Offentlig-Privat Samarbejde om Miljøfremme*, Copenhagen:
Københavns Universitet.

Vejle Amt (1999), *Miljøtilsyn 2002: Principper for Vejle Amts Miljøtilsyn med
Industrivirksomheder*, Vejle: Udvalget for Teknik og Miljø, Vejle Amt.

Weick, Karl E. (1982), 'Management of organisational change among loosely
coupled elements', in Paul S. Goodman and Associates (eds), *Change in
Organisations: New Perspectives on Theory, Research and Practice*, San Francisco,
CA: Jossey-Bass Publishers, 375–408.

Zollo, M. and S.G. Winter (2002), 'Deliberate learning and the evolution of
dynamic capabilities', *Organization Science*, **13**(3), 339–51.

Index

quality
  management and firm performance
    157–64, 170–76
  manufacturing capabilities 190, 203,
    205
  standards 142

radical innovations 266, 267–8, 269
'rationalized environments' 290
reactive environmental strategies
  101
'reflexive modernization' 288–9
regional
  alliances 293
  clusters/environmental innovations
    273
  networks 289
regulation 32–3, 43–4,
  circumvention 52
  compliance 186, 187–8, 195, 202,
    235, 236
  flexible approaches 12, 34–5
  focus on 211
regulative institutions 290–91
regulatory
  capability 278
  regimes, shift in 286, 288
  stakeholders 87
reinforcement theory 89–90
reinsurance industry 246–7, 250
relational skills 275
reputation, concern with 41, 105
research methodology, eco-
    manufacturing strategies 191–9
'resilience management' 248, 250
resource-based view
  competitive environmental
    management 29–31
  corporate environmental strategies
    101–2
  of the firm (RBV) 3, 6–7, 9–12, 20,
    29, 30, 33
  of SMEs 96, 99–100
resources
  and competitive advantage 173–5
  concept of 29
  visible commitment of 60
Responsible Care Program, chemical
    industry 265
retail food industry 30

'risk societies' 288–9
Royal Dutch/Shell 54, 56, 60, 61

sane, humane, ecological paradigm
    (SHE) 2
SARS 251
Scandic 121–2
Schmidheiny, Stephen 4–5
Scientific American 5
self-efficacy beliefs 78–9
self-regulation 211, 212–15
service
  differentiation 117
  improvements 121
  failsafing 119
service firms 115–16
  characteristics 117–19, 131–2
  customer loyalty/satisfaction 119–20
service–profit chain 120–22, 131–2
services, enlargement of 145–6
shared
  responsibility 104
  vision 103–4
Shell Expro (UK) 53–4, 56, 60, 61
Silent Spring 1, 234
situational strength 75, 79–80, 89
Small Business Administration, US 98
small and medium-sized enterprises
    (SMEs) 21, 96–8
  competitive advantage 99–100
  corporate environmental strategies
    101–7
  delimitation 98
  strategic management literature
    98–9
social
  equity 267
  issues 237–8, 264
  stakeholders 64
  sustainability 239–42
Social Science Research Council,
    Netherlands 281
socialization process 75, 77
socio-economic activities 210, 211–12
sociological literature on organizations
    262
source-reduction programmes 175
Spain
  large firms 106
  tourism 141